Microbiomes of Soils, Plants and Animals

An Integrated Approach

Through a long history of co-evolution, multicellular organisms form a complex of host cells plus many associated microorganism species. Consisting of algae, bacteria, archaea, fungi, protists and viruses, and collectively referred to as the microbiome, these microorganisms contribute to a range of important functions in their hosts, from nutrition to behaviour and disease susceptibility. In this book, a diverse and international group of active researchers outline how multicellular organisms have become reliant on their microbiomes to function, and explore this vital interdependence across the breadth of soil, plant, animal and human hosts. They draw parallels and contrasts across hosts in different environments, and discuss how this invisible microbial ecosystem influences everything from the food we eat, to our health, to the correct functioning of ecosystems we depend on. This insightful read also pertinently encourages students and researchers in microbial ecology, ecology and microbiology to consider how this interdependence may be key to mitigating environmental changes and developing microbial biotechnology to improve life on Earth.

RACHAEL E. ANTWIS is a microbial ecologist at the University of Salford, Manchester, UK. Her research encompasses a range of host systems, including soil, plants, invertebrates and vertebrates. She is the co-founder and co-secretary of the British Ecological Society's Microbial Ecology Special Interest Group, together with Dr Xavier Harrison.

XAVIER A. HARRISON is a molecular ecologist at the University of Exeter, UK. He is fascinated by the potential of host-associated microbes to drive variation among individuals in life-history trajectory. He is co-founder of the British Ecological Society's Microbial Ecology Special Interest Group, alongside Dr Rachael Antwis.

MICHAEL J. COX is a microbial ecologist at the University of Birmingham, UK. His expertise is in applying microbial ecology techniques to understand the respiratory microbiome in chronic and acute respiratory diseases. He is an editor at *FEMS Microbiology Letters* and author of *The Lung Microbiome* (2019), a monograph for the European Respiratory Society.

Ecological Reviews

Ecological Reviews publishes books at the cutting edge of modern ecology, providing a forum for volumes that discuss topics that are focal points of current activity and likely long-term importance to the progress of the field. The series is an invaluable source of ideas and inspiration for ecologists at all levels from graduate students to more-established researchers and professionals. The series has been developed jointly by the British Ecological Society and Cambridge University Press and encompasses the Society's Symposia as appropriate.

Microbiomes of Soils, Plants and Animals

An Integrated Approach

Edited by

RACHAEL E. ANTWIS
University of Salford

XAVIER A. HARRISON
University of Exeter

MICHAEL J. COX
University of Birmingham

CAMBRIDGE
UNIVERSITY PRESS

University Printing House, Cambridge CB2 8BS, United Kingdom

One Liberty Plaza, 20th Floor, New York, NY 10006, USA

477 Williamstown Road, Port Melbourne, VIC 3207, Australia

314–321, 3rd Floor, Plot 3, Splendor Forum, Jasola District Centre,
New Delhi – 110025, India

79 Anson Road, #06–04/06, Singapore 079906

Cambridge University Press is part of the University of Cambridge.

It furthers the University's mission by disseminating knowledge in the pursuit of
education, learning, and research at the highest international levels of excellence.

www.cambridge.org
Information on this title: www.cambridge.org/9781108473712
DOI: 10.1017/9781108654418

First published 2020

Printed in the United Kingdom by TJ International Ltd, Padstow Cornwall

A catalogue record for this publication is available from the British Library.

Library of Congress Cataloging-in-Publication Data
Names: Antwis, Rachael E., editor. | Harrison, Xavier A., editor. | Cox, Michael J. (Ecologist),
editor.
Title: Microbiomes of soils, plants and animals : an integrated approach / edited by Rachael
E Antwis, Xavier A. Harrison, Michael J. Cox.
Description: 1. | New York, NY : Cambridge University Press, 2020. | Series: Ecological
reviews | Includes index.
Identifiers: LCCN 2019055603 (print) | LCCN 2019055604 (ebook) | ISBN 9781108473712
(hardback) | ISBN 9781108654418 (ebook)
Subjects: LCSH: Microbial ecology. | Microorganisms. | Microbial technology. | Soil
microbiology. | Plants – Microbiology.
Classification: LCC QR100 .M532 2020 (print) | LCC QR100 (ebook) | DDC 579/.1757–dc23
LC record available at https://lccn.loc.gov/2019055603
LC ebook record available at https://lccn.loc.gov/2019055604

ISBN 978-1-108-47371-2 Hardback
ISBN 978-1-108-46248-8 Paperback

Contents

Colour plates can be found between pages 114 and 115.

Contributors

RACHAEL E. ANTWIS
School of Science, Engineering and
Environment
University of Salford
Salford
United Kingdom
r.e.antwis@salford.ac.uk

SIMON J. S. CAMERON
Institute for Global Food Security
School of Biological Sciences
Queen's University Belfast
Belfast
United Kingdom
s.cameron@qub.ac.uk

SOPHIA CARRYL
Department of Surgery
University of Chicago
Chicago
Illinois
United States of America
scarryl@uchicago.edu

MICHAEL J. COX
Institute of Microbiology and
Infection
University of Birmingham
Birmingham
United Kingdom
M.J.Cox@bham.ac.uk

ELLA K DEUTSCH
School of Life Sciences
University of Nottingham
Nottingham
United Kingdom
Ella.Deutsch1@nottingham.ac.uk

MEAGAN DEWAR
School of Health and Life Sciences
Federation University Australia
Berwick
Australia
meagandewar@hotmail.com

PHILIP DONKERSLEY
Lancaster Environment Centre
Lancaster University
Lancaster
United Kingdom
donkersleyp@gmail.com

JAMES DOONAN
Department of Geoscience and
Nature Management
University of Copenhagen
Copenhagen
Denmark
School of Biological
Sciences
Bangor University
Bangor
UK
j.doonan@bangor.ac.uk

NATALIE FERRY
School of Science, Engineering and
Environment
University of Salford

Salford
United Kingdom
n.ferry@salford.ac.uk

ELLEN L. FRY
School of Earth and Environmental
Sciences
University of Manchester
Manchester
United Kingdom
ellen.fry@manchester.ac.uk

ALASTAIR T GIBBONS
School of Life Sciences
University of Nottingham
Nottingham
United Kingdom
alastair.gibbons@nottingham.ac.uk

JACK A. GILBERT
Department of Surgery
University of Chicago
Chicago
Illinois
United States of America
gilbertjack@uchicago.edu

BETHAN GREENWOOD
Coral Reef Research Unit
School of Biological Sciences
University of Essex
Colchester
United Kingdom
bgreenc@essex.ac.uk

REID N. HARRIS
Department of Biology
James Madison University
Harrisonburg
Virginia
United States of America
harrisrn@jmu.edu

XAVIER A. HARRISON
School of Biosciences
University of Exeter

Exeter
United Kingdom
x.harrison@exeter.ac.uk

CHLOË E. JAMES
School of Science, Engineering and
Environment
University of Salford
Salford
United Kingdom
C.James@salford.ac.uk

ZENOBIA LEWIS
School of Life Sciences
Institute of Integrative Biology
University of Liverpool
Liverpool
United Kingdom
z.lewis@liverpool.ac.uk

ANNE LIZÉ
Ecosystèmes, Biodiversité, Evolution
University of Rennes
Rennes
France
Anne.Lize@liverpool.ac.uk

REUBEN MARGERISON
School of Earth and Environmental
Sciences
University of Manchester
Manchester
United Kingdom
Reuben.margerison@manchester.ac.
uk

JAMES E. MCDONALD
School of Biological Sciences
Bangor University
Bangor
United Kingdom
j.mcdonald@bangor.ac.uk

VALERIE MCKENZIE
Department of Ecology and
Evolutionary Biology

University of Colorado
Boulder
Colorado
United States of America
valerie.mckenzie@colorado.edu

OCÉANE NICOLITCH
School of Earth and Environmental
Sciences
University of Manchester
Manchester
United Kingdom
oceane.nicolitch@manchester.ac.uk

SAM ROBINSON
Lancaster Environment Centre
Lancaster University
Lancaster
United Kingdom
s.robinson1@lancaster.ac.uk

MARC SZE
Department of Microbiology and
Immunology

University of Michigan
Ann Arbor
Michigan
United States of America
marcsze@med.umich.edu

YAQIAN ZHANG
School of Earth and Environmental
Sciences
University of Manchester
Manchester
United Kingdom
yaqian.zhang@postgrad.manche
ster.ac.uk

FENG ZHU
Center for Agricultural Resources
Research
Institute of Genetics and
Developmental Biology
Chinese Academy of Sciences
Shijiazhuang
China
zhufeng@sjziam.ac.cn

Preface

Although microbiology is an old discipline, research into host-associated microbiomes has become a particularly active field in the last 10 years or so, largely as a result of improved sequencing technologies. Given that every living organism and environmental system has a microbiome (we think!), this area of research transcends traditional organism-based silos. The motivation behind this book was to integrate our current knowledge and understanding of microbiomes across taxa and environments within different biological or functional themes. Given the relative youth and rapid evolution of this field of research, there is still much to be learnt about host microbiomes, and we hope that we have gone some way to summarising these gaps and identifying directions of interest.

We would like to thank the 23 co-authors who contributed to producing this work, as well as Gerard Clarke, Alejandra Escobar, Nicole Gerardo, Peter Graystock, Joseph Hoyt, Joe Taylor, Christian Voolstra and Gemma Walton for reviewing the chapters, and Elizabeth Meade, Joshua Harrop, David Johnson and Ully Kritzler for contributing images. We are very grateful to the British Ecological Society for the opportunity to write this book, and to Philip Warren and Kate Harrison for initially approaching us about the work and helping to construct its contents. We are also extremely grateful to Olivia Boult, Maeve Sinnott and Aleksandra Serocka from Cambridge University Press for their assistance in compiling the book.

Abbreviations

AMF	arbuscular mycorrhizal fungi
AMP	antimicrobial peptide
AMR	arbuscular mycorrhizal
AOD	Acute Oak Decline
ASD	autism spectrum disorder
ASV	amplicon sequence variant
BNF	biological N fixation
BSC	biological soil crust
CCD	colony collapse disorder
CDI	*Clostridium difficile* infection
CRC	colorectal cancer
DAPG	2,4-diacetylphloroglucinol
EAA	essential amino acid
EMF	ectomycorrhizal fungi
GABA	gamma-aminobutyric acid
GRAS	generally regarded as safe
HCN	hydrogen cyanide
IAA	indole-3-acetic acid
IBS	irritable bowel syndrome
IIT	incompatible insect technique
ITS	internal transcribed spacer
JA-Ile	jasmonoyl-isoleucine
MAG	metagenomic assembled genome
MALDI-TOF MS	matrix-assisted laser desorption/ionisation time-of-flight mass spectrometry
MERS	Middle East respiratory syndrome
MIC	minimum inhibitory concentration
NMR	nuclear magnetic resonance
NRP	non-ribosomal peptide
OTU	operational taxonomic unit
PGPR	plant growth–promoting rhizobacteria

PHZ	phenazines
PK	polyketide
PRN	pyrrolnitrin
RHESt	root hair endophyte stack
ROS	reactive oxygen species
SCFA	short-chain fatty acid
SST	sea-surface temperature
T3SS	type III secretion system
TMAO	trimethylamine-N-oxide
WMS	whole metagenome shotgun

CHAPTER ONE

Microbiomes of soils, plants and animals: an introduction

RACHAEL E. ANTWIS
University of Salford
XAVIER A. HARRISON
University of Exeter
MICHAEL J. COX
University of Birmingham
SOPHIA CARRYL
University of Chicago
MEAGAN DEWAR
Federation University Australia, Berwick
JAMES DOONAN
Bangor University
ELLEN L. FRY
University of Manchester
JACK A. GILBERT
University of Chicago
BETHAN GREENWOOD
University of Essex
REID N. HARRIS
James Madison University, Harrisonburg
ZENOBIA LEWIS
University of Liverpool
ANNE LIZÉ
University of Rennes
JAMES E. MCDONALD
Bangor University
VALERIE MCKENZIE
University of Colorado
MARC SZE
University of Michigan
and
FENG ZHU
Chinese Academy of Sciences

As pioneers of life, microorganisms have been established on our planet for c. 3.5 billion years. As a result, plants and animals have co-evolved with trillions of associated microorganisms for millions of years (Chisholm et al., 2006), and multicellular organisms can be considered as meta-organisms; a complex of host cells plus many symbiotic species (Rohwer et al., 2002). These communities have been termed the 'microbiota', and their associated genomes the 'microbiome'. The microbiota can consist of algae, bacteria, archaea, fungi, protists and viruses, and collectively these microorganisms by far surpass the number of host cells (Bosch & McFall-Ngai, 2011; Sender et al., 2016). As a result of this co-evolution, significant interdependency has arisen between hosts and their associated microbiota, and host-associated microbiomes profoundly affect host biology and function (Gilbert et al., 2012; McFall-Ngai et al., 2013; Turner et al., 2013). Across all meta-organisms, the host microbiota contributes significant functional diversity and performs critical roles through the provision of microbial 'ecosystem services', including the synthesis of important molecules required by the host, catabolism and bioconversion of complex polysaccharides, immune regulation and colonisation resistance from potentially pathogenic microorganisms (Lynch & Pedersen, 2016; Young, 2017). As such, multicellular organisms have become reliant on the genetic diversity of their microbiome, requiring the associated immune stimulation and products of microbial metabolism to function. For example, in the human microbiota, >10,000 different microbial strains are associated with the host, conferring around 8 million unique protein-encoding genes; 360 times more protein-coding genes than the human genome (Human Microbiome Consortium, 2012). Within this framework, the host and its microbiota together are defined as the 'holobiont', while the genomes of the host and microbiota within the holobiont represent the hologenome (Rosenberg & Zilber-Rosenberg, 2016). These selected relationships may be interpreted as evidence of a summed unit of evolutionary selection, whereby all the organisms that make up the intra-organismal ecosystem are under super-selection, shaping the evolution of each genotype. This has been termed the hologenome concept of evolution, and may define a level of selection in the evolution of both plants and animals (Bordenstein & Theis, 2015; Berg et al., 2016; Osborne et al., 2018; Rosenberg & Zilber-Rosenberg, 2018). Although this concept remains the subject of debate (Douglas & Werren, 2016), it is compelling to view our shared journey through the world as a co-dependence, a symbiosis, in which both the microbes and the host are entirely dependent on each other.

Recent rapid advances in both nucleic acid sequencing technologies and the identification of proteins and metabolites have transformed our ability to characterise the structure and function of the host microbiome. These have allowed biologists to characterise complex microbial communities associated with a vast array of plant and animal taxa (including humans), offering increased insight into the role of microbes in host development and physiology (Grice & Segre, 2012; McFall-Ngai et al., 2013; Thompson et al., 2015; Chen et al., 2016; Esposti & Romero, 2017). Molecular tools such as amplicon sequencing (metabarcoding), metagenomics and metatranscriptomics can be used to construct species abundance and functional networks, and measure fine-scale changes in community microbiota with ever-increasing resolution, providing greater understanding of ecological trends between hosts and their microbiota. Such advances in DNA sequencing, proteomics and metabolomics, coupled with advances in computational analysis and modelling, have allowed unprecedented access to the microbiome, provoking new hypotheses on the role of microbiomes in health and disease (Autenrieth, 2017). Consequently, great progress has been made in our understanding of plant and animal holobionts. In Chapter 2, we outline and discuss the range of current methods available to researchers for characterising the composition and functional traits of host microbiomes.

One of the most well-studied and yet complex of all microbiomes is not in fact associated with plant or animal hosts, but with the soil that forms the basis of our terrestrial ecosystems. Soil microbiomes play numerous vital roles in the decomposition of soil organic matter and circulation of global carbon and nitrogen stores (Thakuria et al., 2010). Moreover, soil microbiome composition is inherent to plant health and associated biodiversity (Fierer, 2017) and as such supports animal diversity and associated ecosystem health, as well as ultimately providing almost all human sustenance through crop production and livestock feed. Given the vital importance of soil health to ecosystem and human health, Chapter 3 is dedicated to understanding the diversity and function of soil microbiomes across a range of ecosystems and habitat types.

Within a host organism there is a gradient in the strength of the interactions between individual microorganisms and the host, from dependence to independence, which highlights the huge ecological dynamics that shape these interactions. Different host species usually contain unique microbial assemblages (Davenport et al., 2017; Youngblut et al., 2019), and even within hosts, different regions can host different communities. For example, plants support different microbiota in their below-ground and above-ground components, and animals, including humans, have different communities associated with their skin, gut and other organs (Gopal & Gupta, 2016; Gilbert et al., 2018). For both plants and animals, a range of intrinsic and extrinsic factors can influence microbiome composition, including host genetics, development stage, social interactions, behaviour, diet, environmental temperatures and other abiotic factors. The consequences of these for host function are just beginning to be understood, and we discuss these ideas in Chapter 4. Of these factors, diet and associated nutrition are particularly important. The animal microbiome generally reflects the lifestyle of the host (Douglas, 2015; Hammer & Bowers, 2015; Macke et al., 2017), and host diet is one of the key factors that shape the composition and structure of the animal gut microbiome (Ley et al., 2008; McFall-Ngai et al., 2013; Baldo et al., 2017). Indeed, the gut microbiome of animals, including humans, has been most widely studied due to its key role in modulating nutritional intake from food sources, often accessing molecules that would otherwise be unavailable to the host. For example, ruminant guts contain unique cellulolytic bacteria that exude enzymes capable of breaking down tough grassy material (Flint et al., 2008). Another classic example is that of aphid species, which carry *Buchnera* as an obligate bacterial symbiont that synthesises certain essential amino acids, thus allowing the host to feed on nutrient-poor phloem diets that would otherwise not sustain development (Oliver et al., 2010). Similarly, the gut microbiome people from rural areas of Africa and South America have distinct gut microbiota for digestion of complex carbohydrates, whereas those of a large population of humans in the United States is optimised to process fat- and protein-rich diets (Yatsunenko et al., 2012). Furthermore, recent studies in human microbiomes showed that disruption of particular microbiome functions may result in malnutrition, obesity and other metabolic syndromes (Grice & Segre, 2012; Blaser et al., 2016). Although devoid of a gut, plant nutrition is also intrinsically linked to the microbiome of both itself and its associated soil (Pii et al., 2015). Indeed, plants have strong associations with a range of microbial partners, most notably mycorrhizal fungi and rhizobia bacteria, between which nutrients flow. Broadly speaking, plants provide microbial partners with carbon substrates in exchange for mobilising otherwise inaccessible nitrogen and phosphorous (Turner et al., 2013). In Chapter 5, the interactions between microbiome composition and host nutrition for plants and animals is expanded upon.

Perhaps one of the more intriguing areas of research in this field involves the interactions between host microbiomes and host behaviours. Behaviours that can affect and be affected by microbiome composition and function can include foraging decisions, appetite and food choice. The role of microbiomes in synthesising and regulating hormone production as well as influencing reproductive behaviours is also a growing field of research. Furthermore, microbes interact with host mood and stress, and can have profound implications for memory and cognitive function, all of which can influence host health and disease susceptibility. There are also some remarkable examples of behavioural manipulation of the host by parasitic microbes to facilitate their dispersal and transmission. We explore this further in Chapter 6.

As discussed above, the traditional dogma of microorganisms as largely pathogenic no longer stands. Indeed, an increasing body of research is showing that host-associated microbes are in fact critical for preventing infectious and non-infectious disease. In Chapter 7, we examine the symbiotic interactions between hosts and their microbial communities, and highlight the broad suite of mechanisms by which the microbiome protects against invasion by bacterial, fungal and viral pathogens across plants and animals. This chapter also addresses the use of probiotics and microbiome manipulation (through microbiome transplants, personalised medicine, environmental management and host genotype selection) in order to prevent and treat human and wildlife diseases. This is particularly important in the context of the rapid increase in crop and wildlife diseases that we are currently experiencing, largely as a result of increased global trade and climate change (Tompkins et al., 2015; Fisher et al., 2016). Indeed, our planet is currently undergoing a plethora of extreme environmental changes, and the effect of these on host microbiome composition, as well as the potential for the microbiome to mitigate these changes for their hosts, are explored in Chapter 8. Furthermore, given the enormous and diverse functional power provided by microbes, the potential to harness these attributes to solve real-world problems, such as crop production, human and livestock health, antibiotic resistance, and biofuel production, is a highly active area of novel research. The field remains in its infancy; the application of microbes and microbially derived products is still fraught with problems, both biological and technical, in addition to a range of ethical considerations. We discuss this in more detail in Chapter 9. Finally, we conclude in Chapter 10 by bringing together research questions and future directions for the field of microbiome research inspired by our chapter authors. We hope you will enjoy reading this book as much as we enjoyed putting it together!

References

Autenrieth IB. (2017) The microbiome in health and disease: A new role of microbes in molecular medicine. *Journal of Molecular Medicine*, 95, 1–3.

Baldo L, Pretus JL, Riera JL, et al. (2017) Convergence of gut microbiotas in the adaptive radiations of African cichlid fishes. *The ISME Journal*, 11, 1975–1987.

Berg G, Rybakova D, Grube M, et al. (2016) The plant microbiome explored: Implications for experimental botany. *Journal of Experimental Botany*, 67, 995–1002.

Blaser MJ, Cardon ZG, Cho MK, et al. (2016) Toward a predictive understanding of Earth's microbiomes to address 21st century challenges. *mBio*, 7, e00714–16.

Bordenstein SR, Theis KR. (2015) Host biology in light of the microbiome: Ten principles of holobionts and hologenomes. *PLoS Biology*, 13, 1–23.

Bosch TCG, McFall-Ngai MJ. (2011) Metaorganisms as the new frontier. *Zoology*, 114, 185–190.

Chen BS, Teh BS, Sun C, et al. (2016) Biodiversity and activity of the gut microbiota across the life history of the insect herbivore *Spodoptera littoralis*. *Scientific Reports*, 6, 14.

Chisholm ST, Coaker G, Day B, et al. (2006) Host–microbe interactions: Shaping the evolution of the plant immune response. *Cell*, 124, 803–814.

Davenport ER, Sanders JG, Song SJ, et al. (2017) The human microbiome in evolution. *BMC Biology*, 15, 1–12.

Douglas AE. (2015) Multiorganismal insects: Diversity and function of resident microorganisms. *Annual Review of Entomology*, 60, 17–34.

Douglas AE, Werren JH. (2016) Holes in the hologeome: Why host–microbe symbioses are not holobionts. *mBio*, 7, e02099–15.

Esposti MD, Romero EM. (2017) The functional microbiome of arthropods. *PLoS ONE*, 12, 26.

Fierer N. (2017) Embracing the unknown: Disentangling the complexities of the soil microbiome. *Nature Reviews Microbiology*, 15, 579–590.

Fisher MC, Gow NAR, Gurr SJ. (2016) Tackling emerging fungal threats to animal health, food security and ecosystem resilience. *Philosophical Transactions of the Royal Society B: Biological Sciences*, 371, 20160332.

Flint HJ, Bayer EA, Rincon MT, et al. (2008) Polysaccharide utilisation by gut bacteria: Potential for new insights from genomic analysis. *Nature Reviews Microbiology*, 6, 121–131.

Gilbert SF, Sapp J, Tauber AI. (2012) A symbiotic view of life: We have never been individuals. *Quarterly Review of Biology*, 87, 325–341.

Gilbert JA, Blaser MJ, Caporaso JG, et al. (2018) Current understanding of the human microbiome. *Nature Medicine*, 24, 392–400.

Gopal M, Gupta A. (2016) Microbiome selection could spur next-generation plant breeding strategies. *Frontiers in Microbiology*, 7, 1–10.

Grice EA, Segre JA. (2012) The human microbiome: Our second genome. *Annual Review of Genomics and Human Genetics*, 13, 151–170.

Hammer TJ, Bowers MD. (2015) Gut microbes may facilitate insect herbivory of chemically defended plants. *Oecologia*, 179, 1–14.

Human Microbiome Consortium. (2012) Structure, function and diversity of the healthy human microbiome. *Nature*, 486, 207–214.

Ley R, Hamady M, Lozupone C. (2008) Evolution of mammals and their gut microbes. *Science*, 320, 1647–1651.

Lynch SV, Pedersen O. (2016) The human intestinal microbiome in health and disease. *New England Journal of Medicine*, 375, 2369–2379.

Macke E, Tasiemski A, Massol F, et al. (2017) Life history and eco-evolutionary dynamics in light of the gut microbiota. *Oikos*, 126, 508–531.

McFall-Ngai M, Hadfield MG, Bosch TCG, et al. (2013) Animals in a bacterial world, a new imperative for the life sciences. *Proceedings of the National Academy of Sciences*, 110, 3229–3236.

Oliver KM, Degnan PH, Burke GR, Moran NA. (2010) Facultative symbionts in aphids and the horizontal transfer of ecologically important traits. *Annual Review of Entomology*, 55, 247–266.

Osborne OG, De-Kayne R, Bidartondo MI, et al. (2018) Arbuscular mycorrhizal fungi promote coexistence and niche divergence of sympatric palm species on a remote oceanic island. *New Phytologist*, 217, 1254–1266.

Pii Y, Mimmo T, Tomasi N, et al. (2015) Microbial interactions in the rhizosphere: Beneficial influences of plant growth-promoting rhizobacteria on nutrient acquisition process: A review. *Biology and Fertility of Soils*, 51, 403–415.

Rohwer F, Seguritan V, Azam F, Knowlton N. (2002) Diversity and distribution of coral-associated bacteria. *Marine Ecology Progress Series*, 243, 1–10.

Rosenberg E, Zilber-Rosenberg I. (2016) Microbes drive evolution of animals and plants: The hologenome concept. *mBio*, 7, e01395-15.

Rosenberg E, Zilber-Rosenberg I. (2018) The hologenome concept of evolution after 10 years. *Microbiome*, 6, 78.

Sender R, Fuchs S, Milo R. (2016) Are we really vastly outnumbered? Revisiting the ratio of bacterial to host cells in humans. *Cell*, 164, 337–340.

Thakuria D, Schmidt O, Finan D, et al. (2010) Gut wall bacteria of earthworms: A natural selection process. *The ISME Journal*, 4, 357–366.

Thompson JR, Rivera HE, Closek CJ, Medina M. (2015) Microbes in the coral holobiont: Partners through evolution, development, and ecological interactions. *Frontiers in Cellular and Infection Microbiology*, 4, 20.

Tompkins DM, Carver S, Jones ME, et al. (2015) Emerging infectious diseases of wildlife: A critical perspective. *Trends in Parasitology*, 31, 149–159.

Turner TR, James EK, Poole PS. (2013) The plant microbiome. *Genome Biology*, 14, 1–10.

Yatsunenko T, Rey FE, Manary MJ, et al. (2012) Human gut microbiome viewed across age and geography. *Nature*, 486, 222–227.

Young VB. (2017) The role of the microbiome in human health and disease: An introduction for clinicians. *BMJ*, 356, j831.

Youngblut ND, Reischer GH, Walters W, et al. (2019). Host diet and evolutionary history explain different aspects of gut microbiome diversity among vertebrate clades. *Nature Communications*, 10, 2200.

CHAPTER TWO

Analytical approaches for microbiome research

XAVIER A. HARRISON
University of Exeter
and
SIMON J. S. CAMERON
Queen's University Belfast

2.1 Introduction

The study of microbes and how they interact with the environment and their hosts has a fascinating history. Remarkably, we first managed to visualise microorganisms over 300 years ago. In the mid seventeenth century, Robert Hooke used a microscope to present the first scientific depiction of a fungus (Hooke, 1665), and shortly thereafter, Antonie van Leeuwenhoek used a single-lens microscope to describe the 'animalcules' that we now know to have been bacteria and protists (Van Leeuwenhoek, 1677; Lane, 2015). Two hundred years later, Angelina Fanny Hesse pioneered the use of agar media instead of a gelatin-based alternative to culture bacteria (Hitchens & Leikind, 1939) that subsequently allowed the isolation of the bacterium responsible for tuberculosis (Koch, 1882). It is on these foundations of visualisation and isolation that much of modern-day microbiology still rests. Contemporary microbiological work continues to rely on the ability to isolate individual bacterial colonies on agar media to assay their function and interactions with other microbes (e.g. Antwis et al., 2015). Hesse's work, although never formally acknowledged by Koch (Hitchens & Leikind, 1939), continues to help us study the fundamental biology of bacteria and fungi.

Advances in molecular tools over the last few decades have revolutionised our ability to study microbes. As Handelsman (2009) stated, 'the glory of the last 50 years of microbiology is founded, in large part, on genetic analysis'. We can now use metagenome sequencing to assay the composition of an entire microbial community without having to culture any of its members (e.g. Handelsman, 2004). Similarly, both mass spectrometry (Cameron et al., 2016) and Raman spectroscopy (Jarvis & Goodacre, 2004) can be used not only to identify bacterial species in a sample, but can often discriminate among different strains of a particular bacterium. The application of so-called 'culture-independent' approaches to the study of microbes has risen dramatically in recent years (Xu, 2006; Escobar-Zepeda et al., 2015), allowing us to measure the structure and function of microbial communities in unprecedented detail.

Modern genomic tools allow us to generate huge volumes of high-resolution data about microbial communities. Concurrent advances in modern computational power also allow us to analyse those data quickly. However, often viewed as one of the major strengths of modern molecular biology, generating enormous quantities of genomic data does not automatically guarantee we are tackling fundamental questions about the biology of microbes. That is, we are not suddenly free from our obligation to ensure sound study design, adequate replication and sufficient statistical power (see Mallick et al., 2017). Hundreds of gigabases of sequencing effort do us little benefit if we spend them on the wrong samples, or at the wrong level of replication (see Prosser, 2010). Cogent study design means we can leverage the strengths of genomic tools to probe questions previously unanswerable by microbial biologists, rather than rely on the tools themselves to somehow overcome the limitations of study design. As with many things, robust microbial ecology is about picking the right tool for the job. This chapter will briefly introduce several approaches available to researchers seeking to investigate the structure and function of microbial communities, and discuss how analytical approaches might differ depending on the question(s) being asked. We summarise the methods discussed in Figure 2.1, which conceptualises the hierarchical framework of the analytical tools available to microbial biologists.

2.2 High-throughput amplicon sequencing and microbial community structure

In many ways the sorts of questions we are asking in microbial ecology have changed very little since van Leeuwenhoek and Hooke first began to make observations of microscopic organisms over 300 years ago, and Koch was attempting to isolate pathogenic bacteria. Microbial ecologists are fascinated with describing the diversity found within microbial communities living in association with plants, animals and the environment. We want to know which microbes are there, and more importantly, *why* they are there and *what* they are doing. High-throughput amplicon sequencing, often referred to as 'metabarcoding' or 'metagenetics', is the tool that allows us to tackle the first of these three questions through the use of highly conserved gene regions for the taxonomic group of interest (e.g. bacteria, fungi, etc.).

Amplicon sequencing has vastly improved the precision with which we can study the diversity of microbial communities (Handelsman, 2009), and the locations we can study them. In recent years we have seen studies describing how mammals vary in their gut microbiome (Nishida & Ochman, 2018), how ocean currents shape the marine sediment microbiome in the Arctic (Hamdan

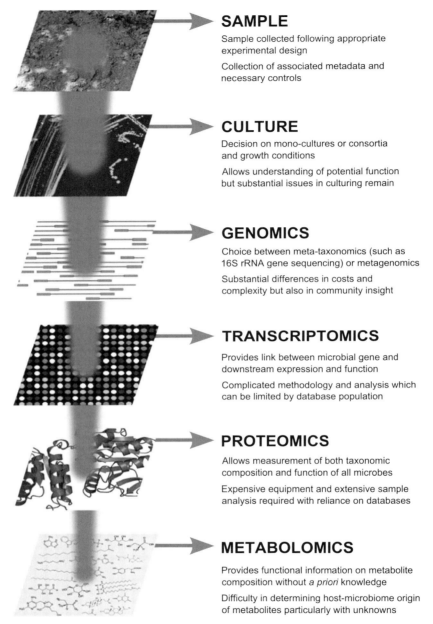

SAMPLE

Sample collected following appropriate experimental design

Collection of associated metadata and necessary controls

CULTURE

Decision on mono-cultures or consortia and growth conditions

Allows understanding of potential function but substantial issues in culturing remain

GENOMICS

Choice between meta-taxonomics (such as 16S rRNA gene sequencing) or metagenomics

Substantial differences in costs and complexity but also in community insight

TRANSCRIPTOMICS

Provides link between microbial gene and downstream expression and function

Complicated methodology and analysis which can be limited by database population

PROTEOMICS

Allows measurement of both taxonomic composition and function of all microbes

Expensive equipment and extensive sample analysis required with reliance on databases

METABOLOMICS

Provides functional information on metabolite composition without *a priori* knowledge

Difficulty in determining host-microbiome origin of metabolites particularly with unknowns

Figure 2.1 Schematic of tools available to researchers interesting in exploring traits of microbiome structure and function. Note the hierarchical nature of these tools, from raw sample to proteomics and metabolomics. We briefly summarise the advantages and disadvantages of each tool, which are expanded upon in the main text (figure compiled by Simon Cameron from images in the public domain). (A black and white version of this figure will appear in some formats. For the colour version, please refer to the plate section.)

et al., 2013) and even how humans transfer our microbial communities to our mobile phones (Meadow et al., 2014). Not only can we characterise microbial communities at a single point in time, but we can also ask how they may shift over time in response to host life history (Maurice et al., 2015) or perturbation by a pathogen (Jani & Briggs, 2014; Bates et al., 2018). Designing an amplicon sequencing project requires consideration of the technical and biological issues that affect the choice of sequencing technology, phylogenetic marker and downstream analysis pipeline. For sequencing technology, the read length, sequencing yield and error rate of the output reads are the main features that require consideration. Illumina is currently the most popular technology used in metabarcoding projects, yielding single or paired-end reads of length around 75–300 bp, with a low error rate (<0.1%), and high sequencing yield (~25 million reads per run on a MiSeq sequencer). Alternative sequencing technologies popular in metabarcoding publications are Ion Torrent, PacBio and the now obsolete 454 (known as 'pyrosequencing'; see Ghurye et al., 2016 for further information on read lengths and accuracies associated with different technologies). Given there are only a limited number of platforms on which to sequence, and this is currently dominated by one or two, arguably decisions regarding phylogenetic marker and downstream analysis ('bioinformatics') are more pertinent to amplicon sequencing.

Two general rules govern the precision of amplicon sequencing approaches to microbial ecology. First, our ability to discriminate among closely related microbes can only ever be as precise as the marker gene is variable among the organisms we are trying to separate taxonomically. If two strains of bacterium are identical across the 16S rRNA gene then we simply cannot separate them. Second, our ability to classify the microbes at a fine resolution of taxonomy can only ever be as good as the database we are using (Kunin et al., 2008). Not surprisingly, it is difficult to use 16S rRNA amplicon sequencing to classify bacteria to species and strain level, especially for environments that have not previously been well studied. This problem is exacerbated by the fact that most next-generation sequencing workflows for amplicon sequencing can only sequence a partial region of the marker gene (e.g. Kozich et al., 2013), and so 'miss out' on a lot of the variability in that gene. As we are only sequencing a portion of what is already a highly conserved gene, taxonomic assignment of those sequences beyond genus level becomes problematic (Escobar-Zepeda et al., 2018). But the vital question here is how much taxonomic resolution is really needed? If the goal is to describe taxonomic diversity in a sample, or the change of that diversity over time, or how that diversity is associated with environmental variables, relative abundance at the genus, family and phylum levels is more than sufficient (e.g. Jani & Briggs, 2014). Metabarcoding is the right tool for that particular job.

Taxonomic marker gene selection requires two things. First, we need a barcoding gene that is unique to a particular type of microbe (e.g. bacteria or fungi) that can be sequenced. But not just any gene will do: it needs to be conserved enough that every member of that group contains at least one copy of that gene (so that we don't 'miss' anyone), but variable enough that it allows us to distinguish between closely related members of a particular taxonomic group with relative precision, so that we don't underestimate diversity. The presence of variable and conserved regions along the taxonomic marker gene is fundamental for the design of flanking primers that fit well with the sequencing read length. 'Universal' primer design is one of the most important bias sources in the reconstruction of the original microbial community structure (Shakya et al., 2013). Examples of such marker genes include the variable regions from the 16S rRNA gene for bacteria, and the internal transcribed spacer (ITS) rRNA gene for metabarcoding of fungi. Indeed, a major breakthrough in prokaryotic barcoding occurred in the late 1970s when Carl Woese discovered the usefulness of the 16S rRNA gene as a phylogenetic marker, and the DNA Sanger sequencing method by chain termination method was developed (Sapp & Fox, 2013). Since then, the databases of ribosomal sequences began to be populated. Indeed, this is the second requirement; we need a reference database of existing genetic diversity that has been described for that barcoding gene, which we can use to cross-reference against the genetic diversity found in our metabarcoded sample. This database can be constructed from full-length gene sequences of the marker gene from either cultured bacteria, or those recovered from metagenomics sequencing and reconstruction of microbial genomes. As such, we don't have to be able to culture the bacterium for it to be represented in the database. A variety of public databases are available for the 16S rRNA marker gene including RDP, SILVA, GreenGenes and the 16S Ribosomal RNA Sequences from the NCBI.

The bioinformatics of amplicon sequencing data involves taking the short contigs (~300–550 bp) that have been generated and joining the overlapping paired-end reads. There are some fairly intuitive rules for sequence trimming and what to do when overlapping bases from paired end reads do not match (e.g. Schloss et al., 2009). There is a range of tools for doing this, including DADA2 (Callahan et al., 2016), QIIME or QIIME2 (Caporaso et al., 2010), and mothur (Schloss et al., 2009). All are relatively straightforward to use and supported by numerous online tutorials and GitHub pages. However, each of these tools makes different assumptions about the data, and models them in different ways. For example, mothur attempts to cluster sequences into operational taxonomic units (OTUs) based on 97% sequence similarity, whereas DADA2 infers amplicon sequence variants (ASVs) based on single base-pair differences while controlling for sequencing errors. Consequently, using different tools on the same data set can yield different estimates of diversity

(Golob et al., 2017), or overestimate the diversity in a sample (Krohn et al., 2016), making comparisons among studies difficult. Analytical repositories such as *Microbiome Helper* (Comeau et al., 2017) provide streamlined workflows for the analysis of amplicon sequence data to standardise practices across studies and to facilitate research in this field. It is worth noting that standardising computational analysis does not address bias introduced due to sample collection and storage, DNA extraction protocols, primer selection and sequencing effort (see Pollock et al., 2018).

Differences in sequencing yield (or sequencing effort, i.e. number of reads) between samples can make comparisons of results both within and across studies difficult. Such differences occur because of normal variability in the output of the sequencer equipment and library preparation. To deal with this problem, normalisation methods have been proposed in order to make the data comparable and to detect microbial signatures related to sample groups. Selection of normalisation methods is not trivial because not all methods are appropriate for all kinds of microbial data (see Weiss et al., 2017 for a nice review of normalisation methods). It is always important to bear in mind that the more diverse the sample, the more sampling effort will be required to detect taxonomic groups of lower abundance. Furthermore, the accurate and robust analysis of these types of community data, limited by what the sequencing machine can provide, is an evolving discipline. We refer readers to a number of recent publications that discuss this (Plaly & Shankar, 2016; Gloor et al., 2017; Weiss et al., 2017; McKnight et al., 2018; Carr et al., 2019; Nguyen & Holmes, 2019; Sankaran & Holmes, 2019).

On the other hand, problems can arise when we ask too much of amplicon sequencing data. For example, there are statistical tools for inferring predicted function from partial 16S rRNA gene sequences (PICRUSt: Langille et al., 2013; Tax4FUN: Aßhauer et al., 2015; and Piphillin: Iwai et al. 2016) and ITS rRNA gene sequences (FUNGulid: Nguyen et al. 2016), but their accuracy in predicting function remains untested over a wide variety of environments and contexts. We know, for example, that bacteria with even 99% identical full-length 16S rRNA gene sequences often have vastly different functional phenotypes, such as the ability to inhibit the growth of a pathogen (Antwis & Harrison, 2018) or to fix nitrogen (Mehnaz et al., 2001). How do we resolve this apparent disparity with the observation that functional prediction from 16S rRNA gene sequencing can often yield a 'good approximation' of function gleaned from shotgun metagenomics data sets (Iwai et al., 2016)? The answer is that it depends on the resolution of function that we are trying to estimate. A trait such as bacteria-mediated resistance to a pathogen is a functional phenotype comprising many genes and metabolic pathways from a bacterial isolate. Software such as PICRUSt can approximate genome-level function from a 16S rRNA gene sequence based on its closest relative in a database of functions (e.g. KEGG) but, (a) often that relative will be phylogenetically quite distant from the gene sequence in question (e.g. Hiraoka et al., 2016) and (b) depending on the completeness of functional information of that relative in the database, it may not recover the functions you are actually interested in measuring (Xu et al., 2014). Although the rate at which we are accumulating microbial genomes is increasing, functional annotations of those genomes are poor (see Baric et al., 2016). Part of the reason why 16S-predicted gene function can be a reasonable approximation to function derived from metagenomes (e.g. the prediction of digestive function in mammals; Finlayson-Trick et al., 2017) is because they only have to approximate incomplete functional information. It is expected that as the microbial genome annotation improves, the disparity between 16S rRNA predicted and actual function may increase. However, we must not forget that the resolution of the 16S rRNA marker gene is, at best, at the genus level. This means that the functional inference from these sequences will be a function of the probability that the specific metabolic pathways of species would be represented in the corresponding taxonomic group at genus or family rank.

Strengths of amplicon sequencing: Cheap per-sample cost and high multiplexing ability; fairly detailed taxonomic profile of community; straightforward bioinformatics and statistical toolsets available.

Weaknesses of amplicon sequencing: Limited ability to distinguish between closely related 'species' and strains; comparing results from studies that sequenced different regions of the same marker gene, or used different bioinformatics tools, is problematic; limited information on microbial function.

2.3 Metagenomics and microbial function

Unlike amplicon sequencing, metagenomics approaches afford us direct access to the functional genetic repertoire present in a microbial community without having to infer probabilistic function from marker genes such as the 16S rRNA gene (Hiraoka et al., 2016). By definition, a metagenomic study implies the recovery and analysis of the collective genomes from the microorganisms that share a particular environment, but does not always entail complete reconstruction of genomes. However, some 'metagenomics' studies are in fact just single-gene amplicon sequencing studies that have been labelled incorrectly (see Esposito & Kirschberg, 2014), probably because 'metagenomics' tends to be used as a catch-all term for simultaneous high-throughput sequencing and because the step prior to amplicon sequencing is the extraction of metagenomic DNA. True whole metagenome shotgun (WMS) studies of microbial communities yield valuable insights into the biology of the plants and animals that act as hosts to such microbes. Bacteria and fungi can provide a huge range of 'hologenomic adaptations' to their hosts, for example allowing vampire bats to digest blood meals (Mendoza et al., 2018) or allowing plants to liberate nutrients from the environment that would otherwise not have been bioavailable (reviewed in Bulgarelli et al., 2013).

Recent advances in next-generation sequencing technology and the concomitant decrease in the cost-per-Gb of sequencing data has led to a proliferation of shotgun metagenomics studies (Quince et al., 2017). The availability of bioinformatics tools specific to these data is also rising (Hiraoka et al., 2016). However, the analysis of shotgun metagenomics data is more complicated than for amplicon sequencing because the sample will contain sequences from entire genomes of organisms that could be closely related phylogenetically, sharing a high portion of their genomes. Additionally, the genomes come from organisms that form part of the microbial community in distinct abundances. The lower the strain abundance, the worse the representation of that strain's genome in the data set, making reconstruction of their genomic fragments more challenging. As in metabarcoding projects, the more diverse the community, the more sequencing effort is required to generate robust assemblies. Finally, depending on the sample origin, contaminant sequences from the host organism could also be present (e.g. Rebollar et al., 2018). Traditional genome assembly tools such as RAST were unsuitable for metagenome assembly because they were designed to assemble single, clonal genomes and not mixtures of genomes (Thomas et al., 2012). However, the recent development of MG-RAST and other de-Bruijn assemblers such as metaVELVET overcome these limitations and allow de-novo metagenomic assembly of complex genomic mixtures (Namiki et al., 2012; Thomas et al., 2012; Ghurye et al., 2016). Assemblers vary markedly in their requirements for computational resources, and different assemblers can produce different results based on the assumptions they make (see van der Walt et al., 2017). As such, it is relatively difficult to standardise the analytical approaches used for these kinds of data, and consequently the inferences made from those data. This presents issues if we ever need to compare results from multiple studies on the same environment, which may require a so-called 'meta-analysis of metagenomes' (Hiraoka et al., 2016).

A huge advantage of the whole-genome shotgun sequencing protocols is the possibility to reconstruct genomes from new and unculturable strains, which usually dominate environmental samples (Konstantinidis et al., 2017). These genomic sequences have contributed in recent years to the expansion of the prokaryotic tree of life (Hug et al., 2016) and to the improvement in our classification methods (Parks et al., 2018). The reconstruction of metagenomic assembled genomes (MAGs) have become an important part of whole-genome shotgun analysis, and some pipelines have been developed in order to automate metagenomic assembly and binning-improvement procedures (Uritskiy et al., 2018). This approach leads to the direct link of function with taxonomy, answering the questions, 'who is there?' and 'what is the metabolic potential of each strain?'

Independent of the recovery of MAGs, downstream analysis after metagenomic assembly commonly involves the prediction of coding sequences. Having identified the microbial gene content in a sample, a primary goal of shotgun metagenomics analysis is to link that gene content to putative metabolic function (Hiraoka et al., 2016). Once genes in a metagenomics sample have been identified (see Thomas et al., 2012), the simplest means to infer gene function is to cross reference the genes against pathway databases such as KEGG or SEED (Hiraoka et al., 2016). Much like amplicon sequencing, our ability to characterise these pathways will only ever be as robust as the reference database is detailed. Consequently, using different databases will yield different functional information. Nonetheless, we can find coincidences in the highly reliable annotations. This is why it is important to select a well-curated database for function inference based on sequence identity.

Another consideration is that shotgun metagenomics alone does not provide us with a direct 1–1 link between genes and the metabolome or proteome. This is because it cannot distinguish between expressed and non-expressed genes, only telling us about the microbial gene content of the sample but not which genes are (going to be) switched on. That is why we refer to the functional inference from WMS data as 'metabolic potential' and should be understood as the potential functions of the whole community. Metatranscriptomic approaches allow us to sequence expressed microbial RNA but come with their own limitations, such as the need to remove rRNA prior to reverse transcription (see Zhou et al., 2015) and are still only an approximation of eventual metabolome, or the gene expression profile at the point of sampling. We can use metabolomics to look at 'end-product' metabolites in a sample, but without metagenomic/metatranscriptomic data it can be impossible to identify *which* microbe in a sample was responsible for manufacturing that metabolite, or even whether it was a fungus or a bacterium. The assumption, in this case, is that the closest orthologue found in the database corresponds to the same organism in the environmental sample, but this is not necessarily true. How much of a problem this poses depends on whether mapping metabolomic function to microbial identity/genome was the central question. As mentioned before, the best alternative to link function and taxonomy in WMS projects is using the information deduced from MAGs.

Strengths of metagenomics: Direct estimates of microbial gene content and diversity without having to infer function from 16S rRNA gene sequences; ability to reconstruct whole microbial genomes given sufficient coverage; ability to concurrently sequence multiple kingdoms; availability of online portals for uploading and automated analysis of raw metagenomic data, e.g. MG-RAST and MGnify.

Weaknesses of metagenomics: Analytically more complex than metabarcoding; more expensive per-sample sequencing cost; variety of analytical tools and functional reference databases are a barrier to methodological standardisation; gene content does not imply gene expression; lots of sequencing effort 'wasted' on host DNA when only microbial DNA may be of interest.

2.4 Moving beyond nucleic acids to measure function

For a truly holistic view of microbial communities, and particularly of their interactions with their environment, analytical approaches that capture the functional activity of microbiomes are essential. Amplicon sequencing, metagenomics and metatranscriptomics are all concerned with understanding what *genes* are in a sample. Whether we have only studied a single gene (amplicon sequencing), a whole suite of genes (metagenomics) or the expressed products of those genes (metatranscriptomics), our ability to measure the function of a microbial community is constrained by only using information from the nucleic acids in that sample. Defining function in a gene-centric fashion risks missing important emergent functional properties, both of single bacterial species and assemblages of multiple species. Elucidating these properties requires that we use different tools.

2.4.1 Cultures and consortia

Culturing microbes such as bacteria is a technique that predates modern nucleic acid–based approaches to microbiome studies by a long way (e.g. Koch, 1882). Yet even in the age of next-generation sequencers, culture-based approaches yield detailed information about the two key questions in microbiome studies: *which* microbes are there, and *what* are they doing? Once microbes have been isolated in culture, they can be identified using sequencing methods (e.g. full-length 16S rRNA sequencing for bacteria, or whole-genome sequencing), and then used in the functional assay of choice. This might include quantifying inhibition of a pathogen (Antwis et al., 2015; Antwis & Harrison, 2018), or enzymatic activity (Mehnaz et al., 2001). The advantage of this approach is that we can test for functions we are actually interested in and link that function to individual microbiome members, rather than brute-force sequencing a microbiome and hoping we recover relevant functional information.

Challenge assays using cultures also allow you to ask questions about how interactions between microbes may change depending on additional factors such as variation in temperature (e.g. Muletz-Wolz et al., 2017) or the addition of other microbes comprising microbial consortia (Antwis & Harrison, 2018).

This approach means we can move beyond describing the function of individual community members to predicting how function might change under altered conditions, whether abiotic such as temperature or biotic such as the presence of microbial competitors. The ability to scale up individual microbial challenge assays into community-level challenges is limited only by the number of microbes that can be cultured, providing near-endless combinations of microbial communities that permit the researcher to test the effect of community composition on the functional trait of interest. 'Leave one out' approaches can be very powerful for quantifying the effect of individual microbes on overall function (Piovia-Scott et al., 2017).

One of the issues with culture-based methods is that, depending on the origin of the sample, only a small proportion of the microbes may be capable of being cultured, and/or those microbes may be very sensitive to culture conditions. Culture-based approaches to identifying the composition of a microbiome may be biased in its assessment of diversity to those microbes that can grow on particular media or at a particular temperature. Culture-based studies are also more time-consuming compared to sequencing-based community studies if your goal is to gain a complete a picture of which microbes are present. However, if one is simply isolating microbes to screen for functional activity, relatively little culturing effort can yield isolates from multiple taxonomic groups, e.g. genera or phyla of bacteria (Antwis et al., 2015). Issues arise when attempting to combine these isolates into consortia – although testing individual bacteria for functional activity, the combinations of consortia possible for a set of individual isolates soon becomes quite large. It may not always be feasible to test every combination of bacterial isolate for a given assay, and it is advisable to design the consortia based on the research question at hand. Cogent study design will mean you often won't need to test every combination of isolates to tackle your chosen research question.

The more genomic information we have about the isolated strains, the better our experimental design will be to test specific functions. In some cases, it is important to know the genomic context of the genes of interest, for which it is convenient to have the assembled genomes of the isolated strains as continuous as possible. This is achievable by combining second-generation technologies (such as Illumina: short reads, low error rate), with third-generation technologies (such as PacBio or Oxford Nanopore: long reads, high error rate), in an approach known as hybrid assembly. Also, genome sequencing of isolates is worthy because it can be used in studies of comparative genomics versus reference genomes publicly available from the RefSeq database from the NCBI. This kind of analysis allows us to establish conclusions about bacterial species evolution and to understand how strain lineages segregate according to their environmental origin. Finally, an in-silico approach is independent of changes that can occur to the genome of the bacterial isolate due to the adaptation to laboratory conditions (Liu et al., 2017).

Strengths of culture-based methods: Direct functional information for traits of interest (e.g. enzyme activity, pathogen inhibition); ability to differentiate microbes based on functional activity rather than marker genes such as 16S rRNA; permits scaling up of cultures to multi-isolate consortia to test the effect of microbial interactions on functional activity; cheaper than deep-sequencing entire microbial communities.

Weaknesses of culture-based methods: Requires that the microbes in a sample can be cultured; single isolate assays only give functional information from a subset of the microbiome; in-vitro function of a single isolate of consortium may not represent microbial function in the microbiome as a whole; difficult to track microbial dynamics (e.g. relative abundance) of individual isolates in multi-isolate consortia.

2.4.2 Proteomics and metabolomics

While metatranscriptomics is concerned with understanding gene expression of communities, both proteomics and metabolomics are associated with the end-product of gene expression and how the interplay between these pillars of systems biology affect the overall interaction of the microbiome with its associated environment – be it host or ecological niche. Exploring the functional relationship between microbiome and environment was a pressing issue before the widespread adoption of high-throughput next-generation sequencing platforms. In fact, in his early studies of infant diarrhoea, Theodore Escherich offered functional differences between bacterial strains as the reason behind why some readily cause disease while others exist as harmless commensal community members.

For proteomic and metabolomic analysis, researchers have the choice of either nuclear magnetic resonance (NMR) spectroscopy or mass spectrometry. Typically, NMR is a powerful technique for the study of metabolites in terms of analytical robustness and potential for quantification. It does, however, suffer from a low level of analytical sensitivity and thus the fields of proteomics and metabolomics are highly reliant on the higher sensitivity of mass spectrometry instruments. Mass spectrometry is a molecular spectroscopy technique that determines the mass-to-charge (m/z) ratios of molecular species as molecular ions. To increase the analytical resolution of mass spectrometry, chromatographic techniques, such as liquid or gas chromatography, are usually employed to separate the chemical constituents of a sample based on their chemical and/or physical properties prior to ion generation and subsequent mass spectrometry analysis. As with all other analytical methods including DNA sequencing, the choice of sample type, sampling methodology, sample storage and sample extraction are essential considerations in both proteomic and metabolomic studies and have major implications for the reproducibility and comparability of results (Cameron & Takáts, 2018).

2.4.2.1 *Proteomics*

In the same way as metagenomics, metaproteomic analysis is concerned with the characterisation of the entire protein component of a sample (see Wilmes et al., 2015). The cell lysate for analysis is usually obtained from the lysis of differentially separated cells. It is then subjected to a protein digest using trypsin to obtain peptide fragments of proteins. Metaproteomic analysis usually couples liquid chromatography with a high-resolution mass spectrometer capable of tandem mass spectrometry for analysis of these peptide fragments. Due to the complexity of samples, very long analytical run times of up to 22 hours can be required. This makes metaproteomics lower-throughput than many DNA sequencing techniques. However, due to the taxonomic information obtained from analysis of ribosomal proteins, the technique allows for both the determination of microbiome composition and function at the protein level, such as the expression of antimicrobial resistance proteins. Furthermore, in the case of microbiomes associated with a eukaryotic host (parasite, plant, animal, etc.), metaproteomics is also capable of assessing host–microbiome responses at the protein level. Metaproteomics has been powerfully applied to the study of microbiomes from a wide range of environmental niches, from activated sludge to marine systems and from soil to faeces.

Strengths of proteomics: Ability to measure both taxonomic composition and function; covers host and microbiome interactions and responses; high analytical sensitivity; potential to cover all microbes, e.g. eukaryotic, prokaryotic, viruses.

Weaknesses of proteomics: High capital expenditure needed for instrumentation; extensive sample extraction and preparation; long analytical runtimes; reliance on annotation of database entries; a-priori knowledge of functional characteristics of proteins required.

2.4.2.2 *Metabolomics*

Metabolomics is concerned with the detection of the entire component of metabolic processes within a sample. Due to the chemical and physical nature of metabolites, there is no one single methodology to obtain a comprehensive overview of the metabolomic content of a sample. This is due to differential extraction efficiencies, travel through chromatographic separation columns, and ionisation mechanisms and efficiencies. For these reasons, metabolomic analysis of microbial communities has taken longer to become established compared to genomic, transcriptomic and proteomic analysis. However, it is becoming increasingly evident that small molecular-weight metabolites underpin many of the interactions between microbial communities and their environments (Zierer et al., 2018) and offer the potential for mechanistic links to be established. Traditional approaches to metabolomic analysis using mass spectrometry utilise chromatographic separation prior to ion generation and mass spectrometric analysis. This step is typically the one that requires the highest input of time for both sample preparation and sample extraction and purification. Although this increases both analytical sensitivity and resolution, there are drawbacks in terms of introduction of bias and homogenisation of metabolic information. In the field of mass spectrometry–based metabolomics, ambient ionisation and mass spectrometry imaging techniques hold much promise for future research. Ambient ionisation methods are those that allow for the generation of metabolite ions in a normal atmosphere without sample preparation or extraction. This increases the throughput of sample analysis but importantly reduces the potential impact of storage and extraction bias and allows for determination of the 'natural metabolic state' of a sample (Cameron & Takáts, 2018). Imaging mass spectrometry techniques are those that allow for the spatial distribution of metabolites to be determined, which is likely to be of particular importance in microbial communities where there is differential spatial distribution of stimuli or nutrient availability. For imaging mass spectrometry techniques, a pixel of an image represents a separate mass spectrum collected for a spatial region of a sample with different techniques, allowing for spatial resolution ranging from nanometres to millimetres (Watrous & Dorrestein, 2011).

Strengths of metabolomics: Potential for high-throughput sample analysis; no requirement for a-priori knowledge of targets; potential for generation of hypotheses regarding host/microbiome interactions; imaging mass spectrometry provides opportunity for determination of spatial distribution of metabolites.

Weaknesses of metabolomics: No robust system for determination of taxonomic composition; difficulty in identifying host/microbiome origin of metabolites; high number of unknown metabolites; high instrument costs; difficulty in combining multi-omic data sets.

2.5 Structure versus function: what should we be measuring?

As a general rule, then, we can say that amplicon sequencing is very good at measuring taxonomic diversity and microbiome 'structure' with certain resolution, but not as adept at quantifying microbiome function, either of individual members or the community as a whole. Conversely, shotgun metagenomics can give us a stronger approximation of potential gene function, and taxonomic information at species or strain resolution, depending on the labelling method. Metatranscriptomics may give us more detailed insights into our system by revealing which genes are actually expressed, rather than simply present, in a microbial community. Often the goal of microbiome studies, especially those based on amplicon sequencing, is to see if the taxonomic profile of samples varies in concert with a variable of interest, such as biological or environmental variation, or an experimental treatment. But perhaps we should ask if taxonomic diversity of samples is the right variable to be measuring at all; should we instead be trying to group samples based on functional profile (Xu et al., 2014)? Evidence is accumulating that though taxonomic profiles can appear quite variable, functional profiles are often more stable (Turnbaugh et al., 2009). For example, Bletz et al. (2016) transplanted tadpoles between streams and observed a marked shift in the taxonomic profiles of their gut microbiomes, but this was not reflected in a shift in predicted gut microbiome function, which remained stable. Apparent functional redundancy of microbial community structure is biologically very interesting, but also serves to underscore that while we might conclude that an experimental treatment might cause a shift in microbial community structure, it may fail to effect significant change in microbial community function. By extension, if we agree that we should be focusing on function, what 'level' of function should we focus on? We can infer function from gene content (metagenomics/transcriptomics), from proteins and metabolites (proteomics/metabolomics), or from challenge assays (culture-based methods). The appropriateness of each of these methods will depend on the study system under investigation, and the research question. Goodrich et al. (2014) and Knight et al. (2018) both provide additional advice for designing microbiome studies and analysing the resulting data.

Finally, an often overlooked but vital component of any study of microbial dynamics is the importance of high-quality metadata. Gigabases of sequencing data from microbes have a utility far beyond the lifetime of a single study, but can only realise that utility if the metadata for samples are recorded in an accurate and transparent manner. Meta-analyses and comparative studies offer the opportunity to place the data from a single study in context with multiple other data sets to answer questions that were previously out of reach (e.g. Sanders et al., 2015). Online repositories such as EMBL-EBI and SRA have strict standards for the submission of metadata alongside raw sequencing reads, but the onus is on researchers to ensure that as much detail as possible is included alongside samples to maximise the breadth and diversity of questions for which those data can be reused.

2.6 Hypothesis-testing in microbiome studies: what should the null model be?

Following from the above, the apparent discord between shifts in structure and function in studies of microbial ecology raises an interesting question: what should our null model be? It is increasingly clear that host-associated microbial communities are strongly structured by intrinsic traits such as ontogeny, genotype and sex (e.g. Bolnick et al., 2014; Griffiths et al., 2018), but also easily perturbed by factors such as changes in diet (e.g. Spor et al., 2011), drug administration (e.g. Maier et al., 2018), season (e.g. Maurice et al., 2015) and reproductive state (e.g. Maurice et al. 2015; Antwis et al., 2019). Indeed, we now have a fairly reasonable expectation that anything that causes changes in host physiological state will also effect changes in the structure of that host's microbial community. The problem with this expectation is that it means that specifying the hypothesis that '*groups* x *and* y *differ in their microbial community structure*' is often too trivial to be informative. Similarly, the complementary null hypothesis of no difference between groups risks the pitfall of 'silly nulls', often cited as a criticism of the way null-hypothesis significance-testing is used (Stephens et al., 2005). Indeed, discovery of no or limited difference between groups (species, treatments, populations) is often far more interesting, because it may imply some form of constraint is operating on host–microbe co-evolution (see Sanders et al., 2014). In such cases, the null hypothesis of no difference is actually more interesting, and more enlightening with respect to the eco-evolutionary forces shaping host microbiomes. We are at the stage now where the scientific literature is approaching saturation with studies of differences in microbial structure, often based on amplicon markers such as the 16S rRNA gene. However, if we continue to simply look for differences, then our knowledge of the importance of host-associated microbial communities will not increase at the same rate as the publication of studies investigating those communities. We need to be asking more interesting questions, and correspondingly specifying more interesting hypotheses.

So what questions should we be asking? Briefly, these can be divided into questions about either *stability* or *function*. With respect to stability, we have ample evidence to suggest that microbiomes are easily perturbed, but know relatively little about the longer-term temporal dynamics arising as a result of that perturbation. Should we be asking if non-antibiotic drugs change the human gut microbiome, or indeed is it more relevant and interesting to ask *how much* do these drugs perturb microbial communities in the gut (i.e. stability; see Maier et al., 2018)? More importantly, once microbial communities have been perturbed, is there variation among individuals in propensity to return to their initial baseline 'state' (i.e. resilience; Maurice et al., 2015)? And what are the consequences of *not* being able to return to a baseline state? These questions are ones of resolution and require that we gather more detailed temporal data on changes in microbial communities in plant and animal hosts. Cases of functional redundancy in microbial communities represent another example where null hypotheses of 'no difference' suddenly become more interesting. Convergence of function suggests a biological constraint where there is selection for microbes inhabiting a particular host niche to maintain a core functional repertoire.

2.7 How should we be studying microbiomes? A call for an integrated approach

The genetic and genomic toolsets available to researchers now afford us the ability to examine the structure and function of microbial communities in unprecedented detail (Figure 2.1). Robust inference about how microbes inter-act with each other within those communities, or how microbes interact with their hosts, requires cogent application of these toolsets. As microbial ecolo-gists, we need to ask ourselves what it is that we really want to know about these microbial communities. Do we want to know about phylogenetic structure and how that structure changes over time in response to life-history traits and environmental covariates? Or do we wish to understand how microbial func-tion maps on to those traits? And at what level do we want to characterise those functions – microbial gene content (metagenomics), microbial gene expression (metatranscriptomics) or microbe-derived metabolites (metabolomics)? Or do we dispense with the 'omics' tools altogether and rely on functional assays on microbial cultures in vitro? Researchers interested in microbial 'function' may all arrive at different answers if they each use a different approach, each with its own inherent set of limitations. Such single-tool investigations of microbial communities severely limit our ability to compare results across studies.

However, the field of microbial ecology is changing. It is now increas-ingly clear that the most robust inference is gleaned from using 'multi-omics' approaches to probe questions about microbial community dynamics, and the relationship between microbial and host function. For example, combining metagenomics and metabolomics data sets allows us to link metabolites detected in a sample directly to microbial genomes in that sample (Zhou et al., 2015; Lamichhane et al., 2018). This yields a high-resolution map of how microbial community membership and gene con-tent reflects realised biological function in the metabolome. Previously, the higher cost-per-base of meta-omics sequencing and relative scarcity of accessible analytical tools for tackling multi-omics data were substantial constraints on the widespread adoption of multi-omics tools. Yet such financial and computational barriers are gradually being lifted, for example with the introduction of software such as HAllA (Rahnavard et al., 2017) and the R package *mixOmics* (Rohart et al., 2017) designed specifically to integrate data from multiple omics data sets. Although we have come a long way technologically from the days of visualising microbes using single-lens microscopes as van Leeuwenhoek did, until recently we have still been asking 'who's there?' In the metagenomics and multi-omic era, we can begin to answer much more sophisticated questions about the functional repertoire of microbial communities, and how these functions mediate critical biological processes in animal, plant and environmental niches.

References

Antwis RE, Harrison XA. (2018). Probiotic consortia are not uniformly effective against different amphibian chytrid pathogen isolates. *Molecular Ecology*, 27, 577–589.

Antwis RE, Preziosi RF, Harrison XA, et al. (2015) Amphibian symbiotic bacteria do not show a universal ability to inhibit growth of the global panzootic lineage of *Batrachochytrium dendrobatidis*. *Applied and Environmental Microbiology*, 81, 3706–3711.

Antwis RE, Edwards KL, Unwin B, et al. (2019) Rare gut microbiota associated with breeding success, hormone metabolites and ovarian cycle phase in the critically endangered eastern black rhino. *Microbiome*, 7, 27.

Aßhauer KP, Wemheuer B, Daniel R, et al. (2015) Tax4Fun: Predicting functional profiles from metagenomic 16S rRNA data. *Bioinformatics*, 31, 2882–2884.

Baric RS, Crosson S, Damania B, et al. (2016) Next-generation high-throughput functional annotation of microbial genomes. *mBio* 7, e01245–16.

Bates KA, Clare FC, O'Hanlon S, et al. (2018) Amphibian chytridiomycosis outbreak dynamics are linked with host skin bacterial community structure. *Nature Communications*, 15, 693.

Bletz MC, Goedbloed DJ, Sanchez E, et al. (2016) Amphibian gut microbiota shifts differentially in community structure but converges on habitat-specific predicted functions. *Nature Communications*, 7, 13699.

Bolnick DI, Snowberg LK, Caporaso JG, et al. (2014) Major histocompatibility complex class II b polymorphism influences gut microbiota composition and diversity. *Molecular Ecology*, 23, 4831–4845.

Bulgarelli D, Schlaeppi K, Spaepen S, et al. (2013) Structure and functions of the bacterial microbiota of plants. *Annual Review of Plant Biology*, 64, 807–838.

Callahan BJ, McMurdie PJ, Rosen MJ, et al. (2016) DADA2: High-resolution sample inference from Illumina amplicon data. *Nature Methods*, 13, 581.

Cameron SJ, Bolt F, Perdones-Montero A, et al. (2016) Rapid evaporative ionisation mass spectrometry (REIMS) provides accurate direct from culture species identification within the genus *Candida*. *Scientific Reports*, 6, 36788.

Cameron SJ, Takáts Z. (2018) Mass spectrometry approaches to metabolic profiling of microbial communities within the human gastrointestinal tract. *Methods*, 149, 13–24.

Caporaso JG, Kuczynski J, Stombaugh J, et al. (2010) QIIME allows analysis of high-throughput community sequencing data. *Nature Methods*, 7, 335.

Carr A, Diener C, Baliga NS, Gibbons SM. (2019) Use and abuse of correlation analyses in microbial ecology. *The ISME Journal*. DOI:10.1038/s41396-019-0459-z.

Comeau AM, Douglas GM, Langille MG. (2017) Microbiome helper: A custom and streamlined workflow for microbiome research. *mSystems*, 2, e00127–16.

Escobar-Zepeda A, Vera-Ponce de León A, Sanchez-Flores A. (2015) The road to metagenomics: From microbiology to DNA sequencing technologies and bioinformatics. *Frontiers in Genetics*, 6, 348.

Escobar-Zepeda A, Godoy-Lozano EE, Raggi L, et al. (2018) Analysis of sequencing strategies and tools for taxonomic annotation: Defining standards for progressive metagenomics. *Scientific Reports*, 8, 12034.

Esposito A, Kirschberg M. (2014) How many 16S-based studies should be included in a metagenomic conference? It may be a matter of etymology. *FEMS Microbiology Letters*, 351, 145–146.

Finlayson-Trick ECL, Getz LJ, Slaine PD, et al. (2017) Taxonomic differences of gut microbiomes drive cellulolytic enzymatic potential within hind-gut fermenting mammals. *PLoS ONE*, 12, e0189404.

Ghurye JS, Cepeda-Espinoza V, Pop M. (2016) Metagenomic assembly: Overview, challenges and applications. *Yale Journal of Biology and Medicine*, 89, 353–362.

Gloor GB, Macklaim JM, Pawlowsky-Glahn V, et al. (2017) Microbiome datasets are compositional: And this is not optional. *Frontiers in Microbiology*, 8, 2224.

Golob JL, Margolis E, Hoffman NG, et al. (2017). Evaluating the accuracy of amplicon-based microbiome computational pipelines on simulated human gut microbial communities. *BMC Bioinformatics*, 18, 283.

Goodrich JK, Di Rienzi SC, Poole AC, et al. (2014) Conducting a microbiome study. *Cell*, 158, 250–262.

Griffiths SM, Harrison XA, Weldon C, et al. (2018) Genetic variability and ontogeny predict microbiome structure in a disease-challenged montane amphibian. *The ISME Journal*, 12, 2506–2517.

Hamdan LJ, Coffin RB, Sikaroodi M, et al. (2013) Ocean currents shape the microbiome of Arctic marine sediments. *The ISME Journal*, 7, 685.

Handelsman J. (2004) Metagenomics: Application of genomics to uncultured microorganisms. *Microbiology and Molecular Biology Reviews*, 68, 669–685.

Handelsman J. (2009) Metagenetics: Spending our inheritance on the future. *Microbial Biotechnology*, 2, 138–139.

Hiraoka S, Yang CC, Iwasaki W. (2016) Metagenomics and bioinformatics in microbial ecology: Current status and beyond. *Microbes and Environments*, 31, 204–212.

Hitchens AP, Leikind MC. (1939). The introduction of agar-agar into bacteriology. *Journal of Bacteriology*, 37, 485.

Hooke R. (1665) *Micrographia or Some Physiological Descriptions of Minute Bodies Made by Magnifying Glasses with Observations and Inquiries Thereupon*. Royal Society, London.

Hug LA, Baker BJ, Anantharaman K, et al. (2016) A new view of the tree of life. *Nature Microbiology*, 1, 16048.

Iwai S, Weinmaier T, Schmidt BL, et al. (2016) Piphillin: Improved prediction of metagenomic content by direct inference from human microbiomes. *PLoS ONE*, 11, e0166104.

Jani AJ, Briggs CJ. (2014) The pathogen *Batrachochytrium dendrobatidis* disturbs the frog skin microbiome during a natural epidemic and experimental infection. *Proceedings of the National Academy of Sciences*, 111, E5049–E5058.

Jarvis RM, Goodacre R. (2004) Discrimination of bacteria using surface-enhanced Raman spectroscopy. *Analytical Chemistry*, 76, 40–47.

Knight R, Vrbanac A, Taylor BC, et al. (2018) Best practices for analysing microbiomes. *Nature Reviews Microbiology*, 16, 410–422.

Koch R. (1882) Die Ätiologie der Tuberkulose. *Berliner Klinische Wochenschrift*, 15, 221–230.

Konstantinidis KT, Rosselló-Móra R, Amann R. (2017) Uncultivated microbes in need of their own taxonomy. *The ISME Journal*, 11, 2399.

Kozich JJ, Westcott SL, Baxter NT, et al. (2013) Development of a dual-index sequencing strategy and curation pipeline for analyzing amplicon sequence data on the MiSeq Illumina sequencing platform. *Applied and Environmental Microbiology*, 79, 5112–5120.

Krohn A, Stevens B, Robbins-Pianka A, et al. (2016) Optimization of 16S amplicon analysis using mock communities: Implications for estimating community diversity. *PeerJ Preprints*, 4, e2196v3.

Kunin V, Copeland A, Lapidus A, et al. (2008) A bioinformatician's guide to metagenomics. *Microbiology and Molecular Biology Reviews*, 72, 557–578.

Lane N. (2015) The unseen world: Reflections on Leeuwenhoek (1677); 'concerning little animals'. *Philosophical Transactions of the Royal Society B: Biological Sciences*, 370, 20140344.

Lamichhane S, Sen P, Dickens AM, et al. (2018) Gut metabolome meets microbiome: A methodological perspective to understand the relationship between host and microbe. *Methods*, 149, 3–12.

Langille MG, Zaneveld J, Caporaso JG, et al. (2013) Predictive functional profiling of microbial communities using 16S rRNA marker gene sequences. *Nature Biotechnology*, 31, 814.

Liu B, Eydallin G, Maharjan RP, et al. (2017) Natural *Escherichia coli* isolates rapidly acquire genetic changes upon laboratory domestication. *Microbiology*, 163, 22–30.

Maier L, Pruteanu M, Kuhn M, et al. (2018) Extensive impact of non-antibiotic drugs on human gut bacteria. *Nature*, 555, 623.

Mallick H, Ma S, Franzosa EA, et al. (2017) Experimental design and quantitative analysis of microbial community multiomics. *Genome Biology*, 18, 228.

Maurice CF, Knowles SC, Ladau J, et al. (2015) Marked seasonal variation in the wild mouse gut microbiota. *The ISME Journal*, 9, 2423.

McKnight DT, Huerlimann R, Bower DS, et al. (2019) Methods for normalizing microbiome data: An ecological perspective. *Methods in Ecology and Evolution*, 10, 389–400.

Meadow JF, Altrichter AE, Green JL. (2014) Mobile phones carry the personal microbiome of their owners. *PeerJ*, 2, e447.

Mehnaz S, Mirza MS, Haurat J, et al. (2001) Isolation and 16S rRNA sequence analysis of the beneficial bacteria from the rhizosphere of rice. *Canadian Journal of Microbiology*, 47, 110–117.

Mendoza ML, Xiong Z, Escalera-Zamudio M, et al. (2018) Hologenomic adaptations underlying the evolution of sanguivory in the common vampire bat. *Nature Ecology & Evolution*, 2, 659.

Muletz-Wolz CR, Almario JG, Barnett SE, et al. (2017) Inhibition of fungal pathogens across genotypes and temperatures by amphibian skin bacteria. *Frontiers in Microbiology*, 8, 1551.

Namiki T, Hachiya T, Tanaka H, Sakakibara Y. (2012) MetaVelvet: An extension of Velvet assembler to de novo metagenome assembly from short sequence reads. *Nucleic Acids Research*, 40, e155.

Nguyen LH, Holmes S. (2019) Ten quick tips for effective dimensionality reduction. *PLoS Computational Biology*, 15, e1006907.

Nguyen NH, Song Z, Bates ST, et al. (2016) FUNGuild: An open annotation tool for parsing fungal community datasets by ecological guild. *Fungal Ecology*, 20, 241–248.

Nishida AH, Ochman H. (2018) Rates of gut microbiome divergence in mammals. *Molecular Ecology*, 27, 1884–1897.

Paliy O, Shankar V. (2016) Application of multivariate statistical techniques in microbial ecology. *Molecular Ecology*, 25, 1032–1057.

Parks DH, Chuvochina M, Waite DW, et al. (2018) A standardized bacterial taxonomy based on genome phylogeny substantially revises the tree of life. *Nature Biotechnology*, 36, 996–1004.

Piovia-Scott J, Rejmanek D, Woodhams DC, et al. (2017) Greater species richness of bacterial skin symbionts better suppresses the amphibian fungal pathogen *Batrachochytrium dendrobatidis*. *Microbial Ecology*, 74, 217–226.

Pollock J, Glendinning L, Wisedchanwet T, et al. (2018) The madness of microbiome: Attempting to find consensus 'best practice' for 16S microbiome studies. *Applied and Environmental Microbiology*, 84, e02627–17.

Prosser JI. (2010) Replicate or lie. *Environmental Microbiology*, 12, 1806–1810.

Quince C, Walker AW, Simpson JT, et al. (2017) Shotgun metagenomics, from sampling to analysis. *Nature Biotechnology*, 35, 833.

Rahnavard G, Franzosa EA, McIver LJ, et al. (2017) High-sensitivity pattern discovery in large multi-omic datasets. Available at https://huttenhower.sph.harvard.edu /halla.

Rebollar EA, Gutiérrez-Preciado A, Noecker C, et al. (2018) The skin microbiome of the neotropical frog *Craugastor fitzingeri*:

Inferring potential bacterial–host–pathogen interactions from metagenomic data. *Frontiers in Microbiology*, 9, 466.

Rohart F, Gautier B, Singh A, et al. (2017) mixOmics: An R package for 'omics feature selection and multiple data integration. *PLoS Computational Biology*, 13, e1005752.

Sanders JG, Powell S, Kronauer DJ, et al. (2014) Stability and phylogenetic correlation in gut microbiota: Lessons from ants and apes. *Molecular Ecology*, 23, 1268–1283.

Sanders JG, Beichman AC, Roman J, et al. (2015) Baleen whales host a unique gut microbiome with similarities to both carnivores and herbivores. *Nature Communications*, 6, 8285.

Sankaran K, Holmes SP. (2019) Multitable methods for microbiome data integration. *Frontiers in Genetics*, 10, 627.

Sapp J, Fox GE. (2013) The singular quest for a universal tree of life. Microbiology and *Molecular Biology Reviews*, 77, 541–550.

Schloss PD, Westcott SL, Ryabin T, et al. (2009) Introducing mothur: Open-source, platform-independent, community-supported software for describing and comparing microbial communities. *Applied and Environmental Microbiology*, 75, 7537–7541.

Shakya M, Quince C, Campbell JH, et al. (2013) Comparative metagenomic and rRNA microbial diversity characterization using archaeal and bacterial synthetic communities. *Environmental Microbiology*, 15, 1882–1899.

Spor A, Koren O, Ley R. (2011) Unravelling the effects of the environment and host genotype on the gut microbiome. *Nature Reviews Microbiology*, 9, 279.

Stephens PA, Buskirk SW, Hayward GD, et al. (2005) Information theory and hypothesis testing: A call for pluralism. *Journal of Applied Ecology*, 42, 4–12.

Thomas T, Gilbert J, Meyer F. (2012) Metagenomics – A guide from sampling to data analysis. *Microbial Informatics and Experimentation*, 2, 3.

Turnbaugh PJ, Hamady M, Yatsunenko T, et al. (2009) A core gut microbiome in obese and lean twins. *Nature*, 457, 480.

Uritskiy GV, DiRuggiero J, Taylor J. (2018) MetaWRAP – A flexible pipeline for genome-resolved metagenomic data analysis. *Microbiome*, 6, 158.

Van der Walt AJ, Van Goethem MW, Ramond JB, et al. (2017) Assembling metagenomes, one community at a time. *BMC Genomics*, 18, 521.

Van Leeuwenhoek A. (1677) Observations, communicated to the publisher by Mr. Antony van Leeuwenhoek, in a Dutch letter of the 9th of October, 1677. Here English'd: Concerning little animals by him observed in rain-well-sea, and snow water; as also in water wherein pepper had lain infused. *Philosophical Transactions*, 12, 821–831.

Watrous JD, Dorrestein PC. (2011) Imaging mass spectrometry in microbiology. *Nature Reviews Microbiology*, 9, 683.

Weiss S, Xu ZZ, Peddada S, et al. (2017) Normalization and microbial differential abundance strategies depend upon data characteristics. *Microbiome*, 5, 27.

Wilmes P, Heintz-Buschart A, Bond PL. (2015). A decade of metaproteomics: Where we stand and what the future holds. *Proteomics*, 15, 3409–3417.

Xu J. (2006) Microbial ecology in the age of genomics and metagenomics: Concepts, tools, and recent advances. *Molecular Ecology*, 15, 1713–1731.

Xu Z, Malmer D, Langille MG, et al. (2014) Which is more important for classifying microbial communities: Who's there or what they can do? *The ISME Journal*, 8, 2357.

Zhou J, He Z, Yang Y, et al. (2015) High-throughput metagenomic technologies for complex microbial community analysis: Open and closed formats. *mBio*, 6, e02288–14.

Zierer J, Jackson MA, Kastenmüller G, et al. (2018) The fecal metabolome as a functional readout of the gut microbiome. *Nature Genetics*, 50, 790.

CHAPTER THREE

Microbiomes of soils

REUBEN MARGERISON, OCÉANE NICOLITCH
AND YAQIAN ZHANG
University of Manchester

3.1 Introduction

The soil microbiome is intimately involved in global nutrient cycling and plant nutrition, and supports a vast range of ecosystem functions that vary depending on the environmental context. Soil broadly comprises minerals, organic matter, biological organisms, gas and water, which provides nutrients and structure that form niches and habitats for microorganisms to flourish (Needelman, 2013). As such, soil is an incredibly heterogeneous environment at both the micro and macro scales, and this is mirrored in the diversity of microorganisms that dwell in it. Bacteria and fungi predominate in soil, with a lower abundance of archaea, followed by protists and viruses (Fierer, 2017). Despite being incredibly diverse, around 500 bacterial phylotypes (about 2% of global soil 'species') account for half of soil bacterial communities globally (Delgado-Baquerizo et al., 2018). That said, there is also wide global variation in soil microbiomes, with taxonomic and functional (gene) diversity of soil bacteria highest at mid-latitudes, and lower at the poles and equator (Bahram et al., 2018). The same is also true for fungal taxonomic diversity, although intriguingly, fungal functional diversity shows the opposite pattern, peaking at the poles and equator (Bahram et al., 2018). For both kingdoms, however, environmental variables rather than geographic location appear to be more important in determining community composition and function (Bahram et al., 2018). For bacteria, pH is the predominant environmental variable that drives community composition, along with carbon and oxygen quality/quantity, soil moisture, and N and P availability (Fierer, 2017; Bahram et al., 2018). Bacterial functional diversity is strongly associated with mean annual precipitation (with decreasing diversity as precipitation increases), which may explain the latitudinal gradient exhibited (Bahram et al., 2018). For fungi, C/N ratio is the strongest predictor of community composition and function, which may reflect higher energy requirements and niche specialisation compared with bacteria (Bahram et al., 2018). Indeed, fungal and bacterial functional diversity have opposite relationships to one another with both mean annual precipitation and pH, suggesting considerable niche separation between these two key soil kingdoms.

In this chapter, we consider the soil itself as a host for a microbiome, as well as interactions between soil and plant hosts, more of which is also covered in Chapter 4. We first outline the general roles of the soil microbiome in global nutrient cycling and ecosystem functioning. We then look at the soil microbiomes of two of the dominant terrestrial ecosystems: grasslands and forests, where critical interactions between plants and soil microorganisms determine plant community structure and plant species diversity (Klironomos, 2002; Reynolds et al., 2003; van der Heijden et al., 2008; Bardgett & Wardle, 2010; Augusto et al., 2015; Tedersoo et al., 2016; Uroz et al., 2016; van der Putten et al., 2016). Further, we also briefly look at how soil microbiomes differ in other environments including deserts, tundra and peatlands.

3.2 Importance of the soil microbiome for global nutrient cycling and ecosystem functioning

The soil microbiome plays vital roles in the provision and sustenance of ecosystem services and functions through primary (plant) productivity, nutrient cycling and the maintenance of plant diversity in ecosystems (e.g. van der Heijden et al., 2008; Singh et al., 2010; Bates et al., 2011; van der Putten et al., 2016; Geisen et al., 2018). Plant diversity is closely related to soil microbial diversity (van der Heijden et al., 1998; Vogelsang et al., 2006; Millard & Singh, 2010; Prober et al., 2015; Semchenko et al., 2018), although the precise mechanisms by which soil biodiversity enhances ecosystem functioning are still unclear (Bardgett & van der Putten, 2014). Soil microorganisms also promote plant growth and increase crop yield and quality through nutrient mobilisation and transport (Berg et al., 2013). Bacteria that support root and plant growth are generally regarded as plant growth–promoting rhizobacteria (PGPR), and PGPR communities are often engineered by plants through the release of root exudates (Shukla et al., 2011). Some PGPR can also enter root interior tissues (the endosphere; Rhoden et al, 2015), and these endophytes play an important role in host plants, usually by promoting growth potential and biocontrol activities against phytopathogens (Falcäo et al., 2014; see Chapters 4 and 7 for more on this).

More direct symbiotic systems also occur; for nitrogen-fixing, the root nodules created by leguminous (family Fabaceae) plants facilitate rhizobium symbiosis, as well as rhizothamnia produced by the association between actinorhizal plants (e.g. Elaeagnaceae) and *Frankia* bacteria. Indeed, soil microorganisms have important roles in regulating the cycling of carbon (C), nitrogen (N), phosphorus (P) and other nutrients. Many soil microorganisms (e.g. bacteria and saprotrophic and symbiotic mycorrhizal fungi) produce extracellular enzymes that breakdown complex organic forms of C, N and P from dead organic matter (e.g. leaf and root litter) (Schimel & Schaeffer, 2012) to release forms that are more readily available for uptake by plants and soil microorganisms. For example, a major group of soil microorganisms involved in N cycling via the regulation of nitrate supply and losses in/from grasslands ecosystems are the nitrifying bacteria (e.g. *Nitrosomonas* spp. and *Nitrobacter* spp.) and archaea (ammonia-oxidising; e.g. *Nitrososphaera* spp.). During the nitrification process, these microorganisms oxidise reduced forms of N (i.e. ammonia) into nitrates (and may also alter soil pH and other soil chemical properties indirectly). In addition, soil microorganisms respire soil C during decomposition to sustain growth and cellular activity that, in turn, has implications on the storage or release of C from the ecosystem and consequently, global C stocks (Schlesinger & Andrews, 2000; Cheng et al., 2012). Furthermore, plant-associated microorganisms can benefit plants through the suppression of diseases by occupying physical space that would otherwise be taken up by pathogens and promoting biotic stress resistance (Berg et al., 2013). Thus, soil microbiomes underpin our global ecosystems that support biodiversity and provide the vast array of ecosystem services that are essential for humans. Two types of (semi-)natural terrestrial habitats that are particularly important and well-studied include grasslands and forests, and we will now look at these soil microbiomes in more detail.

3.3 Microbiomes of grassland soils

Grasslands are largely defined by their plant communities, consisting predominantly of grasses (members of the family Poaceae) and other low-growing, non-woody plant species (Gibson, 2008). Grassland habitats are estimated to occupy ~40% of the Earth's terrestrial surface (White et al., 2000; Gibson, 2008) and can be found at a wide range of altitudes, and in all continents except Antarctica (White et al., 2000; Gibson, 2008). Grassland ecosystems provide highly valuable services and functions such as the regulation of hydrology, nutrient cycling, C sequestration, food production and social–cultural services (e.g. Sala et al., 1997; Gibson, 2008; Grigulis et al., 2013). The soil microbiome is a critical component of the decomposition process and nutrient cycling of grassland ecosystems (van der Heijden et al., 2008; Freschet et al., 2013). Furthermore, the below-ground component of grasslands form a substantial sink of global C stocks, and modelling studies suggest that grassland ecosystems remain a highly reliable sink of C in future climate change scenarios (Hu et al., 2001; Dass et al., 2018) as they possess a greater ability to adapt to extreme weather events than other vegetation types (Vicente-Serrano et al., 2013).

Many grasses and non-woody plant species occurring in grasslands form symbiotic plant–root associations with arbuscular mycorrhizal fungi and, as such, the arbuscular mycorrhizal fungi form an important component of the microbiome of grassland soils (Brundrett, 2002; Smith & Read, 2008). Symbiotic associations involving other mycorrhizal fungal types such as ecto- and ericoid mycorrhizal fungi are less usual in grasslands, as these tend to associate with woody and ericaceous plant species, respectively (Brundrett, 2002; Smith & Read, 2008). Arbuscular mycorrhizal fungi possess the ability to enhance the performance of their plant–host symbiont by assisting the uptake of limiting nutrients from the soil (Smith & Read, 2008). This is achieved through the production of external mycelia by the arbuscular mycorrhizal fungi, which increase the effective absorptive surface area of the roots (Smith & Gianinazzi-Pearson, 1988) and help the plant–host 'scavenge' the soil solution for pockets of limiting nutrients (e.g. inorganic N or P) that are distant from the plant roots or within soil pores that are too small for plant roots to access (Lambers et al., 2008a; Smith & Read, 2008). Although arbuscular mycorrhizal fungi, when compared with ecto- and ericoid mycorrhizal fungi, possess relatively lower capacity to produce extracellular enzymes that break down complex organic substrates to assist plant nutrient uptake (Lambers et al., 2008b), several studies showed that arbuscular mycorrhizal fungi contribute substantially to the breakdown of organic matter (e.g. Hodge et al., 2001; Talbot et al., 2008). In addition to nutrient uptake, arbuscular mycorrhizal fungi also benefit plants by enhancing their ability to acquire water (e.g. Augé, 2001; Ruiz-Lozano, 2003), reducing their susceptibility to soil-borne pathogens (e.g. Newsham et al., 1995; Azcón-Aguilar & Barea, 1997; Wehner et al., 2011; Cameron et al., 2013) and/or enabling inter-plant signalling through a common mycelial (or mycorrhizal) network that boosts plant-defence responses against herbivory and diseases (e.g. Gorzelak et al., 2015; Johnson & Gilbert, 2015). In return, the plant–host supplies the obligate biotrophic arbuscular mycorrhizal fungi symbiont with C in the form of plant-derived photosynthates (Smith & Read, 2008). By enhancing growth of their plant symbionts, arbuscular mycorrhizal fungi have a crucial role in driving the primary productivity and C sequestration of grasslands through the increased capture and input of C by plants into the soil as organic C stocks.

Nitrogen is an essential nutrient for driving primary productivity in grasslands, but is continually lost through grazing activity, leaching and background volatilisation (Whitehead, 1995; Carlsson & Huss-Danell, 2003; LeBauer & Treseder, 2008; Fay et al., 2015). While dinitrogen (N_2) is highly abundant in the atmosphere, eukaryotes – including vascular plants – are unable to directly access this gaseous form, and gaseous N_2 must be 'fixed' into ammonia (NH_3) that can then be further converted to other more assimilable forms of N. In grasslands, where N limits productivity, below-ground symbiotic and asymbiotic diazotrophic microorganisms are responsible for the biological N fixation (BNF) of atmospheric N – via the nitrogenase enzyme complex – and account for substantial inputs of N (aside from anthropogenic inputs) (Ledgard & Steele, 1992; Cleveland et al., 1999). Symbiotic N fixation is a key pathway for BNF in grasslands where 'N-fixing' plants (i.e. plant species with the ability to form symbiotic relationships with N-fixing bacteria) are either naturally abundant or have been introduced as forage crops (Cowling, 1982; Ledgard & Steele, 1992). On the other hand, asymbiotic N-fixing micro-organisms (e.g. free-living cyanobacteria) are a more important source of biological N input in certain grasslands where 'N-fixing' plants are extremely low in abundance or absent (Reed et al., 2011; Keuter et al., 2014). Moreover, BNF pathways via N-fixing soil microorganisms (e.g. *Azospirillum* spp. and *Herbaspirillum* spp.) that 'colonise' plant roots extracellularly and/or form asymbiotic endophytic associations are often overlooked. However, these asymbiotic BNF pathways have been increasingly found to occur in many non-symbiotic 'N-fixing' plant species (including grasses) (e.g. van Dommelen & Vanderleyden, 2007) and may also contribute substantially towards the BNF of grasslands containing little or no symbiotic 'N-fixing' plant species (e.g. Marques et al., 2017). Nitrifying bacteria have been shown to be more impor-tant than archaea in driving the nitrification process in fertile, intensively managed grassland soils; conversely, ammonia-oxidising archaea were sug-gested to be more important in nutrient-poor grasslands due to their compe-titive advantage in 'stressful' environments (Di et al., 2009; Sterngren et al., 2015). As such, nitrifying bacteria and archaea are likely to play important roles in influencing the plant diversity of grasslands through soil abiotic properties via N resource partitioning (van der Heijden et al., 2008; Boudsocq et al., 2012). This is because certain plant species (and their mycor-rhizal symbionts) preferentially uptake nitrate over ammonia or dissolved organic forms of N for their N requirement, and certain plants may be pro-moted or disadvantaged depending on the soil nitrate availability (e.g. Tilman & Wedin, 1991; Weigelt et al., 2005; Gubsch et al., 2011). Therefore, improving our mechanistic understanding of the controls and responses of BNF via symbiotic and asymbiotic N-fixing microorganisms and soil-nitrifying micro-organisms may improve sustainable management practices of productive/ intensively managed grasslands, and potentially enable the use of highly effective N-fixing microorganisms as 'biofertilisers' to enhance BNF (e.g. Richardson et al., 2009; Lüscher et al., 2014). These developments will, in turn, reduce the dependency on the use of chemical fertilisers associated with negative environmental impacts (Ledgard & Steele, 1992; Vance, 2001).

The rate of decomposition and the consequent release (or immobilisation) of nutrients into the soil solution may vary depending on the environment and land-use/management practices of the grassland (e.g. Anderson, 1991; Chapin et al., 2002; Cheng et al., 2012; Ochoa-Hueso et al., 2019). For example, decom-position responses of soil microorganisms to the quality of soil organic matter could, in part, explain weaker soil nutrient retention abilities of intensively-managed grasslands (e.g. fertilised pastures) when compared with relatively nutrient-poor natural grasslands (of high conservation quality) (de Vries & Bardgett, 2012). That is, intensively managed grasslands that contain high N content in excess of microbial demands will experience net microbial excretion of inorganic forms of N (i.e. N mineralisation) that are prone to leaching losses (Schimel & Bennett, 2004). Additionally, because greater temperature and soil moisture promote microbial decomposition activity (Bontti et al., 2009; Craine & Gelderman, 2011; Solly et al., 2014), decomposition rates in semi-arid alpine grasslands are expected to be comparatively lower than those of mesic grasslands of similar nutrient status occurring at a lower altitude.

Competitiveness and dominance of plant species in grassland communities have been related to the differences in degree of dependency on mycorrhizal fungi by plants for nutrient uptake and the species identity of the associated mycorrhizal symbiont(s) (e.g. Klironomos, 2003; Scheublin et al., 2007; Smith & Read, 2008; van der Heijden & Horton, 2009), which could result in differing effectiveness of the plant at acquiring nutrients. Mycorrhizal fungal networks among plants may also play an important role in facilitative plant–plant interactions by assisting the transfer of resources among plants connected to the mycorrhizal network (e.g. Leake et al., 2004; Brooker et al., 2008; van der Heijden & Horton, 2009), which could help promote species co-existence in grassland ecosystems with stressful environmental conditions (van der Heijden & Horton, 2009). Further, host-specific soil-borne pathogens (e.g. fungi, oomycetes) that negatively affect plant performance also play a critical role in shaping plant diversity in many grassland ecosystems via biotic plant–soil feedback mechanisms (e.g. Bever, 1994; Klironomos, 2002; Kardol et al., 2006; Harrison & Bardgett, 2010; Maron et al., 2011; Reinhart, 2012). Biotic plant–soil feedback occurs when the rhizosphere is modified by a plant (e.g. litter or root activity), which in turn influences the performance of itself and/or other plant species (Kulmatiski & Kardol, 2008; van der Putten et al., 2013). Positive biotic feedback occurs when the soil microbial community, conditioned by a plant, improves the growth performance of conspecific plants more than its competitors (e.g. suppression of host-specific pathogens via litter leachates or root exudates, or the accumulation of beneficial mycorrhizal fungi in the rhizosphere), promoting dominance of that species. Conversely, negative feedback is typically linked to the accumulation of host-specific pathogens, which promotes species coexistence in plant communities by reducing the growth performance (or competitiveness) of conspecific plant species (Bever et al., 1997; Ehrenfeld et al., 2005; Mangan et al., 2010; van der Putten et al., 2013). It is critical to understand the roles of soil microorganisms in these processes that drive plant community dynamics and vice versa, because the effects of greater biodiversity (particularly of plants) have been widely demonstrated to enhance the functioning (e.g. productivity, C sequestration, etc.) of grassland ecosystems and their resistance and resilience to disturbances (e.g. Hooper et al., 2005; Bardgett & Wardle, 2010; Isbell et al., 2015; Oliver et al., 2015).

Soil protists are also a functionally important and diverse (polyphyletic) group of eukaryotic unicellular microorganisms that occur in grasslands (Venter et al., 2017; Fiore-Donno et al., 2019). For example, the various functional groups of heterotrophic protists, in terms of their feeding traits (e.g. bacterivores, omnivores, plant parasites), are part of soil food webs and are expected to have important roles in driving the community structures of plants and other soil microorganisms such as bacteria, fungi and algae (Trap et al., 2016; Dassen et al., 2017; Geisen et al., 2018). Likewise, the community structures of soil protists are closely related to that of other groups of microorganisms and the abiotic edaphic factors (e.g. moisture, texture, N content) that affect these (and plant communities) (Dassen et al., 2017; Venter et al., 2017; Geisen et al., 2018; Fiore-Donno et al., 2019). Moreover, soil protist diversity has been shown to be associated with plant functional group diversity in grasslands (Ledeganck et al., 2003). However, current knowledge of soil protists and their ecological roles in grasslands (and other terrestrial biomes) is largely limited compared with that of soil fungi and bacteria. This could be attributed to the difficulty in identifying molecular markers for the vast diversity of polyphyletic protist groups (Pawlowski et al., 2012; Geisen et al., 2018; Fiore-Donno et al., 2019).

Recent advancements in molecular techniques to better study the various groups of soil microorganisms and their functional roles (Fierer et al., 2013; Jansson & Hofmockel, 2018; Chapter 2), together with many long-term grassland biodiversity experiments (e.g. Jena Experiment (Weisser et al., 2017), Cedar Creek Ecosystem Science Reserve (Tilman et al., 2001), Buxton Climate Change Impacts Lab (Booth & Grime, 2003), Park Grass Experiment (Silvertown et al., 2006), etc.) means we can gain better insights into the interactions between plants and the soil microbiome of grassland ecosystems. Knowledge gained will provide novel opportunities, such as better manipulation of the soil microbial and plant communities to effectively restore degraded grasslands (Fierer et al., 2013; Bender et al., 2016; French et al., 2017; Koziol & Bever, 2017) and to enhance the resilience and resistance of grassland ecosystems to global change (Isbell et al., 2015; Craven et al., 2016).

3.4 Microbiomes of forest soils

Forests cover four billion hectares globally and are often considered as one of the most important C sinks on Earth. Each year, approximately two billion tonnes of carbon dioxide (CO_2) equivalent are absorbed through the leaves of trees (FAO, 2018). While a large proportion of this C is allocated to the above-ground and below-ground biomass of a tree (~42%), a similar amount of this is exuded by the roots into the rhizosphere soil (~44%), where it can be miner-alised by microbial communities (Pan et al., 2011). However, characterising the complexity of the forest soil microbiome remains challenging considering the highly contrasting environmental conditions where different types of forests occur.

At global scales, forest ecosystems are mainly shaped by climatic conditions and soil types, resulting in three extensive biomes: tropical, temperate and boreal (in order of distance from the equator). The importance of temperature in shaping the structure of the forest soil microbiome has been shown in a recent continental-scale study, where bacterial and fungal diversities increased along a temperature-gradient (Zhou et al., 2016). Those temperature-driven variations can be explained directly and indirectly through the meta-bolic theory of ecology, which predicts a higher metabolic activity of organ-isms exposed to higher temperatures (Brown et al., 2004). In boreal forests, low temperatures restrict microbial activities, organic matter decomposition and nutrient cycling, resulting in C accumulation in soil organic matter and N depletion. In contrast, the warm and wet conditions of tropical forests enhance microbial activities and encourage a rapid turnover of soil organic matter and nitrogen enrichment (Malhi et al., 1999; Reinsch et al., 2017). Variation in soil edaphic properties such as pH, texture or nutrient availability are often described as good predictors of microbial community structure (Fierer & Jackson, 2006; Lauber et al., 2008). However, the relative influence of climatic and physicochemical factors on microbial community distribution remains context-dependent as the magnitude of change in temperature, moisture or pH is specific to the biome considered (Delgado-Baquerizo & Eldridge, 2019). Thus, the range of forest biomes possesses a huge diversity of soil microbiomes at the larger geographical scales.

The great complexity and diversity of soil microbiomes also exist at local scales. This is because the dominance of large trees in forests and the unique microhabitats they create (e.g. tree roots, thick litter layers, deadwood) provide high spatial heterogeneity in soils, which in turn enables the existence of a variety of specific microbial communities (Štursová & Baldrian, 2011). In particular, tree roots of boreal, temperate and the majority of tropical forests are known to form symbiotic associations with ectomycorrhizal fungi, which represent 80% of the fungal community and one-third of the total microbial biomass in forest soils (Högberg & Högberg, 2002; Wallander, 2006). Consequently, forest microbiomes are often characterised by high fungal/bac-terial ratios, and consistently harbour a lower bacterial diversity than grasslands or agricultural soils (Roesch et al., 2007; Tedersoo et al., 2012; Delgado-Baquerizo & Eldridge, 2019). In litter and deadwood, the accumulation of organic matter also selects for specific microbial communities, mainly sapro-trophic fungi, which are able to decompose recalcitrant plant-derived biopoly-mers (Lindahl et al., 2007). Litter-derived organic matter accumulates in the first few centimetres of soil and decreases with soil depth, creating a sharp vertical stratification in forest soils and an alteration of microbial composition accom-panied by an increasing fungal/bacterial ratio (Lindahl et al., 2007; Šnajdr et al., 2008). However, this effect is dampened in tropical forests due to the high turnover of organic matter (Tedersoo et al., 2012). In temperate and boreal ecosystems, microbial community composition follows an annual cycle due to seasonal changes in photosynthesis rates, root exudation and litter production, which alter C and N cycling through the soil microbiome (Kaiser et al., 2010; Rasche et al., 2011).

Symbiotic interactions between ectomycorrhizal fungi and their hosts are relatively well studied (Finlay et al., 1990; Tibbett, 2002). Fossil evidence indicates that this type of interaction is approximately 50 million years old, although molecular clock data suggest it may have originated over 180 million years ago (Strullu-Derrien et al., 2018). Throughout evolution, ectomycorrhizal fungi have lost a large portion of their enzymatic toolkit and their ability to degrade complex carbohydrates remains limited. However, the oxidation of organic matter remains possible through Fenton reactions or peroxidase activity (Kohler et al., 2015; Lindahl & Tunlid, 2015). The mycelia of ectomy-corrhizal fungi can cover several square metres and are able to reach extended areas of soil where they can assist the acquisition of soluble nutrients (e.g. N, P) and water, mobilise nutrients from organic matter via the release of extra-cellular enzymes, or effect mineral weathering (Hagerberg et al., 2016; Nehls & Plassard, 2018). The exchange of nutrients, C, and water between the ectomycorrhizal fungi and host tree occurs via the 'Hartig net', which is composed of the hyphae of the ectomycorrhizal fungi that enclose the host's root cells (Hobbie & Högberg, 2012). Some studies have also demonstrated nutrient transfer between trees through their associated fungal mycelia net-work (Leake et al., 2004). Ectomycorrhizal fungi can also enhance the tree's defence against soil-borne pathogens, and may play a role in maintaining the tree species diversity in tropical forests (i.e. pathogen-mediated negative den-sity dependence) (Lambers et al., 2018).

The decomposition and recycling of organic matter contained in litter or deadwood are crucial steps in the C cycle of forest soils. This process is highly complex due to the seasonal dynamics of litter composition and quality, leading to a succession of decomposer microorganisms, among which sapro-trophic fungi are the main actors (Urbanová et al., 2015). Labile carbon com-pounds, such as simple carbohydrates or amino acids, are taken up first, and favour competitive and fast-growing microorganisms (Hobbie, 1996). Among complex carbohydrates, cellulose and hemicellulose are rapidly decomposed by a range of microorganisms through exoenzymes like cellulase, hemicellulose or glucosidase. However, the most recalcitrant compounds such as lignin or chitin require peroxidases or *N*-acetyl-glycosaminidases to be decomposed. While saprotrophic fungi are usually considered the most important actors of organic matter decomposition, recent findings also suggest a key role of bacteria in the degradation of recalcitrant organic matter in forest soils. In litter of a coniferous forest, Betaproteobacteria, Bacteroidetes and Acidobacteria incorporated more C than fungi (Štursová et al., 2012). Understanding the factors regulating the mechanisms of organic matter degradation in the soil by the microbiota is a key question in the context of global change, as C contained in leaf litter can either be mineralised and released in the form of CO_2, or immobilised in the microbial biomass for long-term storage in soils.

Nutrients such as phosphorus, potassium, magnesium, calcium and iron often occur as insoluble minerals in forest soils. As such, mineral weathering, occurring through biotic or abiotic processes, increases soil nutrient availability, and is a key process in biogeochemical cycles in forest ecosystems. Microbial communities are strongly involved in this process through the production of siderophores, protons or organic acids (citrate, gluconate, oxalate, succinate; Richardson & Simpson, 2011). An increasing range of studies have identified specific microbial communities that colonise minerals depending on their chemical composition, leading to the advancement of the 'mineralosphere' concept (Uroz et al., 2015; Colin et al., 2016; Whitman et al., 2018). While this ability seems to be widespread in fungal communities, only a few members of the bacterial kingdom exhibit efficient mineral weathering in forest soils, such as members of the genera *Burkholderia* and *Collimonas* (Adamo & Violante, 2000; Uroz et al., 2009). This mineral-weathering ability, through the mobilisation of inorganic nutrients, is essential for tree growth, particularly in nutrient-limited conditions. In the case of ectomycorrhizal symbiosis, those nutrients are directly allocated to the tree in exchange for carbon (Landeweert et al., 2001). Enrichment of mineral-weathering microbial communities, dependent on the soil nutrient conditions, has also been suggested in the rhizosphere of beech trees (Nicolitch et al., 2016; Colin et al., 2017).

3.5 Soil microbiomes in other environments

3.5.1 Desert soils

Desert soils – comprising mostly sand – generally represent an extreme environment for soil microorganisms. While deserts are present in many different parts of the world, they all share a combination of extreme temperatures and low water availability (Lugtenberg, 2015). As there is little plant litter in desert soils, soil microorganisms here inhabit a very different environment to those found in other habitats (Aguirre-Garrido et al., 2012).

Extremophiles (bacteria and archaea) are the first colonisers in desert environments (Mapelli et al., 2012), due to their adaptations to survive in harsh physical and chemical conditions (Colica et al., 2014). The soil develops slowly to later include multicellular organisms including fungi, lichens and mosses, which form biological soil crusts (BSCs) that play key roles in the ecological security and health of the desert region (Li et al., 2018). Some examples include stabilising soil against erosion, improving germination in the niches created by BSCs, providing habitat for a large number of microorganisms (Xu et al., 2013). Thus, BSCs are regarded as the key biotic component of desert ecosystems by helping to maintain soil stability, fix C and N, and aid establishment of vascular plants (Li et al., 2018).

Soil microbiomes of deserts are primarily influenced by abiotic processes, although some desert plants or animals can also shape soil microbial diversity (Lugtenberg, 2015). Shifts in temperature and precipitation affect the function of desert ecosystems by altering the species composition of BSCs. For example, an experiment that simulated warming and reduced precipitation over a 10-year period showed that mosses in crustal communities would be more impacted under climate change when compared with lichens and cyanobacteria, which would lead to a direct alteration of the hydrological performance of BSCs (Li et al., 2018). However, the extent to which other important components of desert soil microbiomes may respond to climate change is still not well understood.

While the complexity of desert plants is related to environmental factors such as moisture, pH, climate, lithology, temperature, and nutrient and organic matter content (Kaplan et al., 2013), the ability of desert plants to adapt to drought stress in desert environments has also been shown to be related to the bacterial composition of the soil microbiome (Shelef et al., 2013). Conversely, plants in desert ecosystems can also strongly influence the microbial community composition and enhance microbial growth in their rhizosphere (Jorquera et al., 2012; Mapelli et al. 2013). For example, Ferjani et al. (2015) showed that date palms (*Phoenix dactylifera*) from the southern Tunisian desert possess a rhizosphere community completely different to that in the surrounding soil.

Research into desert soil microbiomes may also improve food production in desert regions through understanding the complex microbial diversity that are naturally exposed to extreme climatic conditions (de Vries & Wallenstein, 2017). Many studies have shown the importance of associated root bacteria in increasing crop yield and soil fertility (Kumar et al., 2014; Nadeem et al., 2014). This is currently applied in desert farming, as well as restoration and reforestation of eroded desert lands. For example, a study looking at rhizobacteria associated with desert plants in Saudi Arabia has identified *Bacillus* spp., *Enterobacter* spp. and *Pseudomonas* spp. that inhibit phytopathogenic fungi (El-

Sayed et al., 2014). Based on plant growth promotion properties, resilience to harsh conditions and antagonistic potentials, the strains have been proposed for use as biofertilisers (El-Sayed et al., 2014).

3.5.2 Peatland soils

Peatlands are characterised by an accumulation of dead organic material on the soil surface due to water-saturated conditions that prevent the complete decomposition of plant material (Joosten & Clarke, 2002). Although covering only 2.84% of land, representing 4.23 million km^2 (Xu et al., 2018), peatlands play a significant role in soil C storage and cycling (Page et al., 2011). The sequestration of carbon arises from the imbalance between inputs by primary productivity and losses through decomposition by microorganisms. Peatland microorganisms not only directly control the turnover of organic C, they are also instrumental in nutrient mineralisation and uptake, and can therefore feedback on plant productivity and overall ecosystem functioning (Andersen et al., 2013). Although all types of peatlands have the capacity to sequester C and produce methane (CH_4), the composition of microbial communities that drive this is sensitive to changes in pH, hydrologic regime, trophic levels, mineral element concentration and vegetation (Andersen et al., 2013). For example, temperature influences organic matter decomposition through the inherent mediation of microbial activity and biochemical reactions (Davidson & Janssens, 2006).

Microbial populations of peatlands possess a large diversity of metabolic rates (Williams & Crawford, 1983). However, the relative contribution of each of the different microbial groups to decomposition and nutrient cycling processes are still unknown (Winsborough & Basiliko, 2010). This is because relatively few studies have examined peatland microbial communities as a whole, with most focusing on particular functional or trophic groups (e.g. methanogens or heterotrophic bacteria) or looking at particular processes from a strictly functional point of view (e.g. litter decomposition or carbon utilisation patterns). Moreover, it is unclear whether fungal (Golovchenko et al., 2007) or bacterial (Winsborough & Basiliko, 2010) biomass plays a more important structural and functional role overall in peatland ecosystems.

The microbial communities and related decomposition processes of all peatland types are influenced by depth, redox conditions and carbon quality (Morales et al., 2006). In natural peatlands, as organic matter accumulates, microorganisms at greater depths are challenged with increasing energetic constraints driven by a reduction in availability of oxygen and other electron acceptors (Artz, 2009). Fungal vertical stratification is generally characterised by a reduction in biomass rather than an alteration of the community, with spore numbers, biomass and hyphal length decreasing with increasing depth

(Golovchenko et al., 2002). On the other hand, bacterial communities change both in composition and size with depth, with studies showing a general decrease in biomass and diversity with depth (Jaatinen et al., 2007).

Microbial activity and functional decomposition differ among peatlands dominated by different plant growth forms, with shrub and sphagnum moss sites harbouring significantly different communities from forested and sedge peatlands (Fisk et al., 2003). Changes in the composition of the fungal community between peatland types are related to changes in litter type (Andersen et al., 2013), and evidence suggests that litter type may be an even more important driver of below-ground fungal community structure as a whole than abiotic factors such as groundwater levels (Trinder et al., 2008).

Many aspects of peatland soil microbiomes remain enigmatic, however. For example, little is known about the function(s) of dark septate endophytic fungi, despite being found widely distributed in roots in many boreal peatlands (Grunig & Sieber, 2005). In peatlands, any impact on microbial communities has the potential to alter carbon dynamics and nutrient cycling. As such, there is considerable need to further unravel the role and importance of fungi, bacteria and archaea in organic matter degradation and nutrient acquisition processes in this environment.

3.5.3 Tundra soils

Tundra refers to all kinds of rock and soil containing ice that experience temperatures below 0°C for a significant portion of the year. According to the duration of freezing state, tundra can be generally divided into short-term freeze, seasonal tundra and permafrost. The tundra is a highly heterogeneous and dynamic landscape with unique hydrothermal characteristics. As tundra soil microorganisms play important functions in biochemical cycling, studying the diversity and structure of microorganisms in the tundra will help to detect environmental changes and potentially develop effective measures to deal with these (Lydolph et al., 2005; Li et al., 2011).

Permafrost is characterised by stable low temperatures, low nutrient inputs and continuous exposure to low levels of radiation (Gilichinsky, 2002). Microbial abundance is relatively low; in the Arctic, Antarctic, Qinghai–Tibet Plateau and Siberian permafrost, the total number of microorganisms ranged from ~100 to 400 cells per gram of dry weight (Vishnivetskaya et al., 2006; Hansen et al., 2007; Zhang et al., 2007; Ganzert et al., 2011). Bacterial taxa included *Cellulomonas*, *Arthrobacter*, *Planococcus*, *Pseudomonas*, and genera from Acidobacteria, Firmicutes, Bacteroidetes, Proteobacteria and Gammaproteobacteria (Vishnivetskaya et al., 2006; Hansen et al., 2007; Zhang et al., 2007; Ganzert et al., 2011). Despite this low abundance, diversity and endemism is surprisingly high. High-throughput sequencing of bacterial communities in the front of Glacier No. 1 in the Urumqi River Source of Tianshan Mountains revealed 31 phyla, of which 19 were common bacteria and the rest were endemic to different regions of the same glacial valley (Wu et al., 2012). Zhang et al. (2007) found differences in microbial community composition between the layers of the permafrost on the Qinghai–Tibet Plateau, suggesting that the structural characteristics of microbial communities can also reflect the thickness of the active layer of tundra soil.

Soil temperature is perhaps the most important factor in permafrost microbial communities, affecting soil respiration, decomposition of soil organic matter, nitrogen mineralisation, denitrification, plant productivity and nutrient uptake by vegetation (Callesen et al., 2003). It is generally believed that the critical point of microbial metabolic activity is $-8°C$, and no microbial activity below $-12°C$ has been detected (Margesin, 2012). Bakermans et al. (2003) found that the growth of microorganisms in the Siberian permafrost was normal at $22°C$ and slowed to negligible at $-10°C$. Further research from the Siberian permafrost showed two-thirds of micro-organisms are active at $-2.5°C$, indicating many are cold-adapted bacteria (Vishnivetskaya et al., 2006). The upper, or 'active', layer of permafrost undergoes an annual freeze–thaw process, which leads to changes in temperature, water, organic matter, and pH in the active layer or seasonal tundra soil (Gilichinsky, 2002; Yergeau & Kowalchuk, 2008). These changes affect the formation of microbial cell membranes, as well as the growth and metabolism of microorganisms. Studies have shown that freeze–thaw cycles can significantly reduce microbial biomass and change the metabolic level of soil microbial communities (Jenkinson, 1990). Similarly, freeze–thaw cycles decrease the metabolic activity of microorganisms and affect the expression of deaminase, resulting in the release of nitrous oxide, a greenhouse gas (Sharma et al., 2006). Furthermore, Wagner et al. (2007) showed that higher permafrost temperatures resulted in significant increases in methanogenesis, and Rivkina et al. (2007) showed that the formation of CH_4 was closely related to microbial activity and temperature. Indeed, climate change has a direct impact on the metabolism of microbial physiological activities, and also affects the composition of microbial communities. Simulated experiments suggest that climate warming will significantly change the microbial community structure and increase soil microbial biomass in the tundra soil region by the mid twenty-first century (Anisimov, 2007). Lipson et al. (2000) also showed that changes in microbial diversity was correlated with changes in climatic factors, and Schadt et al. (2003) demonstrated similar results in the study of fungal community structure in tundra permafrost soil. Under warming conditions, freeze–thaw cycles in permafrost regions are intensifying, altering microorganism activity and associated biogeochemical cycles in permafrost, thus increasing the potential for climate change. It is predicted that the permafrost in the northern hemisphere will be reduced by 15–30% by the middle of the twenty-first century, and greenhouse gases will be released in large quantities (Anisimov, 2007).

Soil total C is another primary regulator of the structure of soil bacterial community in some tundra soils (Ganzert et al., 2011), which influences C mineralisation and thus plays an important role in soil microbial diversity (Jangid et al., 2008). Furthermore, Barns et al. (1999) suggest microflora differences in tundra soil are related to the variation in soil type and pH. The pH in tundra soil is mainly determined by the content of organic acids (Hobbie & Gough, 2004) and varies depending on locale; the Arctic and Siberian permafrost soils are acidic, while Antarctic and Chinese Qinghai–Tibet Plateau permafrost soils are alkaline (Hobbie & Gough, 2004). Water is one of the most important limiting factors for bacterial growth in tundra soil. There is a significant positive correlation between the number of microorganisms in permafrost and soil moisture content, potentially as the liquid water film in permafrost is too thin to encapsulate microorganisms or enable microbial cells to migrate within it (Wang et al., 2011). The degradation of permafrost leads to changes in soil water environments, which affects species composition and community succession in permafrost regions (Sturm et al., 2001). The unfrozen water in permafrost plays an important role in the transformation of microbial biomass and is an important determinant of heterotrophic microbial metabolism (Oquist et al., 2009). The heterotrophic activity of microorganisms is limited when soil moisture content is low and long-term water shortage can also cause the death or dormancy of microorganisms in permafrost (Graham et al., 2012). Low water content in permafrost additionally affects the fluidity of protein and soil enzyme activities, and the low temperatures affect the fluidity of cell membranes, which together are essential for the survival of soil microorganisms.

3.6 Conclusions

The microbiome of soils is highly diverse, and its constituent community varies greatly between habitats in both form and function. It both affects, and is influenced by, the substrate and environment, creating a complex whole that is greater than the sum of its parts. Soils also represent an incredible reservoir of biodiversity, with many constituents of the microbiome endemic to their specific locale. Advances in community characterisation and analysis will continue to illuminate the complexities of this diverse and heterogeneous environment, and enable a better understanding of how the functioning of the soil microbiome changes under a changing climate.

References

Adamo P, Violante P. (2000) Weathering of rocks and neogenesis of minerals associated with lichen activity. *Applied Clay Science*, 16, 229–256.

Aguirre-Garrido JF, Montiel-Lugo D, Hernández-Rodríguez C, et al. (2012) Bacterial community structure in the rhizosphere of three cactus species from semi-arid highlands in central Mexico. *Antonie van Leeuwenhoek*, 101, 891–904.

Anderson JM. (1991) The effects of climate change on decomposition processes in grassland and coniferous forests. *Ecological Applications*, 1, 326–347.

Andersen R, Chapman S, Artz RRE. (2013) Microbial communities in natural and disturbed peatlands: A review. *Soil Biology and Biochemistry*, 57, 979–994.

Anisimov OA. (2007) Potential feedback of thawing permafrost to the global climate system through methane emission. *Environmental Research Letters*, 2, 045016.

Artz RRE. (2009) Microbial community structure and carbon substrate use in Northern peatlands. In: Baird AJ, Belya LR, Comas X, et al. (Eds.), *Carbon Cycling in Northern Peatlands. Geophysical Monograph Series*, vol. 184. Washington, DC: American Geophysical Union.

Augé RM. (2001) Water relations, drought and vesicular–arbuscular mycorrhizal symbiosis. *Mycorrhiza*, 11, 3–42.

Augusto L, De Schrijver A, Vesterdal L, et al. (2015) Influences of evergreen gymnosperm and deciduous angiosperm tree species on the functioning of temperate and boreal forests. *Biological Reviews*, 90, 444–466.

Azcón-Aguilar C, Barea JM. (1997) Arbuscular mycorrhizas and biological control of soil-borne plant pathogens – an overview of the mechanisms involved. *Mycorrhiza*, 6, 457–464.

Bahram M, Hildebrand F, Forslund SK, et al. (2018) Structure and function of the global topsoil microbiome. *Nature*, 560, 233.

Bakermans C, Tsapin AI, Souza-Egipsy V, et al. (2003) Reproduction and metabolism at −10°C of bacteria isolated from Siberian permafrost. *Environmental Microbiology*, 5, 321–326.

Bardgett RD, Wardle DA. (2010) *Aboveground–Belowground Linkages: Biotic Interactions, Ecosystem Processes, and Global Change*. Oxford: Oxford University Press.

Bardgett RD, van der Putten WH. (2014) Belowground biodiversity and ecosystem functioning. *Nature*, 515, 505–511.

Barns SM, Takala SL, Kuske CR. (1999) Wide distribution and diversity of members of the bacterial kingdom *Acidobacterium* in the environment. *Applied Environmental Microbiology*, 65, 1731–1737.

Bates ST, Berg-Lyons D, Caporaso JG, et al. (2011) Examining the global distribution of dominant archaeal populations in soil. *The ISME Journal*, 5, 908–917.

Bender SF, Wagg C, van der Heijden MGA. (2016) An underground revolution: Biodiversity and soil ecological engineering for agricultural sustainability. *Trends in Ecology & Evolution*, 31, 440–452.

Berg G, Zachow C, Müller H, et al. (2013) Next-generation bio-products sowing the seeds of success for sustainable agriculture. *Agronomy*, 3, 648–656.

Bever JD. (1994) Feedback between plants and their soil communities in an old field community. *Ecology*, 75, 1965–1977.

Bever JD, Westover KM, Antonovics J. (1997) Incorporating the soil community into plant population dynamics: The utility of the feedback approach. *Journal of Ecology*, 85, 561–573.

Bontti EE, Decant JP, Munson SM, et al. (2009) Litter decomposition in grasslands of Central North America (US Great Plains). *Global Change Biology*, 15, 1356–1363.

Booth RE, Grime JP. (2003) Effects of genetic impoverishment on plant community diversity. *Journal of Ecology*, 91, 721–730.

Boudsocq S, Niboyet A, Lata JC, et al. (2012) Plant preference for ammonium versus nitrate: A neglected determinant of ecosystem functioning? *The American Naturalist*, 180, 60–69.

Brooker RW, Maestre FT, Callaway RM, et al. (2008) Facilitation in plant communities: The past, the present, and the future. *Journal of Ecology*, 96, 18–34.

Brown JH, Gillooly JF, Allen AP, et al. (2004) Toward a metabolic theory of ecology. *Ecology*, 85, 1771–1789.

Brundrett MC. (2002) Coevolution of roots and mycorrhizas of land plants. *New Phytologist*, 154, 275–304.

Callesen I, Liski J, Raulund-Rasmussen K, et al. (2003) Soil carbon stores in Nordic well-drained forest soils – Relationships with climate and texture class. *Global Change Biology*, 9, 358–370.

Cameron DD, Neal AL, van Wees SCM, et al. (2013) Mycorrhiza-induced resistance: More than the sum of its parts? *Trends in Plant Science*, 18, 539–545.

Carlsson G, Huss-Danell K. (2003) Nitrogen fixation in perennial forage legumes in the field. *Plant and Soil*, 253, 353–372.

Chapin FS, Matson PA, Mooney HA. (Eds.) (2002) Terrestrial decomposition. In: *Principles of Terrestrial Ecosystem Ecology*. New York, NY: Springer.

Cheng L, Booker FL, Tu C, et al. (2012) Arbuscular mycorrhizal fungi increase organic carbon decomposition under elevated CO_2. *Science*, 337, 1084–1087.

Cleveland CC, Townsend AR, Schimel DS, et al. (1999) Global patterns of terrestrial biological nitrogen (N_2) fixation in natural ecosystems. *Global Biogeochemical Cycles*, 13, 623–645.

Colica G, Li H, Rossi F, et al. (2014) Microbial secreted exopolysaccharides affect the hydrological behavior of induced biological soil crusts in desert sandy soils. *Soil Biology and Biochemistry*, 68, 62–70.

Colin Y, Nicolitch O, Turpault MP, et al. (2016) Mineral type and tree species determine the functional and taxonomic structure of forest soil bacterial communities. *Applied and Environmental Microbiology*, 83, 1–23.

Colin Y, Nicolitch O, Van Nostrand JD, et al. (2017) Taxonomic and functional shifts in the beech rhizosphere microbiome across a natural soil toposequence. *Scientific Reports*, 7, 1–17.

Cowling DW. (1982) Biological nitrogen fixation and grassland production in the United Kingdom. *Philosophical Transactions of the Royal Society Series B: Biological Sciences*, 296, 397–404.

Craine JM, Gelderman TM. (2011) Soil moisture controls on temperature sensitivity of soil organic carbon decomposition for a mesic grassland. *Soil Biology and Biochemistry*, 43, 455–457.

Craven D, Isbell F, Manning P, et al. (2016) Plant diversity effects on grassland productivity are robust to both nutrient enrichment and drought. *Philosophical Transactions of the Royal Society B: Biological Sciences*, 371, 20150277.

Dass P, Houlton BZ, Wang Y, et al. (2018) Grasslands may be more reliable carbon sinks than forests in California. *Environmental Research Letters*, 13, 074027.

Dassen S, Cortois R, Martens H, et al. (2017) Differential responses of soil bacteria, fungi, archaea and protists to plant species richness and plant functional group identity. *Molecular Ecology*, 26, 4085–4098.

Davidson EA, Janssens IA. (2006) Temperature sensitivity of soil carbon decomposition and feedbacks to climate change. *Nature*, 440, 165–173.

de Vries FT, Bardgett RD. (2012) Plant–microbial linkages and ecosystem nitrogen retention: Lessons for sustainable agriculture. *Frontiers in Ecology and the Environment*, 10, 425–432.

de Vries FT, Wallenstein MD. (2017) Below-ground connections underlying above-ground food production: A framework for optimising ecological connections in the rhizosphere. *Journal of Ecology*. 105, 913–920.

Delgado-Baquerizo M, Eldridge DJ. (2019) Cross-biome drivers of soil bacterial alpha diversity on a worldwide scale. *Ecosystems*, 22, 1220–1231.

Delgado-Baquerizo M, Oliverio AM, Brewer TE, et al. (2018) A global atlas of the dominant bacteria found in soil. *Science*, 359, 320–325.

Di HJ, Cameron KC, Shen JP, et al. (2009) Nitrification driven by bacteria and not archaea in nitrogen-rich grassland soils. *Nature Geoscience*, 2, 621–624.

Ehrenfeld JG, Ravit B, Elgersma K. (2005) Feedback in the plant–soil system. *Annual Review of Environment and Resources*, 30, 75–115.

El-Sayed WS, Akhkha A, El-Naggar MY, et al. (2014) *In vitro* antagonistic activity, plant growth promoting traits and phylogenetic affiliation of rhizobacteria associated with wild plants grown in arid soil. *Frontiers in Microbiology*, 5, 651.

Falcão LL, Silva-Werneck JO, Vilarinho BR, et al. (2014) Antimicrobial and plant growth-promoting properties of the cacao endophyte *Bacillus subtilis* ALB 629. *Journal of Applied Microbiology*, 116, 1584–1592.

Fay PA, Prober SM, Harpole WS, et al. (2015) Grassland productivity limited by multiple nutrients. *Nature Plants*, 1, 15080.

Ferjani R, Marasco R, Rolli E, et al. (2015) The date palm tree rhizosphere is a niche for plant growth promoting bacteria in the oasis ecosystem. *BioMed Research International*, 2015, 153851.

Fierer N. (2017) Embracing the unknown: Disentangling the complexities of the soil microbiome. *Nature Reviews Microbiology*, 15, 579.

Fierer N, Jackson RB. (2006) The diversity and biogeography of soil bacterial communities. *Proceedings of the National Academy of Sciences*, 103, 626–631.

Fierer N, Ladau J, Clemente JC, et al. (2013) Reconstructing the microbial diversity and function of pre-agricultural tallgrass prairie soils in the United States. *Science*, 342, 621–624.

Finlay RD, Ek H, Odham G, et al. (1990) Mycelial uptake, translocation and assimilation of ^{15}N-labelled nitrogen by ectomycorrhizal *Pinus sylvestris* plants. *Agriculture, Ecosystems & Environment*, 28, 133–137.

Fiore-Donno AM, Richter-Heitmann T, Degrune F, et al. (2019) Functional traits and spatio-temporal structure of a major group of soil protists (Rhizaria: Cercozoa) in a temperate grassland. *Frontiers in Microbiology*, 10, 1332.

Fisk MC, Ruether KF, Yavitt JB. (2003) Microbial activity and functional composition among northern peatland ecosystems. *Soil Biology and Biochemistry*, 35, 591–602.

Food and Agriculture Organisation of the United Nations (FAO). (2018) *The State of the World's Forests*. Rome: Food and Agriculture Organization of the United Nations.

French KE, Tkacz A, Turnbull LA. (2017) Conversion of grassland to arable decreases microbial diversity and alters community composition. *Applied Soil Ecology*, 110, 43–52.

Freschet GT, Cornwell WK, Wardle DA, et al. (2013) Linking litter decomposition of above- and below-ground organs to plant–soil feedbacks worldwide. *Journal of Ecology*, 101, 943–952.

Ganzert L, Lipsk A, Hubberten HW, Wagner D. (2011) The impact of different soil parameters on the community structure of dominant bacteria from nine different soils located on Livingston Island, South Shetland Archipelago, Antarctica. *FEMS Microbiology Ecology*, 76, 476–491.

Geisen S, Mitchell EA, Adl S, et al. (2018) Soil protists: A fertile frontier in soil biology research. *FEMS Microbiology Reviews*, 42, 293–323.

Gibson DJ. (2008) *Grasses and Grassland Ecology*. Oxford: Oxford University Press.

Gilichinsky DA. (2002) Permafrost model of extraterrestrial habitat. In: Horneck G, Baumstark-Khan C. (Eds.) *Astrobiology*. Berlin: Springer.

Golovchenko AV, Semenova TA, Polyakova AV, et al. (2002) The structure of the micromycete complexes of oligotrophic peat deposits in the southern Taiga subzone of west Siberia. *Microbiology*, 71, 575–581.

Golovchenko AV, Tikhonova EY, Zvyaginster DG. (2007) Abundance, biomass, structure and activity of the microbial complexes of minerotrophic and ombrotrophic peatlands. *Microbiology*, 76, 630–637.

Gorzelak MA, Asay AK, Pickles BJ, et al. (2015) Inter-plant communication through mycorrhizal networks mediates complex adaptive behaviour in plant communities. *Annals of Botany Plants*, 7, plv050.

Graham DE, Wallenstein MD, Vishnivetskaya TA, et al. (2012) Microbes in thawing permafrost: The unknown variable in the climate change equation. *The ISME Journal*, 6, 709.

Grigulis K, Lavorel S, Krainer U, et al. (2013) Relative contributions of plant traits and soil microbial properties to mountain grassland ecosystem services. *Journal of Ecology*, 101, 47–57.

Grunig CR, Sieber TN. (2005) Molecular and phenotypic description of the widespread root symbiont *Acephala applanata* gen. et sp. nov., formerly known as dark-septate endophyte Type 1. *Mycologia*, 97, 628–640.

Gubsch M, Roscher C, Gleixner G, et al. (2011) Foliar and soil δ^{15}N values reveal increased nitrogen partitioning among species in diverse grassland communities. *Plant, Cell & Environment*, 34, 895–908.

Hagerberg D, Thelin G, Wallander H. (2016) The production of ectomycorrhizal mycelium in forests: Relation between forest nutrient status and local mineral sources. *Plant and Soil*, 252, 279–290.

Hansen AA, Herbert RA, Mikkelsen K, et al. (2007) Viability, diversity and composition of the bacterial community in a high Arctic permafrost soil from Spitsbergen, Northern Norway. *Environmental Microbiology*, 9, 2870–2884.

Harrison KA, Bardgett RD. (2010) Influence of plant species and soil conditions on plant–

soil feedback in mixed grassland communities. *Journal of Ecology*, 98, 384–395.

Hobbie EA, Högberg P. (2012). Nitrogen isotopes link mycorrhizal fungi and plants to nitrogen dynamics. *New Phytologist*, 296, 367–382.

Hobbie SE. (1996) Temperature and plant species control over litter decomposition in Alaskan tundra. *Ecological Monographs*, 66, 503–522.

Hobbie SE, Gough L. (2004) Litter decomposition in moist acidic and non-acidic tundra with different glacial histories. *Oecologia*. 140, 113–24.

Hodge A, Campbell CD, Fitter AH. (2001) An arbuscular mycorrhizal fungus accelerates decomposition and acquires nitrogen directly from organic material. *Nature*, 413, 297–299.

Högberg MN, Högberg P. (2002) Extramatrical ectomycorrhizal mycelium contributes one-third of microbial biomass and produces, together with associated roots, half the dissolved organic carbon in a forest soil. *New Phytologist*, 154, 791–795.

Hooper DU, Chapin FS, Ewel JJ, et al. (2005) Effects of biodiversity on ecosystem functioning: A consensus of current knowledge. *Ecological Monographs*, 75, 3–35.

Hu S, Chapin III FS, Firestone MK, et al. (2001) Nitrogen limitation of microbial decomposition in a grassland under elevated CO_2. *Nature*, 409, 188–191.

Isbell F, Craven D, Connolly J, et al. (2015) Biodiversity increases the resistance of ecosystem productivity to climate extremes. *Nature*, 526, 574–577.

Jaatinen K, Fritze H, Laine J, Laiho R. (2007) Effects of short- and long-term water-level drawdown on the populations and activity of aerobic decomposers in a boreal peatland. *Global Change Biology*, 13, 491–510.

Jangid K, Williams MA, Franzluebbers AJ, et al. (2008) Relative impacts of land-use, management intensity and fertilization upon soil microbial community structure in agricultural systems. *Soil Biology and Biochemistry*, 40, 2843–2853.

Jansson JK, Hofmockel KS. (2018) The soil microbiome – From metagenomics to metaphenomics. *Current Opinion in Microbiology*, 43, 162–168.

Jenkinson DS. (1990) The turnover of organic carbon and nitrogen in soil. Philosophical *Transactions of the Royal Society Series B: Biological Sciences*, 329, 361–368.

Johnson D, Gilbert L. (2015) Interplant signalling through hyphal networks. *New Phytologist*, 205, 1448–1453.

Joosten H, Clarke D. (2002) *Wise Use of Mires and Peatlands: Background and Principles Including a Framework for Decision-making.* Greifswald: International Mire Conservation Group.

Jorquera MA, Shaharoona B, Nadeem SM, et al. (2012) Plant growth-promoting rhizobacteria associated with ancient clones of creosote bush (*Larrea tridentata*). *Microbial Ecology*, 64, 1008–1017.

Kaiser C, Koranda M, Kitzler B, et al. (2010) Belowground carbon allocation by trees drives seasonal patterns of extracellular enzyme activities by altering microbial community composition in a beech forest soil. *New Phytologist*, 187, 843–858.

Kaplan D, Maymon M, Agapakis CM, et al. (2013) A survey of the microbial community in the rhizosphere of two dominant shrubs of the Negev Desert highlands, *Zygophyllum dumosum* (Zygophyllaceae) and *Atriplex halimus* (Amaranthaceae), using cultivation-dependent and cultivation-independent methods. *American Journal of Botany*, 100, 1713–1725.

Kardol P, Martijn Bezemer T, van der Putten WH. (2006) Temporal variation in plant–soil feedback controls succession. *Ecology Letters*, 9, 1080–1088.

Keuter A, Veldkamp E, Corre MD. (2014) Asymbiotic biological nitrogen fixation in a temperate grassland as affected by management practices. *Soil Biology and Biochemistry*, 70, 38–46.

Klironomos JN. (2002) Feedback with soil biota contributes to plant rarity and invasiveness in communities. *Nature*, 417, 67–70.

Klironomos JN. (2003) Variation in plant response to native and exotic arbuscular mycorrhizal fungi. *Ecology*, 84, 2292–2301.

Kohler A, Kuo A, Nagy LG, et al. (2015) Convergent losses of decay mechanisms and rapid turnover of symbiosis genes in mycorrhizal mutualists. *Nature Genetics*, 47, 410–415.

Koziol L, Bever JD. (2017) The missing link in grassland restoration: Arbuscular mycorrhizal fungi inoculation increases plant diversity and accelerates succession. *Journal of Applied Ecology*, 54, 1301–1309.

Kulmatiski A, Kardol P. (2008) Getting plant–soil feedbacks out of the greenhouse: Experimental and conceptual approaches. *Progress in Botany*, 69, 449–472.

Kumar A, Maurya BR, Raghuwanshi R. (2014) Isolation and characterization of PGPR and their effect on growth, yield and nutrient content in wheat (*Triticum aestivum* L.). *Biocatalysis and Agricultural Biotechnology*, 3, 121–128.

Lambers H, Chapin FS, Pons TL. (2008a) *Plant Physiological Ecology.* New York, NY: Springer.

Lambers H, Raven JA, Shaver GR, et al. (2008b) Plant nutrient-acquisition strategies change with soil age. *Trends in Ecology & Evolution*, 23, 95–103.

Lambers H, Albornoz F, Kotula L, et al. (2018) How belowground interactions contribute to the coexistence of mycorrhizal and non-mycorrhizal species in severely phosphorus-impoverished hyperdiverse ecosystems. *Plant and Soil*, 424, 11–33.

Landeweert R, Hoffland E, Finlay RD, et al. (2001) Linking plants to rocks: Ectomycorrhizal fungi mobilize nutrients from minerals. *Trends in Ecology & Evolution*, 16, 248–254.

Lauber CL, Strickland MS, Bradford MA, et al. (2008) The influence of soil properties on the structure of bacterial and fungal communities across land-use types. *Soil Biology and Biochemistry*, 40, 2407–2415.

Leake J, Johnson D, Donnelly D, et al. (2004) Networks of power and influence: The role of mycorrhizal mycelium in controlling plant communities and agroecosystem functioning. *Canadian Journal of Botany*, 82, 1016–1045.

LeBauer DS, Treseder KK. (2008) Nitrogen limitation of net primary productivity in terrestrial ecosystems is globally distributed. *Ecology*, 89, 371–379.

Ledeganck P, Nijs I, Beyens L. (2003) Plant functional group diversity promotes soil protist diversity. *Protist*, 154, 239–249.

Ledgard SF, Steele KW. (1992) Biological nitrogen fixation in mixed legume/grass pastures. *Plant and Soil*, 141, 137–153.

Li M, Feng H, Yang Z, et al. (2011) Diversity of culturable bacteria in the typical frozen soil areas in China. *Acta Microbiologica Sinica*, 51, 1595–1604.

Li XR, Jia RL, Zhang ZS, et al. (2018) Hydrological response of biological soil crusts to global warming: A ten-year simulative study. *Global Change Biology*, 24, 4960–4971.

Lindahl BD, Ihrmark K, Boberg J, et al. (2007) Spatial separation of litter decomposition and mycorrhizal nitrogen uptake in a boreal forest. *New Phytologist*, 173, 611–620.

Lindahl BD, Tunlid A. (2015) Ectomycorrhizal fungi – Potential organic matter decomposers, yet not saprotrophs. *New Phytologist*, 205, 1443–1447.

Lipson DA, Schmidt SK, Monson RK. (2000) Carbon availability and temperature control the post-snowmelt decline in alpine soil microbial biomass. *Soil Biology and Biochemistry*, 32, 441–448.

Lugtenberg B. (2015) Introduction to plant–microbe interactions. In: Lugtenberg B. (Ed.) *Principles of Plant–Microbe Interactions*. Cham: Springer.

Lüscher A, Mueller-Harvey I, Soussana JF, et al. (2014) Potential of legume-based grassland–livestock systems in Europe:

A review. *Grass and Forage Science*, 69, 206–228.

Lydolph MC, Jacobsen J, Arctander P, et al. (2005) Beringian paleoecology inferred from permafrost-preserved fungal DNA. *Applied and Environmental Microbiology*, 71, 1012–1017.

Malhi Y, Baldocchi DD, Jarvis PG. (1999) The carbon balance of tropical, temperate and boreal forests. *Plant, Cell & Environment*, 22, 715–740.

Mangan SA, Schnitzer SA, Herre EA, et al. (2010) Negative plant–soil feedback predicts tree-species relative abundance in a tropical forest. *Nature*, 466, 752–755.

Mapelli F, Marasco R, Balloi A, et al. (2012) Mineral–microbe interactions: Biotechnological potential of bioweathering. *Journal of Biotechnology*, 157, 473–481.

Mapelli F, Marasco R, Rolli E, et al. (2013) Potential for plant growth promotion of Rhizobacteria associated with *Salicornia* growing in Tunisian hypersaline soils. *BioMed Research International*, 2013, 248078.

Margesin R. (2012) Psychrophilic microorganisms in alpine soils. In: Lütz C. (Ed.) *Plants in Alpine Regions*. Vienna: Springer.

Maron JL, Marler M, Klironomos JN, et al. (2011) Soil fungal pathogens and the relationship between plant diversity and productivity. *Ecology Letters*, 14, 36–41.

Marques AC, de Oliveira LB, Nicoloso FT, et al. (2017) Biological nitrogen fixation in C4 grasses of different growth strategies of South America natural grasslands. *Applied Soil Ecology*, 113, 54–62.

Millard P, Singh BK. (2010) Does grassland vegetation drive soil microbial diversity? *Nutrient Cycling in Agroecosystems*, 88, 147–158.

Millet M, Wortham H, Sanusi A, et al. (1997) Low molecular weight organic acids in fogwater in an urban area: Strasbourg (France). *Science of the Total Environment*, 206, 57–65.

Morales SE, Mouser PJ, Ward N, et al. (2006) Comparison of bacterial communities in

New England Sphagnum bogs using terminal restriction fragment length polymorphism (T-RFLP). *Microbial Ecology*, 52, 34–44.

Nadeem SM, Ahmad M, Zahir ZA, et al. (2014) The role of mycorrhizae and plant growth promoting rhizobacteria (PGPR) in improving crop productivity under stressful environments. *Biotechnology Advances*, 32, 429–448.

Needelman BA. (2013) What are soils? *Nature Education Knowledge*, 4, 2.

Nehls U, Plassard C. (2018) Nitrogen and phosphate metabolism in ectomycorrhizas. *New Phytologist*, 220, 1047–1058.

Newsham KK, Fitter AH, Watkinson AR. (1995) Arbuscular mycorrhiza protect an annual grass from root pathogenic fungi in the field. *Journal of Ecology*, 83, 991–1000.

Nicolitch O, Colin Y, Turpault MP, et al. (2016) Soil type determines the distribution of nutrient mobilizing bacterial communities in the rhizosphere of beech trees. *Soil Biology and Biochemistry*, 103, 429–445.

Ochoa-Hueso R, Delgado-Baquerizo M, King PT, et al. (2019) Ecosystem type and resource quality are more important than global change drivers in regulating early stages of litter decomposition. *Soil Biology and Biochemistry*, 129, 144–152.

Oliver TH, Heard MS, Isaac NJ, et al. (2015) Biodiversity and resilience of ecosystem functions. *Trends in Ecology & Evolution*, 30, 673–684.

Oquist MG, Sparrman T, Klemedtsson L, et al. (2009) Water availability controls microbial temperature responses in frozen soil CO_2 production. *Global Change Biology*, 15, 2715–2722.

Page SE, Rieley JO, Banks CJ. (2011) Global and regional importance of the tropical peatland carbon pool. *Global Change Biology*, 17, 798–818.

Pan Y, Birdsey RA, Fang J, et al. (2011) A large and persistent carbon sink in the world's forests. *Science*, 333, 988–993.

Pawlowski J, Audic S, Adl S, et al. (2012) CBOL protist working group: Barcoding eukaryotic richness beyond the animal, plant, and fungal kingdoms. *PLoS Biology*, 10, e1001419.

Prober SM, Leff JW, Bates ST, et al. (2015) Plant diversity predicts beta but not alpha diversity of soil microbes across grasslands worldwide. *Ecology Letters*, 18, 85–95.

Rasche F, Knapp D, Kaiser C, et al. (2011) Seasonality and resource availability control bacterial and archaeal communities in soils of a temperate beech forest. *The ISME Journal*, 5, 389–402.

Reed SC, Cleveland CC, Townsend AR. (2011) Functional ecology of free-living nitrogen fixation: A contemporary perspective. *Annual Review of Ecology, Evolution, and Systematics*, 42, 489–512.

Reinhart KO. (2012) The organization of plant communities: Negative plant–soil feedbacks and semiarid grasslands. *Ecology*, 93, 2377–2385.

Reinsch S, Koller E, Sowerby A, et al. (2017) Shrubland primary production and soil respiration diverge along European climate gradient. *Scientific Reports*, 7, 43952.

Reynolds HL, Packer A, Bever JD, et al. (2003) Grassroots ecology: Plant-microbe–soil interactions as drivers of plant community structure and dynamics. *Ecology*, 84, 2281–2291.

Rhoden SA, Garcia A, Santos E, et al. (2015) Phylogenetic analysis of endophytic bacterial isolates from leaves of the medicinal plant *Trichilia elegans* A. Juss. (Meliaceae). *Genetics and Molecular Research*, 14, 1515–1525.

Richardson AE, Simpson RJ. (2011). Update on microbial phosphorus soil microorganisms mediating phosphorus availability. *Plant Physiology*, 156, 989–996.

Richardson AE, Barea J-M, McNeill AM, et al. (2009) Acquisition of phosphorus and nitrogen in the rhizosphere and plant growth promotion by microorganisms. *Plant and Soil*, 321, 305–339.

Rivkina E, Shcherbakova V, Laurinavichius K, et al. (2007) Biogeochemistry of methane and methanogenic archaea in permafrost. *FEMS Microbiology Ecology*, 61, 1–5.

Roesch LF, Fulthorpe RR, Riva A, et al. (2007) Pyrosequencing enumerates and contrasts soil microbial diversity. *The ISME Journal*, 1, 283–290.

Ruiz-Lozano JM. (2003) Arbuscular mycorrhizal symbiosis and alleviation of osmotic stress. New perspectives for molecular studies. *Mycorrhiza*, 13, 309–317.

Sala OE, Paruelo JM, Sala OE, et al. (1997) Ecosystem services in grasslands. In: Daily GC (Ed.) *Nature's Services: Societal Dependence on Natural Ecosystems*. Washington, DC: Island Press.

Schadt CW, Martin AP, Lipson DA, et al. (2003) Seasonal dynamics of previously unknown fungal lineages in tundra soils. *Science*, 301, 1359–1361.

Scheublin TR, Logtestijn RSPV, van der Heijden MGA. (2007) Presence and identity of arbuscular mycorrhizal fungi influence competitive interactions between plant species. *Journal of Ecology*, 95, 631–638.

Schimel JP, Bennett J. (2004) Nitrogen mineralization: Challenges of a changing paradigm. *Ecology*, 85, 591–602.

Schimel J, Schaeffer SM. (2012) Microbial control over carbon cycling in soil. *Frontiers in Microbiology*, 26, 348.

Schlesinger WH, Andrews JA. (2000) Soil respiration and the global carbon cycle. *Biogeochemistry*, 48, 7–20.

Semchenko M, Leff JW, Lozano YM, et al. (2018) Fungal diversity regulates plant–soil feedbacks in temperate grassland. *Science Advances*, 4, eaau4578.

Sharma S, Szele Z, Schilling R, et al. (2006) Influence of freeze–thaw stress on the structure and function of microbial communities and denitrifying populations in soil. *Applied and Environmental Microbiology*, 72, 2148–2154.

Shelef O, Helman Y, Behar A, et al. (2013) Tri-party underground symbiosis between a weevil, bacteria and a desert plant. *PLoS ONE*, 8, e76588.

Shukla KP, Sharma S, Singh NK, et al. (2011) Nature and role of root exudates: Efficacy in bioremediation. *African Journal of Biotechnology*, 10, 9717–9724.

Silvertown J, Poulton P, Johnston E, et al. (2006) The Park Grass Experiment 1856–2006: Its contribution to ecology. *Journal of Ecology*, 94, 801–814.

Singh BK, Bardgett RD, Smith P, et al. (2010) Microorganisms and climate change: Terrestrial feedbacks and mitigation options. *Nature Reviews Microbiology*, 8, 779–790.

Smith SE, Gianinazzi-Pearson V. (1988) Physiological interactions between symbionts in vesicular–arbuscular mycorrhizal plants. *Annual Review of Plant Physiology and Plant Molecular Biology*, 39, 221–244.

Smith SE, Read DJ. (2008) *Mycorrhizal Symbiosis*, 3rd edition. New York, NY: Academic Press.

Šnajdr J, Valášková V, Merhautová V, et al. (2008) Spatial variability of enzyme activities and microbial biomass in the upper layers of *Quercus petraea* forest soil. *Soil Biology and Biochemistry*, 40, 2068–2075.

Solly EF, Schöning I, Boch S, et al. (2014) Factors controlling decomposition rates of fine root litter in temperate forests and grasslands. *Plant and Soil*, 382, 203–218.

Sterngren AE, Hallin S, Bengtson P. (2015) Archaeal ammonia oxidizers dominate in numbers, but bacteria drive gross nitrification in N-amended grassland soil. *Frontiers in Microbiology*, 6, 1350.

Strullu-Derrien C, Selosse MA, Kenrick P, Martin FM. (2018) The origin and evolution of mycorrhizal symbioses: From palaeomycology to phylogenomics. *New Phytologist*, 220, 1012–1030.

Sturm M, Racine C, Tape K. (2001) Climate change: Increasing shrub abundance in the Arctic. *Nature*, 411, 546–547.

Štursová M, Baldrian P. (2011) Effects of soil properties and management on the activity of soil organic matter transforming enzymes and the quantification of soil-bound and free activity. *Plant and Soil*, 338, 99–110.

Štursová M, Žifčáková L, Leigh MB, et al. (2012) Cellulose utilization in forest litter and soil: Identification of bacterial and fungal decomposers. *FEMS Microbiology Ecology*, 80, 735–746.

Talbot JM, Allison SD, Treseder KK. (2008) Decomposers in disguise: Mycorrhizal fungi as regulators of soil C dynamics in ecosystems under global change. *Functional Ecology*, 22, 955–963.

Tedersoo L, Bahram M, Toots M, et al. (2012) Towards global patterns in the diversity and community structure of ectomycorrhizal fungi. *Molecular Ecology*, 21, 4160–4170.

Tedersoo L, Bahram M, Cajthaml T, et al. (2016) Tree diversity and species identity effects on soil fungi, protists and animals are context dependent. *The ISME Journal*, 10, 346–362.

Tibbett M. (2002) Ectomycorrhizal symbiosis can enhance plant nutrition through improved access to discrete organic nutrient patches of high resource quality. *Annals of Botany*, 89, 783–789.

Tilman D, Wedin D. (1991) Dynamics of nitrogen competition between successional grasses. *Ecology*, 72, 1038–1049.

Tilman D, Reich PB, Knops J, et al. (2001) Diversity and productivity in a long-term grassland experiment. *Science*, 294, 843–845.

Trap J, Bonkowski M, Plassard C, et al. (2016) Ecological importance of soil bacterivores for ecosystem functions. *Plant and Soil*, 398, 1–24.

Trinder CJ, Johnson D, Artz RR. (2008) Interactions among fungal community structure, litter decomposition and depth of water table in a cutover peatland. *FEMS Microbiology Ecology*, 64, 433–448.

Urbanová M, Šnajdr J, Baldrian P. (2015) Composition of fungal and bacterial communities in forest litter and soil is largely determined by dominant trees. *Soil Biology and Biochemistry*, 84, 53–64.

Uroz S, Calvaruso C, Turpault MP, et al. (2009) Efficient mineral weathering is a distinctive functional trait of the bacterial genus *Collimonas*. *Soil Biology and Biochemistry*, 41, 2178–2186.

Uroz S, Kelly LC, Turpault MP, et al. (2015) The mineralosphere concept: Mineralogical control of the distribution and function of mineral-associated bacterial communities. *Trends in Microbiology*, 23, 751–762.

Uroz S, Oger P, Tisserand E, et al. (2016) Specific impacts of beech and Norway spruce on the structure and diversity of the rhizosphere and soil microbial communities. *Scientific Reports*, 6, 27756.

van der Heijden MGA, Horton TR. (2009) Socialism in soil? The importance of mycorrhizal fungal networks for facilitation in natural ecosystems. *Journal of Ecology*, 97, 1139–1150.

van der Heijden MG, Klironomos JN, Ursic M, et al. (1998) Mycorrhizal fungal diversity determines plant biodiversity, ecosystem variability and productivity. *Nature*, 396, 69–72.

van der Heijden MGA, Bardgett RD, van Straalen NM. (2008) The unseen majority: Soil microbes as drivers of plant diversity and productivity in terrestrial ecosystems. *Ecology Letters*, 11, 296–310.

van der Putten WH, Bardgett RD, Bever JD, et al. (2013) Plant–soil feedbacks: The past, the present and future challenges. *Journal of Ecology*, 101, 265–276.

van der Putten WH, Bradford MA, Pernilla Brinkman E, et al. (2016) Where, when and how plant–soil feedback matters in a changing world. *Functional Ecology*, 30, 1109–1121.

van Dommelen A, Vanderleyden J. (2007) Associative nitrogen fixation. In: Bothe H,

Ferguson SJ, Newton WE. (Eds.) *Biology of the Nitrogen Cycle*. Amsterdam: Elsevier.

Vance CP. (2001) Symbiotic nitrogen fixation and phosphorus acquisition: Plant nutrition in a world of declining renewable resources. *Plant Physiology*, 127, 390–397.

Venter PC, Nitsche F, Domonell A, et al. (2017) The protistan microbiome of grassland soil: Diversity in the mesoscale. *Protist*, 168, 546–564.

Vicente-Serrano SM, Gouveia C, Camarero JJ, et al. (2013) Response of vegetation to drought time-scales across global land biomes. *Proceedings of the National Academy of Sciences*, 110, 52–57.

Vishnivetskaya TA, Petrova MA, Urbance J, et al. (2006) Bacterial community in ancient Siberian permafrost as characterized by culture and culture-independent methods. *Astrobiology*, 6, 400–414.

Vogelsang KM, Reynolds HL, Bever JD. (2006) Mycorrhizal fungal identity and richness determine the diversity and productivity of a tallgrass prairie system. *New Phytologist*, 172, 554–562.

Wagner D, Gattinger A, Embacher A, et al. (2007) Methanogenic activity and biomass in Holocene permafrost deposits of the Lena Delta, Siberian Arctic and its implication for the global methane budget. *Global Change Biology*, 13, 1089–1099.

Wallander H. (2006) External mycorrhizal mycelia – The importance of quantification in natural ecosystems. *New Phytologist*, 171, 240–242.

Wang L, Dong XP, Zhang W, et al. (2011) Quantitative characters of microorganisms in permafrost at different depths and their relation to soil physicochemical properties. *Journal of Glaciology and Geocryology*, 2, 436–441.

Wehner J, Antunes PM, Powell JR, et al. (2011) Indigenous arbuscular mycorrhizal fungal assemblages protect grassland host plants from pathogens. *PLoS ONE*, 6, e27381.

Weigelt A, Bol R, Bardgett RD. (2005) Preferential uptake of soil nitrogen forms by grassland plant species. *Oecologia*, 142, 627–635.

Weisser WW, Roscher C, Meyer ST, et al. (2017) Biodiversity effects on ecosystem functioning in a 15-year grassland experiment: Patterns, mechanisms, and open questions. *Basic and Applied Ecology*, 23, 1–73.

White RP, Murray S, Rohweder M. (2000) *Pilot Analysis of Global Ecosystems: Grassland Ecosystems*. Washington, DC: World Resources Institute.

Whitehead DC. (1995) *Grassland Nitrogen*. Wallingford: CAB International.

Whitman T, Neurath R, Perera A, et al. (2018) Microbial community assembly differs across minerals in a rhizosphere microcosm. *Environmental Microbiology*, 20, 4444–4460.

Williams RT, Crawford RL. (1983) Microbial diversity of Minnesota peatlands. *Microbial Ecology*, 9, 201–214.

Winsborough C, Basiliko N. (2010) Fungal and bacterial activity in northern peatlands. *Geomicrobiology Journal*, 27, 315–320.

Wu X, Zhang W, Liu G, et al. (2012) Bacterial diversity in the foreland of the Tianshan No. 1 glacier, China. *Environmental Research Letters*, 7, 014038.

Xu J, Morris PJ, Liu J, et al. (2018) PEATMAP: Refining estimates of global peatland distribution based on a meta-analysis. *Catena*, 160, 134–40.

Xu Y, Rossi F, Colica G, et al. (2013) Use of cyanobacterial polysaccharides to promote shrub performances in desert soils: A potential approach for the restoration of desertified areas. *Biology and Fertility of Soils*, 49, 143–152.

Yergeau E, Kowalchuk GA. (2008) Responses of Antarctic soil microbial communities and associated functions to temperature and freeze–thaw cycle frequency. *Environmental Microbiology*, 10, 2223–2235.

Zhang G, Niu F, Ma X, et al. (2007) Phylogenetic diversity of bacteria isolates from the Qinghai–Tibet Plateau permafrost region.

Canadian Journal of Microbiology, 53, 1000–1010.

Zhang N, Wang D, Liu Y, et al. (2014) Effects of different plant root exudates and their organic acid components on chemotaxis, biofilm formation and colonization by beneficial rhizosphere-associated bacterial strains. *Plant and Soil*, 374, 689–700.

Zhou J, Deng Y, Shen L, et al. (2016) Temperature mediates continental-scale diversity of microbes in forest soils. *Nature Communications*, 7, 12083.

CHAPTER FOUR

Factors that shape the host microbiome

MARC SZE
University of Michigan
JAMES DOONAN, JAMES E. MCDONALD
Bangor University
REID N. HARRIS
James Madison University, Harrisonburg
and
MEAGAN DEWAR
Federation University Australia, Berwick

4.1 Introduction

From the time that Antonie van Leeuwenhoek first stared down his microscope at a previously invisible world in the seventeenth century, we have been enthralled with studying and observing microbes in action. Historically, interest in microbes has focused on the infections, morbidity and mortality they cause in hosts (Ellner, 1998; House et al., 2001; Bula-Rudas et al., 2015; Gabutti et al., 2016; Bollaerts et al., 2017; Yang et al., 2017), yet pathogens comprise only a small overall percentage of the microbiota living in association with animals, plants and soils (Gevers et al., 2012; Human Microbiome Consortium, 2012). In fact, the majority of multicellular organisms can be considered meta-organisms because of the diverse repertoire of symbiotic and parasitic micro-organisms associated with them (Bosch & McFall-Ngai, 2011). For example, there exist approximately 10^{14} bacteria within the human gastrointestinal tract, not including viruses, fungi and archaea (Sender et al., 2016a, 2016b). The genetic diversity and complexity contained within this microscopic community or microbiome is astounding.

The microbiome has been studied in a range of environments including the Arctic (Tveit et al., 2015), European lake systems (Zwirglmaier et al., 2015) and soils (Gómez-Brandón et al., 2012), as well a diverse suite of plant and animal hosts (e.g. Ley et al., 2008a; Turnbaugh et al., 2009a; Kwong & Moran, 2015; Thompson et al., 2017; Zheng et al., 2017). The enormous proliferation of research directed at host-associated microbes over the last two decades has revealed the myriad functions they perform that are critical to hosts, including protection from pathogens, nutrient and energy metabolism, and regulation of homeostasis (reviewed in Feng et al., 2018). In humans, microbial communities can be used to help classify people at highest risk of developing a disease (Shah et al., 2018; Sze & Schloss, 2018), but can also exacerbate disease (Feng et al., 2018) and actively degrade drug treatments designed to alleviate disease (Geller et al., 2017). Although this focus on the human microbiome may lead to important medical advances, research into a wide variety of plant, animal and environmental hosts is critical for understanding the diverse mechanisms by which microbes can influence important biological processes. Non-human animal research over the past decade has started to increase with studies focusing on domestic animals (48%), model animals such as mice and pigs (38%), and wild animals (14%) (Ley et al., 2008a, 2008b; Pascoe et al., 2017). Domestic and model animal research has predominately focused on studying the response of the microbiome to a perturbation such as infection, inflammation, antibiotics or diet (Turnbaugh et al., 2006; Sze et al., 2014; Schubert et al., 2015). In contrast, wild animal research has focused on observational studies that investigate changes in the microbiome due to ecological interactions and life-history traits including moulting (Dewar et al., 2014), foraging (Costello et al., 2010), sociality (Antwis et al., 2018), transition to captivity (McKenzie et al., 2017) and infection with pathogens (Bates et al., 2018; Campbell et al., 2019).

Within this chapter, we provide a broad overview of the various environmental and host factors that influence the microbiome of plants and animals. Some of these aspects are explored in greater detail in later chapters. This chapter will highlight that host-associated microbiomes are ubiquitous in nature, that they are highly variable in both space and time, and that they are crucial for the optimal biological function of the hosts they inhabit.

4.2 Factors influencing plant microbiomes

Microbial assemblages of plants occupy niche environments that can be broadly divided into three physical levels: (1) the rhizosphere, the soil environment in close proximity to and influenced by the plant; (2) the phyllosphere, the above-ground parts of the plant; and (3) the endosphere, within the plant (Figure 4.1; Turner et al., 2013). The assemblage of microbial cells at the three physical levels comprise bacteria, viruses, fungi, protozoa, algae and archaea, alongside multicellular organisms including nematodes, oomycetes and arthropods (Mendes et al., 2011). The plant host itself is an active participant in microbiome composition and directly attracts microbes that suit its nutritional requirements across natural environments and across the three plant-associated physical environments (Sasse et al., 2018). Community microbiota differ between physical environments as rhizosphere microbes benefit from soil nutrients and are often incapable of surviving on the phyllosphere. Some rhizosphere community members can avoid immune rejection by the host and enter the plant through natural openings or hydrolysis to live as

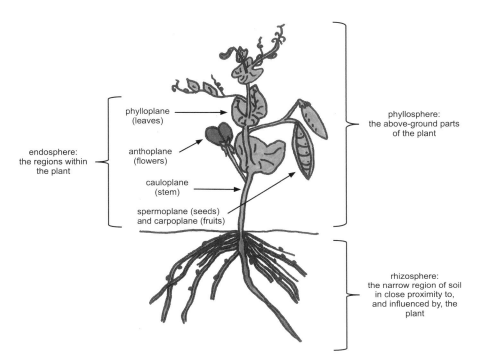

Figure 4.1 Niche environments of plants that are colonised by microbial communities (illustration by Elizabeth Meade and Rachael Antwis). (A black and white version of this figure will appear in some formats. For the colour version, please refer to the plate section.)

endophytes, usually as commensals, or in some cases, they become mutualists (as is the case with rhizobia which migrate from rhizosphere to endosphere) or pathogens (Rosenblueth & Martinez-Romero, 2006). Within each niche, the plant microbiome is shaped by biotic and abiotic factors, and each community is subject to idiosyncratic flux through perturbations. As a result, the microbiota can vary substantially both temporally within a niche and spatially across small geographic distances (Fraust & Raes, 2012). Communities continually change as they are shaped by ecological processes including perturbation by external forces and competitive exclusion within communities (Gause, 1934; Bennett, 1997), which push these assemblages towards new equilibria. Here we will look at the factors that influence the microbial communities associated with each of these three plant regions: the rhizosphere, phyllosphere and endosphere.

4.2.1 Rhizosphere microbiota
Rhizosphere microbiota exist at the interface between plant roots and soil. These are among the most diverse host microbiomes recorded and the richest

of the three plant-associated environments (Philippot et al., 2013). Of the three regions, the rhizosphere is by far the most studied due to its critical role in the interactions between soil and plant. Natural ecosystem rhizosphere communities are shaped by multiple factors, which vary in importance to community formation. Ranked in order of influence to community formation, these are: (1)–(3) biotic interactions, plant diversity and plant species (with equal weighting), (4) soil type, (5) climate and (6) agricultural practices (Philippot et al., 2013). Interestingly, geographic location does not have a notable influence on species composition (Weinert et al., 2011). Survival in the rhizosphere depends on the ability to utilise fluctuating amounts of root exudates in the form of carbon compounds known as rhizodeposits. Fast-growing bacteria from the phylum Proteobacteria are best positioned to dominate, as are the fungal phyla Ascomycota and Glomeromycota (Philippot et al., 2013). Rhizosphere interactions can be mutually beneficial as community members have access to carbon-rich rhizodeposits, and plants benefit as symbionts prevent colonisation by pathogens, strengthen the plants' defensive capacity, facilitate uptake of phosphorus, nitrogen and minerals, and degrade recalcitrant organic compounds (Berendsen et al., 2012).

Rhizosphere biotic interactions between mutualistic symbionts and legumes are among the most extensively characterised symbiotic interactions, particularly legume-associated nitrogen-fixing polyphyletic proteobacteria called rhizobia, and legume-arbuscular mycorrhizal fungi (AMR) (Larrainzar & Wienkoop, 2017). These endosymbiotic relationships co-evolved with early land plants beginning ~407 million years ago, and ~80% of extant land plants have endosymbionts evolved from these origins (Martin et al., 2017). These primitive symbioses led to the formation of N-fixing symbiotic nodules that have a common evolutionary origin, but multiple gains and losses of N-fixing symbioses, explaining the varied mechanisms of root colonisation, nodule ontology and development (Oldroyd et al., 2011). Plant–rhizobia symbioses produce differentiated bacteria that transition into endosymbionts within intracellular compartments (symbiosomes) of root nodules – an environment that allows nitrogen fixation by facilitating nitrogenase activity (Oldroyd et al., 2011). Plant–AMR interactions allow invasion of fungi to the inner root cortex, where they expedite the acquisition of nutrients (see Chapter 5 for more information). These symbioses are formed through the release of signalling molecules, flavonoids (rhizobia) and strigolactones (AMR), which activate bidirectional signal transduction pathways beginning with the production of nodulation compounds in rhizobia and mycorrhizal chitin oligomers in AMR (Froussart et al., 2016).

Rhizosphere communities are formed from a subset of bulk soil constituents; taxonomic separation of rhizosphere and bulk soil microbiomes is known as the rhizosphere effect (Berendsen et al., 2012; Sasse et al., 2018).

Plants such as maize and barley have a strong rhizosphere effect, with rhizospheres varying substantially in species composition and abundance to bulk soil, whereas others such as *Arabidopsis* and rice have a weak rhizosphere effect. Accumulating evidence has revealed that the below-ground microbiota is as heavily managed by multi-trophic interactions as those above ground. For example, Zgadzaj et al. (2016) revealed that host selection of rhizosphere symbionts was more extensive than recruitment of nitrogen-fixing rhizobia because systematic deletion of nodulation pathway genes formed taxonomically distinct rhizosphere communities. Furthermore, nodule pathway–mediated selection of rhizosphere symbionts resulted in reduced abundance of six bacterial orders, including substantial reduction in the two most abundant orders, Flavobacteriales and Burkholderiales. The power of plants to influence their rhizosphere microbiota compared to environmental conditions has been measured in pairwise comparisons, yet variability between plant species and environments make generalisations difficult because each niche is context-dependent (Borruso et al., 2014; Sasse et al., 2018).

4.2.2 Endosphere microbiota

Adaptation to life inside plant tissues offers mutual benefits: the host develops immunity through exposure to epitopes, while endophytes live within a reduced stress environment and are shielded from external perturbations (Hallmann et al., 1997). The composition of the endosphere can be influenced by temperature, O_2 and CO_2 availability, soil type, and biogeography (Gottel et al., 2011; Ren et al., 2015; Coleman-Derr et al., 2016). Furthermore, the endosphere is host-specific, and beneficial bacteria such as *Gluconacetobacter diazotrophicus* and *Herbaspirillum rubrisubalbicans* are actively encouraged to colonise to assist with nitrogen assimilation, carbon metabolism and plant growth (Hallmann et al., 1997). Conversely, prospective endophytes or previously internalised endophytes can be rejected through failure to interact appropriately with the host and extracellular components, which triggers ethylene signalling and repulsion from the endosphere (Iniguez et al., 2005). Symbionts that assimilate into host tissue can stimulate growth through the regulation of plant hormones or the direct synthesis of phytohormones such as indole-3-acetic acid (IAA), cytokinins and gibberellins (Santoyo et al., 2016). Bacterial genera with proven benefits to host growth and biomass include *Azoarcus*, *Burkholderia*, *Gluconobacter*, *Herbaspirillum*, *Klebsiella*, *Pantoea* and *Rahnella* (Kandel et al., 2017).

An interesting example is that of soybean, a leguminous crop with substantial economic importance to worldwide food and biodiesel supplies, which benefits from legume–rhizobium symbioses through increased growth and nutrition. High salinity reduces root growth, number of root hairs, nodule development and recruitment of rhizobia to nodules (Parvaiz & Satyawati,

2008). The salt-tolerant endophyte *Stenotrophomonas rhizophila* facilitates recruitment of the symbiotic rhizobium, *Bradyrhizobium japonicum*, in salt-stressed conditions, overriding the deleterious effects of salinity and boosting root growth, nodulation and nitrogen uptake (Egamberdieva et al., 2016). This legume–rhizobium–endophyte tripartite symbiosis is mediated by chemical and nutrient interaction as plant exudates incite spermidine and glucosylglycerol production by *S. rhizophila*, leading a to *B. japonicum*-mediated increase in nitrogen and phosphorus availability. Soybean plants are responsive to phytohormone-mediated physiological stimulus released via the IAA-producing endophytes *Sphingomonas* sp. LK11 and *Serratia marcescens* (Asaf et al., 2017). Endophytic phytohormone production triggers upregulation of abscisic acid and downregulation of jasmonic acid, resulting in increased shoot/root growth, fresh/dry weight and chlorophyll content within the soybean host.

4.2.3 Phyllosphere microbiota

The phyllosphere includes all above-ground parts of the plant; the external components of the phyllosphere can be subdivided into the phylloplane (leaves), cauloplane (stem), anthoplane (flowers), spermoplane (seeds) and carpoplane (fruits) (Figure 4.1; Vacher et al., 2016). Phylloplane microbiota are the most extensively documented communities among phyllosphere components. In comparison to the rhizosphere and endosphere, the phylloplane is subject to greater atmospheric perturbations, including cycles of hydration and desiccation (Burch et al., 2014; Vacher et al., 2016). Additionally, anthropogenic perturbations such as climate change, air pollution and spraying of crops with, for example, fungicidal agents all impact phylloplane communities (Vacher et al., 2016). Phylloplane environments are usually dominated by the bacterial phylum Proteobacteria and the fungal phylum Ascomycota, with the genera *Aureobasidium*, *Cladosporium*, *Taphrina*, and the Basidiomycete yeast genera *Cryptococcus* and *Sporobolomyces* also highly abundant. These genera have important roles in nutrient cycling, and some, such as *Aureobasidium pullulans*, outcompete pathogens and limit available space for colonisation (Cordier et al., 2012; Vacher et al., 2016). Phylloplane communities are adapted to lower carbohydrate concentrations and a more heterogeneous environment than endophytes. For example, *Pseudomonas syringae* pv. *syringae* B728a increases leaching of moisture and nutrients through the waxy leaf cuticle by releasing a hygroscopic biosurfactant, syringafactin (Burch et al., 2014).

Bacterial phylloplane pathogens penetrate internal tissues through stomatal openings, hydathodes or wounds (Melotto et al., 2017). Host recognition of conserved bacterial epitopes triggers an immune response, closing stomatal openings and gas exchanges. Pathogen-elicited closure of stomata is positively regulated through the plant hormones abscisic acid and salicylic acid, and negatively regulated via jasmonoyl-isoleucine (JA-Ile) (Pieterse et al., 2014). To negate stomatal closure, pathogens release phytotoxins and type III secretion system effectors, allowing their proliferation within intercellular spaces (Melotto et al., 2006). *Pseudomonas syringae* pathovars are well-characterised pathogenic microbiota from which many bacterial–host interactions were first identified, including the release of coronatine that mimics JA-Ile, reopening stomatal pores, even those that have been closed at night through the plant's circadian rhythm (Melotto et al., 2006; Panchal et al., 2016; Vacher et al., 2016). To exploit plant resources, pathogens must first attach to available space on the leaf cuticle. This is often limited by symbionts such as growth-promoting species from the genera *Pseudomonas*, *Bacillus* and *Serratia*, or fungi such as non-pathogenic strains of *Fusarium oxysporum*, *Trichoderma* and *Piriformospora indica*, which can also be introduced artificially as biocontrol agents. Widespread characterisation of phylloplane constituents is surprisingly lacking, to the extent that composition and function of this microbiota remains largely unknown (Vacher et al., 2016). This is particularly surprising as leaf microbiota are more readily cultured than rhizosphere constituents, with one study finding >85% similarity between OTUs from the culture-independent microbiome and recovery of culturable microbiome constituents, in comparison to 21% recovery of culture-independent OTUs from soil communities (Burch et al., 2016).

4.3 Factors influencing animal microbiomes

4.3.1 Host phylogeny and genetics

Genetic variation influences microbiome composition of many vertebrates and invertebrates, both in terms of differences between species (i.e. phylogenetic variation or the 'phylobiome'), as well as variation between different genotypes within the same species (Ley et al., 2008b; Nelson et al., 2013; Davenport et al., 2017; Mazel et al., 2018; Youngblut et al., 2019). At the broad phylogenetic scale, the microbiome of invertebrate species is characterised by a very low species richness compared to vertebrate species. For example, the *Drosophila* gut microbiome comprises only around 20 species, compared to hundreds or thousands in vertebrates (Broderick & Lemaitre, 2012). Lower microbiome diversity in invertebrates is typically associated with the lack of an adaptive immune system found in vertebrates (McFall-Ngai et al., 2013). At the finer scale, species identity is a particularly strong determinant of microbiome composition (e.g. Kueneman et al., 2014; Yildirim et al., 2014; Thomas et al., 2016), and at an even finer scale, host genotype can influence microbiome composition. For example, Banks et al. (2009) found that the microbial communities of Adelie penguins (*Pygoscelis adeliae*) were strongly negatively correlated with genetic distance between host species, which suggests that microbial communities are inherited. Differences in gut microbiome composition due to host phylogeny were also observed in parasitic wasps *Nasonia*, where the microbiota of hybrid offspring differed from their parents (Brucker & Bordenstein, 2013). Similarly, the hybridisation of sika and elk deer resulted in distinct hybrid microbial communities, which differed from their parents and may have resulted from vertical transmission (Li et al., 2016). In stickleback fish, host genotype influences the microbial composition at the population level, with genetically divergent populations exhibiting a more divergent microbiome, and lower among-individual microbial variation in populations with greater genetic heterozygosity (Smith et al., 2015). Similarly, Bolnick et al. (2014) found that individuals with more diverse Major Histocompatibility Complex Class II alleles have less-diverse gut microbial communities. Host genotype also influences the microbiome composition of the Phofung river frog (*Amietia hymenopus*) (Griffiths & Harrison et al., 2018), and in gopher tortoises (*Gopherus polyphemus*), inbreeding and relatedness, but not population genetic structure, influence gut microbiome composition (Yuan et al., 2015). Griffiths et al. (2019) demonstrated a significant relationship between genetic distance and microbiome composition in the Caribbean sponge *Ircinia campana*; however, Noyer and Becerro (2012) showed there was no effect of host genotype and microbiome composition of the Mediterranean sponge *Spongia lamella*.

In humans, the role of host phylogeny is still hotly debated. Zoetendal et al. (2001) and Goodrich et al. (2014) have found specific members of the gut microbiome are influenced by host genetics. Using the twin-based ACE model, which partitions total variance into three sources: genetic effects (A), common (C) and unique (E) environments (Eaves et al., 1978), Goodrich et al. (2014) identified that some taxa, such as Christensenellaceae, are highly genetically inheritable while other taxa, such as Bacteroidetes, are environmentally inherited. However, Turnbaugh et al. (2009a) reported that host genetics had a negligible effect on the composition of human microbial communities.

4.3.2 Initial colonisation and developmental changes

Some of the most interesting questions in microbiome research are focused on the colonisation dynamics of organisms by microbes; how the early microbiome is formed and how it changes throughout ontogeny. Microbiomes can be acquired either horizontally (via the environment or other host organisms) or vertically from parent to offspring. For example, there is evidence of vertical transmission in amphibian species with nest attendance by adults (Banning et al., 2008), as well as early and continuous colonisation pressure of microbes from environmental sources (Walke et al., 2011, 2014; Fitzpatrick & Allison, 2014). The amphibian skin microbiome experiences subtle changes throughout the larval (tadpole) stages (Griffiths et al., 2018) as well as pro-nounced changes on metamorphosis from tadpole to juvenile frog or toad (e.g. Kohl et al., 2013; Kueneman et al., 2014; Bates et al., 2018). In viviparous lizards, a significant portion of the microbiome is acquired via vertical trans-mission and communal rearing (Colston, 2017). In juvenile ostriches (*Struthio camelus*), microbial colonisation is aided by vertical transmission of microbes through coprophagy of their parents' faeces (Cooper, 2004), and their micro-biome composition changes throughout growth and development (Videvall et al., 2019). Conversely, chickens and turkeys develop a similar microbial composition to adults simply via horizontal transfer from the environment (Lu et al., 2003). In the hoatzin (*Opisthocomus hoazin*), vertical transmission of microbes via regurgitation initiates microbial colonisation of the crop (part of the digestive tract; Godoy-Vitorino et al., 2010).

Elegant experiments in *Hydra* species have revealed that early colonisation in embryos is shaped by maternally encoded antimicrobial peptides (AMPs) (Augustin et al., 2017), whereas downstream microbiome control is affected by zygotically expressed AMPs. After hatching, a stable microbiota is quickly established, acquired by vertical or horizontal transmission, or both. Peptides secreted by neurons play an important structuring role (Augustin et al., 2017), suggesting that selection for the evolution of a nervous system in early metazoans was, in part, to control the microbiome. Another mechanism of controlling colonisation is the host's ability to modify a bacterial quorum-sensing signal, with different modifications leading to either increased or decreased likelihood of colonisation, with the potential to structure the micro-bial community (Pietschke et al., 2017).

Microbiome colonisation, however, is probably most well studied in humans. The foetus is presumed to be sterile *in utero*, although there is evidence to challenge this (Aagaard et al., 2014). Neonates can present with relatively high microbial diversity in the oral and gut cavity immediately postpartum that diminishes with time, suggesting a potential microbial asso-ciation prior to birth (Dominguez-Bello et al., 2016). Immediately post-delivery, there is a substantial signature of either vaginal or caesarean section on the infant microbiota (Dominguez-Bello et al., 2010). Subsequent to this, the human microbiome receives exogenous input from multiple envir-onments. Many microbial taxa have the potential to colonise the baby and may play a role in immune activation and stimulation, which can feedback on the endogenous microbiota causing dynamic changes in composition and struc-ture. The physical and dietary influences that pervade early life do, however, play a substantial role in shaping both colonisation and immune education, including breast milk (Funkhouser & Bordenstein, 2013), and exposure to the microbiomes of other people (Lax et al., 2014) and animals or plants (von Mutius, 2016). Indeed, following the transition to solid foods and non-breast milk fluids, the baby continues to be exposed to a diversity of microbial sources that may be beneficial for development (Hehemann et al., 2012).

Interestingly, while host genetics plays a role in shaping the colonisation of the host, homozygote twins have only slightly more similar faecal microbiota than heterozygote twins (Goodrich et al., 2014). This suggests that the environment occupied by the host plays a considerable role in colonisation and/or composition. However, the colonisation of germ-free animals is far from non-selective. Although a tiny fraction of non-host–associated bacteria are capable of colonising the mouse gut, they are rapidly out-competed by bacteria that are adapted to the mammalian gut (Seedorf et al., 2014). This provides compelling evidence for directed evolutionary dependence of microbes in the animal ecosystem. Indeed, a recent survey of the microbial life of Earth revealed striking differences in the structure and richness of free-living and host-associated microbiomes, indicating the huge influence of symbiotic interaction on microbial evolution (Thompson et al., 2017).

4.3.3 Diet

The gut microbiome is key to increasing the nutritional intake from food sources, often accessing molecules that would otherwise be unavailable to the host (see Chapter 5 for more information). The animal gut microbiome generally reflects the feeding style of the host (Douglas, 2015; Hammer & Bowers, 2015; Macke et al., 2017), and dietary differences among hosts are a major factor influencing the microbial composition of many animals including humans (Ley et al., 2008a; Muegge et al., 2011; David et al., 2014; Wong et al., 2015). Marked differences in the microbial composition of herbivores, omnivores and carnivores have been observed for a number of vertebrate animals, with animal microbiomes clustering by feeding strategy (Ley et al., 2008a, 2008b). Increases in microbial diversity are also observed from carnivores through to omnivores and herbivores, with herbivorous mammals harbouring the highest diversity (Ley et al., 2008b; Muegge et al., 2011). Soil animals contain rich gut microbiota that play vital roles in the decomposition of soil organic matter and circulation of global carbon (Thakuria et al., 2010). Ruminant guts harbour unique cellulolytic bacteria that exude enzymes designed to break down tough, grassy material (Flint et al., 2008). Almost all aphid species carry *Buchnera* as an obligate gut bacterial symbiont synthesising certain essential amino acids, thus allowing the host to feed on nutrient-poor phloem diets that otherwise would not sustain development (Oliver et al., 2010).

Studies on captive and laboratory animals have demonstrated the relationship between dietary changes and changes in animal microbiome. Studies on mice have shown that changes from a low-fat diet rich in plant polysaccharides to a diet high in fat and sugar results in drastic changes in the microbial composition in one day, especially within the classes of bacteria in the phylum Firmicutes (Turnbaugh et al., 2009b). In giant pandas (*Ailuropoda melanoleuca*), Williams et al. (2013) found that a dietary shift from bamboo to leaf resulted in a significant linear relationship between *Lactobacillus* and *Bacteroides* spp. Xue et al. (2015) observed large variation in diversity and structure in the giant panda microbiome when bamboo shoots were absent from their diet, with different microbial composition associated with seasonal dietary variation. Variation in the gut microbiome of Mexican black howler monkeys (*Alouatta pigra*) from four distinct habitats was influenced by dietary differences (Amato et al., 2013). The reduced diversity of the diet of captive monkeys and those from fragmented habitats were associated with changes in the microbial composition and reduced microbial richness and diversity. Furthermore, monkeys feeding on a variety of different plant species had distinct microbial profiles, with higher species richness and diversity in comparison to monkey groups that consumed a less-diverse diet (Amato et al., 2013). The authors also suggested that dietary shifts associated with habitat fragmentation influenced the howler monkey microbiome, presumably due to differences in the diversity of plants in the diet (Amato et al., 2013). Short- and long-term changes in diet have been associated with alterations in the composition and activity of the human microbiome (Ley et al., 2005; Duncan et al., 2007; Muegge et al., 2011; Wu et al., 2011; David et al., 2014). David et al. (2014) showed that short-term consumption of diets completely composed of plant material or animal products significantly influenced microbial community structure in humans. Increased abundances of bile-tolerant microorganisms such as *Bacteroides*, *Bilophila*, and *Alistipes* and decreased levels of members of the phylum Firmicutes that specialise in metabolism of plant polysaccharides were observed in people consuming animal-based diets.

4.3.4 Metabolism

Many animals reduce their metabolic rates during times of nutrient deprivation, undergoing hibernation or torpor as a process to survive. In leopard frogs (*Rana pipiens*), Banas et al. (1988) and Gossling et al. (1982a, 1982b) observed a significant reduction in the abundance and composition of the microbiome as a response to hibernation. Similarly, ground squirrels (*Citellus tridecemlineatus*) undergo a 100-fold reduction in the abundance of aerobic flora during hibernation (Barnes & Burton, 1970). In Arctic squirrels (*Spermophilus parryii*), the microbial composition of active and hibernating squirrels forms distinct clusters (Sonoyama et al., 2009). Sit-and-wait predators like snakes consume large infrequent meals and undergo long periods of fasting in between meals. Costello et al. (2010) found that fasting resulted in an overall reduction in overall microbial diversity in Burmese pythons

(*Python molurus*) and a marked increase in the abundance of Bacteroides, Rikenella, Synergistes and Akkermansia. Following re-feeding, a significant change in the microbial composition and structure was observed, with an increase in microbial diversity and a shift from a Bacteroidetes-dominated microbiome to a Firmicutes-dominated micro-biome (Costello et al., 2010).

Unlike many other vertebrates, penguins do not hibernate during fast-ing, which occurs regularly during egg incubation and early stages of chick brooding, as well as annually when moulting. During the moult, penguins replace their entire plumage while fasting on land, which can last any-where from two to five weeks depending on the species (Groscolas & Robin, 2001; Gauthier-Clerc et al., 2002). During this time, penguins must rely on endogenous fat and protein reserves for feather synthesis and nourishment (Cherel et al., 1994), and moult-associated fasting signifi-cantly reduces the gut microbial diversity and composition of king (*Aptenodytes patagonicus*) and little (*Eudyptula minor*) penguins (Dewar et al., 2014). For king penguins, the majority of the genera observed were only present pre- or post-moult, with not many genera present at both time points. In little penguins, only moderate differences were observed in the genera present at each time point. Moreover, clear differences were observed between king and little penguins in response to fasting, with no 'core' fasting microbiome observed between the host species (Dewar et al., 2014).

4.3.5 Social interactions

Social interactions among colonial species influences microbiome composi-tion through microbial transfer via grooming, co-residency, shared environ-ments and sexual transmission (White et al., 2010, 2011; Archie & Tung, 2015; Tung et al., 2015; Grieneisen et al., 2017; see Chapter 6 for more details). Colonial species, such as chimpanzees (*Pan troglodytes schweinfurthii*) and baboons (*Papio cynocephalus*), share more similar microbial communities with other members of their social group than members from other groups, even when living in similar habitat types and consuming similar diets (Degnan et al., 2012; Archie & Tung, 2015). In yellow baboons (*Papio cynocephalus*), males newly immigrated to a social group have lower microbial similarities to males that immigrated earlier (Grieneisen et al., 2017). Furthermore, increased levels of social interaction promote a more diverse microbiome in comparison to lower levels of interaction (Archie & Tung, 2015), and grooming partners have a more similar microbiome compared to those who rarely groom each other (Tung et al., 2015). For bees, close social contact with nest mates enhances bacterial transfer between individuals and leads to direct transfer of symbiotic bacteria from one generation to the next (Billiet et al.,

2017). Reduced social interaction in bumblebees (*Bombus terrestris*) lowered the abundance of *Lactobacillus bombicola* and *Lactobacillus bombi*, while a significant decrease in microbial diversity was observed in individuals that were completely excluded from the colony (Billiet et al., 2017). Co-habiting humans also exhibit more similar microbiomes to one another when compared to humans in other households, and this is particularly true for couples (Song et al., 2013). Interestingly, dog owners also share a more similar skin microbiome with their own dogs than other dogs, and dog ownership increases the shared microbiome between co-habiting individuals (Song et al., 2013), highlighting an interesting example of cross-species microbiome transfer. Most research on the sexual transmission of microbes has focused heavily on sexually transmitted diseases in humans; however, recent research has shown that in some animal species, copulation can also influence the microbial composition of the cloaca of birds and reptiles (White et al., 2010, 2011). To observe whether microbes can be sexually transmitted in birds, Kulkarni and Heeb (2007) infected the cloaca of either male or female captive zebra finches (*Taeniopygia guttata*) with *Bacillus licheniformis* PWD1 prior to copulation. Results indicated that sexual transmission of microbes was four times higher from male to female than female to male (Kulkarni & Heeb, 2007). In common lizards (*Zootoca vivipara*), polyandrous females harbour more diverse microbial communities in comparison to monandrous females (White et al., 2011). Similarly, the cloacal microbial composition between the two groups differed significantly. It is hypothesised that because different males harbour different microbial communities, polyandrous females will acquire a more diverse microbiome from their different partners than monandrous females (White et al., 2011). In kittiwakes (*Rissa tridactyla*), White et al. (2010) used anti-insemination devices to block the transmission of microbial communities between nesting partners during copulation, and found that dissimilarity in microbial communities between nest partners increased while microbial diversity in females decreased and reverted back to pre-copulatory status.

4.3.6 Captivity

Captivity has pronounced effects on the animal microbiome, principally because captivity represents an artificial environment that does not replicate the natural variation in biotic and abiotic functions conferred by the social, dietary and environmental conditions that may influence a host's microbial community (Clayton et al., 2016; Hird, 2017; McKenzie et al., 2017). Moreover, captive animals are exposed to a variety of non-endemic microbes through human interactions with keepers and the general public (Delport et al., 2016), poor-quality and altered dietary sources (Hird, 2017; McKenzie et al., 2017), and microbes from the built environment (McKenzie et al., 2017). Captivity has been shown to reduce microbial diversity and alter microbial composition of mammals (Delsuc et al., 2014; Kong et al., 2014; Kreisinger et al., 2014; Clayton et al., 2016; Delport et al., 2016; McKenzie et al., 2017; Wasimuddin et al., 2017), birds (Wienemann et al., 2011; Waite et al., 2014; Wang et al., 2016; Xie et al., 2016), reptiles (Keenan et al., 2013; Kohl et al., 2017) and amphibians (Becker et al., 2014; Loudon et al., 2014; Bataille et al., 2016; Kueneman et al., 2016). For example, Clayton et al. (2016) found that captivity caused the loss of native microbes and a more humanised microbial composition in primates' species in zoological facilities. Moreover, hand-rearing reduces microbial diversity and alters microbiome composition of red-crowned cranes (*Grus japonensis*) and the endangered kakapo (*Strigops habroptilus*) (Waite et al., 2014; Xie et al., 2016). Alterations experienced in captivity may negatively affect the digestive physiology, immune function and fitness of individuals reintroduced into the wild (McKenzie et al., 2017). Recent studies in captive cheetahs (*Acinonyx jubatus*) have shown that captivity not only significantly alters the microbial composition and diversity of the host, but also alters the functional pathways related to immunity, resulting in captive individuals having higher incidences of pathogenic bacteria (Menke et al., 2017). In reptiles, captivity has also been associated with the introduction of pathogenic bacteria such as *Enterobacter*, *Salmonella* and *Trabulsiella* into the gut microbiota (Kohl et al., 2017). This suggests that the reintroduction of individuals from captivity into the wild may also introduce non-native and potentially pathogenic microbes into wild populations. Given this, together with the strong effects of captivity on microbial communities, there have been calls to consider the host microbiome when planning and implementing reintroductions (Redford et al., 2012; Bahrndorff et al., 2016; Antwis et al., 2017; Trevelline et al., 2019). Furthermore, as the microbiomes of captive individuals often do not provide a true representation of the microbiomes associated with their wild counterparts, or the natural variation that exists, one must be cautious about the assumptions made using these models for understanding the microbiome of wild animals (Amato, 2013; Amato et al., 2013).

The influence of captivity on host microbiomes also has indirect consequences for humans in terms of experimental outcomes from biomedical studies. Turnbaugh et al. (2006) showed that microbial communities associated with obesity could be transferred to non-obese mice, that these newly transferred communities caused weight gain, and that energy metabolism was different between the microbiota of lean and obese mice (Turnbaugh et al., 2009a). These surprising findings provided what many believed to be a clear link between the microbiota and obesity, and supported the initial case–control studies reported in humans (Ley et al., 2006). However, these specific studies with mice have been difficult for other groups to reliably replicate (Duca et al., 2014, 2016). This may not be surprising, because there is not only variation in the microbiota of mice from facility to facility (Hufeldt et al., 2010) but also a large amount of variability within both lean and obese humans (Finucane et al., 2014; Walters et al., 2014; Sze & Schloss, 2016). Experiments trying to recapitulate findings with mice also have to account for microbiome differences based on the strain of mouse being used and how they are housed (Hufeldt et al., 2010), as well as common genetic or maternal background effects (Mamantopoulos et al., 2017). Nevertheless, faecal microbiome transfer has successfully been used to repopulate specific pathogen-free laboratory mice with a microbiome from wild mouse populations, which subsequently improved resistance to viral infection and remained stable over multiple years (Rosshart et al., 2017). Directly manipulating the microbiome as an experimental variable is a highly powerful approach for detecting and quantifying host–microbe interactions, but there is a clear need to control for a multitude of confounding effects, and attempt to replicate findings across multiple labs (e.g. Mamantopoulos et al., 2017) to ensure any detected effects are robust.

4.4 Conclusions

Research directed at understanding the structure of microbial communities associated with animals, plants and soils, and the forces that shape them, has advanced rapidly over the last decade. As quantitative evidence from a diverse range of host taxonomic groups has accumulated, broad patterns have begun to emerge that highlight the immensely labile and plastic nature of microbiomes, as well as common drivers of change across diverse hosts and environments. Critically, although our knowledge of the forces shaping such plasticity is increasing, data on the consequences of microbiome variation for the host are relatively scarce. In this chapter, we have only scratched the surface of describing the intimate relationship between host and microbiome. Understanding the complex dynamics between these two agents is vital for elucidating the functional roles microbes play in affecting the health and fitness of their hosts.

References

Aagaard K, Ma J, Antony KM, et al. (2014) The placenta harbors a unique microbiome. *Science Translational Medicine*, 6, 237ra65.

Amato KR. (2013) Co-evolution in context: The importance of studying the gut microbiome of wild animals. *Microbiome Science*, 1, 10–29.

Amato KR, Yeoman CJ, Kent A, et al. (2013) Habitat degradation impacts black howler monkey (*Alouatta pigra*) gastrointestinal microbiomes. *The ISME Journal*, 7, 1344–1353.

Antwis RE, Griffiths SM, Harrison XA, et al. (2017) 50 important research questions in microbial ecology. *FEMS Microbiology Ecology*, 93,fix044.

Antwis RE, Lea JM, Unwin B, et al. (2018) Gut microbiome composition is associated with spatial structuring and social interactions in semi-feral Welsh Mountain ponies. *Microbiome*, 6, 207.

Archie EA, Tung J. (2015) Social behavior and the microbiome. *Current Opinion in Behavioral Sciences*, 6, 28–34.

Asaf S, Khan MA, Khan AL, et al. (2017) Bacterial endophytes from arid land plants regulate endogenous hormone content and promote growth in crop plants: An example of *Sphingomonas* sp. and *Serratia marcescens*. *Journal of Plant Interactions*, 12, 31–38.

Augustin R, Schröder K, Rincón AP, et al. (2017) A secreted antibacterial neuropeptide shapes the microbiome of *Hydra*. *Nature Communications*, 8, 698.

Bahrndorff S, Bahrndorff S, Alemu T, et al. (2016) The microbiome of animals: Implications for conservation biology. *International Journal of Genomics*, 2016, 5304028.

Banas JA, Loesche WJ, Nace GW. (1988) Possible mechanisms responsible for the reduced intestinal flora in hibernating leopard frogs (*Rana pipiens*). *Applied and Environmental Microbiology*, 54, 2311–2317.

Banks JC, Craig S, Cary I, et al. (2009) The phylogeography of Adelie penguin faecal flora. *Environmental Microbiology*, 11, 577–588.

Banning JL, Weddle AL, Wahl GW, et al. (2008) Antifungal skin bacteria, embryonic survival, and communal nesting in four-toed salamanders, *Hemidactylium scutatum*. *Oecologia*, 156, 423–429.

Barnes EM, Burton GC. (1970). The effect of hibernation on the caecal flora of the thirteen-lined ground squirrel (*Citellus tridecemlineatus*). *Journal of Applied Bacteriology*, 33, 505–514.

Bataille A, Lee-Cruz L, Tripathi B, et al. (2016) Microbiome variation across amphibian skin regions: Implications for chytridiomycosis mitigation efforts. *Microbial Ecology*, 71, 221–232.

Bates KA, Clare FC, O'Hanlon S, et al. (2018) Amphibian chytridiomycosis outbreak dynamics are linked with host skin bacterial community structure. *Nature Communications*, 9, 693.

Becker MH, Richards-Zawacki CL, Gratwicke B, et al. (2014) The effect of captivity on the cutaneous bacterial community of the critically endangered Panamanian golden frog (*Atelopus zeteki*). *Biological Conservation*, 176, 199–206.

Bennett KD. (1997) *Evolution and Ecology: The Pace of Life*. Cambridge: Cambridge University Press.

Berendsen RL, Pieterse CM, Bakker PA. (2012) The rhizosphere microbiome and plant health. *Trends in Plant Science*, 17, 478–486.

Billiet A, Meeus I, Van Nieuwerburgh F, et al. (2017) Colony contact contributes to the diversity of gut bacteria in bumblebees (*Bombus terrestris*). *Insect Science*, 24, 270–277.

Bollaerts K, Riera-Montes M, Heininger U, et al. (2017) A systematic review of varicella seroprevalence in European countries before universal childhood immunization: Deriving incidence from seroprevalence data. *Epidemiology & Infection*, 145, 2666–2677.

Bolnick DI, Snowberg LK, Caporaso JG, et al. (2014) Major Histocompatibility Complex class IIb polymorphism influences gut microbiota composition and diversity. *Molecular Ecology*, 23, 4831–4845.

Borruso L, Bacci G, Mengoni A, et al. (2014) Rhizosphere effect and salinity competing to shape microbial communities in *Phragmites australis* (Cav.) Trin. ex-Steud. *FEMS Microbiology Letters*, 359, 193–200.

Bosch TCG, McFall-Ngai MJ. (2011) Metaorganisms as the new frontier. *Zoology*, 114, 185–190.

Broderick NA, Lemaitre B. (2012) Gut-associated microbes of *Drosophila melanogaster*. *Gut Microbes*, 3, 307–321.

Brucker RM, Bordenstein SR. (2013) The hologenomic basis of speciation: Gut bacteria cause hybrid lethality in the genus *Nasonia*. *Science*, 341, 667–669.

Bula-Rudas FJ, Rathore MH, Maraqa NF. (2015) *Salmonella* infections in childhood. *Advances in Pediatrics*, 62, 29–58.

Burch AY, Zeisler V, Yokota K, et al. (2014) The hygroscopic biosurfactant syringafactin produced by *Pseudomonas syringae* enhances fitness on leaf surfaces during fluctuating humidity. *Environmental Microbiology*, 16, 2086–2098.

Burch AY, Do PT, Sbodio A, et al. (2016) High-level culturability of epiphytic bacteria and frequency of biosurfactant producers on leaves. *Applied and Environmental Microbiology*, 82, 5997.

Campbell LJ, Garner TW, Hopkins K, et al. (2019) Outbreaks of an emerging viral disease covary with differences in the composition of the skin microbiome of a wild UK amphibian. *Frontiers in Microbiology*, 10, 1245.

Cherel Y, Charrassin JB, Challet E. (1994) Energy and protein requirements for molt in the king penguin *Aptenodytes patagonicus*. *American Journal of Physiology: Regulatory, Integrative and Comparative Physiology*, 266, R1182–1188.

Clayton JB, Vangay P, Huang H, et al. (2016) Captivity humanizes the primate microbiome. *Proceedings of the National Academy of Sciences*, 113, 10376–10381.

Coleman-Derr D, Desgarennes D, Fonseca-Garcia C, et al. (2016) Plant compartment and biogeography affect microbiome composition in cultivated and native *Agave* species. *New Phytologist*, 209, 798–811.

Colston TJ. (2017) Gut microbiome transmission in lizards. *Molecular Ecology*, 26, 972–974.

Cooper RG. (2004) Ostrich (*Struthio camelus*) chick and grower nutrition. *Animal Science Journal*, 75, 487–490.

Cordier T, Robin C, Capdevielle X, et al. (2012) The composition of phyllosphere fungal assemblages of European beech (*Fagus sylvatica*) varies significantly along an elevation gradient. *New Phytologist*, 196, 510–519.

Costello EK, Gordon JI, Secor SM, et al. (2010) Postprandial remodeling of the gut microbiota in Burmese pythons. *The ISME Journal*, 4, 1375–1385.

Davenport ER, Sanders JG, Song SJ, et al. (2017) The human microbiome in evolution. *BMC Biology*, 15, 1–12.

David LA, Maurice CF, Carmody RN, et al. (2014) Diet rapidly and reproducibly alters the human gut microbiome. *Nature*, 505, 559.

Degnan PH, Pusey AE, Lonsdorf EV, et al. (2012) Factors associated with the diversification of the gut microbial communities within chimpanzees from Gombe National Park. *Proceedings of the National Academy of Sciences*, 109, 13034–13039.

Delport TC, Power ML, Harcourt RG, et al. (2016) Colony location and captivity influence the gut microbial community composition of the Australian sea lion (*Neophoca cinerea*). *Applied and Environmental Microbiology*, 82, 3440–3449.

Delsuc F, Metcalf JL, Wegener Parfrey L, et al. (2014) Convergence of gut microbiomes in myrmecophagous mammals. *Molecular Ecology*, 23, 1301–1317.

Dewar ML, Arnould JP, Krause L, et al. (2014) Influence of fasting during moult on the faecal microbiota of penguins. *PLoS ONE*, 9, e99996.

Dominguez-Bello MG, Costello EK, Contreras M, et al. (2010) Delivery mode shapes the acquisition and structure of the initial microbiota across multiple body habitats in newborns. *Proceedings of the National Academy of Sciences*, 107, 11971–11975.

Dominguez-Bello MG, De Jesus-Laboy KM, Shen N, et al. (2016) Partial restoration of the microbiota of cesarean-born infants via vaginal microbial transfer. *Nature Medicine*, 22, 250.

Douglas AE. (2015) Multiorganismal insects: Diversity and function of resident microorganisms. *Annual Review of Entomology*, 60, 17–34.

Duca FA, Sakar Y, Lepage P, et al. (2014) Replication of obesity and associated signaling pathways through transfer of microbiota from obese-prone rats. *Diabetes*, 63, 1624–36.

Duca FA, Sakar Y, Lepage P, et al. (2016) Statement of retraction. Replication of obesity and associated signaling pathways through transfer of microbiota from obese-prone rats. *Diabetes*, 63, 1624–1636.

Duncan SH, Belenguer A, Holtrop G, et al. (2007) Reduced dietary intake of carbohydrates by obese subjects results in decreased concentrations of butyrate and butyrate-producing bacteria in feces. *Applied and Environmental Microbiology*, 73, 1073–1078.

Eaves LJ, Last KA, Young PA, Martin NG. (1978) Model-fitting approaches to the analysis of human behaviour. *Heredity*, 41, 249–320.

Egamberdieva D, Jabborova D, Berg G. (2016) Synergistic interactions between *Bradyrhizobium japonicum* and the endophyte *Stenotrophomonas rhizophila* and their effects on growth, and nodulation of soybean under salt stress. *Plant and Soil*, 405, 35–45.

Ellner PD. (1998) Smallpox: Gone but not forgotten. *Infection*, 26, 263–269.

Feng Q, Chen WD, Wang YD. (2018) Gut microbiota: An integral moderator in health and disease. *Frontiers in Microbiology*, 9, 151.

Finucane MM, Sharpton TJ, Laurent TJ, et al. (2014) A taxonomic signature of obesity in the microbiome? Getting to the guts of the matter. *PLoS ONE*, 9, e84689.

Fitzpatrick BM, Allison AL. (2014) Similarity and differentiation between bacteria associated with skin of salamanders (*Plethodon jordani*) and free-living assemblages. *FEMS Microbiology Ecology*, 88, 482–94.

Flint HJ, Bayer EA, Rincon MT, et al. (2008) Polysaccharide utilization by gut bacteria: Potential for new insights from genomic analysis. *Nature Reviews Microbiology*, 6, 121–131.

Fraust K, Raes J. (2012) Microbial interactions: From networks to models. *Nature Reviews Microbiology*, 10, 538–550.

Froussart E, Bonneau J, Franche C, et al. (2016) Recent advances in actinorhizal symbiosis signaling. *Plant Molecular Biology*, 90, 613–22.

Funkhouser LJ, Bordenstein SR. (2013) Mom knows best: The universality of maternal microbial transmission. *PLoS Biology*, 11, e1001631.

Gabutti G, Franchi M, Maniscalco L, et al. (2016) Varicella-zoster virus: Pathogenesis, incidence patterns and vaccination programs. *Minerva Pediatrica*, 68, 213–225.

Gause G. (1934) *The Struggle for Existence.* New York, NY: Dover Publications.

Gauthier-Clerc M, Le Maho Y, Clerquin Y, et al. (2002) Seabird reproduction in an unpredictable environment: How king penguins provide their young chicks with food. *Marine Ecology Progress Series*, 237, 291–300.

Geller LT, Barzily-Rokni M, Danino T, et al. (2017) Potential role of intratumor bacteria in mediating tumor resistance to the chemotherapeutic drug gemcitabine. *Science*, 357, 1156–1160.

Gevers D, Knight R, Petrosino JF, et al. (2012) The Human Microbiome Project: A community resource for the healthy human microbiome. *PLoS Biology*, 10, e1001377.

Godoy-Vitorino F, Goldfarb KC, Brodie EL, et al. (2010) Developmental microbial ecology of the crop of the folivorous hoatzin. *The ISME Journal*, 4, 611.

Goodrich JK, Waters JL, Poole AC, et al. (2014) Human genetics shape the gut microbiome. *Cell*, 159, 789–99.

Gossling J, Loesche WJ, Nace GW. (1982a) Large intestine bacterial flora of nonhibernating and hibernating leopard frogs (*Rana pipiens*). *Applied and Environmental Microbiology*, 44, 59–66.

Gossling J, Loesche WJ, Nace GW. (1982b) Response of intestinal flora of laboratory-reared leopard frogs (*Rana pipiens*) to cold and fasting. *Applied and Environmental Microbiology*, 44, 67–71.

Gottel NR, Castro HF, Kerley M, et al. (2011) Distinct microbial communities within the endosphere and rhizosphere of *Populus deltoides* roots across contrasting soil types. *Applied and Environmental Microbiology*, 77, 5934–5944.

Grieneisen LE, Livermore J, Alberts S, et al. (2017) Group living and male dispersal predict the core gut microbiome in wild baboons. *Integrative and Comparative Biology*, 57, 770–785.

Griffiths SM, Harrison XA, Weldon C, et al. (2018) Genetic variability and ontogeny predict microbiome structure in a disease-challenged montane amphibian. *The ISME Journal*, 12, 2506.

Griffiths SM, Antwis RE, Lenzi L, et al. (2019) Host genetics and geography influence microbiome composition in the sponge Ircinia campana. *Journal of Animal Ecology*, DOI:10.1111/1365-2656.13065.

Groscolas R, Robin JP. (2001) Long-term fasting and re-feeding in penguins. *Comparative Biochemistry and Physiology Part A: Molecular and Integrative Physiology*, 128, 645–655.

Gómez-Brandón M, Lores M, Domínguez J. (2012) Species-specific effects of epigeic earthworms on microbial community structure during first stages of decomposition of organic matter. *PLoS ONE*, 7, e31895.

Hallmann J, Quadt-Hallmann A, Mahaffee WF, et al. (1997) Bacterial endophytes in agricultural crops. *Canadian Journal of Microbiology*, 43, 895–914.

Hammer TJ, Bowers MD. (2015) Gut microbes may facilitate insect herbivory of chemically defended plants. *Oecologia*, 179, 1–14.

Hehemann JH, Kelly AG, Pudlo NA, et al. (2012) Bacteria of the human gut microbiome catabolize red seaweed glycans with carbohydrate-active enzyme updates from extrinsic microbes. *Proceedings of the National Academy of Sciences*, 109, 19786–19791.

Hird SM. (2017) Evolutionary biology needs wild microbiomes. *Frontiers in Microbiology*, 8, 725.

House D, Bishop A, Parry C, et al. (2001) Typhoid fever: Pathogenesis and disease. *Current Opinion in Infectious Diseases*, 14, 573–578.

Hufeldt MR, Nielsen DS, Vogensen FK, et al. (2010) Variation in the gut microbiota of laboratory mice is related to both genetic and environmental factors. *Comparative Medicine*, 60, 336–347.

Human Microbiome Consortium. (2012) Structure, function and diversity of the healthy human microbiome. *Nature*, 486, 207–214.

Iniguez AL, Dong Y, Carter HD, et al. (2005) Regulation of enteric endophytic bacterial colonization by plant defenses. *Molecular Plant–Microbe Interactions*, 18, 169–178.

Kandel S, Joubert P, Doty S. (2017) Bacterial endophyte colonization and distribution within plants. *Microorganisms*, 5, 77.

Keenan SW, Engel AS, Elsey RM. (2013) The alligator gut microbiome and implications for archosaur symbioses. *Scientific Reports*, 3, 2877.

Kohl KD, Cary TL, Karasov WH, et al. (2013) Restructuring of the amphibian gut microbiota through metamorphosis. *Environmental Microbiology Reports*, 5, 899–903.

Kohl KD, Brun A, Magallanes M, et al. (2017) Gut microbial ecology of lizards: Insights into diversity in the wild, effects of captivity, variation across gut regions and transmission. *Molecular Ecology*, 26, 1175–1189.

Kong F, Zhao J, Han S, et al. (2014) Characterization of the gut microbiota in the red panda (*Ailurus fulgens*). *PLoS ONE*, 9, e87885.

Kreisinger J, Čížková D, Vohánka J, et al. (2014) Gastrointestinal microbiota of wild and inbred individuals of two house mouse subspecies assessed using high-throughput parallel pyrosequencing. *Molecular Ecology*, 23, 5048–5060.

Kueneman JG, Parfrey LW, Woodhams DC, et al. (2014) The amphibian skin-associated microbiome across species, space and life history stages. *Molecular Ecology*, 23, 1238–1250.

Kueneman JG, Woodhams DC, Harris R, et al. (2016) Probiotic treatment restores protection against lethal fungal infection lost during amphibian captivity. *Proceedings of the Royal Society B: Biological Sciences*, 283, 20161553.

Kulkarni S, Heeb P. (2007) Social and sexual behaviours aid transmission of bacteria in birds. *Behavioral Processes*, 74, 88–92.

Kwong WK, Moran NA. (2015) Evolution of host specialization in gut microbes: The bee gut as a model. *Gut Microbes*, 6, 214–220.

Larrainzar E, Wienkoop S. (2017) A proteomic view on the role of legume symbiotic interactions. *Frontiers in Plant Science*, 8, 1267.

Lax S, Smith DP, Hampton-Marcell J, et al. (2014) Longitudinal analysis of microbial interaction between humans and the indoor environment. *Science*, 345, 1048–1052.

Ley RE, Bäckhed F, Turnbaugh P, et al. (2005) Obesity alters gut microbial ecology. *Proceedings of the National Academy of Sciences*, 102, 11070–11075.

Ley RE, Turnbaugh PJ, Klein S, et al. (2006) Microbial ecology: Human gut microbes associated with obesity. *Nature*, 444, 1022.

Ley RE, Hamady M, Lozupone C, et al. (2008a) Evolution of mammals and their gut microbes. *Science*, 320, 1647–1651.

Ley RE, Lozupone CA, Hamady M, et al. (2008b) Worlds within worlds: Evolution of the vertebrate gut microbiota. *Nature Reviews Microbiology*, 6, 776.

Li Z, Wright AD, Si H, et al. (2016) Changes in the rumen microbiome and metabolites reveal the effect of host genetics on hybrid crosses. *Environmental Microbiology Reports*, 8, 1016–1023.

Loudon AH, Woodhams DC, Parfrey LW, et al. (2014) Microbial community dynamics and effect of environmental microbial reservoirs on red-backed salamanders (*Plethodon cinereus*). *The ISME Journal*, 8, 830.

Lu J, Idris U, Harmon B, et al. (2003) Diversity and succession of the intestinal bacterial community of the maturing broiler chicken. *Applied and Environmental Microbiology*, 69, 6816–6824.

Macke E, Tasiemski A, Massol F, et al. (2017) Life history and eco-evolutionary dynamics in light of the gut microbiota. *Oikos*, 126, 508–531.

Mamantopoulos M, Ronchi F, Van Hauwermeiren F, et al. (2017) Nlrp6-and ASC-dependent inflammasomes do not shape the commensal gut microbiota composition. *Immunity*, 47, 339–348.

Martin FM, Uroz S, Barker DG. (2017) Ancestral alliances: Plant mutualistic symbioses with fungi and bacteria. *Science*, 356, eaad4501.

Mazel F, Davis KM, Loudon A, et al. (2018) Is host filtering the main driver of phylosymbiosis across the tree of life? *mSystems*, 3, e00097–18.

McFall-Ngai M, Hadfield MG, Bosch TC, et al. (2013) Animals in a bacterial world, a new imperative for the life sciences. *Proceedings of the National Academy of Sciences*, 110, 3229–3236.

McKenzie VJ, Song SJ, Delsuc F, et al. (2017) The effects of captivity on the mammalian gut microbiome. *Integrative and Comparative Biology*, 57, 690–704.

Melotto M, Underwood W, Koczan J, et al. (2006) Plant stomata function in innate immunity against bacterial invasion. *Cell*, 126, 969–980.

Melotto M, Zhang L, Oblessuc PR, et al. (2017) Stomatal defense a decade later. *Plant Physiology*, 174, 561–571.

Mendes R, Kruijt M, De Bruijn I, et al. (2011) Deciphering the rhizosphere microbiome for disease-suppressive bacteria. *Science*, 332, 1097–1100.

Menke S, Melzheimer J, Thalwitzer S, et al. (2017) Gut microbiomes of free-ranging and captive Namibian cheetahs: Diversity, putative functions and occurrence of potential pathogens. *Molecular Ecology*, 26, 5515–5527.

Muegge BD, Kuczynski J, Knights D, et al. (2011) Diet drives convergence in gut microbiome functions across mammalian phylogeny and within humans. *Science*, 332, 970–974.

Nelson TM, Rogers TL, Carlini AR, et al. (2013) Diet and phylogeny shape the gut microbiota of Antarctic seals: A comparison of wild and captive animals. *Environmental Microbiology*, 15, 1132–1145.

Noyer C, Becerro MA. (2012) Relationship between genetic, chemical, and bacterial diversity in the Atlanto-Mediterranean bath sponge *Spongia lamella*. *Hydrobiologia*, 687, 85–99.

Oldroyd GE, Murray JD, Poole PS, et al. (2011) The rules of engagement in the legume–rhizobial symbiosis. *Annual Review of Genetics*, 45, 119–144.

Oliver KM, Degnan PH, Burke GR, et al. (2010) Facultative symbionts in aphids and the horizontal transfer of ecologically important traits. *Annual Review of Entomology*, 55, 247–266.

Panchal S, Roy D, Chitrakar R, et al. (2016) Coronatine facilitates *Pseudomonas syringae* infection of *Arabidopsis* leaves at night. *Frontiers in Plant Science*, 7, 880.

Parvaiz A, Satyawati S. (2008) Salt stress and phyto-biochemical responses of plants – A review. *Plant Soil Environment*, 54, 89–99.

Pascoe EL, Hauffe HC, Marchesi JR, Perkins SE. (2017) Network analysis of gut microbiota literature: An overview of the research landscape in non-human animal studies. *The ISME Journal*, 11, 2644.

Philippot L, Raaijmakers JM, Lemanceau P, et al. (2013) Going back to the roots: The microbial ecology of the rhizosphere. *Nature Reviews Microbiology*, 11, 789.

Pieterse CM, Zamioudis C, Berendsen RL, et al. (2014) Induced systemic resistance by beneficial microbes. *Annual Review of Phytopathology*, 52, 347–375.

Pietschke C, Treitz C, Forêt S, et al. (2017) Host modification of a bacterial quorum-sensing signal induces a phenotypic switch in bacterial symbionts. *Proceedings of the National Academy of Sciences*, 114, E8488–8497.

Redford KH, Segre JA, Salafsky N, et al. (2012) Conservation and the microbiome. *Conservation Biology*, 2012, 195–197.

Ren G, Zhang H, Lin X, et al. (2015) Response of leaf endophytic bacterial community to elevated CO_2 at different growth stages of rice plant. *Frontiers in Microbiology*, 6, 855.

Rosenblueth M, Martínez-Romero E. (2006) Bacterial endophytes and their interactions with hosts. *Molecular Plant–Microbe Interactions*, 19, 827–837.

Rosshart SP, Vassallo BG, Angeletti D, et al. (2017) Wild mouse gut microbiota promotes host fitness and improves disease resistance. *Cell*, 171, 1015–1028.

Santoyo G, Moreno-Hagelsieb G, del Carmen Orozco-Mosqueda M, et al. (2016) Plant growth-promoting bacterial endophytes. *Microbiological Research*, 183, 92–99.

Sasse J, Martinoia E, Northen T. (2018) Feed your friends: Do plant exudates shape the root microbiome? *Trends in Plant Science*, 23, 25–41.

Schubert AM, Sinani H, Schloss PD. (2015) Antibiotic-induced alterations of the murine gut microbiota and subsequent effects on colonization resistance against *Clostridium difficile*. *mBio*, 6, e00974–15.

Seedorf H, Griffin NW, Ridaura VK, et al. (2014) Bacteria from diverse habitats colonize and compete in the mouse gut. *Cell*, 159, 253–266.

Sender R, Fuchs S, Milo R. (2016a) Are we really vastly outnumbered? Revisiting the ratio of bacterial to host cells in humans. *Cell*, 164, 337–340.

Sender R, Fuchs S, Milo R. (2016b) Revised estimates for the number of human and bacteria cells in the body. *PLoS Biology*, 14, e1002533.

Shah MS, DeSantis TZ, Weinmaier T, et al. (2018) Leveraging sequence-based faecal microbial community survey data to identify a composite biomarker for colorectal cancer. *Gut*, 67, 882–891.

Smith CC, Snowberg LK, Caporaso JG, et al. (2015) Dietary input of microbes and host genetic variation shape among-population differences in stickleback gut microbiota. *The ISME Journal*, 9, 2515.

Song SJ, Lauber C, Costello EK, et al. (2013) Cohabiting family members share microbiota with one another and with their dogs. *eLife*, 2, e00458.

Sonoyama K, Fujiwara R, Takemura N, et al. (2009) Response of gut microbiota to fasting and hibernation in Syrian hamsters. *Journal of Applied Environmental Microbiology*, 75, 6451–6456.

Sze MA, Schloss PD. (2016) Looking for a signal in the noise: Revisiting obesity and the microbiome. *mBio*, 7, e01018–16.

Sze MA, Schloss PD. (2018) Leveraging existing 16S rRNA gene surveys to identify reproducible biomarkers in individuals with colorectal tumors. *mBio*, 9, e00630–18.

Sze MA, Tsuruta M, Yang SW, et al. (2014) Changes in the bacterial microbiota in gut, blood, and lungs following acute LPS instillation into mice lungs. *PLoS ONE*, 9, e111228.

Thakuria D, Schmidt O, Finan D, et al. (2010) Gut wall bacteria of earthworms: A natural selection process. *The ISME Journal*, 4, 357.

Thomas T, Moitinho-Silva L, Lurgi M, et al. (2016) Diversity, structure and convergent evolution of the global sponge microbiome. *Nature Communications*, 7, 11870.

Thompson LR, Sanders JG, McDonald D, et al. (2017) A communal catalogue reveals Earth's multiscale microbial diversity. *Nature*, 551, 457.

Trevelline BK, Fontaine SS, Hartup BK, et al. (2019) Conservation biology needs a microbial renaissance: A call for the consideration of host-associated microbiota in wildlife management practices. *Proceedings of the Royal Society B: Biological Sciences*, 286, 20182448.

Tung J, Barreiro LB, Burns MB, et al. (2015) Social networks predict gut microbiome composition in wild baboons. *eLife*, 4, e05224.

Turnbaugh PJ, Ley RE, Mahowald MA, et al. (2006) An obesity-associated gut microbiome with increased capacity for energy harvest. *Nature*, 444, 1027.

Turnbaugh PJ, Hamady M, Yatsunenko T, et al. (2009a) A core gut microbiome in obese and lean twins. *Nature*, 457, 480.

Turnbaugh PJ, Ridaura VK, Faith JJ, et al. (2009b) The effect of diet on the human gut microbiome: A metagenomic analysis in humanized gnotobiotic mice. *Science Translational Medicine*, 1, 6ra14.

Turner TR, James EK, Poole PS. (2013) The plant microbiome. *Genome Biology*, 14, 209.

Tveit AT, Urich T, Frenzel P, et al. (2015) Metabolic and trophic interactions modulate methane production by Arctic peat microbiota in response to warming. *Proceedings of the National Academy of Sciences*, 112, E2507–2516.

Vacher C, Hampe A, Porté AJ, et al. (2016) The phyllosphere: Microbial jungle at the plant–climate interface. *Annual Review of Ecology, Evolution, and Systematics*, 47, 1–24.

Videvall E, Song SJ, Bensch HM, et al. (2019) Major shifts in gut microbiota during development and its relationship to growth in ostriches. *Molecular Ecology*, 28, 2653–2667.

Von Mutius E. (2016) The microbial environment and its influence on asthma prevention in early life. *The Journal of Allergy and Clinical Immunology*, 137, 680–689.

Waite DW, Eason D, Taylor MW. (2014) Influence of hand rearing and bird age on the fecal microbiota of the critically endangered kakapo. *Applied and Environmental Microbiology*, 80, 4650–4658.

Walke JB, Harris RN, Reinert LK, et al. (2011) Social immunity in amphibians: Evidence for vertical transmission of innate defenses. *Biotropica*, 43, 396–400.

Walke JB, Becker MH, Loftus SC, et al. (2014) Amphibian skin may select for rare environmental microbes. *The ISME Journal*, 8, 2207.

Walters WA, Xu Z, Knight R. (2014) Meta-analyses of human gut microbes associated with obesity and IBD. *FEBS Letters*, 588, 4223–4233.

Wang W, Zheng S, Sharshov K, et al. (2016) Distinctive gut microbial community structure in both the wild and farmed swan goose (*Anser cygnoides*). *Journal of Basic Microbiology*, 56, 1299–1307.

Wasimuddin, Menke S, Melzheimer J, et al. (2017) Gut microbiomes of free-ranging and captive Namibian cheetahs: Diversity, putative functions and occurrence of potential pathogens. *Molecular Ecology*, 26.

Weinert N, Piceno Y, Ding GC, et al. (2011) PhyloChip hybridization uncovered an enormous bacterial diversity in the rhizosphere of different potato cultivars: Many common and few cultivar-dependent taxa. *FEMS Microbiology Ecology*, 75, 497–506.

White J, Mirleau P, Danchin E, et al. (2010) Sexually transmitted bacteria affect female cloacal assemblages in a wild bird. *Ecology Letters*, 13, 1515–1524.

White J, Richard M, Massot M, Meylan S. (2011) Cloacal bacterial diversity increases with multiple mates: Evidence of sexual transmission in female common lizards. *PLoS ONE*, 6, e22339.

Wienemann T, Schmitt-Wagner D, Meuser K, et al. (2011) The bacterial microbiota in the ceca of Capercaillie (*Tetrao urogallus*) differs between wild and captive birds. *Systematic and Applied Microbiology*, 34, 542–551.

Williams CL, Willard S, Kouba A, et al. (2013) Dietary shifts affect the gastrointestinal microflora of the giant panda (*Ailuropoda melanoleuca*). *Journal of Animal Physiology and Animal Nutrition*, 97, 577–585.

Wong S, Stephens WZ, Burns AR, et al. (2015) Ontogenetic differences in dietary fat influence microbiota assembly in the zebrafish gut. *mBio*, 6, e00687–15.

Wu GD, Chen J, Hoffmann C, et al. (2011) Linking long-term dietary patterns with gut microbial enterotypes. *Science*, 334, 105–108.

Xie Y, Xia P, Wang H, et al. (2016) Effects of captivity and artificial breeding on microbiota in feces of the red-crowned crane (*Grus japonensis*). *Scientific Reports*, 6, 33350.

Xue Z, Zhang W, Wang L, et al. (2015) The bamboo-eating giant panda harbors a carnivore-like gut microbiota, with

excessive seasonal variations. *mBio*, 6, e00022–15.

Yang SC, Lin CH, Aljuffali IA, Fang JY. (2017). Current pathogenic *Escherichia coli* foodborne outbreak cases and therapy development. *Archives of Microbiology*, 199, 811–825.

Yildirim S, Yeoman CJ, Janga SC, et al. (2014) Primate vaginal microbiomes exhibit species specificity without universal *Lactobacillus dominance*. *The ISME Journal*, 8, 2431–2444.

Youngblut ND, Reischer GH, Walters W, et al. (2019). Host diet and evolutionary history explain different aspects of gut microbiome diversity among vertebrate clades. *Nature Communications*, 10, 2200.

Yuan ML, Dean SH, Longo AV, et al. (2015) Kinship, inbreeding and fine-scale spatial structure influence gut microbiota in a hindgut-fermenting tortoise. *Molecular Ecology*, 24, 2521–2536.

Zgadzaj R, Garrido-Oter R, Jensen DB, et al. (2016) Root nodule symbiosis in *Lotus japonicus* drives the establishment of distinctive rhizosphere, root, and nodule bacterial communities. *Proceedings of the National Academy of Sciences*, 113, E7996.

Zheng H, Powell JE, Steele MI, et al. (2017) Honeybee gut microbiota promotes host weight gain via bacterial metabolism and hormonal signaling. *Proceedings of the National Academy of Sciences*, 114, 4775–4780.

Zoetendal EG, Akkermans ADL, Vliet WMA, et al. (2001) The host genotype affects the bacterial community in the human gastrointestinal tract. *Microbial Ecology in Health and Disease*, 13, 129–134.

Zwirglmaier K, Keiz K, Engel M, et al. (2015) Seasonal and spatial patterns of microbial diversity along a trophic gradient in the interconnected lakes of the Osterseen Lake District, Bavaria. *Frontiers in Microbiology*, 6, 1168.

CHAPTER FIVE

Microbial symbioses and host nutrition

PHILIP DONKERSLEY, SAM ROBINSON
Lancaster University
ELLA K. DEUTSCH and ALASTAIR
T. GIBBONS
University of Nottingham

5.1 Introduction

Classical ecology can look at an ecosystem in terms of food webs, where the movement of energy between trophic levels describes the content and structure of an ecosystem. These reductionist descriptions typically use unidirectional flows of nutrients (i.e. energy) from primary producers to higher consumers. Given that all environments and multicellular organisms support microbial communities, and that these are innately linked to nutrient processing, microbiomes play a key role in regulating the flow of nutrients within entire ecosystems (McFall-Ngai et al., 2013; Sommer & Bäckhed, 2013). For example, primary producers – plants – have evolved symbioses with fungal arbuscular mycorrhizae to increase nutrient absorption from the soil, and most herbivorous animals require a microbial symbiosis to retrieve sufficient nutrients to survive. Furthermore, predators and parasites of lower trophic levels often host complex microbial communities as both commensal and mutualistic symbionts to more efficiently exploit nutrients acquired from other organisms (i.e. herbivores). Some parasites and parasitoids (i.e. ticks or parasitoid wasps) even employ microbial pathogens of their hosts as a parasitism co-factor. All of this biological complexity is supported by fundamental nutrient cycles such as carbon and nitrogen, which are driven by environmental and soil-associated microbial communities. Furthermore, the critical pressure to produce sufficient nutrition for a rapidly growing human population makes this is a particularly timely topic. Present solutions attempt to develop sustainable agriculture, reducing pressure on already constrained land and water resources (Whitacre et al., 2010). By better understanding the links between nutrition and microbial symbioses (Muegge et al., 2011), we might address this need for efficiency on a novel axis. This chapter will specifically consider soil biogeochemical nutrient cycling in the context of plant hosts (see Chapters 3 and 4 for additional information), as well as invertebrates as both herbivores and predators, with a brief comment on microbially mediated vertebrate nutrition.

5.2 Microbial mediation of plant–soil nutrient dynamics

The regulation of plant productivity, diversity and community composition by soil microbes is well recognised, largely resulting from the supply of key nutrients required for plant growth and survival by microbial decomposers and symbionts (Van Der Heijden et al., 2008). Soil microbial communities themselves are mutually influenced by plants through reciprocal feedbacks to the soil, as plant inputs via litter and roots may alter soil biotic and abiotic characteristics (Bever et al., 2010; Van Der Putten et al., 2013; Cortois et al., 2016). Subsequently, the microbial mediation of plant–soil interactions underpins vital biogeochemical cycles, affecting nutrient and carbon flows through entire ecosystems (Wardle et al., 2004).

Beyond the indirect provision of plant-available nutrients by free-living soil microbes, for example through mineralisation of organic matter (Schimel & Bennett, 2004; Van Der Heijden et al., 2008), direct symbioses arising from plant–microbe co-evolution (Brundrett, 2002) can be crucial for plant acquisition of essential (co-)limiting nutrients such as nitrogen (N) and phosphorus (P), required for the building of proteins, DNA and RNA (Davidson & Howarth, 2007). These associations predominantly involve plant partnerships with N-fixing bacteria and mycorrhizal fungi. The majority of terrestrial plant species benefit from such symbioses, and estimates suggest at least 20,000 of these are completely dependent on colonisation by microbial partners for survival and growth (approximately 1 in 20 plant species based on 391,000 known globally; RGB Kew, 2016), especially in nutrient-poor environments (Van Der Heijden et al., 2008).

5.2.1 Symbiotic nitrogen fixation

Nitrogen is abundantly found throughout the planet, making up the majority of our atmosphere, but this nitrogen is not bioavailable. Plants have co-evolved with a combination of endosymbionts, ectosymbionts and other soil-borne microbial organisms that can 'fix' non-bioavailable sources of nitrogen (Wardle et al., 1999; Nannipieri et al., 2003; Macé et al., 2016). In terrestrial ecosystems, symbiotic N fixation involves the root nodulation of some vascular plant species by bacteria able to convert atmospheric dinitrogen (N_2) into bioavailable forms (Nasto et al., 2014). This typically occurs between leguminous plants and rhizobia, and between non-legumes and the actinomycete *Frankia* spp., offering a solution to N deficiency for both woody and herbaceous plant species across tropical, temperate and boreal biomes (Vitousek et al., 2002). However, plant associations with N-fixing bacteria come at a price. Maintaining these partnerships is energy-demanding for host plants, with microbial symbionts requiring costly investments of both carbon (C) and P (Vitousek & Howarth, 1991). For this reason, plants may downregulate acquisition of N from bacterial symbionts when it becomes more readily available in the soil (Gerber et al., 2010).

5.2.2 Mycorrhizal symbiosis

Mycorrhizae are ubiquitous symbiotic associations between fungi and terrestrial plants (Smith & Read, 2008; Calvaruso et al., 2010; Wurzburger & Clemmensen, 2018; Meier et al., 2019). They play a major role in plant development, growth, behaviour and evolution (Gorzelak et al., 2015; Sędzielewska-Toro & Delaux, 2016), providing a 'functional link' to the soil they inhabit (Wurzburger & Clemmensen, 2018) through which the initial colonisation of land by plants may have been made possible (Redecker et al., 2000; Humphreys et al., 2010). Fungal symbionts supply nutrients in exchange for photosynthates produced by their plant hosts (Smith & Read, 2008). This exchange is vital for both partners; heterotrophic fungi must obtain C from external sources for growth and survival (Itoo & Reshi, 2013), while roots extended by foraging fungal hyphae increase plant acquisition of key nutrients that are often limiting to productivity (Lambers et al., 2008; Nasto et al., 2014; Wurzburger & Clemmensen, 2018). These are obtained either from distant nutrient 'hotspots', or through the release of bioavailable nutrients from inaccessible organic pools by fungal symbionts (e.g. mineralisation of organic P through production of the extracellular phosphatase enzyme). As most vegetation has been shown to form mycorrhizal associations (Smith & Read, 2008), these relationships are instrumental in shaping nutrient dynamics across multiple tropic levels (e.g. Maxwell Stevens et al., 2018), with huge implications for biogeochemical cycling and carbon storage at the ecosystem scale (Averill et al., 2014; Dickie et al., 2014).

There are two main mycorrhizal classes. Arbuscular mycorrhizal fungi (AMF), obligate symbionts in the Glomeromycota, are considerably the most widespread (associated with 74% of angiosperms) and are the dominant class in tropical forests, temperate grasslands and agricultural land (Smith & Read, 2008; Brundrett, 2009). Ectomycorrhizal fungi (EMF) are comparatively less common, but comprise a greater number of fungal species (Smith & Read, 2008) and often form partnerships with hosts that dominate the vegetation communities in which they are present, for example the Pinacea of boreal ecosystems and the Dipterocaceae of some tropical forests (Brearley, 2012; Wallander et al., 2013; Gorzelak et al., 2015). AMF characteristically form arbuscules within the cortical cells of plants, and produce microscopic branching hyphae (mycelium) into the soil. EMF instead construct a distinctive mantle around roots from which hyphae grow inwardly between cortical cells of the plant (the Hartig net; Smith & Read, 2008), as well as an extramatrical mycelium that can often be extensive and macroscopic (Peterson et al., 2004), in some cases even forming dense mats across forest floors (Ekblad et al., 2013; see Chapter 3 for more).

Mycorrhizal partnerships form by way of two-directional messaging between plant roots and fungi at the molecular level. Coordination is provided within the rhizosphere as plant root exudates influence amount and direction of fungal growth, and root surface conditions promote mycorrhizal colonisation. Plants and fungi regulate their own roles in these partnerships, including the fungal rejection of a potential plant symbiont through mechanisms of resistance (Anderson, 1992; Koske & Gemma, 1993), while plants may also vary the amount of carbon and nutrients invested in fungal partners depending on soil conditions (Nasto et al., 2014). Species-specificity in mycorrhizae tends to be low as both plants and fungi associate with a broad range of partners, with a few exceptions (Lang et al., 2011; Gorzelak et al., 2015). Plants may simultaneously form symbioses with a broad range of fungal species and functional types, including both AMF and EMF, selected by plant hosts according to environmental conditions (Albornoz et al., 2016). Selection mechanisms and regulation result in contrasting nutrient foraging strategies within plant communities, promoting complementarity among plant species with different root functional traits and mycorrhizal types (Chen et al., 2016). Moreover, recent studies have shown nutrients may be transferred between individual plants of the same or different species that are linked by a continuous AMF or EMF mycelium (Barto et al., 2012; Gorzelak et al., 2015), known as a 'common mycelial network' (Bever et al., 2010; Babikova et al., 2013). These networks can influence plant growth and survival through inter-plant exchanges of nitrogen, phosphorous and micronutrients over long distances between donor and receiver plants, as well as plant establishment as seedlings tap into existing mycelial networks (reviewed by Gorzelak et al., 2015).

5.2.3 Symbiotic synergies and interactions with the wider soil microbiome

Recent mycorrhizal research has expanded beyond plant nutrient acquisition to include consideration of their multifunctionality within, and indirect effects upon, wider ecosystem processes that affect nutrient dynamics. This includes their influence on surrounding microbial functional diversity, plant community assemblage and quality of soil organic matter (Itoo & Reshi, 2013; Wurzburger & Clemmensen, 2018). While other soil microorganisms have been found to regulate both the formation and function of mycorrhizal partnerships (Azcón-Aguilar & Barea, 1993), mycorrhizae themselves are known to synergistically select surrounding rhizosphere microbial communities, known as the 'mycorrhizosphere effect' (Duponnois et al., 2008), through an alteration of soil physical, chemical and biological conditions (Calvaruso et al., 2007). For example, the structure of bacterial communities within the mycorrhizosphere of the widespread EMF *Scleroderma citrinium* have been shown to include strains more efficient in P- and iron- (Fe-)mobilisation in temperate environments, including oak stands (Calvaruso et al., 2007, 2010; Uroz et al., 2007). Furthermore, although mycorrhizal colonisation is not necessarily a prerequisite to nodulation of plant roots by N-fixing bacteria (de Oliveira Júnior et al., 2017), the close interactions between these symbioses also may have far-reaching impacts for plant nutrition. AMF have been found to facilitate greater N-fixation in legumes, mainly through increasing supply of plant-available P in limited conditions required by rhizobia symbionts (e.g. Püschel et al., 2017). Conversely, symbiotic N-fixation has been shown to increase P acquisition by trees in tropical forest ecosystems through increasing N investment to AMF partners, explaining the paradoxical abundance of N-fixing plant species in ecosystems that are P- rather than N-limited (Nasto et al., 2014).

5.3 Microbial symbionts in invertebrate nutrition

Part of the holobiont concept for organisms is based on the assumption that host organisms require the additional genetic pool of enzymes and resources provided by their symbionts (Macdonald et al., 2012). This is certainly true for invertebrates which, being the most diverse group of multicellular organisms on the planet, have evolved to live on a similarly diverse suite of hosts, food plants and prey. The scope of this diversity of nutritional sources was certainly made possible through the co-evolution of a variety of microbial endosymbionts (Moran et al., 2005; Russell et al., 2013; Duplouy & Hornett, 2018).

Of all the food sources insects have evolved to contend with, the most common nutrient found lacking in insect diets is nitrogen (Joern & Behmer, 1998). As with plants, microbial symbionts of invertebrates most commonly fulfil this lack of nitrogen, using nitrogen in the form of proteins and non-essential amino acids from host plants as a substrate for the synthesis of essential amino acids (EAAs) or other high-value nitrogenous compounds, and then releasing these back to the host (Douglas, 1998). In a manner similar to plant endosymbionts, some insects (i.e. Hemiptera, in particular the aphids) have even evolved cell bodies for hosting microbial symbionts (Douglas, 1998). Other symbioses within the insects can support production of other nutrients, from methane-sequestering bacteria in cockroaches and termites (Zurek & Keddie, 1998; Shinzato et al., 2001) to complex community associations in higher social insects (Anderson et al., 2013; Kaltenpoth & Engl, 2014; Salem et al., 2015).

5.3.1 Aphids and nutrient-fixing symbionts

Aphids provide some of the best-known examples of insect–microbial symbioses. Almost all aphids are infected with an obligate nutritional symbiont: *Buchnera aphidicola* (Moran et al., 2008). *Buchnera* symbionts are fundamental for aphid development. They are responsible for biosynthesis of EAAs that cannot be sufficiently acquired from the natural aphid food source: phloem (Douglas, 1998). Aphid species may also harbour facultative symbionts that co-exist with *Buchnera*. Although quite common among invertebrates as a whole, the role of secondary symbionts in aphid biology remains poorly understood in the majority of cases, particularly with regard to their contribution towards aphid nutritional ecology (Najar-Rodríguez et al., 2009; Brady et al., 2014; Hansen & Moran, 2014).

The most well-studied facultative symbionts of aphids are *Hamiltonella defensa*, *Serratia symbiotica* and *Regiella insecticola*. In the pea aphid (*Acyrthosiphon pisum*) the secondary bacterial symbiont *H. defensa* infects the larvae of a parasitoid *Aphidius ervi*, leading to high mortality during early stage parasitoid larval development (Oliver et al., 2003, 2005). *Serratia symbiotica* protects hosts from parasitoids, fungi and heat stress (Montllor et al., 2002; Oliver et al., 2003), and *R. insecticola* protects against fungal pathogens (Scarborough et al., 2005). *Ricketsiella* can even alter host aphid body colour (Tsuchida et al., 2010).

The diversity of facultative bacterial symbionts found within aphids can differ wildly across species and populations (Brady et al., 2014). *Acyrthosiphon pisum*, *Microlophium carnosum* and *Sitobion avenae* all harbour diverse facultative symbionts; for example, *A. pisum* harbours up to eight facultative symbionts, either singly or in multiple infections (Ferrari et al., 2012; Russell et al., 2013). Some factors known to influence the aphid–symbiont association include host and symbiont genotypes, host plant, and geographical niche (Henry et al., 2013). Surveys of facultative symbionts clearly show that particular species are strongly associated with aphids feeding on certain food sources (McLean et al., 2011; Guidolin & Cônsoli, 2017).

5.3.2 Fungal gardens of leafcutter ants and termites

The evolution of nest-building and provisioning behaviour in Hymenoptera and Isoptera has led to the storage of large amounts of food within nests, which facilitates contact between nest mates and consequently within-colony transfer of microbes (Kaltenpoth & Engl, 2014; Salem et al., 2015). The ecto-microbial communities associated with their food sources are highly complex and can be formed of distinct members in different locations. Leafcutter ants (*Atta* and *Acromyrmex*; Hymenoptera: Formicidae: Attini) nurture a symbiotic monocultural fungus garden (Agaricales: primarily Lepiotaceae and Leucocoprineae) that converts vegetative material collected by the workers into a food source for the colony (Mueller, 2002). This fungal garden is threatened by specialised fungal pathogens; *Escovopsis* (Ascomycota: ana-morphic Hypocreales) that co-opt the environment established by ants and reduce host fitness (Currie et al., 1999; Haeder et al., 2009). A third player in the form of symbiotic microorganisms was also discovered on the integument of the ants (Currie et al., 1999). Those microorganisms (*Pseudonocardia* spp.) were suggested to be part of a 50 million-year-old tripartite co-evolutionary com-munity. Similar to the growing body of evidence within aphids that broad bacterial communities are more important than single key players, a complex community of bacteria has been detected within ant fungal gardens, which produces antifungal compounds that inhibit the growth of the parasitic fun-gus (Haeder et al., 2009). Recent studies provide strong evidence that these protective microbial communities are actually flexible, highly diverse, and variable between nests (Kost et al., 2007; Mueller et al., 2008).

Similarly, Termites (Isoptera: Blattodea) can associate with a wide diversity of symbiotic microorganisms such as fungi, flagellated protists and prokar-yotes, as well as bacteria and archaea (De Fine Licht et al., 2007). Termites are only capable of their eponymous digestion of wood through the cooperation of the host and gut microbiota. The microbial community in the hindgut of the termite can break down lignocellulose into acetate and methane, which can then be metabolised by its host (Leadbetter & Breznak, 1996). Different lineages of termites have evolved different microbial symbionts; primitive termites use Protista to digest wood, whereas more advanced lineages are colonised exclusively by prokaryotic bacteria (Brune, 2014).

5.3.3 Honeybees and pollen digestion

Within honeybee colonies, the bee gut (McFrederick et al., 2013), body surface (McFrederick et al., 2012), food stores (Donkersley et al., 2018) and hive infra-structure (Powell et al., 2014) all harbour distinct microbial communities. In their guts, honeybees (*Apis mellifera* L.) possess a core set of eight bacterial phylotypes: Gammaproteobacteria 1, Gammaproteobacteria 2, Betaproteobacteria, Alphaproteobacteria 1, Alphaproteobacteria 2, Firmicutes 1, Firmicutes 2 and Actinobacteria (Cox-Foster et al., 2007). These eight members of the core gut community are now known to be *Snodgrassella alvi*, *Gilliamella apicola*, *Frischella perrara*, Alphaproteobacteria and Lactobacillae. They constitute 95% of bacterial 16S rRNA gene sequences that have been cultured from within honeybee abdo-mens (Cox-Foster et al., 2007; Olofsson & Vásquez, 2009; Moran et al., 2012). Moreover, these core groups have been observed in honeybees from the USA, Australia, South Africa, Germany, Sweden, Switzerland and the United Kingdom (Jeyaprakash et al., 2003; Mohr & Tebbe, 2006; Martinson et al., 2011; Moran et al., 2012).

Gilliamella, *Erwinia* and *Frischella* (Order: Enterobacteriales) demonstrate com-plimentary metabolic pathways for the metabolism of carbohydrates (Henry et al., 2013), which suggests a direct contribution towards the nutritional intake of their honeybee hosts. When foraging on flowers, honeybees collect both nectar and pollen (Donkersley et al., 2014). However, an important point to make here is that while adult bees collect pollen, the pollen is stored in the hive where it is consumed by younger nurse bees, who feed it to larvae (Martinson et al., 2012). The honeybee genome does not possess the genes necessary to digest the complex polymer wall that surrounds pollen grains (Kunieda et al., 2006). The necessary enzymatic pathways to digest this compound (sporopollenin) can be found within certain members of the microbial community associated with both the honeybee gut (Olofsson & Vásquez, 2008; Hamdi et al., 2011; McFrederick et al., 2013) and the pollen stores themselves (i.e. *Lactobacillus* and *Acetobacter*; Vásquez & Olofsson, 2009; Donkersley et al., 2018). These may therefore play an important role in helping bees to access the nutritious core of pollen grains, which form the primary source of dietary protein to the hive (Donkersley et al., 2014, 2017). The gut microbiome of larvae is highly variable dependent on life stage (Vojvodic et al., 2013), clearly highlighting the importance of the bacteria found within stored pollen in contributing to the digestion of pollen. Furthermore, solitary bees, lacking in regular contact with nestmates, do not share a core microbiome seen in honeybees (Kwong et al., 2017). Consequently, variation in the microbiome of these bees is more closely associated with the microbes coming in on pollen grains (Graystock et al., 2017; McFrederick et al., 2017).

Further to the core community found in the guts of honeybees, microbial symbionts including some Firmicutes (*Lactobacillus*), Enterobacteriales (*Enterobacter*) and Bifidobacteriales (*Actinobacteria*) have also been found within the floral nectaries and surfaces of pollen grains of insect-pollinated plants (Ambika Manirajan et al., 2016; Lenaerts et al., 2016). As with many other microbial symbioses, there is debate over the hereditary transmission of these microorganisms and the novel external sources of microbes. It is likely that honeybees maintain the core microbial community in their gut through vertical transmission (McFrederick et al., 2012), but that the wider microbial community in the hive is in a state of constant flux due to the regular influx of 'wild' bacteria from incoming forage (Anderson et al., 2013; McFrederick et al., 2017).

Although microbial symbioses can be described in terms of the singular benefits of specific members (Douglas, 1998; Montllor et al., 2002), it is likely that a broader community composition with multiple symbioses may be key to host fitness (Chandler et al., 2011). For example, dysbiosis (the disruption of microbial community structure) can lead to increased disease susceptibility (Hamdi et al., 2011; Anderson & Ricigliano, 2017). Although a specific link between dysbiosis and colony collapse disorder (CCD) in honeybees has not been identified (Johnson et al., 2009), there are examples of a direct link between gut dysbiosis and honeybee health. There is evidence that both *S. alvi* and *G. apicola* protect bees from opportunistic infections, possibly by forming a biofilm on host gut lining and establishing a physical barrier to opportunity infection (Anderson et al., 2013). *Frischella perrera* is an opportunistic pathogen that (under high abundances) causes symptoms parallel to emerging models of dysbiosis (Maes et al., 2016). Evidence from recent studies of honeybee gut dysbiosis suggests *S. alvi* and *G. apicola* bacteria from stored pollen may protect from *F. perrera* dysbiosis by early establishment of a stable gut microflora (Anderson et al., 2013; Maes et al., 2016). Likewise, bumblebee workers that have reduced abundances of the typical *S. alvi* and *G. apicola* have a greater chance of hosting enteric pathogens (Cariveau et al., 2014), and removal of the bumblebee gut microbiome can lead to increased susceptibility to another pathogen; *Crithidia bombi* (Koch & Schmid-Hempel, 2011).

5.3.4 Endosymbionts of arachnids

Arachnids are a highly diverse group of animals that include spiders, ticks, mites and scorpions. They are variable in their morphology, feeding preferences, and behaviour, and represent another exciting opportunity to study endosymbionts (Goodacre & Martin, 2013). Symbiotic bacteria occupy a wide array of arachnid orders and, similar to those previously discussed within insects, are able to manipulate the host in a variety of ways bearing evolutionary significance (Goodacre & Martin, 2012; Bolaños et al., 2016). These can include factors that influence their dispersal, abundance, behaviour and reproduction, as well as allowing them to perform daily biological processes such as breaking down food (Goodacre & Martin, 2012; Attia et al., 2013). A recent study on ticks by Andreotti et al. (2011) identified 121 genera of bacteria found in different tissues and stages of *Rhipicephalus microplus*, an important vector of veterinary pathogens. This is important because it is likely that there are many more hidden symbioses to be found. However, to date, nutritional symbionts have received little attention in arachnid–symbiont research even though the effects of these relationships are likely extensive. Furthermore, in almost all studies, the focus has been on characteristic endosymbionts for a given species of arachnid and not much attention has been given to their full microbiome. Endosymbionts of arachnids are often localised to specific specialised tissues, including the gut, ovaries and Malphigian tubes (Burgdorfer et al., 1973; Noda et al., 1997), and evidence suggests that most of the commonly studied endosymbionts are vertically transmitted. Many arachnids (with the exception of spiders) have poor dispersal capabilities, hence the need for an intimate relationship between extant intracellular bacteria and host as exposure to novel symbionts is greatly reduced, leading to the evolution of endosymbioses (Taylor et al., 2012).

Mites are capable of vectoring human and animal diseases and can, in high numbers, also cause severe losses to crops and livestock in agriculture due to disease transmission and host parasitism (Flamini, 2006). Mites are very small arachnids that can be found in a variety of habitats including water and soil, and are parasites of plants or animals (Flamini, 2006; George et al., 2015). While plant and animal material does form a large part of the diet of many mites, fungi can also be exploited as an additional food resource (Momen & Abdelkhader, 2010). Mites have been commonly recorded feeding on fungal matter, with the bulb mite *Rhyzoglyphus robini* feeding almost exclusively on plants with fungal infections (Okabe & Amano, 1991). Not only did mites show a preference for the infected plants in a laboratory culture, they also gained higher fecundity from the association (Hanuny et al., 2008; Zindel et al., 2013). The chitinous walls of fungi are an excellent source of nitrogen for those with the ability to break it down, as most animals are unable to produce the necessary enzymes for digestion. Many mites have been found to break down fungal wall tissue within the gut, with digested remnants of fungal tissue found within their faecal matter (Zindel et al., 2013). It appears that bacterial symbiosis is integral for this digestion. Chitinase-producing bacteria are found commonly across mite taxa, supporting a cooperative association between the mites and bacteria and allowing for the digestion of advantageous tissues (Zindel et al., 2013).

Unlike other arachnids, ticks feed exclusively on the blood of vertebrates, during which they can transmit a wide variety of pathogens to vertebrate hosts. Yet, from this blood meal, it is not clear how they are able to overcome a diet that is lacking in essential vitamins, nucleosides and enzyme co-factors (Zhong et al., 2007; Smith et al., 2015). In the past it has been hypothesised that the occurrence of intracellular bacteria in ticks may play a role in nutrient acquisition (De Meillon & Golberg, 1947). However, despite several bacteria being suspected endosymbionts, it is still not clear whether they provision the host with nutrients (Rounds et al., 2012; Smith et al., 2015). A recent and promising example has been reported in the lone star tick, *Amblyomma americanum*, where an intracellular CLEAA (*Coxiella*-like bacterium) has been detected ubiquitously across the majority of studies (Taylor et al., 2012; Smith et al., 2015). CLEAA is of interest because eliminating it from ticks using the antibiotics rifampin or tetracycline causes a severe reduction in tick fecundity and fitness (Zhong et al., 2007). The authors reconstructed the vitamin and co-factor biosynthesis pathways and found that CLEAA has complete (or almost complete) pathways for B-vitamin complex synthesis. As such, it has been proposed that CLEAA may be a primary endosymbiont (Zhong et al., 2007; Rounds et al., 2012), and one that also plays a crucial role in the provision of essential nutrients unattainable from a nutrient-poor mammalian blood diet.

Although preliminary studies have recorded the nutritional effects of endo-symbionts associated with the Acari (mites and ticks), there is still much to learn concerning the interactions that govern arachnid nutrition generally, as well as how bacterial symbiosis affects the distribution and abundance of this diverse and important group. More research is required to isolate the bacterial species responsible for Acari nutrient provisioning, as well as understanding its origin and how this has shaped the development of both the host and the symbiont.

5.4 Vertebrates and microbially derived nutrition

Microbial community symbioses are a key factor in the digestive system of vertebrates (Hooper & Gordon, 2001). The gastrointestinal tract of young mammals is thought to be sterile or near-sterile *in utero*, with bacteria readily acquired from the mother during the birth process (Mändar & Mikelsaar, 1996; Palmer et al., 2007; Voreades et al., 2014). Initially the digestive tract is colonised by facultative anaerobes (Hooper & Gordon, 2001). Following weaning, there is a shift towards a more complex community structure in which facultative anaerobes are replaced by obligate anaerobes including species of Bacteroides and Bifidobacteria, for example (Louis & Flint, 2009; Walter & Ley, 2011), a process that is influenced by diet, host-specific and environmental factors (Mackie et al., 1999; Walter & Ley, 2011). Although the digestive systems of different mammals differ somewhat in their physiology, the similarity of their early microbiota could be a function of similar physiochemical anaerobic conditions encountered within the gut. The gastrointestinal systems of adult mammals also exhibit complex communities of obligate anaerobes, which have the potential to impact upon health, for example by reducing susceptibility to enteropathogens (Collins & Gibson, 1999; Conlon & Bird, 2015).

As has been discussed previously with numerous other taxa, the gut microflora of vertebrates is crucial for the harvesting and absorption of nutrients from food sources (Turnbaugh et al., 2006; Cani & Delzenne, 2009). Bacteria in the mammalian gastrointestinal tract have the ability to influence nutrient absorption in a number of ways, by modifying the physiology of the intestines (Torok et al., 2008; Round & Mazmanian, 2009) or breaking down indigestible compounds. For example, the gut bacteria present in Japanese people have acquired an enzyme from marine bacteria that allows them to digest the polysaccharides found in seaweed, which is prevalent in their diet (Hehemann et al., 2012). Most work with vertebrate hosts centres around humans, but there is a large body of work looking at the gut microbial community of agriculturally important species, including ruminant livestock (particularly cows and sheep) and poultry (particularly chickens). Ruminants are heavily reliant on the complex microbial communities of their guts to break down tough plant material, converting even relatively poor-quality feed into high-quality protein, ultimately for human consumption (reviewed in

Huws et al., 2018). These communities form complex biofilms comprised of bacteria, archaea, bacteriophages, protozoa and fungi, which contain high concentrations of enzymes such as glycosyl hydrolases to break down plant material (reviewed in Huws et al., 2018). Furthermore, the ruminant microbiome shows huge diurnal variability and niche specialisation, responding to changes in nutrient availability and metabolite production according to food intake by the host (Pereira & Berry, 2017; Huws et al., 2018; Shaani et al., 2018). Given this critical role of microbes in converting feed into protein, there is growing interest in identifying pathways to manipulate these communities to maximise the efficiency of this process and increase productivity (reviewed in Huws et al., 2018). Furthermore, a significant by-product of this process is methane, a powerful greenhouse gas, and thus potential exists to alter microbiomes that reduce methane emissions to minimise the environmental impact of livestock production (Belanche et al., 2012, 2014; Huws et al., 2018).

The accessibility and economic value of poultry has also resulted in extensive research into the dynamics and influences of gut bacterial communities in this system (Mead, 2000). Chickens represent captive birds whose lifestyle and environment are highly controlled. The composition and diversity of the poultry gut microbiome was initially characterised by a core set of studies conducted between 1950 and 1970 (Lev & Briggs, 1956; Smith, 1965; Harry et al., 1972) and has since been supplemented by studies using molecular-based methods (e.g. Gong et al., 2002; Zhu et al., 2002). The bacteria present in the microbiome are known to play a significant role in the growth and health of birds within this poultry system (Yegani & Korver, 2008; Jankowski et al., 2009; Kers et al., 2018) affecting both the uptake and use of energy and nutrients by the avian host (Smits & Annison, 1996; Torok et al., 2008).

5.5 Conclusions

All multicellular organisms, whether heterotroph or autotroph, saprophyte or detritivore, or herbivore or carnivore, harbour a distinct microbiome that is adapted to aid the flow of nutrients to its host. Often these symbioses have a long evolutionary history. This microbially mediated release of nutrients has implications for host health at the organismal scale, as well as environmental turnover and regulation of nutrient cycles on the global scale.

References

Albornoz FE, Lambers H, Turner BL, et al. (2016) Shifts in symbiotic associations in plants capable of forming multiple root symbioses across a long-term soil chronosequence. *Ecology and Evolution*, 6, 2368–2377.

Ambika Manirajan B, Ratering S, Rusch V, et al. (2016) Bacterial microbiota associated with flower pollen is influenced by pollination type, and shows a high degree of diversity and species-specificity. *Environmental Microbiology*, 18, 5161–5174.

Anderson AJ. (1992) The influence of the plant root on mycorrhizal formation. In: Allen MF. (Ed.) *Mycorrhizal Functioning: An Integrative Plant–Fungal Process.* New York, NY: Chapman & Hall.

Anderson KE, Sheehan TH, Mott BM, et al. (2013) Microbial ecology of the hive and pollination landscape: Bacterial associates from floral nectar, the alimentary tract and stored food of honey bees (*Apis mellifera*). *PLoS ONE*, 8, e83125.

Anderson KE, Ricigliano VA. (2017) Honey bee gut dysbiosis: A novel context of disease ecology. *Current Opinion in Insect Science*, 22, 125–132.

Andreotti R, Pérez de León AA, Dowd SE, et al. (2011) Assessment of bacterial diversity in the cattle tick *Rhipicephalus (Boophilus) microplus* through tag-encoded pyrosequencing. *BMC Microbiology*, 11, 6.

Attia S, Grissa KL, Lognay G, et al. (2013) A review of the major biological approaches to control the worldwide pest *Tetranychus urticae* (Acari: Tetranychidae) with special reference to natural pesticides: Biological approaches to control *Tetranychus urticae*. *Journal of Pest Science*, 86, 361–386.

Averill C, Turner BL, Finzi AC. (2014) Mycorrhiza-mediated competition between plants and decomposers drives soil carbon storage. *Nature*, 505, 543.

Azcón-Aguilar C, Barea JM. (1993) Interactions between mycorrhizal fungi and other rhizosphere micro-organisms. In: Allen MF. (Ed.) *Mycorrhizal Functioning: An Integrative Plant–Fungal Process.* New York, NY: Chapman & Hall, pp. 163–198.

Babikova Z, Gilbert L, Bruce TJA, et al. (2013) Underground signals carried through common mycelial networks warn neighbouring plants of aphid attack. *Ecology Letters*, 16, 835–843

Barto EK, Weidenhamer JD, Cipollini D, et al. (2012) Fungal superhighways: Do common mycorrhizal networks enhance below ground communication? *Trends in Plant Science*, 17, 633–637.

Belanche A, Doreau M, Edwards JE, et al. (2012) Shifts in the rumen microbiota due to the type of carbohydrate and level of protein ingested by dairy cattle are associated with changes in rumen fermentation. *Journal of Nutrition*, 142, 1684–1692.

Belanche A, De La Fuente G, Newbold CJ. (2014) Study of methanogen communities associated with different rumen protozoal populations. *FEMS Microbiology Ecology*, 90, 663–677.

Bever JD, Dickie IA, Facelli E, et al. (2010) Rooting theories of plant community ecology in microbial interactions. *Trends in Ecology & Evolution*, 25, 468–478.

Bolaños LM, Rosenblueth M, Castillo-Ramírez S, et al. (2016) Species-specific diversity of novel bacterial lineages and differential abundance of predicted pathways for toxic compound degradation in scorpion gut microbiota. *Environmental Microbiology*, 18, 1364–1378.

Brady CM, Asplen MK, Desneux N, et al. (2014) Worldwide populations of the aphid *Aphis craccivora* are infected with diverse facultative bacterial symbionts. *Microbial Ecology*, 67, 195–204.

Brearley FQ. (2012) Ectomycorrhizal associations of the Dipterocarpaceae. *Biotropica*, 44, 637–648.

Brundrett MC. (2002) Coevolution of roots and mycorrhizas of land plants. *New Phytologist*, 154, 275–304.

Brundrett M. (2009) Mycorrhizal associations and other means of nutrition of vascular plants: Understanding the global diversity of host plants by resolving conflicting information and developing reliable means of diagnosis. *Plant and Soil*, 320, 37–77.

Brune A. (2014) Symbiotic digestion of lignocellulose in termite guts. *Nature Reviews Microbiology*, 12, 168–180.

Burgdorfer W, Brinton LP, Hughes LE. (1973) Isolation and characterization of symbiotes from the Rocky Mountain wood tick, *Dermacentor andersoni. Journal of Invertebrate Pathology*, 22, 424–434.

Calvaruso C, Turpault MP, Leclerc E, et al. (2007) Impact of ectomycorrhizosphere on the functional diversity of soil bacterial and fungal communities from a forest stand in relation to nutrient mobilization processes. *Microbial Ecology*, 54, 567–577.

Calvaruso C, Turpault MP, Leclerc E, et al. (2010) Influence of forest trees on the distribution of mineral weathering-associated bacterial communities of the *Scleroderma citrinum* mycorrhizosphere. *Applied and Environmental Microbiology*, 76, 4780.

Cani P, Delzenne N. (2009) The role of the gut microbiota in energy metabolism and metabolic disease. *Current Pharmaceutical Design*, 15, 1546–1558.

Cariveau DP, Powell JE, Koch H, et al. (2014) Variation in gut microbial communities and its association with pathogen infection in wild bumblebees (*Bombus*). *The ISME Journal*, 8, 2369–2379.

Chandler JA, Lang J, Bhatnagar S, et al. (2011) Bacterial communities of diverse *Drosophila* species: Ecological context of a host–microbe model system. *PLoS Genetics*, 7, e1002272.

Chen W, Koide RT, Adams TS, et al. (2016) Root morphology and mycorrhizal symbioses together shape nutrient foraging strategies of temperate trees. *Proceedings of the National Academy of Sciences*, 113, 8741.

Collins MD, Gibson GR. (1999) Probiotics, prebiotics, and synbiotics: Approaches for modulating the microbial ecology of the gut. *American Journal of Clinical Nutrition*, 69, 1052s–1057s.

Conlon MA, Bird AR. (2015) The impact of diet and lifestyle on gut microbiota and human health. *Nutrients*, 7, 17–44.

Cortois R, Schröder-Georgi T, Weigelt A, et al. (2016) Plant–soil feedbacks: Role of plant functional group and plant traits. *Journal of Ecology*, 104, 1608–1617.

Cox-Foster DL, Conlan S, Holmes EC, et al. (2007) A metagenomic survey of microbes in honey bee colony collapse disorder. *Science*, 318, 283–287.

Currie CR, Scott JA, Summerbell RC, Malloch D. (1999) Fungus-growing ants use antibiotic-producing bacteria to control garden parasites. *Nature*, 398, 701–704.

Davidson EA, Howarth RW. (2007) Nutrients in synergy: A literature meta-analysis of the effects of nitrogen and phosphorus on plant growth prompts a thought-provoking inference – That the supply of, and demand for, these nutrients are usually in close balance. *Nature*, 449, 1000.

De Fine Licht HH, Boomsma JJ, Aanen DK. (2007) Asymmetric interaction specificity between two sympatric termites and their fungal symbionts. *Ecological Entomology*, 32, 76–81.

De Meillon B, Golberg L. (1947) Preliminary studies on the nutritional requirements of the bedbug (*Cimex lectularius*) and the tick (*Ornithodoros moubata*). Journal of Experimental Biology, 24, 41–63.

de Oliveira Júnior JQ, Jesus EC, Lisboa FJ, et al. (2017) Nitrogen-fixing bacteria and arbuscular mycorrhizal fungi in *Piptadenia gonoacantha* (Mart.). *Brazilian Journal of Microbiology*, 48, 95–100.

Dickie I, Koele N, Blum JD, et al. (2014) Mycorrhizas in changing ecosystems. *Botany*, 92, 149–160.

Donkersley P, Rhodes G, Pickup RW, et al. (2014) Honeybee nutrition is linked to landscape composition. *Ecology and Evolution*, 4, 4195–4206.

Donkersley P, Rhodes G, Pickup RW, et al. (2017) Nutritional composition of honey bee food stores vary with floral composition. *Oecologia*, 185, 1–13.

Donkersley P, Rhodes G, Pickup RW, et al. (2018) Bacterial communities associated with honey bee food stores are correlated with land use. *Ecology and Evolution*, 8, 4743–4756.

Douglas AE. (1998) Nutritional interactions in insect-microbial symbioses: Aphids and their symbiotic bacteria *Buchnera*. *Annual Review of Entomology*, 43, 17–37.

Duplouy A, Hornett EA. (2018) Uncovering the hidden players in Lepidoptera biology: The heritable microbial endosymbionts. *PeerJ*, 6, e4629.

Duponnois R, Galiana A, Prin YCN. (2008) The mycorrhizosphere effect: A multitrophic interaction complex improves mycorrhizal symbiosis and plant growth. In: Siddiqui ZA, Akhtar MS, et al. (Eds.) *Mycorrhizae: Sustainable Agriculture and Forestry*. New York, NY: Springer.

Ekblad A, Wallander H, Godbold D, et al. (2013) The production and turnover of extramatrical mycelium of ectomycorrhizal fungi in forest soils: Role in carbon cycling. *Plant and Soil*, 366, 1–27.

Ferrari J, West JA, Via S, et al. (2012) Population genetic structure and secondary symbionts in host-associated populations of the pea aphid complex. *Evolution*, 66, 375–390.

Flamini G. (2006) Acaricides of natural origin, part 2, review of the literature (2002–2006). *NPC Natural Product Communications*, 1, 1151–1158.

George DR, Finn RD, Graham KM, et al. (2015) Should the poultry red mite *Dermanyssus gallinae* be of wider concern for veterinary and medical science? *Parasites and Vectors*, 8, 178.

Gerber S, Hedin LO, Oppenheimer M, et al. (2010) Nitrogen cycling and feedbacks in a global dynamic land model. *Global Biogeochemical Cycles*, 24, GB1001.

Gong J, Forster RJ, Yu H, et al. (2002) Molecular analysis of bacterial populations in the ileum of broiler chickens and comparison with bacteria in the cecum. *FEMS Microbiology Ecology*, 41, 171–179.

Goodacre SL, Martin OY. (2012) Modification of insect and arachnid behaviours by vertically transmitted endosymbionts: Infections as drivers of behavioural change and evolutionary novelty. *Insects*, 3, 246–261.

Goodacre SL, Martin OY. (2013) Endosymbiont infections in spiders. In: Nentwig W. (Ed.) *Spider Ecophysiology*. Berlin: Springer.

Gorzelak MA, Asay AK, Pickles BJ, Simard SW. (2015) Inter-plant communication through mycorrhizal networks mediates complex adaptive behaviour in plant communities. *AoB Plants*, 7, plv050.

Graystock P, Rehan SM, McFrederick QS. (2017) Hunting for healthy microbiomes: Determining the core microbiomes of *Ceratina*, *Megalopta*, and *Apis* bees and how they associate with microbes in bee collected pollen. *Conservation Genetics*, 18, 701–711.

Guidolin AS, Cônsoli FL. (2017) Symbiont diversity of *Aphis* (*Toxoptera*) *citricidus* (Hemiptera: Aphididae) as influenced by host plants. *Microbial Ecology*, 73, 201–210.

Haeder S, Wirth R, Herz H, et al. (2009) Candicidin-producing *Streptomyces* support leaf-cutting ants to protect their fungus garden against the pathogenic fungus *Escovopsis*. *Proceedings of the National Academy of Sciences*, 106, 4742–4746.

Hamdi C, Balloi A, Essanaa J, et al. (2011) Gut microbiome dysbiosis and honeybee health. *Journal of Applied Entomology*, 135, 524–533.

Hansen AK, Moran NA. (2014) The impact of microbial symbionts on host plant utilization by herbivorous insects. *Molecular Ecology*, 23, 1473–1496.

Hanuny T, Inbar M, Tsror L, et al. (2008) Complex interactions between *Rhizoglyphus robini* and *Fusarium oxysporum*: Implications on onion pest management. *Integrated Control in Protected Crops, Temperature Climate IOBC/wprs Bulletin*, 32, 71–74.

Harry EG, Mead GC, Barnum DA. (1972) The intestinal flora of the chicken in the period 2 to 6 weeks of age, with particular reference to the anaerobic bacteria. *British Poultry Science*, 13, 311–326.

Hehemann JH, Kelly AG, Pudlo NA, et al. (2012) Bacteria of the human gut microbiome catabolize red seaweed glycans with carbohydrate-active enzyme updates from extrinsic microbes. *Proceedings of the National Academy of Sciences*, 109, 19786–19791.

Henry LM, Peccoud J, Simon JC, et al. (2013) Horizontally transmitted symbionts and host colonization of ecological niches. *Current Biology*, 23, 1713–1717.

Hooper LV, Gordon JI. (2001) Commensal host–bacterial relationships in the gut. *Science*, 292, 1115–1118.

Humphreys CP, Franks PJ, Rees M, et al. (2010) Mutualistic mycorrhiza-like symbiosis in the most ancient group of land plants. *Nature Communications*, 1, 103.

Huws SA, Creevey CJ, Oyama LB, et al. (2018) Addressing global ruminant agricultural challenges through understanding the rumen microbiome: Past, present, and future. *Frontiers in Microbiology*, 9, 2161.

Itoo Z, Reshi Z. (2013) The multifunctional role of ectomycorrhizal associations in forest ecosystem processes. *Botanical Reviews*, 79, 371–400.

Jankowski J, Juskiewicz J, Gulewicz K, et al. (2009) The effect of diets containing soybean meal, soybean protein concentrate, and soybean protein isolate of different oligosaccharide content on growth performance and gut function of young turkeys. *Poultry Science*, 88, 2132–2140.

Jeyaprakash A, Hoy MA, Allsopp MH. (2003) Bacterial diversity in worker adults of *Apis mellifera capensis* and *Apis mellifera scutellata* (Insecta: Hymenoptera) assessed using 16S rRNA sequences. *Journal of Invertebrate Pathology*, 84, 96–103.

Joern A, Behmer ST. (1998) Impact of diet quality on demographic attributes in adult grasshoppers and the nitrogen limitation hypothesis. *Ecological Entomology*, 23, 174–184.

Johnson RM, Evans JD, Robinson GE, et al. (2009) Changes in transcript abundance relating to colony collapse disorder in honey bees (*Apis mellifera*). *Proceedings of the National Academy of Sciences*, 106, 14790–14795.

Kaltenpoth M, Engl T. (2014) Defensive microbial symbionts in Hymenoptera. *Functional Ecology*, 28, 315–327.

Kers JG, Velkers FC, Fischer EAJ, et al. (2018) Host and environmental factors affecting the intestinal microbiota in chickens. *Frontiers in Microbiology*, 9, 235.

Koch H, Schmid-Hempel P. (2011) Socially transmitted gut microbiota protect bumblebees against an intestinal parasite. *Proceedings of the National Academy of Sciences*, 108, 19288–19292.

Koske RE, Gemma, JN. (1993) Fungal reactions to plants prior to mycorrhizal formation. In: Allen MF. (Ed.) *Mycorrhizal Functioning: An Integrative Plant–Fungal Process*, New York, NY: Chapman & Hall.

Kost C, Lakatos T, Böttcher I, et al. (2007) Non-specific association between filamentous bacteria and fungus-growing ants. *Naturwissenschaften*, 94, 821–828.

Kunieda T, Fujiyuki T, Kucharski R, et al. (2006) Carbohydrate metabolism genes and pathways in insects: Insights from the honey bee genome. *Insect Molecular Biology*, 15, 563–576.

Kwong WK, Medina LA, Koch H, et al. (2017) Dynamic microbiome evolution in social bees. *Science Advances*, 3, e1600513.

Lambers H, Raven JA, Shaver GR, Smith SE. (2008) Plant nutrient-acquisition strategies change with soil age. *Trends in Ecology & Evolution*, 23, 95–103.

Lang C, Seven J, Polle A. (2011) Host preferences and differential contributions of deciduous tree species shape mycorrhizal species richness in a mixed Central European forest. *Mycorrhiza*, 21, 297–308.

Leadbetter JR, Breznak JA. (1996) Physiological ecology of *Methanobrevibacter cuticularis* sp. nov. and *Methanobrevibacter curvatus* sp. nov., isolated from the hindgut of the termite *Reticulitermes flavipes*. *Applied and Environmental Microbiology*, 62, 3620–3631.

Lenaerts M, Pozo MI, Wäckers F, et al. (2016) Impact of microbial communities on floral nectar chemistry: Potential implications for biological control of pest insects. *Basic and Applied Ecology*, 17, 189–198.

Lev M, Briggs CAE. (1956) The gut flora of chicks. II. The establishment of the flora. *Journal of Applied Bacteriology*, 19, 224–230.

Louis P, Flint HJ. (2009) Diversity, metabolism and microbial ecology of butyrate-producing bacteria from the human large intestine. *FEMS Microbiology Letters*, 294, 1–8.

Macdonald SJ, Lin GG, Russell CW, et al. (2012) The central role of the host cell in symbiotic nitrogen metabolism. *Proceedings of the Royal Society B: Biological Sciences*, 279, 2965–2973.

Macé OG, Steinauer K, Jousset A, et al. (2016) Flood-induced changes in soil microbial functions as modified by plant diversity. *PLoS ONE*, 11, e0166349.

Mackie RI, Sghir A, Gaskins HR. (1999) Developmental microbial ecology of the neonatal gastrointestinal tract. *American Journal of Clinical Nutrition*, 69, 1035s–1045s.

Maes PW, Rodrigues PAP, Oliver R, et al. (2016) Diet-related gut bacterial dysbiosis correlates with impaired development, increased mortality and Nosema disease in the honeybee (*Apis mellifera*). *Molecular Ecology*, 25, 5439–5450.

Mändar R, Mikelsaar M. (1996) Transmission of mother's microflora to the newborn at birth. *Neonatology*, 69, 30–5.

Martinson VG, Danforth BN, Minckley RL, et al. (2011) A simple and distinctive microbiota associated with honey bees and bumblebees. *Molecular Ecology*, 20, 619–628.

Martinson VG, Moy J, Moran NA. (2012) Establishment of characteristic gut bacteria during development of the honeybee worker. *Applied and Environmental Microbiology*, 78, 2830–2840.

Maxwell Stevens B, Propster J, Wilson GWT, et al. (2018) Mycorrhizal symbioses influence the trophic structure of the Serengeti. *Journal of Ecology*, 106, 536–546.

McFall-Ngai M, Hadfield MG, Bosch TCG, et al. (2013) Animals in a bacterial world, a new imperative for the life sciences. *Proceedings of the National Academy of Sciences*, 110, 3229–3236.

McFrederick QS, Wcislo WT, Taylor DR, et al. (2012) Environment or kin: Whence do bees obtain acidophilic bacteria? *Molecular Ecology*, 21, 1754–1768.

McFrederick QS, Cannone JJ, Gutell RR, et al. (2013) Specificity between *Lactobacilli* and Hymenopteran hosts is the exception rather than the rule. *Applied and Environmental Microbiology*, 79, 1803–1812.

McFrederick QS, Thomas JM, Neff JL, et al. (2017) Flowers and wild megachilid bees share microbes. *Microbial Ecology*, 73, 188–200.

McLean AHC, van Asch M, Ferrari J, et al. (2011) Effects of bacterial secondary symbionts on host plant use in pea aphids. *Proceedings of the Royal Society B: Biological Sciences*, 278, 760–766.

Mead GC. (2000) Prospects for 'competitive exclusion' treatment to control salmonellas and other foodborne pathogens in poultry. *The Veterinary Journal*, 159, 111–123.

Meier IC, Brunner I, Godbold DL, et al. (2019) Roots and rhizospheres in forest ecosystems: Recent advances and future challenges. *Forest Ecology and Management*, 431, 1–5.

Mohr KI, Tebbe CC. (2006) Diversity and phylotype consistency of bacteria in the guts of three bee species (Apoidea) at an oilseed rape field. *Environmental Microbiology*, 8, 258–272.

Momen F, Abdelkhader M. (2010) Fungi as food source for the generalist predator *Neoseiulus barkeri* (Hughes) (Acari: Phytoseiidae). *Acta Phytopathologica et Entomologica Hungarica*, 45, 401–409.

Montllor CB, Maxmen A, Purcell AH. (2002) Facultative bacterial endosymbionts benefit pea aphids *Acyrthosiphon pisum* under heat stress. *Ecological Entomology*, 27, 189–195.

Moran NA, Degnan PH, Santos SR, et al. (2005) The players in a mutualistic symbiosis:

Insects, bacteria, viruses, and virulence genes. *Proceedings of the National Academy of Sciences*, 102, 16919–16926.

Moran NA, McCutcheon JP, Nakabachi A. (2008) Genomics and evolution of heritable bacterial symbionts. *Annual Review of Genetics*, 42, 165–190.

Moran NA, Hansen AK, Powell JE, et al. (2012) Distinctive gut microbiota of honey bees assessed using deep sampling from individual worker bees. *PLoS ONE*, 7, e36393.

Muegge BD, Kuczynski J, Knights D, et al. (2011) Diet drives convergence in gut microbiome functions across mammalian phylogeny and within humans. *Science*, 332, 970–974.

Mueller UG. (2002) Ant versus fungus versus mutualism: Ant-cultivar conflict and the deconstruction of the Attine ant–fungus symbiosis. *The American Naturalist*, 160, S67–98.

Mueller UG, Dash D, Rabeling C, et al. (2008) Coevolution between Attine ants and actinomycete bacteria: A re-evaluation. *Evolution*, 62, 2894–2912.

Najar-Rodríguez AJ, McGraw EA, Mensah RK, et al. (2009) The microbial flora of *Aphis gossypii*: Patterns across host plants and geographical space. *Journal of Invertebrate Pathology*, 100, 123–126.

Nannipieri P, Ascher J, Ceccherini MT, et al. (2003) Microbial diversity and soil functions. *European Journal of Soil Science*, 54, 655.

Nasto MK, Alvarez-Clare S, Lekberg Y, et al. (2014) Interactions among nitrogen fixation and soil phosphorus acquisition strategies in lowland tropical rain forests. *Ecology Letters*, 17, 1282.

Noda H, Munderloh UG, Kurtti TJ. (1997) Endosymbionts of ticks and their relationship to *Wolbachia* spp. and tick-borne pathogens of humans and animals. *Applied and Environmental Microbiology*, 63, 3926–3932.

Okabe K, Amano H. (1991) Penetration and population growth of the robine bulb mite, *Rhizoglyphus robini* Claparède (Acari: Acaridae), on healthy and *Fusarium*-infected rakkyo bulbs. *Applied Entomology and Zoology*, 26, 129–136.

Oliver KM, Russell JA, Moran NA, et al. (2003) Facultative bacterial symbionts in aphids confer resistance to parasitic wasps. *Proceedings of the National Academy of Sciences*, 100, 1803–1807.

Oliver KM, Moran NA, Hunter MS. (2005) Variation in resistance to parasitism in aphids is due to symbionts not host genotype. *Proceedings of the National Academy of Sciences*, 102, 12795–12800.

Olofsson TC, Vásquez A. (2008) Detection and identification of a novel lactic acid bacterial flora within the honey stomach of the honeybee *Apis mellifera*. *Current Microbiology*, 57, 356–363.

Olofsson TC, Vásquez A. (2009) Phylogenetic comparison of bacteria isolated from the honey stomachs of honey bees *Apis mellifera* and bumblebees *Bombus* spp. *Journal of Apicultural Research*, 48, 233–237.

Palmer C, Bik EM, DiGiulio DB, et al. (2007) Development of the human infant intestinal microbiota. *PLoS Biology*, 5, e177.

Peterson RL, Massicotte HB, Melville LH. (2004) Mycorrhizas: Anatomy and cell biology, *Mycologist*, 19, 133.

Pereira FC, Berry D. (2017). Microbial nutrient niches in the gut. *Environmental Microbiology*, 19, 1366–1378.

Powell JE, Martinson VG, Urban-Mead K, et al. (2014) Routes of acquisition of the gut microbiota of the honey bee *Apis mellifera*. *Applied and Environmental Microbiology*, 80, 7378–7387.

Püschel D, Janoušková M, Voříšková A, et al. (2017) Arbuscular mycorrhiza stimulates biological nitrogen fixation in two *Medicago* spp. through improved phosphorus acquisition. *Frontiers in Plant Science*, 8, 390.

Redecker D, Kodner R, Graham LE. (2000) Glomalean fungi from the Ordovician. *Science*, 289, 1920–1921.

RGB Kew (2016) *The State of the World's Plants Report – 2016*. Kew: Royal Botanic Gardens.

Round JL, Mazmanian SK. (2009) The gut microbiota shapes intestinal immune responses during health and disease. *Nature Reviews Immunology*, 9, 313–323.

Rounds MA, Crowder CD, Matthews HE, et al. (2012) Identification of endosymbionts in ticks by broad-range polymerase chain reaction and electrospray ionization mass spectrometry. *Journal of Medical Entomology*, 49, 843–850.

Russell JA, Weldon S, Smith AH, et al. (2013) Uncovering symbiont-driven genetic diversity across North American pea aphids. *Molecular Ecology*, 22, 2045–2059.

Salem H, Florez L, Gerardo N, et al. (2015) An out-of-body experience: The extracellular dimension for the transmission of mutualistic bacteria in insects. *Proceedings of the Royal Society B: Biological Sciences*, 282, 20142957.

Scarborough CL, Ferrari J, Godfray HCJ. (2005) Ecology: Aphid protected from pathogen by endosymbiont. *Science*, 310, 1781.

Schimel JP, Bennett J. (2004) Nitrogen mineralization: Challenges of a changing paradigm. *Ecology*, 85, 591–602.

Sędzielewska-Toro K, Delaux P. (2016) Mycorrhizal symbioses: Today and tomorrow. *New Phytologist*, 209, 917–920.

Shaani Y, Zehavi T, Eyal S, et al. (2018). Microbiome niche modification drives diurnal rumen community assembly, overpowering individual variability and diet effects. *The ISME Journal*, 12, 2446–2457.

Shinzato N, Matsumoto T, Yamaoka I, et al. (2001) Methanogenic symbionts and the locality of their host lower termites. *Microbes and Environments*, 16, 43–47.

Smith HW. (1965) Observations on the flora of the alimentary tract of animals and factors affecting its composition. *The Journal of Pathology and Bacteriology*, 89, 95–122.

Smith SE, Read DJ. (2008) *Mycorrhizal Symbiosis*, 3rd edition. New York, NY: Academic Press.

Smith TA, Driscoll T, Gillespie JJ, et al. (2015) A *Coxiella*-like endosymbiont is a potential vitamin source for the lone star tick. *Genome Biology and Evolution*, 7, 831–838.

Smits CHM, Annison G. (1996) Non-starch plant polysaccharides in broiler nutrition – Towards a physiologically valid approach to their determination. *World's Poultry Science Journal*, 52, 203–221.

Sommer F, Bäckhed F. (2013) The gut microbiota – Masters of host development and physiology. *Nature Reviews Microbiology*, 11, 227–238.

Taylor M, Mediannikov O, Raoult D, et al. (2012) Endosymbiotic bacteria associated with nematodes, ticks and amoebae. *FEMS Immunology and Medical Microbiology*, 64, 21–31.

Torok VA, Ophel-Keller K, Loo M, et al. (2008) Application of methods for identifying broiler chicken gut bacterial species linked with increased energy metabolism. *Applied and Environmental Microbiology*, 74, 783–791.

Tsuchida T, Koga R, Horikawa M, et al. (2010) Symbiotic bacterium modifies aphid body color. *Science*, 330, 1102–1104.

Turnbaugh PJ, Ley RE, Mahowald MA, et al. (2006) An obesity-associated gut microbiome with increased capacity for energy harvest. *Nature*, 444, 1027–1131.

Uroz S, Calvaruso C, Turpault MP, et al. (2007) Effect of the mycorrhizosphere on the genotypic and metabolic diversity of the bacterial communities involved in mineral weathering in a forest soil. *Applied and Environmental Microbiology*, 73, 3019.

van Der Putten W, Bardgett RD, Bever JD, et al. (2013) Plant–soil feedbacks: The past, the present and future challenges. *Journal of Ecology*, 101, 265–276.

Van Der Heijden MGA, Bardgett RD, Van Straalen NM. (2008) The unseen majority: Soil microbes as drivers of plant diversity and productivity in terrestrial ecosystems. *Ecology Letters*, 11, 296–310.

Vásquez A, Olofsson TC. (2009) The lactic acid bacteria involved in the production of bee pollen and bee bread. *Journal of Apicultural Research*, 48, 189–195.

Vitousek P, Howarth R. (1991) Nitrogen limitation on land and in the sea: How can it occur? *Biogeochemistry*, 13, 87–115.

Vitousek P, Cassman K, Cleveland C, et al. (2002) Towards an ecological understanding of biological nitrogen fixation. *Biogeochemistry*, 57, 1–45.

Vojvodic S, Rehan SM, Anderson KE. (2013) Microbial gut diversity of Africanized and European honey bee larval instars. *PLoS ONE*, 8, e72106.

Voreades N, Kozil A, Weir TL. (2014) Diet and the development of the human intestinal microbiome. *Frontiers in Microbiology*, 5, 494.

Wallander H, Ekblad A, Godbold DL, et al. (2013) Evaluation of methods to estimate production, biomass and turnover of ectomycorrhizal mycelium in forests soils – A review. *Soil Biology and Biochemistry*, 57, 1034–1047.

Walter J, Ley R. (2011) The human gut microbiome: Ecology and recent evolutionary changes. *Annual Review of Microbiology*, 65, 411–429.

Wardle DA, Bonner KI, Barker GM, et al. (1999) Plant removals in perennial grassland: Vegetation dynamics, decomposers, soil biodiversity, and ecosystem properties. *Ecological Monographs*, 69, 535–568.

Wardle DA, Bardgett RD, Klironomos JN, et al. (2004) Ecological linkages between aboveground and belowground biota. *Science*, 304, 1629.

Whitacre PT, Fagen AP, Husbands JL, et al. (2010) Implementing the new biology: Decadal challenges linking food, energy, and the environment: Summary of a workshop, June 3–4, 2010. Washington, DC: National Academies Press.

Wurzburger N, Clemmensen KE. (2018) From mycorrhizal fungal traits to ecosystem properties: And back again. *Journal of Ecology*, 106, 463–467.

Yegani M, Korver DR. (2008) Factors affecting intestinal health in poultry. *Poultry Science*, 87, 2052–2063.

Zhong J, Jasinskas A, Barbour AG. (2007) Antibiotic treatment of the tick vector *Amblyomma americanum* reduced reproductive fitness. *PLoS ONE*, 2, e405.

Zhu XY, Zhong T, Pandya Y, et al. (2002) 16S rRNA-based analysis of microbiota from the cecum of broiler chickens. *Applied and Environmental Microbiology*, 68, 124–137.

Zindel R, Ofek M, Minz D, et al. (2013) The role of the bacterial community in the nutritional ecology of the bulb mite *Rhizoglyphus robini* (Acari: Astigmata: Acaridae). *FASEB Journal*, 27, 1488–1497.

Zurek L, Keddie BA. (1998) Significance of methanogenic symbionts for development of the American cockroach, *Periplaneta americana*. *Journal of Insect Physiology*, 44, 645–651.

CHAPTER SIX

The microbiome and host behaviour

ANNE LIZÉ

University of Rennes and University of Liverpool

and

ZENOBIA LEWIS

University of Liverpool

6.1 Introduction

The potential for microorganisms to affect host behaviour has been recognised for decades, particularly with respect to parasites. The first suggestion that Gordian worms induce their arthropod hosts to jump into water, usually to their death, dates back almost 100 years (Blunk, 1922). In the 1970s it was first shown that rodents infected with the cat protozoan parasite *Toxoplasmosis gondii* exhibited differences in learning capability and memory (e.g. Witting, 1979). Many examples of parasite-mediated alterations of host behaviour were initially presumed to be unintended side effects related to the pathology of infection. It was the seminal work of Poulin (1995, 2010) that indicated such phenomena could actually be adaptations to maximise parasite transmission and/or host fitness. Poulin formulated a framework for determining whether parasite-induced behaviours were adaptive, suggesting that such behaviours should be complex, purposeful, have arisen independently in several lineages of host or parasite, and increase the fitness of either the parasite or the host (Poulin, 1995). We now know that Gordian worms induce their arthropod hosts to seek water to facilitate the reproductive stage of the parasite life cycle (Thomas et al., 2002; Sanchez et al., 2008). In the case of *T. gondii*, infection results in rodents exhibiting suicidal preference for areas exhibiting signs of cat presence (Berdoy et al., 2000), and this preference is of benefit to the parasite as rodent predation by cats results in transmission to the definitive host.

Research into the wider influence of microorganisms on host behaviour and communication is now also gaining more interest. The link between symbiotic bacteria and olfactory communication in the small Indian mongoose (*Herpestes auropunctatus*) was first hypothesised in the 1970s (e.g. Gorman, 1976). Since then, commensal bacteria have been proposed to affect a wide array of brain functions (Cryan & Dinan, 2012; Ezenwa et al., 2012; Mayer et al., 2014;

Sampson & Mazmanian, 2015; Wong et al., 2015), ranging from bulk food intake (Vijay-Kumar et al., 2010) to anxiety (Heijtz et al., 2011; Neufeld et al., 2011), neurodevelopmental disorders (Hsiao et al., 2013) and social behaviour (Archie & Theis, 2011; Lizé et al., 2013, 2014; Desbonnet et al., 2014; Arentsen et al., 2015; Stilling et al., 2018). Furthermore, communication in various animal species is contingent on the presence or absence of appropriate host–microorganism interactions (e.g. Archie & Theis, 2011; Lizé et al., 2013; Desbonnet et al., 2014; Archie & Tung, 2015; Arentsen et al., 2015).

Here we discuss recent advances in the study of the effects of the microbiome on the behaviour of both animals and plants. We cover five key areas of interest with respect to the ways the microbiome can impact host behaviour: foraging, dispersal, reproduction, social interactions, and learning and memory. Our coverage is not, however, exhaustive. Similar to the rest of this book, where possible we cover both animals and plants, although it should be noted that the study of the effects of the microbiome on plant behaviour is still in its infancy. For the purposes of this chapter, we define behaviour in the context of both animals and plants as every action performed by an organism in order to survive and reproduce, and these behaviours can be induced by environmental or internal stimuli, innate or learnt, voluntary or not (reviewed in Trewavas, 2009).

6.2 Foraging and nutrient acquisition

In most animals, the largest reservoir of microbes is found in the gut, and it is now well-established that the gastrointestinal microbiome can assist in host feeding, in some cases permitting utilisation of food resources that would not otherwise be accessible (see Chapters 3–5). The interaction of the microbiome with ingested nutrients has emerged as a major determinant of human health and disease (Ley et al., 2006; Turnbaugh et al., 2006; Kau et al., 2011; Clemente et al., 2012; Sharon et al., 2014; Goyal et al., 2015; Subramanian et al., 2015). However, despite being an intensive field of research, the importance of microbiome–nutrient interactions in influencing behaviour remains poorly understood. In vertebrates, the complexity of the microbiome, and the large set of nutritional parameters that could influence their function, renders this field of research a challenge. Furthermore, research on the microbiome has mainly focused on its role in carbohydrate homeostasis (Turnbaugh et al., 2006; Huang & Douglas, 2015). More recently, however, the importance of commensal bacteria in controlling growth (Shin et al., 2011; Storelli et al., 2011; Schwarzer et al., 2016) and in protecting children from symptoms of malnutrition (Smith et al., 2013) indicate that the microbiome could also play a pivotal role in protein homeostasis (Yamada et al., 2015). Other evidence comes from the implication of the gut microbiome in the degradation of dietary proteins through the release of tryptophan, which is converted into various catabolites by the gut microbiome (Roager & Licht, 2018). Metabolites produced by gut microbes such as tryptophan catabolites have been shown to activate the immune system, enhance the intestinal epithelial barrier, stimulate gastrointestinal motility, and exert anti-inflammatory, antioxidative or antitoxic effects in systemic circulation (Roager & Licht, 2018).

There is also evidence that the gut microbiome could influence host food preferences more widely. Microorganisms are under selective pressure to increase their fitness. As microorganisms are harboured by their host, one way of increasing fitness could be through the manipulation of host feeding behaviours to enhance the microorganism fitness, sometimes at the expense of the host fitness (reviewed in Alcock et al., 2014). Indeed, when host and microorganism interests diverge, conflicts may arise over resource acquisition and resource allocation. This could lead the host to be attracted or repulsed by certain food items that may or may not benefit host and/or microorganism fitness, depending on the host–microorganism interaction. Alcock et al. (2014) hypothesise that in a diverse gut microbiome, more energy will be expended on competition between species. Conversely, in a less-diverse microbiome, the decrease in competition between microorganisms will promote population growth, which may render them better able to manipulate host feeding behaviour by inducing cravings or dysphoria for food more beneficial to the bacteria in question. Indeed, the gut microbiomes of obese individuals have been shown to be less diverse than those of lean individuals in both humans (e.g. Turnbaugh et al., 2009) and mice (e.g. Ley et al., 2005). This field of research is predicted to explode in the next years as there is the potential for health solutions through microbiome management. A similar phenomenon has been shown in *Drosophila melanogaster*, the gut microbiome of which is primarily composed of *Acetobacter* spp. and *Lactobacillus* spp. (Wong et al., 2011). These gut bacteria influence the food preferences and foraging decisions of flies (Wong et al., 2017). Flies harbouring an intact, non-manipulated microbiome or those inoculated with a mixture of *Acetobacter* spp. and *Lactobacillus* sp. preferred food that was optimal for the host, while flies that had their gut microbiome suppressed, or mono-associated with one or other of the bacteria, showed preference for suboptimal food (Wong et al., 2017). This suggests that bacteria can alter the foraging decisions made by the host in a manner that is potentially advantageous to the bacteria. As flies need to trade-off between acquiring beneficial microorganisms and balancing nutrients in foraging, this can have detrimental effects on the nutrient acquisition of the fly (Wong et al., 2017).

The extent to which the microbiome affects appetite for specific nutrients remains underexplored. That said, microorganisms have been shown to alter host taste and odour receptors in mammal species such as mice, rats and even humans (Rousseaux et al., 2007; Swartz et al., 2012). In insects, the microbiome affects both odour emission and food preferences in larvae and adult *D. melanogaster* (Farine et al. 2017; Wong et al., 2017). The greater appetite for sugar observed in flies with an unaltered microbiome, as opposed to axenic flies, resulted in a decrease in the ratio of protein to carbohydrate intake, an important determinant of life-history traits such as somatic growth and reproduction in animals including vertebrates (Simpson & Raubenheimer, 2012). Given that a reduction in yeast and amino acid intake has been shown to lead to an increase in lifespan, the observation that commensal bacteria reduce the host intake ratio of protein to carbohydrate could account for the shorter lifespan exhibited by axenic flies (Brummel et al., 2004). It is interesting to note that flies harbouring a microbiome are also able to increase their reproductive output (Elgart et al., 2016; Leitão-Gonçalves et al., 2017) despite their lower protein intake. Commensal bacteria could therefore have a highly beneficial impact on the fly, enabling it to simultaneously maximise lifespan and reproductive output. The increase in sugar appetite observed in gnotobiotic flies associated with only one species of gut bacteria could simply arise from the bacteria utilising the sugar in the food, therefore inducing a carbohydrate deficit in flies. The decrease in yeast appetite, however, is more difficult to explain. One possibility could be that bacteria themselves act as nutrients, which has been proposed for yeast and other fungi (Yamada et al., 2015). The finding that heat-killed (inactivated) bacteria do not induce a change in feeding behaviour, and that only specific commensal bacteria change yeast appetite, indicates that the microbiome acts in a very specific way to alter food choice. Furthermore, previous data showing that microbes can improve the uptake of amino acids (Erkosar et al., 2015; Yamada et al., 2015) are not sufficient to explain the suppression of yeast appetite in flies pretreated with commensals, as generally holidic media are used that are completely devoid of essential amino acids. A key question is thus: what could be the mechanisms by which gut bacteria change yeast appetite and increase egg-laying?

Microorganisms can also induce the alteration of host feeding behaviour. The bacteria *Wolbachia* has been shown to alter host olfactory cues leading to either an enhanced or a decreased attraction to food cues in *D. simulans* and *D. melanogaster*, respectively (Peng et al., 2008). The authors suggest the difference could be the result of different levels of *Wolbachia* tissue tropism in the two hosts. The protozoa *Plasmodium falciparum* has also been shown to alter blood-seeking and feeding behaviour of the insect vector *Anopheles gambiae*. *Caenorhabditis elegans*, which feeds on bacteria, can discriminate between pathogenic and non-pathogenic food sources, avoiding the consumption of pathogens (Zhang et al., 2005), or being more attracted to them (Caldwell et al., 2003). While self-medication with secondary metabolites of plants to control nematode and tapeworm infections is well documented in vertebrates, in particular the primates (reviewed in Forbey et al., 2009), less is known about it in insects. However, there is evidence that following infection with parasitic microorganisms, some insect species similarly alter their food preferences to control infection (reviewed in de Roode et al., 2013; Abbott, 2014). For example, *Spodoptera littoralis* armyworms infected with nucleopolyhedrovirus prefer food containing more protein, which increases their resistance to the virus, and in turn increases their survival (Lee et al., 2006). Monarch butterflies, *Danaus plexippus*, infected with the protozoan parasite *Ophryocystis elektroscirrpha* are unable to cure themselves through altered feeding behaviours, but females will oviposit on more toxic species of their milkweed host plants (Lefèvre et al., 2010), resulting in survival benefits for their infected offspring. Thus, it appears some insects also exhibit self-medicating foraging behaviours when infected with pathogenic microorganisms.

Some plants appear to have behavioural control over their ancient symbioses with nitrogen-fixing bacteria. The mutualistic associations between land plants and microorganisms are probably some of the oldest, likely having developed early in the emergence of plants on land, in the Mid-Ordovician period around 470 million years ago (Martin et al., 2017). Diverse plant taxa exhibit such symbioses that allow them to acquire nutrients in a useable form, yet all plants that do share a highly conserved Common Symbiosis Signalling Pathway. It has been suggested that a single evolutionary event over ~100 million years ago resulted in all nitrogen-fixing symbioses that we see in extant plants today (Werner et al., 2014). Although we are beginning to understand the interactions between plants and their symbiotic microorganisms at a molecular level (reviewed in Vandenkoornhuyse et al., 2015; Martin et al., 2017; Plett & Martin, 2017), important questions remain unanswered. For example, it is still unclear how plants differentiate between beneficial and pathogenic microorganisms and then respond accordingly. In an elegant study, Sachs et al. (2010) experimentally inoculated the lotus *Acmispon strigosus* with nitrogen-fixing *Bradyrhizobium* strains that varied in their provision of symbiotic benefits to the plant. 'Cheater' strains, exploiting the benefits provided by others while avoiding the costs of supplying resources, exhibited lower infection rates of hosts than beneficial strains, suggesting that plants potentially punish cheating bacteria by reducing carbon provision, a behaviour termed 'sanctioning' that had long been theorised to occur (Denison, 2000). In the same way, *Medicago truncatula* roots can detect, discriminate and reward the best arbuscular mycorrhizal fungal partners with more carbohydrates. In turn, the fungal symbionts enforce cooperation by increasing nutrient transfer only to those roots providing more carbohydrates (Kiers et al., 2011). A more recent study suggests that, rather than limiting carbon allocation, some plants limit infection rate of uncooperative bacterial strains by upregulating defence compounds (Hortal et al., 2017). Given the close association between plants and the microbial community of the surrounding soil, there are widespread and fundamental impacts of microorganisms on plant nutrient acquisition, both positive and negative, and these are covered in more detail in Chapters 3 and 5.

6.3 Host movement

One of the most spectacular illustrations of microbial-induced changes in host behaviour is the manipulation of ants by fungus of the genus *Ophiocordiceps* (Hughes et al., 2011; reviewed in Hughes et al., 2016). For example, the parasitic *O. unilateralis* develops inside the ant by feeding on its non-vital organs (Andersen et al., 2012). When the fungus is ready to produce reproductive spores, it grows into its host brain, resulting in the host behaving like a 'zombie' and causing it to leave the nest and climb to the top of a plant. It then kills its host by devouring its brain, before sprouting a mushroom from the top of its head, which disperses its spores widely below the 'zombie ant'. Entomopathogenic fungi manipulating their hosts have also been described in other insect and arachnid species (reviewed in Hughes et al., 2016). Fungal parasites do not always kill their host before dispersing spores onto the environment. For instance, *Strongwellsea castrans* parasitises the Diptera *Hylemya brassicae* and *H. platura*. This fungus keeps its hosts alive despite creating a sizeable hole in the abdomen through which the fungal spores are released during flight, therefore using the host as a vector for distribution (Araújo & Hughes, 2016). Similar behavioural manipulations of the host have been described for the fungus *Massospora cicadina*, which infects cicadas (Araújo & Hughes, 2016). Again, despite infection and associated necrosis, the host retains the ability to fly, forage and mate (Soper, 1963; Soper et al., 1976; Humber, 1982).

As noted previously, rodents infected with the protozoan *Toxoplasma gondii* lose their innate aversion to cats (Berdoy et al., 2000). Similarly, chimpanzees (*Pan troglodytes troglodytes*) infected by *T. gondii* lose their innate aversion towards the urine of leopards (*Panthera pardus*), their only natural predator (Poirotte et al., 2016). Parasitic nematomorphs manipulate their insect hosts' water-seeking behaviour, leading the host to jump into water (Thomas et al., 2002). Ants infected by the trematode *Dicrocoelium dendricum* climb to the top of grass blades to be eaten by ruminants, the definitive host (Moore, 1995; Libersat et al., 2009), and the parasitic worm *Pomphorhynchus laevis* induces phototactic behaviour in its intermediate host *Gammarus pulex*, thereby increasing risk of predation by the fish definitive host (Cézilly et al., 2000). *Wolbachia* infection decreases locomotion activity of the parasitoid wasp *Leptopilina heterotoma* (Fleury et al., 2000), whereas it enhances locomotor activity in the mosquito *Aedes aegypti* (Evans et al., 2009). Viruses have also been shown to alter their host movements, such as baculoviruses that are responsible for the enhanced locomotion activity observed in the caterpillars they infect (Kamita et al., 2005; Hoover et al., 2011).

The impact of commensal and/or symbiotic microorganisms on host movement has received far less attention than parasites or pathogens. However, some studies have demonstrated that symbiotic microorganisms play a role in regulating host responses to stressful situations (Dinan & Cryan, 2012; Foster & McVey Neufeld, 2013; Sampson & Mazmanian, 2015), such that dysbiosis leads to associated changes in locomotion (Heijtz et al., 2011). In zebrafish (*Danio rerio*; Davis et al., 2016) and stinkbug nymphs (Hosokawa et al., 2007), the absence of a microbiome increases locomotor activity, for example.

6.4 Hormones and stress

The role of microorganisms in regulating hormone and steroid production is becoming increasingly recognised, particularly in the context of human health, on which there are a number of recent reviews (e.g. Sandrini et al., 2015; Kunc et al., 2016). A number of publications have also looked at this in the context of wild animals, and those of conservation concern (e.g. Stothart et al., 2016; Miller et al., 2017; Noguera et al., 2018; Vlčková et al., 2018; Antwis et al., 2019). Not only do host hormones shape the structure and function of the host microbiome, the microbiome can also alter host production and regulation of hormones (e.g. catecholamines, cortisol/corticosterone, oestrogens, testosterone, thyroid and growth hormones) and alter hormone-associated host gene expression profiles. For example, female zebrafish (*D. rario*) fed with *Lactobacillus rhamnosus* experience increased transcription of various genes involved in sex determination and fertility (Carnevali et al., 2013). Microbial communities can also synthesise hormones that are analogous in structure and function to those produced by the host, as well as degrade or metabolise host-derived hormones (Lyte, 2013; Kunc et al., 2016). For example, norepinephrine, a critical neurotransmitter in the sympathetic nervous system, is conserved across all taxa from microorganisms to mammals, and signalling pathways in humans are thought to have originated from microbial-derived lateral gene transfer (Lyte, 2013). That the gut microbiome is critical for the correct functioning of the central nervous system is becoming increasingly recognised, as well as its role in the development and regulation of the hypothalamic–pituitary–adrenal axis and subsequent host behaviour (Sudo, 2014). Therefore, hormonal communication between the host and its microbiome can have wide-ranging impacts on host function and behaviour, as well as development, health and immunity.

Perhaps surprisingly, the microbiome has also been implicated in host mood and stress, which is of particular interest given the role of stress in pathogen susceptibility, as well as the potential for altering host microbiomes in order to treat, for example, anxiety disorders and other mental health issues. Chronic stress exposure is also known to increase susceptibility to bacterial infection while altering the gut microbiome community (Bailey et al., 2010). Observed changes in host–gut microbiome interactions when rats are exposed to stress include an increased bacterial attachment and internalisation in the epithelium (Soderholm et al., 2002), which can be restored by probiotic administration (Zareie et al., 2006). In zebrafish (*D. rerio*), anxious behaviour in axenic fish can also be reversed through probiotic supplementation (Davis et al., 2016). Indeed, probiotic administration has been repeatedly demonstrated to markedly reduce the level of depressive-like behaviours of hosts. For example, in young rats, probiotic administration (*Bifidobacterium bifidum*, *B. lactis*, *Lactobacillus acidophilus*, *L. brevis*, *L. casei*, *L. salivarus*, *Lactococcus lactis*) has an antidepressant effect measured by an increase in swimming activity, a standard measure of depression-like behaviours in rats (Abildgaard et al., 2017). In rats and mice, probiotics have also been shown to ameliorate stress-induced depressive-like behaviour (Desbonnet et al., 2010; Bravo et al., 2011; Arseneault-Breard et al., 2012; Savignac et al., 2014; Liang et al., 2015). Therefore, it is no surprise that the novel concept of psychobiotics has received increasing attention in recent years (Dinan et al., 2013; reviewed in Sarkar et al., 2016; but also see Romijn & Rucklidge, 2015). Psychobiotics are defined as live beneficial bacteria, or support for the growth of such bacteria, which when ingested confer mental health benefits through interactions with commensal gut bacteria (reviewed in Sarkar et al., 2016).

It is now clear that the mechanisms by which the microbiome can alter host mental health involve the host gut–brain axis via the vagus nerve (Bonaz et al., 2018; Lowry et al., 2018) and/or the host immune system (Hooper et al., 2012). The vagus nerve is able to sense microbiome metabolites, to transfer this gut information to the central nervous system, and then to generate an adapted or inappropriate response (Bonaz et al., 2018). Several studies report that the microbiome interacts with the host neurohormones such as dopamine, corticosterone, glutamate, glutamine, serotonin and gamma-aminobutyric acid (reviewed in Lu et al., 2013; Lyte, 2013; Sampson & Mazmanian, 2015). For instance, the turnover rates of noradrenaline and dopamine in the brain of germ-free mice is higher compared to mice harbouring an intact, non-manipulated microbiome, which could explain the higher motor activity observed in germ-free mice (Diaz-Heijtz et al., 2011). While the microbiome could directly trigger host neurotransmitter production at distal sites, it is also possible that microbial-derived molecules act as neuroactives. Indeed, some species of gut bacteria are known to produce small molecules such as serotonin, dopamine, norepinephrine, epinephrine, GABA and acetylcholine, which are all possible bioactive neurotransmitters (Wall et al., 2014). In the same way, other microbial metabolites such as short chain fatty acids or microbial catabolism of tryptophan (Roager & Licht, 2018) have also been shown to activate the host immune system and stimulate gut hormone secretion (Roager & Licht, 2018). However, how microbial-derived molecules can reach the host central nervous system, mimic its neurotransmitters, and fit with host neuroreceptors or act as neuroactives, and whether their impacts on the host neurophysiology are comparable to conventional host neurotransmitters, remain unknown.

6.5 Reproduction

Some of the most well-known examples of microorganisms affecting host behaviour are the reproduction-manipulating endosymbionts. The ability of the arthropod endosymbiont *Wolbachia pipientis* to manipulate host behaviour to further its own transmission is one of the more spectacular examples (reviewed in Stouthamer et al., 1999; Werren et al., 2008). It has been suggested that *Wolbachia* could infect up to two-thirds of all insect species (Jeyaprakash & Hoy, 2000; Hilgenboecker et al., 2008), plus other groups of arthropods (e.g. Gotah et al., 2003) and nematodes (e.g. Haegeman et al., 2009). *Wolbachia* is vertically transmitted via the female germline, and as a result, males represent an evolutionary 'dead-end' for the bacterium. Therefore, *Wolbachia* manipulate host reproduction in order to increase reproductive success of infected females in the population, thereby maximising its transmission (reviewed in O'Neill et al., 1997). These manipulations include phenotypic feminisation of genetic males (Rousset et al., 1992), the induction of parthenogenesis (Stouthamer et al., 1990) and the killing of male offspring in early development (Hurst et al., 1999). Most commonly, *Wolbachia* induces cytoplasmic incompatibility; matings between infected males and uninfected females result in the production of inviable offspring, which in turn increases the relative reproductive success of infected females (Hoffmann et al., 1986).

In addition to the direct effects of *Wolbachia* on host reproduction, these bacteria have been shown to affect behaviour, as noted above. For example, in the blue moon butterfly, *Hypolimnas bolina*, the evolution of male-killing *Wolbachia* has resulted in female-biased sex ratios of 100:1, which have remained stable in some populations for over 100 years (Dyson & Hurst, 2004). The biased sex ratios have resulted in males reducing investment in copulation, and in turn, the consequent sperm-depleted females have become more polyandrous (Charlat et al., 2007). So, indirectly, *Wolbachia* has had a strong effect on the mating system of infected populations. In *D. melanogaster* and *D. simulans*, *Wolbachia* has been shown to increase mating rate (de Crespigny et al., 2006), while in *Drosophila paulistorum* (Miller et al., 2010), shrimp (Dunn et al., 2006) and spider mites (Vala et al., 2004) it affects mating preferences.

More recently there is emerging evidence that other microorganisms such as *Cardinium*, *Spiroplasma* and *Arsenophonus* can also affect behaviour (reviewed in Engelstädter & Hurst, 2009). In *Drosophila*, the commensal gut bacteria have been implicated in assortative mating preferences; Dodd (1989) demonstrated that *D. pseudoobscura* exhibit mate preference towards individuals that had developed on the same food. A more recent study in *D. melanogaster* suggested that the recognition process underlying this preference is mediated by the gut bacteria (Sharon et al., 2010), although it has been suggested this effect is population-specific (Najarro et al., 2015; Leftwich et al., 2017). Gut bacteria have also been implicated in kin recognition processes in *D. melanogaster* (Lizé et al., 2014; Heys et al., 2018). *Drosophila subobscura* is a nuptial gift-giving species in which males present an edible droplet formed to females from the contents of the crop (Krimbas, 1993). The commensal gut bacteria have been implicated in female mate choice and fecundity in this species; females with a suppressed gut microbiome mated faster with normal males, but also had higher fecundity than normal females, and it has been suggested that this effect is related to the microbial content of the nuptial gift (Walsh et al., 2017). Symbionts are also involved in determining oviposition behaviour of house flies (*Musca domestica*). During oviposition, *Klebsiella oxytoca* is transferred from females to the surface of the eggs, and chemical cues released from this symbiont inhibit further oviposition in that area (Lam et al., 2007). Interestingly, *K. oxytoca*–enriched diets also increase male sexual competitiveness in Mediterranean fruit flies (*Ceratitis capitata*; Gavriel et al., 2011). Gut bacteria have also been associated with post-zygotic reproductive isolation. When recently diverged species of *Nasonia* parasitic wasp were crossed, hybrids died during the larval stage (Brucker & Bordenstein, 2013). However, lethality could be 'rescued' via antibiotic suppression of the gut bacteria. The authors suggest that the host genome and gut microbiome are co-adapted, and that the breakdown of the relationship between them via hybridisation results in host death. It has been suggested that more widely, microorganism-driven mating preferences could be an important, but thus far neglected, driver of evolution (Rosenberg & Zilber-Rosenberg, 2016; Shropshire & Bordenstein, 2016; but see Leftwich et al., 2017).

Microbial communities also appear to be important in reproduction and fecundity of mammals. For example, relationships between microbial community composition and ovarian cycling and reproductive state have been demonstrated in wild baboons (Miller et al., 2017) and captive black rhino (Antwis et al., 2019), although directionality is difficult to determine. In humans, gut microbes such as *Clostridium scindens* can convert glucocorticoids to androgens (Ridlon et al., 2013). In females, the human gut microbiome secretes enzymes that regulate oestrogen binding to downstream receptors (Flores et al., 2012), and disruption of the gut microbiome can alter circulating oestrogen levels (Baker et al., 2017). Concurrently, manipulation of the gut microbiome can alter fertility and pregnancy outcomes for humans, which may form the basis of promising new fertility treatments for humans (Fox & Eichelberger, 2015; Franasiak & Scott, 2015a, 2015b; Baker et al., 2017).

Apart from the effects of pathogens, very little is known with regard to the effects of microorganisms on plant reproductive behaviour. Indeed, few studies have thus far even characterised the microorganisms found on non-crop plants (although see e.g. Alvarez-Pérez et al., 2012; Junker & Keller, 2015). That said, it has been shown that the forbs *Centaurea jacea* and *C. scabiosa* modulate resource allocation to reproduction in response to inoculation with root-associated microorganisms (Moora et al., 2004), and microorganisms are thought to be able to affect reproduction indirectly, via, for example, alteration of the floral scent that attracts pollinators (Helletsgruber et al., 2017).

6.6 Cognitive behaviours: learning and memory

Cognitive behaviours encompass behaviours (e.g. mate choice, foraging, stress response, etc.) implying cognitive processes such as learning, memory and decision-making. In this section, we focus on the host–microbiome interactions that influence these, with particular regard to the gut microbiome. It is worth noting that most of the literature on the impact of the microbiome on their host cognitive behaviours relates to mammals, and further studies in more taxonomically diverse hosts are needed.

It is now widely recognised that the gut microbiome is essential for normal cognitive development of rodents (Diaz Heijtz et al., 2011; Gareau et al., 2011), insects such as *D. melanogaster* (Wong et al., 2017), and also humans (Dinan et al., 2015; Carlson et al., 2018). The use of germ-free and gnotobiotic animals, as well as antibiotic and probiotic treatments, have facilitated studies of cognitive behaviour (reviewed in Gareau, 2014; Vuong et al., 2017). For example, germ-free mice present a decreased working memory when confronted with a novel object recognition task (Gareau et al., 2011). The same decreased working memory has also been observed in specific pathogen-free mice treated with a cocktail of antibiotics (Frohlich et al., 2016). Several studies suggest that probiotic supplementation can modulate learning and memory in animals. In the context of anxiety and fear behaviours, probiotic supplementation of *Pediococcus acidilactici* in Japanese quails (*Coturnix japonica*) decreased their emotional reactivity and increased their memory (Parois et al., 2017). Similarly, in mice, *Lactobacillus rhamnosus* supplementation regulates emotional behaviours and enhances memory consolidation (Bravo et al., 2011), while germ-free mice have deficits in fear recall (Hoban et al., 2018). Treatment with *L. fermentum* in rats initially exposed to ampicillin restored their impaired spatial memory (Wang et al., 2015). In the same way, treatment with *Bifidobacterium longum* in inbred mice increased spatial and long-term learning and memory (Savignac et al., 2015). Treatment with *Bifidobacterium breve* was observed to have the same effects except for long-term memory (Savignac et al., 2015). Impaired spatial memory of mice fed a high-fat Western diet was restored through *L. helveticus* treatment (Ohland et al., 2013). Additionally, improved learning and memory abilities were observed in mice treated with *Mycobacterium vaccae* (Matthews & Jenks, 2013), and in humans with terminal lung cancer treated with heat-killed *M. vaccae* (O'Brien et al., 2004). In obese humans, who are known to exhibit an altered microbiome, microbiome changes co-varied with their scores in speed, attention, and cognitive flexibility, although sample sizes were small and there were potential confounding factors as a result of the experimental design (Fernandez-Real et al., 2015). Such impact on memory abilities, and particularly on visuospatial memory, have also been demonstrated in patients suffering from irritable bowel syndrome (IBS), who also present with an altered microbiome (Kennedy et al., 2014). Finally, healthy humans receiving a probiotic cocktail (*L. helveticus* and *B. longum*) saw improvements in their mood and cognition (Messaoudi et al., 2011).

Cognitive behaviours are also impacted during infection (reviewed in Hoogland et al., 2015; Frohlich et al., 2016) and chronic stress exposure (reviewed in McEwen, 2008). *Wolbachia* infection in the parasitoid wasp *Trichogramma brassicae* leads to a decrease in memory retention in ovipositing females (Kishani Farahani et al., 2017). In this study, however, the observed decreased memory retention could also be attributed to the reproductive manipulation by *Wolbachia* (Kishani Farahani et al., 2017). *Caenorhabditis elegans* exposure to the pathogenic bacteria *Pseudomonas aeruginosa* induces avoidance and results in aversive olfactory learning behaviour via the production of an intestinal neuropeptide (Lee & Mylonakis, 2017). When infected by the gut protozoan parasite *Crithidia bombi*, bumblebees experience impaired ability to use floral information (Gegear et al., 2006). Maternal infection of pregnant rats with *Escherichia coli* leads to altered cognitive development in offspring (Jiang et al., 2013). In humans, cognitive impairments have been associated with an elevated infection burden, which occurs when individuals have been infected by several pathogenic viruses and bacteria in the past (e.g. cytomegalovirus, *Helicobacter pylori* and herpes simplex virus; Katan et al., 2013). In mice, infection with *Citrobacter rodentium* has no deleterious effects on memory and cognition, but when coupled with psychological stress, this leads to long-term memory impairment (Gareau et al., 2011).

6.7 Social interactions and communication

As noted in the introduction, it was in the 1970s that a link between the microbiome and social behaviour was first hypothesised (Gorman, 1976). However, it is only in the past decade that we have come to appreciate just how important and widespread this phenomenon is (Archie & Tung, 2015). Social behaviours, such as grooming and other interactions, have been shown to influence microbiome composition in yellow baboons (*Papio cynocephalus*; Tung et al., 2015), chimpanzees (*Pan troglodytes*; Degnan et al., 2012; Moeller et al., 2016) and wild ponies (*Equus ferus caballus*; Antwis et al., 2018).

One of the key ways that microorganisms can affect social behaviour is through alteration or mediation of chemical signalling, the major mechanism underpinning social behaviour in many diverse species of animal. Many mammals communicate with conspecifics via scent marking, and while the compounds involved can be secreted by the animal (Steiger, 2012) or derived from the external environment (Wyatt, 2014), there is increasing evidence that in some cases they are the products of microorganisms in the scent glands. The fermentation hypothesis posits that metabolites resulting from bacteria breaking down substrates in the scent gland are co-opted as scent signals (Albone, 1984), and this has been suggested as the mechanism underlying scent communication in, among other species, the European badger (*Meles meles*; Sin et al., 2012), and the big brown bat (*Eptesicus fuscus*; Bloss et al., 2002). It has been suggested that utilising bacterial metabolites as a signalling cue allows fast and effective discrimination of nest-mates compared to unrelated individuals (Archie & Theis, 2011). Recent studies of the striped (*Hyeana hyeana*) and spotted (*Crocuta crocuta*) hyenas suggest this may be the case; next-generation sequencing of the bacterial communities found in the scent glands of these two species have been shown to co-vary with the fatty acid profiles of their respective scent signals (Theis et al., 2012, 2013). In addition, the bacterial communities are more similar in members of the same social group compared to those of others (Theis et al., 2012, 2013).

It is not only mammals that appear to use microbially-derived compounds in odour signalling. In some of the earlier work to demonstrate a link between bacteria and behaviour, it was shown that guaiacol, an important component of the desert locust (*Schistocerca gregaria*) pheromone that induces swarming behaviour, is produced by the gut bacterial community of the host (Dillon et al., 2000, 2002). Similarly, in German cockroaches (*Blatella germanica*), the gut bacterial community plays an important role in the production of the pheromones that induce aggregation in this species (Wada-Katsumata et al., 2015). The commensal gut bacteria also influence host social behaviour in *D. melanogaster*. Manipulation of the gut bacteria via the addition of antibiotics to the growth media suggests that adult kin recognition behaviours (Lizé et al., 2014) and adult and larval social attraction are mediated by the gut bacteria (Venu et al., 2014). Similar techniques have been used in the termite *Hodotermes mossambicus* to demonstrate that nest-mate recognition is likely mediated by gut bacteria (Minkley et al., 2006). As in many insect species, mate preferences in *D. melanogaster* are determined by chemical signals produced by the cuticular hydrocarbons that cover the surface of insects (Ferveur & Cobb, 2010), the primary function of which is desiccation avoidance (Hadley, 1981). Cuticular hydrocarbons are produced by the oenocytes, secretory cells that lie under the epidermis, and their functioning is mediated by the mid-gut. Potentially, therefore, bacterial manipulation of the mid-gut may affect the operation of the oenocytes, which in turn modifies the scent profiles used in mating preferences.

To date, empirical studies demonstrating a link between the animal microbiome and communication are largely restricted to insect taxa and model mammalian species. This is likely in part due to the difficulties presented with conducting empirical and potentially invasive studies in wild animals. However, further studies are needed in diverse taxa in order for us to understand how widespread such interactions are (Ezenwa & Williams, 2014). Intriguingly, there is also emerging evidence that the plant microbiome is utilised in host communication. In the early 1980s, a number of studies suggested that plants damaged by herbivore foraging communicated with undamaged neighbours, who consequently increased levels of defence compounds (Baldwin & Schultz, 1983; Rhoades, 1983). Although largely dismissed at the time, in the past 10 years it has become widely accepted that plants communicate with one another, both within and across species, by emitting volatile organic compounds from their leaves, which can be microbial-derived (reviewed in Trewavas, 2017). This, in addition to the soil or plant microbiome in general, can also influence pollinator and pest visitation (Helletsgruber et al., 2017; Pineda et al., 2017), thus highlighting the power of microorganisms to alter behaviour across multiple trophic levels. Plants can also communicate via the mycorrhizal fungal networks associated with their roots. Babikova et al. (2013) found that broad beans (*Vicia faba*) that were allowed to establish hyphal contact with neighbours were able to transmit information regarding herbivore attack, which in turn elicited defensive behaviours in the receiver. Plants have also been shown to communicate drought stress to neighbours, resulting in defensive closing of the stomata (Falik et al., 2011), and potentially exhibit kin recognition in response to mycorrhizal signalling between relatives (Biedrzycki & Bais, 2010; Biedrzycki et al., 2010).

6.8 Conclusions

A wide diversity of microorganisms alters the behaviour of their hosts in interactions that range from parasitic and pathogenic, to commensal and mutualist. In all cases, a central question arises: what are the mechanisms by which host behavioural alteration occurs? Recent advances in sequencing, mass spectrometry, bioinformatics and gnotobiotic technologies (see Chapter 2) have enabled spectacular advancements in our understanding of such host–microbiome interactions. Indeed, it is now widely recognised that the microbiome modulates host physiology, immunity and metabolism, in addition to brain function and behaviour. However, in many cases, the mechanisms underlying microorganism-mediated behavioural alterations of the host have not yet been defined. Research in this area has expanded rapidly in recent years, but as noted throughout, the literature remains biased towards key model organisms such as mice, the fruit fly *D. melanogaster*, and crop and nitrogen-fixing plants. Determining the mechanisms underlying microorganism-induced host behavioural changes is a promising avenue of research with the potential to provide important health and environmental solutions.

References

Abbott J. (2014) Self-medication in insects: Current evidence and future perspectives. *Ecological Entomology*, 39, 273–280.

Abildgaard A, Elfving B, Hokland M, et al. (2017) Probiotic treatment reduces depressive-like behaviour in rats independently of diet. *Psychoneuroendocrinology*, 79, 40–48.

Albone ES. (1984) *Mammalian Semiochemistry*. London: John Wiley.

Alcock J, Maley CC, Aktipis CA. (2014) Is eating behaviour manipulated by the gastrointestinal microbiota? Evolutionary pressures and potential mechanisms. *BioEssays*, 36, 940–949.

Alvarez-Pérez S, Herrera CM, de Vega C. (2012) Zooming in on floral nectar: A first exploration of nectar-associated bacteria in wild plant communities. *FEMS Microbiology Ecology*, 80, 591–602.

Andersen SB, Ferrari M, Evans HC, et al. (2012) Disease dynamics in a specialized parasite of ant societies. *PLoS ONE*, 7, e36352.

Antwis RE, Lea JMD, Unwin B, et al. (2018) Gut microbiome composition is associated with spatial structuring and social interactions in semi-feral Welsh mountain ponies. *Microbiome*, 6, 207.

Antwis RE, Edwards KL, Unwin B, et al. (2019) Rare gut microbiota associated with breeding success, hormone metabolites and ovarian cycle phase in the critically endangered eastern black rhino. *Microbiome*, 7, 27.

Araújo J, Hughes DP. (2016) Diversity of entomopathogenic fungi: Which groups conquered the insect body? *Advances in Genetics*, 94, 1–39.

Archie EA, Theis KR. (2011) Animal behaviour meets microbial ecology. *Animal Behaviour*, 82, 425–436.

Archie EA, Tung J. (2015) Social behavior and the microbiome. *Current Opinion in Behavioral Sciences*, 6, 28–34.

Arentsen T, Raith H, Qian Y, et al. (2015) Host microbiota modulates development of social preference in mice. *Microbial Ecology in Health and Disease*, 26, 29719.

Arseneault-Bréard J, Rondeau I, Gilbert K, et al. (2012) Combination of *Lactobacillus helveticus* R0052 and *Bifidobacterium longum* R0175 reduces post-myocardial infarction depression symptoms and restores intestinal permeability in a rat model. *The British Journal of Nutrition*, 107, 1793–1799.

Babikova Z, Gilbert L, Bruce TJA, et al. (2013) Underground signals carried through common mycelial networks warn neighbouring plants of aphid attack. *Ecology Letters*, 16, 835–843.

Bailey MT, Dowd SE, Parry NM, et al. (2010) Stressor exposure disrupts commensal microbial populations in the intestines and leads to increased colonization by *Citrobacter rodentium*. *Infection and Immunity*, 78, 1509–1519.

Baker JM, Al-Nakkash L, Herbst-Kralovetz MM. (2017) Estrogen–gut microbiome axis:

Physiological and clinical implications. *Maturitas*, 103, 45–53.

Baldwin IT, Schultz JC. (1983) Rapid changes in tree leaf chemistry induced by damage – Evidence for communication between plants. *Science*, 221, 277–279.

Berdoy M, Webster JP, Macdonald DW. (2000) Fatal attraction in *Toxoplasma*-infected rats: A case of parasite manipulation of its mammalian host. *Proceedings of the Royal Society B: Biological Sciences*, 267, 1591–1594.

Biedrzycki ML, Bais HP. (2010) Kin recognition in plants: A mysterious behaviour unsolved. *The Journal of Experimental Botany*, 61, 4123–4128.

Biedrzycki ML, Jilany TA, Dudley SA, et al. (2010) Root exudates mediate kin recognition in plants. *Communicative & Integrative Biology*, 3, 28–35.

Bloss J, Acree TE, Bloss JM, et al. (2002) Potential use of chemical cues for colony-mate recognition in the big brown bat, *Eptesicus fuscus*. *Journal of Chemical Ecology*, 28, 819–834.

Blunk H. (1922) Die lebensgeschichte der im gelbrand schmarotzenden saitenwürmer. *Zoologische Anzeiger*, 54, 110–132.

Bonaz B, Bazin T, Pellissier S. (2018) The vagus nerve at the interface of the microbiota–gut–brain axis. *Frontiers in Neurosciences*, 12, 49.

Bravo JA, Forsythe P, Chew MV, et al. (2011) Ingestion of *Lactobacillus* strain regulates emotional behaviour and central GABA receptor expression in a mouse via the vagus nerve. *Proceedings of the National Academy of Sciences*, 108, 16050–16055.

Brucker RM, Bordenstein SR. (2013) The hologenomic basis of speciation: Gut bacteria cause hybrid lethality in the genus *Nasonia*. *Science*, 341, 667–669.

Brummel T, Ching A, Seroude L, et al. (2004) *Drosophila* lifespan enhancement by exogenous bacteria. *Proceedings of the National Academy of Sciences*, 101, 12974–12979.

Caldwell KN, Anderson GL, Williams PL, et al. (2003) Attraction of a free-living nematode, *Caenorhabditis elegans*, to foodborne pathogenic bacteria and its potential as a vector of *Salmonella poona* for preharvest contamination of cantaloupe. *Journal of Food Protection*, 66, 1964–1971.

Carlson AL, Xia K, Azcarate-Peril MA, et al. (2018) Infant gut microbiome associated with cognitive development. *Biological Psychiatry*, 83, 148–159.

Carnevali O, Avella MA, Gioacchini G (2013) Effects of probiotic administration on zebra fish development and reproduction. *General and Comparative Endocrinology*, 188, 297–302.

Cézilly F, Grégoire A, Bertin A. (2000) Conflict between cooccurring manipulative parasites? An experimental study of the joint influence of two acanthocephalan parasites on the behaviour of *Gammarus pulex*. *Parasitology*, 120, 625–630.

Charlat S, Reuter M, Dyson EA, et al. (2007) Male-killing bacteria trigger a cycle of increasing male fatigue and female promiscuity. *Current Biology*, 17, 273–277.

Clemente JC, Ursell LK, Parfrey LW, et al. (2012) The impact of the gut microbiota on human health: An integrative view. *Cell*, 148, 1258–1270.

Cryan JF, Dinan TG. (2012) Mind-altering microorganisms: The impact of the gut microbiota on brain and behaviour. *Nature Reviews Neuroscience*, 13, 701–712.

Davis DJ, Bryda EC, Gillepsie CH, et al. (2016) Microbial modulation of behavior and stress responses in zebrafish larvae. *Behavioural Brain Research*, 311, 219–227.

de Crespigny FEC, Pitt TD, Wedell N. (2006) Increased male mating rate in *Drosophila* associated with *Wolbachia* infection. *Journal of Evolutionary Biology*, 19, 1964–1972.

de Roode JC, Lefèvre, Hunter MD. (2013) Self-medication in animals. *Science*, 340, 150–151.

Degnan P, Pusey A, Lonsdorf E, et al. (2012) Factors associated with the diversification of the gut microbial communities within chimpanzees from Gombe National Park.

Proceedings of the National Academy of Sciences, 109, 13034–13039.

Denison RF. (2000) Legume sanctions and the evolution of symbiotic cooperation by rhizobia. *The American Naturalist*, 156, 567–576.

Desbonnet L, Garrett L, Clarke G, et al. (2010) Effects of the probiotic *Bifidobacterium infantis* in the maternal separation model of depression. *Neuroscience*, 170, 1179–1188.

Desbonnet L, Clarke G, Shanahan F, et al. (2014) Microbiota is essential for social development in the mouse. *Molecular Psychiatry*, 19, 146–148.

Diaz-Heijtz R, Wang S, Anuar F, et al. (2011) Normal gut microbiota modulates brain development and behavior. *Proceedings of the National Academy of Sciences*, 108, 3047–3052.

Dillon RJ, Vennard CT, Charnley AK. (2000) Pheromones: Exploitation of gut bacteria in the locust. *Nature*, 403, 851.

Dillon RJ, Vennard CT, Charnley AK. (2002) A note: Gut bacteria produce components of a locust cohesion pheromone. *Journal of Applied Microbiology*, 92, 759–763.

Dinan TG, Cryan JF. (2012) Regulation of the stress response by the gut microbiota: Implications for psychoneuroendocrinology. *Psychoneuroendocrinology*, 37, 1369–1378.

Dinan TG, Stanton C, Cryan JF. (2013) Psychobiotics: A novel class of psychotropic. *Biological Psychiatry*, 74, 720–726.

Dinan TG, Stilling RM, Stanton C, et al. (2015) Collective unconscious: How gut microbes shape human behavior. *Journal of Psychiatric Research*, 63, 1–9.

Dodd DMB. (1989) Reproductive isolation as a consequence of adaptive divergence in *Drosophila pseudoobscura*. *Evolution*, 43, 1308–1311.

Dunn AM, Andrews T, Ingrey H, et al. (2006) Strategic sperm allocation under parasitic sex-ratio distortion. *Biology Letters*, 2, 78–80.

Dyson EA, Hurst GDD. 2004. Persistence of an extreme sex-ratio bias in a natural population. *Proceedings of the National Academy of Sciences*, 101, 6520–6523.

Elgart M, Stern S, Salton O, et al. (2016) Impact of gut microbiota on the fly's germ line. *Nature Communications*, 7, 11280.

Engelstädter J, Hurst GDD. (2009) The ecology and evolution of microbes that manipulate host reproduction. *Annual Review of Ecology and Systematics*, 40, 127–149.

Erkosar B, Storelli G, Mitchell M, et al. (2015) Pathogen virulence impedes mutualist-mediated enhancement of host juvenile growth via inhibition of protein digestion. *Cell Host Microbe*, 18, 445–455.

Evans O, Caragata EP, McMeniman CJ, et al. (2009) Increased locomotor activity and metabolism of *Aedes aegypti* infected with a life-shortening strain of *Wolbachia pipientis*. *Journal of Experimental Biology*, 212, 1436–1441.

Ezenwa VO, Gerardo NM, Inouye DW, et al. (2012) Animal behavior and the microbiome. *Science*, 338, 198–199.

Ezenwa VO, Williams AE. (2014) Microbes and animal olfactory communication: Where do we go from here? *BioEssays*, 36, 847–854.

Falik O, Mordoch Y, Quansah L, et al. (2011) Rumor has it . . .: Relay communication of stress cues in plants. *PLoS ONE*, 6, e23625.

Farine JP, Habbachi W, Cortot J, et al. (2017) Maternally-transmitted microbiota affects odor emission and preference in *Drosophila* larva. *Scientific Reports*, 7, 6062.

Fernandez-Real JM, Serino M, Blasco G, et al. (2015) Gut microbiota interacts with brain microstructure and function. *The Journal of Clinical Endocrinology & Metabolism*, 100, 4505–4513.

Ferveur JF, Cobb M. (2010) Behavioral and evolutionary roles of cuticular hydrocarbons in Diptera. In: Blomqvist GJ, Bagnères AG. (Eds.) *Insect Hydrocarbons*. Cambridge: Cambridge University Press.

Fleury F, Vavre F, Ris N, et al. (2000) Physiological cost induced by the maternally-transmitted endosymbiont *Wolbachia* in the *Drosophila* parasitoid *Leptopilina heterotoma*. *Parasitology*, 121, 493–500.

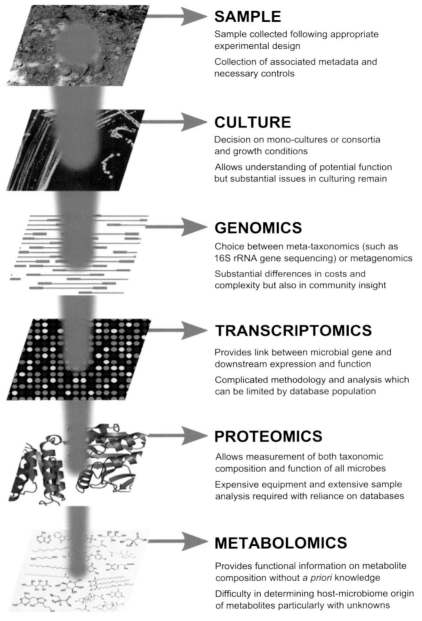

SAMPLE

Sample collected following appropriate experimental design

Collection of associated metadata and necessary controls

CULTURE

Decision on mono-cultures or consortia and growth conditions

Allows understanding of potential function but substantial issues in culturing remain

GENOMICS

Choice between meta-taxonomics (such as 16S rRNA gene sequencing) or metagenomics

Substantial differences in costs and complexity but also in community insight

TRANSCRIPTOMICS

Provides link between microbial gene and downstream expression and function

Complicated methodology and analysis which can be limited by database population

PROTEOMICS

Allows measurement of both taxonomic composition and function of all microbes

Expensive equipment and extensive sample analysis required with reliance on databases

METABOLOMICS

Provides functional information on metabolite composition without *a priori* knowledge

Difficulty in determining host-microbiome origin of metabolites particularly with unknowns

Figure 2.1 Schematic of tools available to researchers interesting in exploring traits of microbiome structure and function. Note the hierarchical nature of these tools, from raw sample to proteomics and metabolomics. We briefly summarise the advantages and disadvantages of each tool, which are expanded upon in the main text (figure compiled by Simon Cameron from images in the public domain). (A black and white version of this figure will appear in some formats.)

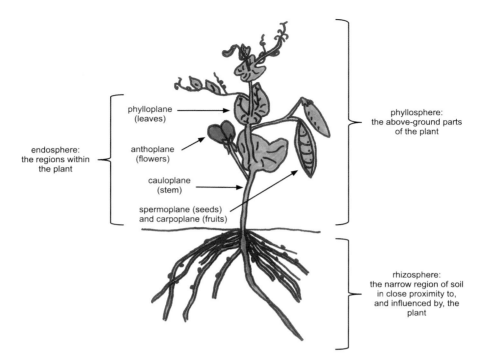

Figure 4.1 Niche environments of plants that are colonised by microbial communities (illustration by Elizabeth Meade and Rachael Antwis). (A black and white version of this figure will appear in some formats.)

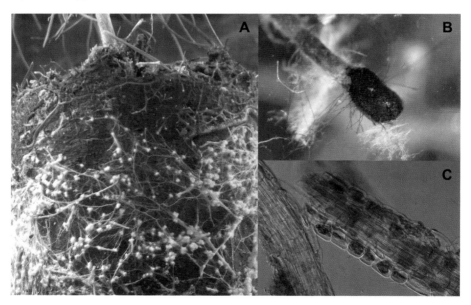

Figure 8.1 Mycorrhizal colonisation of plant roots at different scales. (A) Ectomycorrhizal fungal colonisation of *Pinus sylvestris* (photo credit: Joshua Harrop); (B) ectomycorrhizal fungal colonisation of *Cenococcum geophilum* (black) on *Pinus sylvestris* roots, with a second ectomycorrhizal coloniser visible (white) (photo credit: David Johnson); (C) ericoid mycorrhizal colonisation of *Vaccinium vitis-idaea* root, with mycorrhiza stained blue (photo credit: Ully Kritzler). (A black and white version of this figure will appear in some formats.)

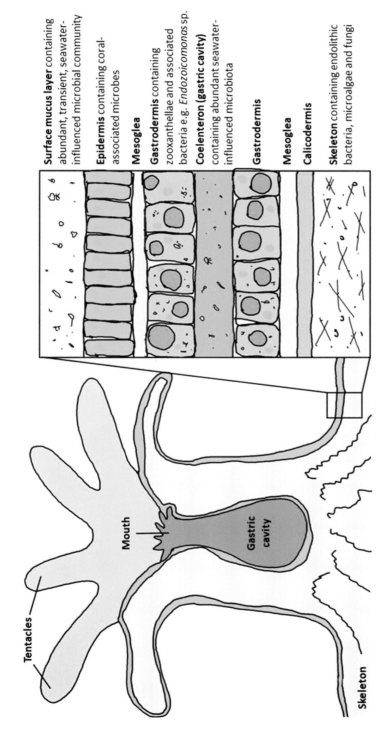

Figure 8.2 Schematic illustration of the coral holobiont depicting a cross-section of a coral polyp and microbial symbionts associated with various compartments: surface mucus layer, epidermis, mesoglea, gastrodermis, gastric cavity, calicodermis and skeleton (illustration by Bethan Greenwood, adapted from Bourne et al., 2016). (A black and white version of this figure will appear in some formats.)

Healthy microbiome
Pathobiome

Coral → Zooxanthellae
Habitat provision
Nitrogenous waste
Expulsion (bleaching)
leading to coral
starvation

Coral → Microbes
Carbon and nutrient
source for microbes
(coral heterotrophy)
Excess DOC, bacterial
opportunism

Microbes → Coral
Nitrogen fixation
Vitamins and minerals
Pathogen inhibition
Reduced antibacterial
capacity
Opportunistic
pathogens
Increased alpha
diversity
Less structured
microbial community
Disease

Microbes → Zooxanthellae
Fixed N from diazotrophs
Nutrient exchange
Less *Endozoicomonas* sp.
Reduced nutrient translocation

Zooxanthellae → Coral
Carbon fixation
(autotrophy)
Oxidative stress
(ROS)

Zooxanthellae → Microbes
Fixed C from autotrophy
DMSP production structures microbiota
Reduced carbon translocation

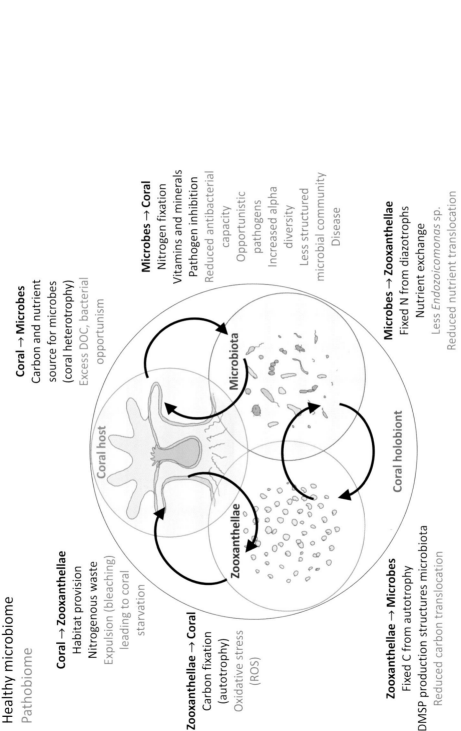

Figure 8.3 Conceptual figure showing purported roles of the coral host and associated microbiome, including both zooxanthellae and other microbiota within the coral holobiont. Functions of a healthy microbiome are shown in black text, and impaired functions due to a disease-associated microbiome or 'pathobiome' (Sweet & Bulling, 2017) during times of environmental stress in pale grey (illustration by Bethan Greenwood, adapted from Vega Thurber et al., 2009). (A black and white version of this figure will appear in some formats.)

Flores R, Shi J, Fuhrman B, et al. (2012) Fecal microbial determinants of fecal and systemic estrogens and estrogen metabolites: A cross-sectional study. *Journal of Translational Medicine*, 10, 1–11.

Forbey JS, Harvey AL, Huffman MA, et al. (2009) Exploitation of secondary metabolites by animals: A response to homeostatic challenges. *Integrative and Comparative Biology*, 49, 314–328.

Foster JA, McVey Neufeld KA. (2013) Gut–brain axis: How the microbiome influences anxiety and depression. *Trends in Neurosciences*, 36, 305–312.

Fox C, Eichelberger K. (2015) Maternal microbiome and pregnancy outcomes. *Fertility and Sterility*, 104, 1358–1363.

Franasiak JM, Scott RT. (2015a) Microbiome in human reproduction. *Fertility and Sterility*, 104, 1341–1343.

Franasiak JM, Scott RT. (2015b) Reproductive tract microbiome in assisted reproductive technologies. *Fertility and Sterility*, 104, 1364–1371.

Frohlich EE, Farzi A, Mayerhofer R, et al. (2016) Cognitive impairment by antibiotic-induced gut dysbiosis: Analysis of gut microbiota–brain communication. *Brain, Behavior, and Immunity*, 56, 140–155.

Gareau MG, Wine E, Rodrigues DM, et al. (2011) Bacterial infection causes stress-induced memory dysfunction in mice. *Gut*, 60, 307–317.

Gareau M. (2014) Microbiota–gut–brain axis and cognitive function. In: Lyte M, Cryan J. (Eds.) *Microbial Endocrinology: The Microbiota–Gut–Brain Axis in Health and Disease*. Advances in Experimental Medicine and Biology. New York, NY: Springer.

Gavriel S, Jurkevitch E, Gazit Y, et al. (2011) Bacterially enriched diet improves sexual performance of sterile male Mediterranean fruit flies. *Journal of Applied Entomology*, 135, 564–573.

Gegear RJ, Otterstatter MC, Thomson JD. (2006) Bumble-bee foragers infected by a gut parasite have an impaired ability to utilize floral information. *Proceedings of the Royal Society B: Biological Sciences*, 273, 1073–1078.

Gorman ML. (1976) A mechanism for individual recognition by odour in *Herpestes auropunctatus* (Carnivora: Viverridae). *Animal Behaviour*, 24, 141–145.

Gotah T, Noda H, Hong XY. (2003) Wolbachia distribution and cytoplasmic incompatibility based on a survey of 42 spider mite species (Acari: Tetranychidae) in Japan. *Heredity*, 91, 208–216.

Goyal MS, Venkatesh S, Milbrandt J, et al. (2015) Feeding the brain and nurturing the mind: Linking nutrition and the gut microbiota to brain development. *Proceedings of the National Academy of Sciences*, 112, 14105–14112.

Hadley NF. (1981) Cuticular lipids of terrestrial plants and arthropods: A comparison of their structure, composition, and waterproofing function. *Biological Reviews*, 56, 23–47.

Haegeman A, Vanholme B, Jacob J, et al. (2009) An endosymbiotic bacterium in a plant-parasitic nematode: Member of a new *Wolbachia* supergroup. *International Journal for Parasitology*, 39, 1045–1054.

Heijtz RD, Wang S, Anuar F, et al. (2011) Normal gut microbiota modulates brain development and behavior. *Proceedings of the National Academy of Sciences*, 108, 3047–3052.

Helletsgruber C, Dötterl S, Ruprecht U, et al. (2017) Epiphytic bacteria alter floral scent emissions. *Journal of Chemical Ecology*, 43, 1073–1077.

Heys C, Lizé A, Colinet H, et al. (2018) Evidence that the microbiota counteracts male outbreeding strategy by inhibiting sexual signaling in females. *Frontiers in Ecology and Evolution*, 6, 29.

Hilgenboecker K, Hammerstein P, Schlattmann P, et al. (2008) How many species are infected with *Wolbachia*? A statistical analysis of current data. *FEMS Microbiology Letters*, 281, 215–220.

Hoban AE, Stilling RM, Moloney G, et al. (2018) The microbiome regulates amygdala-dependent fear recall. *Molecular Psychiatry*, 23, 1134–1144.

Hoffmann AA, Turelli M, Simmons GM. (1986) Unidirectional incompatibility between populations of *Drosophila simulans*. *Evolution*, 40, 692–701.

Hoogland ICM, Houbolt C, van Westerloo DJ, et al. (2015) Systemic inflammation and microglial activation: Systematic review of animal experiments. *Journal of Neuroinflammation*, 12, 114.

Hooper LV, Littman DR, Macpherson AJ. (2012) Interactions between the microbiota and the immune system. *Science*, 336, 1268–1273.

Hoover K, Grove M, Gardner M, et al. (2011) A gene for an extended phenotype. *Science*, 333, 1401.

Hortal S, Plett KL, Plett JM, et al. (2017) Role of plant–fungal nutrient trading and host control in determining the competitive success of ectomycorrhizal fungi. *The ISME Journal*, 11, 2666–2676.

Hosokawa T, Kikuchi Y, Shimada M, et al. 2007. Symbiont acquisition alters behaviour of stinkbug nymphs. *Biology Letters*, 4, 45–48.

Hsiao EY, McBride SW, Hsien S, et al. (2013) Microbiota modulate behavioral and physiological abnormalities associated with neurodevelopmental disorders. *Cell*, 155, 1451–1463.

Huang JH, Douglas AE. (2015) Consumption of dietary sugar by gut bacteria determines *Drosophila* lipid content. *Biology Letters*, 11, 20150469.

Hughes DP, Andersen SB, Hywel-Jones NL, et al. (2011) Behavioral mechanisms and morphological symptoms of zombie ants dying from fungal infection. *BMC Ecology*, 11, 13.

Hughes DP, Araújo JPM, Loreto RG, et al. (2016) From so simple a beginning: The evolution of behavioral manipulation by fungi. In: Lovett B, St Leger RJ. (Eds.) *Genetics and Molecular Biology of Entomopathogenic Fungi, Advances in Genetics*. New York, NY: Academic Press.

Humber R. (1982) *Strongwellsea* vs. *Erynia*: The case for a phylogenetic classification of the Entomophthorales (Zygomycetes). *Mycotaxon*, 15, 167–184.

Hurst GDD, Graf von der Schulenburg JH, Majerus TM, et al. (1999) Invasion of one insect species, *Adalia bipunctata*, by two different male-killing bacteria. *Insect Molecular Biology*, 8, 133–139.

Jeyaprakash A, Hoy MA. (2000) Long PCR improves *Wolbachia* DNA amplification: wsp sequences found in 76% of sixty-three arthropod species. *Insect Molecular Biology*, 9, 393–405.

Jiang PF, Zhu T, Gao JD, et al. (2013) The effect of maternal infection on cognitive development and hippocampus neuronal apoptosis, proliferation and differentiation in the neonatal rats. *Neuroscience*, 246, 422–434.

Junker RR, Keller A. (2015) Microhabitat heterogeneity across leaves and flower organs promotes bacterial diversity. *FEMS Microbiology Ecology*, 91, fiv097.

Kamita SG, Nagasaka K, Chua JW, et al. (2005) A baculovirus encoded protein tyrosine phosphatase gene induces enhanced locomotory activity in a lepidopteran host. *Proceedings of the National Academy of Sciences*, 102, 2584–2589.

Katan M, Moon YP, Paik MC, et al. (2013) Infectious burden and cognitive function: The Northern Manhattan study. *Neurology*, 80, 1209–1215.

Kau AL, Ahern PP, Griffin NW, et al. (2011) Human nutrition, the gut microbiome, and immune system: Envisioning the future. *Nature*, 474, 327–336.

Kennedy PJ, Clarke G, O'Neill A, et al. (2014) Cognitive performance in irritable bowel syndrome: Evidence of a stress-related impairment in visuospatial memory. *Psychological Medicine*, 44, 1553–1566.

Kiers ET, Duhamel M, Beesetty Y, et al. (2011) Reciprocal rewards stabilize cooperation in the mycorrhizal symbiosis. *Science*, 333, 880–882.

Kishani Farahani HK, Ashouri A, Goldansaz SH, et al. (2017) Decrease of memory retention in a parasitic wasp: An effect of host manipulation by *Wolbachia*? *Insect Science*, 24, 569–583.

Krimbas CB. (1993) Drosophila subobscura: *Biology, Genetics and Inversion Polymorphism.* Hamburg: Dr Kovac.

Kunc M, Gabrych A, Witkowski JM. (2016) Microbiome impact on metabolism and function of sex, thyroid, growth and parathyroid hormones. *Acta Biochimica Polonica*, 63, 189–201.

Lam K, Babor D, Duthie B, et al. (2007) Proliferating bacterial symbionts on house fly eggs affect oviposition behaviour of adult flies. *Animal Behaviour*, 74, 81–92.

Lee KP, Cory JS, Wilson K, et al. (2006) Flexible diet choice offsets protein costs of pathogen resistance in a caterpillar. *Proceedings of the Royal Society B: Biological Sciences*, 273, 823–829.

Lee K, Mylonakis E. (2017) An intestine-derived neuropeptide controls avoidance behavior in *Caenorhabditis elegans*. *Cell Reports*, 20, 2501–2512.

Lefèvre T, Oliver L, Hunter MD, et al. (2010) Evidence for trans-generational medication in nature. *Ecology Letters*, 13, 1485–1493.

Leftwich PT, Clarke NVE, Hutchings MI, et al. (2017) Gut microbiomes and reproductive isolation in *Drosophila*. *Proceedings of the National Academy of Sciences*, 114, 12767–12772.

Leitão-Gonçalves R, Carvalho-Santos Z, Francisco AP, et al. (2017) Commensal bacteria and essential amino acids control food choice behavior and reproduction. *PLoS Biology*, 15, e2000862.

Ley RE, Bäckhead F, Turnbaugh P, et al. (2005) Obesity alters gut microbial ecology. *Proceedings of the National Academy of Sciences*, 102, 11070–11075.

Ley RE, Turnbaugh PJ, Klein S, et al. (2006) Microbial ecology: Human gut microbes associated with obesity. *Nature*, 444, 1022–1023.

Liang S, Wang T, Hu X, et al. (2015) Administration of *Lactobacillus helveticus* NS8 improves behavioral, cognitive and biochemical aberrations caused by chronic restraints stress. *Neuroscience*, 310, 561–577.

Libersat F, Delago A, Gal R. (2009) Manipulation of host behavior by parasitic insects and insect parasites. *Annual Review of Entomology*, 54, 189–207.

Lizé A, McKay R, Lewis Z. (2013) Gut microbiota and kin recognition. *Trends in Ecology & Evolution*, 28, 325–326.

Lizé A, McKay R, Lewis, Z. (2014) Kin recognition in *Drosophila*: The importance of ecology and gut bacteria. *The ISME Journal*, 8, 469–477.

Lowry CA, Smith DG, Siebler PH, et al. (2018) The microbiota, immunoregulation, and mental health: Implications for public health. *Current Environmental Health Reports*, 3, 270–286.

Lu B, Nagappan G, Guan X, et al. (2013) BDNF-based synaptic repair as a disease-modifying strategy for neurodegenerative diseases. *Nature Reviews Neuroscience*, 14, 401–416.

Lyte M. (2013) Microbial endocrinology in the microbiome–gut–brain axis: How bacterial production and utilization of neurochemicals influence behavior. *PLoS Pathogens*, 9, e1003726.

Martin FM, Uroz S, Barker DG. (2017) Ancestral alliances: Plant mutualistic symbiosis with fungi and bacteria. *Science*, 356, 819.

Matthews DM, Jenks SM. (2013) Ingestion of *Mycobacterium vaccae* decreases anxiety-related behavior and improves learning in mice. *Behavioural Processes*, 96, 27–35.

Mayer EA, Knight R, Mazmanian SK, et al. (2014) Gut microbes and the brain: Paradigm shift in neuroscience. *Journal of Neuroscience*, 34, 15490–15496.

McEwen BS. (2008) Central effects of stress hormones in health and disease: Understanding the protective and damaging effects of stress and stress mediators. *European Journal of Pharmacology*, 583, 174–185.

Messaoudi M, Lalonde R, Violle N, et al. (2011) Assessment of psychotropic-like properties of a probiotic formulation (*Lactobacillus helveticus* R0052 and *Bifidobacterium longum* R0175) in rats and human subjects. *British Journal of Nutrition*, 105, 755–764.

Miller W, Ehrman L, Schneider D. (2010) Infection speciation revisited: Impact of symbionts-depletion on female fitness and mating behaviour of *Drosophila paulistorum*. *PLoS Pathogens*, 6, e1001214.

Miller EA, Livermore JA, Alberts SC, et al. (2017) Ovarian cycling and reproductive state shape the vaginal microbiota in wild baboons. *Microbiome*, 5, 1–14.

Minkley N, Fujita A, Brune A, et al. (2006) Nest specificity of the bacterial community in termite guts (*Hodotermes mossambicus*). *Insectes Sociaux*, 53, 339–344.

Moeller A, Foerster S, Wilson M, et al. (2016) Social behavior shapes the chimpanzee pan-microbiome. *Science Advances*, 2, e1500997.

Moora M, Öpik M, Zobel M. (2004) Performance of two *Centaurea* species in response to different root-associated microbial communities and to alterations in nutrient availability. *Annales Botanici Fennici*, 41, 263–271.

Moore J. (1995) The behavior of parasitized animals. *BioScience*, 45, 89–96.

Najarro MA, Sumethasorn M, Lamoureux A, et al. (2015) Choosing mates based on the diet of your ancestors: Replication of non-genetic assortative mating in *Drosophila melanogaster*. *PeerJ*, 3, e1173.

Neufeld KM, Kang N, Bienenstock J, et al. (2011) Reduced anxiety-like behavior and central neurochemical change in germ-free mice. *Neurogastroenterology and Motility*, 23, 255–264.

Noguera JC, Aira M, Pérez-Losada M, et al. (2018) Glucocorticoids modulate gastrointestinal microbiome in a wild bird. *Royal Society Open Science*, 5, 171743.

O'Brien ME, Anderson H, Kaukel E, et al. (2004) SRL172 (killed *Mycobacterium vaccae*) in addition to standard chemotherapy improves quality of life without affecting survival, in patients with advanced non-small-cell lung cancer: Phase III results. *Annals of Oncology*, 15, 906–914.

O'Neill SL, Hoffmann AA, Werren JH. (1997) *Influential Passengers: Inherited Microorganisms and Arthropod Reproduction*. Oxford: Oxford University Press.

Ohland CL, Kish L, Bell H, et al. (2013) Effects of *Lactobacillus helveticus* on murine behavior are dependent on diet and genotype and correlate with alterations in the gut microbiome. *Psychoneuroendocrinology*, 38, 1738–1747.

Parois S, Calandreau L, Kraimi N, et al. (2017) The influence of a probiotic supplementation on memory in quail suggests a role of gut microbiota on cognitive abilities in birds. *Behavioural Brain Research*, 331, 47–53.

Peng Y, Nielsen JE, Cunningham JP, et al. (2008) *Wolbachia* infection alters olfactory-cued locomotion in *Drosophila* spp. *Applied and Environmental Microbiology*, 74, 3943–3948.

Pineda A, Kaplan I, Bezemer TM. (2017) Steering soil microbiomes to suppress aboveground insect pests. *Trends in Plant Science*, 22, 770–778.

Plett JM, Martin FM. (2017) Know your enemy, embrace your friend: Using omics to understand how plants respond differently to pathogenic and mutualistic microorganisms. *The Plant Journal*, 93, 729–746.

Poirotte C, Kappeler PM, Ngoubangoye B, et al. (2016) Morbid attraction to leopard urine in *Toxoplasma*-infected chimpanzees. *Current Biology*, 26, 98–99.

Poulin R. (1995) 'Adaptive' changes in the behaviour of parasitized animals: A critical review. *International Journal for Parasitology*, 25, 1371–1383.

Poulin R. (2010) Parasite manipulation of host behaviour: An update and frequently asked questions. In: Brockmann J, Roper TJ, Naguib M, et al. (Eds.) *Advances in the Study of Behaviour*. New York, NY: Academic Press.

Rhoades DF. (1983) Responses of alder and willow to attack by tent caterpillars and webworms: evidence for pheromonal sensitivity of willows. In: Hedin PA. (Ed.) *Plant Resistance to Insects*. Washington, DC: American Chemical Society Symposium Series.

Ridlon JM, Ikegawa S, Alves JMP, et al. (2013) *Clostridium scindens*: A human gut microbe with a high potential to convert glucocorticoids into androgens. *The Journal of Lipid Research*, 54, 2437–49.

Roager HM, Licht TR. (2018) Microbial tryptophan catabolites in health and disease. *Nature Communications*, 9, 3294.

Romijn AR, Rucklidge JJ. (2015) Systematic review of evidence to support the theory of psychobiotics. *Nutrition Reviews*, 73, 675–693.

Rosenberg E, Zilber-Rosenberg I. (2016) Microbes drive evolution of animals and plants: The hologenome concept. *mBio*, 7, e01395–15.

Rousseaux C, Thuru X, Gelot A, et al. (2007) *Lactobacillus acidophilus* modulates intestinal pain and induces opioid and cannabinoid receptors. *Nature Methods*, 13, 35–37.

Rousset F, Bouchon D, Pintereau B, et al. (1992) *Wolbachia* endosymbionts responsible for various alterations of sexuality in arthropods. *Proceedings of the Royal Society B: Biological Sciences*, 250, 91–98.

Sachs JL, Russell JE, Lii YE, et al. (2010) Host control over infection and proliferation of a cheater symbiont. *Journal of Evolutionary Biology*, 23, 1919–1927.

Sampson TR, Mazmanian SK. (2015) Control of brain development, function, and behavior by the microbiome. *Cell Host Microbe*, 17, 565–576.

Sanchez MI, Ponton F, Schmidt-Rhaesa A, et al. (2008) Two steps to suicide in crickets harbouring hairworms. *Animal Behaviour*, 76, 1621–1624.

Sandrini S, Aldriwesh M, Alruways M, et al. (2015) Microbial endocrinology: Host-

bacteria communication within the gut microbiome. *Journal of Endocrinology* 225, R21–R34.

Sarkar A, Lehto SM, Harty S, et al. (2016) Psychobiotics and the manipulation of bacteria–gut–brain signals. *Trends in Neurosciences*, 39, 763–781.

Savignac HM, Kiely B, Dinan TG, et al. (2014) *Bifidobacteria* exert strain-specific effects on stress-related behaviour and physiology in BALB/c mice. *Neurogastroenterology and Motility*, 26, 1615–1627.

Savignac HM, Tramullas M, Kiely B, et al. (2015) *Bifidobacteria* modulate cognitive processes in an anxious mouse strain. *Behavioural Brain Research*, 287, 59–72.

Schwarzer M, Makki K, Storelli G, et al. (2016) *Lactobacillus plantarum* strain maintains growth of infant mice during chronic undernutrition. *Science*, 351, 854–857.

Sharon G, Garg N, Debelius J, et al. (2014) Specialized metabolites from the microbiome in health and disease. *Cell Metabolism*, 20, 719–730.

Sharon G, Segal D, Ringo JM, et al. (2010) Commensal bacteria play a role in mating preference of *Drosophila melanogaster*. *Proceedings of the National Academy of Sciences*, 107, 20051–20056.

Shin SC, Kim S-H, You H, et al. (2011) *Drosophila* microbiome modulates host developmental and metabolic homeostasis via insulin signaling. *Science*, 334, 670–674.

Shropshire JD, Bordenstein SR. (2016) Speciation by symbiosis: The microbiome and behaviour. *mBio*, 7, e01785–15.

Simpson SJ, Raubenheimer D. (2012) *The Nature of Nutrition*. Princeton, NJ: Princeton University Press.

Sin YW, Buesching CD, Burke T, et al. (2012) Molecular characterization of the microbial communities in the subcaudal gland secretion of the European badger (*Meles meles*). *FEMS Microbiology Ecology*, 81, 648–659.

Smith MI, Yatsunenko T, Manary MJ, et al. (2013) Gut microbiomes of Malawian twin pairs discordant for kwashiorkor. *Science*, 339, 548–554.

Soderholm JD, Yang PC, Ceponis P, et al. (2002) Chronic stress induces mast cell-dependent bacterial adherence and initiates mucosal inflammation in rat intestine. *Gastroenterology*, 123, 1099–1108.

Soper RS. (1963) *Massospora laevispora*, a new species of fungus pathogenic to the cicada, *Okanagana rimosa*. *Revue Canadienne de Botanique*, 41, 875–878.

Soper RS, Delyzer AJ, Smith FLR. (1976) The genus *Massospora*, entomopathogenic for cicadas. Part. II. Biology of *Massospora levispora* and its host *Okanagana rimosa*, with notes on *Massospora cicadina* on the periodical cicadas. *Annals of the Entomological Society of America*, 69, 88–95.

Steiger S. (2012) New synthesis – Visual and chemical ornaments: What researchers of signal modalities can learn from each other. *Journal of Chemical Ecology*, 38, 1.

Stilling RM, Moloney GM, Ryan FJ, et al. (2018) Social interaction-induced activation of RNA splicing in the amygdala of microbiome-deficient mice. *eLife*, 7, e33070.

Storelli G, Defaye A, Erkosar B, et al. (2011) *Lactobacillus plantarum* promotes *Drosophila* systemic growth by modulating hormonal signals through TOR-dependent nutrient sensing. *Cell Metabolism*, 14, 403–414.

Stothart MR, Bobbie CB, Schulte-Hostedde AI, et al. (2016) Stress and the microbiome: Linking glucocorticoids to bacterial community dynamics in wild red squirrels. *Biology Letters*, 12, 2016–2019.

Stouthamer R, Breeuwer JA, Hurst GDD. (1999) *Wolbachia pipientis*: Microbial manipulator of arthropod reproduction. *Annual Review of Microbiology*, 53, 71–102.

Stouthamer R, Luck RE, Hamilton WD. (1990) Antibiotics cause parthenogenetic *Trichogramma* (Hymenoptera: Trichogrammatidae) to revert to sex. *Proceedings of the National Academy of Sciences*, 87, 2424–2427.

Subramanian S, Blanton LV, Frese SA, et al. (2015) Cultivating healthy growth and nutrition through the gut microbiota. *Cell*, 161, 36–48.

Sudo N. (2014) Microbiome, HPA axis and production of endocrine hormones in the gut. In: Lyte M, Cryan J. (Eds.) *Microbial Endocrinology: The Microbiota–Gut–Brain Axis in Health and Disease*. Advances in Experimental Medicine and Biology. New York, NY: Springer.

Swartz T, Duca F, de Wouters T, et al. (2012) Up-regulation of intestinal type 1 taste receptor 3 and sodium glucose luminal transporter-1 expression and increased sucrose intake in mice lacking gut microbiota. *British Journal of Nutrition*, 107, 621–630.

Theis KR, Schmidt TM, Holekamp KE. (2012) Evidence for a bacterial mechanism for group-specific social odors among hyenas. *Scientific Reports*, 2, 615.

Theis KR, Venkataraman A, Dycus JA, et al. (2013) Symbiotic bacteria appear to mediate hyena social signals. *Proceedings of the National Academy of Sciences*, 110, 19832–19837.

Thomas F, Schmidt-Rhaesa A, Martin G, et al. (2002) Do hairworms (Nematomorpha) manipulate the water seeking behaviour of their terrestrial hosts? *Journal of Evolutionary Biology*, 15, 356–361.

Trewavas A. (2009) What is plant behaviour? *Plant, Cell & Environment*, 32, 606–616.

Trewavas A. (2017) The foundations of plant intelligence. *Interface Focus*, 7, 20160098.

Tung J, Barreiro L, Burns M, et al. (2015) Social networks predict gut microbiome composition in wild baboons. *eLife*, 4, e05224.

Turnbaugh PJ, Ley RE, Mahowald MA, et al. (2006) An obesity-associated gut microbiome with increased capacity for energy harvest. *Nature*, 444, 1027–1131.

Turnbaugh PJ, Hamady M, Yatsunenko T, et al. (2009) A core gut microbiome in obese and lean twins. *Nature*, 457, 480–484.

Vala F, Egas M, Breeuwer JAJ, et al. (2004) *Wolbachia* affects oviposition and mating behaviour of its spider mite host. *Journal of Evolutionary Biology*, 17, 692–700.

Vandenkoornhuyse P, Quaiser A, Duhamel M, et al. (2015) The importance of the microbiome of the plant holobiont. *New Phytologist*, 206, 1196–1206.

Venu I, Durisko Z, Xu J, et al. (2014) Social attraction mediated by fruit flies' microbiome. *Journal of Experimental Biology*, 217, 1346–1352.

Vijay-Kumar M, Aitken JD, Carvalho FA, et al. (2010) Metabolic syndrome and altered gut microbiota in mice lacking toll-like receptor 5. *Science*, 328, 228–231.

Vlčková K, Shutt-Phillips K, Heistermann M, et al. (2018) Impact of stress on the gut microbiome of free-ranging western lowland gorillas. *Microbiology*, 164, 40–44.

Vuong HE, Yano JM, Fung TC, et al. (2017) The microbiome and host behavior. *Annual Review of Neuroscience*, 40, 21–49.

Wada-Katsumata A, Zurek L, Nalyanya G, et al. (2015) Gut bacteria mediate aggregation in the German cockroach. *Proceedings of the National Academy of Sciences*, 112, 15678–15683.

Wall R, Cryan JF, Ross RP, et al. (2014) Bacterial neuroactive compounds produced by psychobiotics. *Advances in Experimental Medicine and Biology*, 817, 221–239.

Walsh BS, Heys C, Lewis Z. (2017) Gut microbiota influences female choice and fecundity in the nuptial gift-giving species, *Drosophila subobscura* (Diptera: Drosophilidae). *European Journal of Entomology*, 114, 439–445.

Wang T, Hu X, Liang S, et al. (2015) *Lactobacillus fermentum* NS9 restores the antibiotic induced physiological and psychological abnormalities in rats. *Beneficial Microbes*, 6, 707–717.

Werner GDA, Cornwell WK, Sprent JI, et al. (2014) A single evolutionary innovation drives the deep evolution of symbiotic N_2 fixation in angiosperms. *Nature Communications*, 5, 4087.

Werren JH, Baldo L, Clark ME. (2008) *Wolbachia*: Master manipulators of invertebrate biology. *Nature Reviews Microbiology*, 6, 741–751.

Witting PA. (1979) Learning capacity and memory of normal and *Toxoplasma*-infected laboratory rats and mice. *Zeitschrift fur Parasitenkunde*, 61, 29–51.

Wong CNA, Ng P, Douglas AE. (2011) Low-diversity bacterial community in the gut of the fruit fly Drosophila melanogaster. *Environmental Microbiology*, 13, 1889–1900.

Wong AC-N, Holmes A, Ponton F, et al. (2015) Behavioral microbiomics: A multi-dimensional approach to microbial influence on behavior. *Frontiers in Microbiology*, 6, 1359.

Wong AC-N, Wang Q-P, Morimoto J, et al. (2017) Gut microbiota modifies olfactory-guided microbial preferences and foraging decisions in *Drosophila*. *Current Biology*, 27, 2397–2404.

Wyatt TD. (2014) *Pheromones and Animal Behaviour: Chemical Signals and Signature Mixes*. Cambridge: Cambridge University Press.

Yamada R, Deshpande SA, Bruce KD, et al. (2015) Microbes promote amino acid harvest to rescue undernutrition in *Drosophila*. *Cell Reports*, 10, 865–872.

Zareie M, Johnson-Henry K, Jury J, et al. (2006) Probiotics prevent bacterial translocation and improve intestinal barrier function in rats following chronic psychological stress. *Gut*, 55, 1553–1560.

Zhang Y, Lu H, Bargmann CI. (2005) Pathogenic bacteria induce aversive olfactory learning in *Caenorhabditis elegans*. *Nature*, 438, 179–184.

CHAPTER SEVEN

Host microbiomes and disease

JAMES E. MCDONALD
Bangor University
REID N. HARRIS
James Madison University, Harrisonburg
JAMES DOONAN
Bangor University
SOPHIA CARRYL
University of Chicago
MARC SZE
University of Michigan
VALERIE MCKENZIE
University of Colorado
and
JACK A. GILBERT
University of Chicago

7.1 Introduction

The germ theory, which proposed that microorganisms are the cause of infectious disease, was first identified by Louis Pasteur and further developed by Henle and Koch, who devised a series of postulates that represent a standard to ascribe causality of particular organisms in disease. The Henle–Koch postulates specify that the suspected causal microorganism: (1) must occur in every instance of the disease; (2) must not be found in healthy individuals; (3) can be isolated and propagated from a diseased individual, and when inoculated into a healthy host, the microorganism can cause disease anew; and (4) the same pathogen strain used to experimentally infect the host must be re-isolated from the individual. Consequently, the prevailing paradigm has been that disease causation is often mediated by single primary pathogenic agents, often encouraging focus on the cultivation and genetic manipulation of an individual species in order to address disease causality (Autenrieth, 2017). However, it is well known that a large proportion of microbes cannot be isolated and cultivated in the laboratory using conventional approaches. In addition, other pathogens cannot be grown in axenic culture (e.g. viruses), cannot be tested in infection models due to a restricted host range or may instead cause subclinical infection (Fredericks & Relman, 1996). Indeed, Robert Koch also experienced limitations on strict adherence to the postulates due to an inability to isolate *Mycobacterium leprae*, the causal agent of leprosy, from infected hosts, thus preventing fulfilment of the third and fourth postulates. Furthermore, *Vibrio cholerae*, the cause of cholera, was isolated from both healthy and diseased individuals, contravening the second postulate (Fredericks & Relman, 1996).

In contrast, environmental microbial ecology studies have made use of molecular surveys to recognise the importance of entire microbial communities and their syntrophic interactions in ecosystem function, a concept that has been rapidly translated and applied in research on host-associated microbiota (Young, 2017). It is now clear that many diseases of plants and animals are associated with changes in the taxonomic composition and function of the microbiome, and that health and disease are mediated by a dynamic interplay between host factors (including genetics, physiology and immunity), environmental factors (including biotic and abiotic agents), the host microbiota and pathogenic microorganisms. Consequently, understanding these complex host–microbiota and microbiota–microbiota interactions and their influence on health status and disease susceptibility is critical for the maintenance of host homeostasis and for the diagnosis, treatment and prevention of disease. Advances in methodologies for the analysis of host-associated microbiomes has demonstrated the complex and sometimes polymicrobial nature of disease causation. For instance, domestic turkeys co-infected with *Chlamydophila* and *Escherichia coli* suffered greater health deterioration than those infected with a single species (Poiani, 2010). Consequently, several revisions of Koch's postulates have been proposed to incorporate contemporary methodologies and scientific findings that cannot be accommodated by strict adherence to the original postulates (Rivers, 1937; Evans, 1976; Falkow, 1988; Fredericks & Relman, 1996; Autenrieth, 2017). Byrdand Segre (2016) recently evaluated these in light of advances in analytical technologies and their application in microbiome studies, highlighting that the 'one pathogen = one disease' paradigm is not always appropriate. In addition to the direct causation of infectious disease through the activity of a primary pathogen or a microbiome associated with disease (a 'pathobiome'), the role of the microbiota as a contributor or causal agent of chronic disease is also well established (Autenrieth, 2017). For example, positive interactions between a pathogen and either a single pathogen promoter species or a group of microorganisms can facilitate the aetiology of disease. However, there are also scenarios where a challenge by a pathogen does not result in disease due to the presence of a commensal microorganism that protects the host via a process called 'colonisation resistance'. A protective organism or community prevents disease through direct inhibition of the pathogen, or by stimulating host immunity, presenting opportunities to utilise microbiome analysis to identify situations in which disease cannot be induced in the host. Furthermore, microbial consortia also play important roles in colonisation resistance, as demonstrated by the success of faecal transplants for the treatment of *Clostridium difficile* infection. Thus, these scenarios lead to a discussion of how microbial consortia can fulfil Koch's postulates, and how we can adapt these ideas to use contemporary technologies in a systems biology approach to better understand the role of microbiomes in health and disease (see Chapter 2).

A key challenge in microbiome research is disentangling whether changes in microbiome composition are associated with causation of the disease state, or if they are secondary to the cause of disease. To understand this, the isolation and cultivation of members of the microbiota are still essential. In plant biology, combinations of microbiome and infectivity studies, made possible by the high culturability of plant-associated microbiota (Finkel et al., 2017), have enabled fascinating insights into the role of polymicrobial consortia in disease (Denman et al., 2018). Understanding how the microbiome can influence health and disease susceptibility is a rapidly developing area of microbiome research and represents a promising approach for the diagnosis, prevention and treatment of disease. Consequently, the opportunity to directly manipulate the host microbiota is a tantalising challenge with significant potential. A variety of approaches have been tested, including the application of antibiotics, bacteriophages, synthetic communities, prebiotics, probiotics and microbiome transplants (see Chapter 9 for more). Agriculturalists, veterinarians and clinical professionals are starting to consider the microbial inhabitants of their respective ecosystems as essential components of the machine. This is leading to a professional revolution whereby microbial ecology and ecological analysis are becoming paramount for all aspects of plant cultivation, animal husbandry and medical practice. However, we are only just starting to understand how the microbiome influences disease and health in animals and plants. This chapter will consider current knowledge on the role of plant and animal microbiomes in health status and disease susceptibility, in addition to highlighting contemporary approaches for manipulating the host microbiome in order to prevent or treat disease.

7.2 The role of the microbiome in disease prevention

Each individual in a population has a unique and variable microbial community (Raveh-Sadka et al., 2015; Zhu et al., 2015); a unique strain-level assemblage of bacteria, fungi, archaea, viruses and protists that can influence how they respond to the world. This unique microbiome can substantially influence disease susceptibility, as well as responses to treatments and therapies. Gopalakrishnan et al. (2018) provide evidence that human patients with an increase in 'good' gut bacteria showed an improved response to anti-PD-1 immunotherapy compared to patients with unfavourable gut bacteria.

Indeed, the microbes an organism is exposed to can shape their immune system, which in turn can shape the endogenous microbial communities that may be responsible for determining whether a pathogen can establish on a host, or whether a person develops asthma, for example (Stein et al., 2016). The term 'dysbiosis' is often used to describe the shift in microbiome composition between healthy and diseased states within the host; however, interpretations of a dysbiotic state often do not consider if the altered microbiome composition reflects the cause or effect of the disease (Olesen & Alm, 2016), and are not determined by methodological approaches the can determine true shifts in cellular abundance rather than discrepancies in sequence read counts. The ultimate outcome of infection with a pathogen is determined by a combination of host, microbial and environmental interactions. Consequently, virulence is increasingly being observed as an emergent property, where effects on the host are additive and cannot be described by host- or pathogen-centric approaches, as microbial virulence will only occur in a susceptible host, and the same pathogen may be avirulent in another (Casadevall et al., 2011). We will now look at the role that microbiomes of plants and animals can play in disease prevention.

7.2.1 Plants

The plant microbiome is a fundamental driver of plant productivity and health (Turner et al., 2013), contributing significant functional diversity and performing critical roles in host fitness and adaptation through promoting growth and productivity, stress resistance, immune regulation and disease suppression (Berg, 2009; Turner et al., 2013; Berg et al., 2014, 2016). Many diseases of plants are associated with changes in the taxonomic composition and function of the microbiome. Consequently, understanding the complex host–microbiota and microbiota–microbiota interactions, and their influence on health status and disease susceptibility, is critical for the maintenance of host fitness, and for the diagnosis, treatment and prevention of plant disease. Plant microbiota interact with their host according to their lifestyle, which can be characterised as pathogenic or symbiotic (Pérez-Brocal et al., 2013). Strictly speaking, pathogens are symbionts as they live in close proximity and have biological relationships with the host, often only displaying a pathogenic phenotype during certain stages of their life cycle (Hentschel et al., 2000). However, the complexity of host–microbiota relationships has led to definitions of symbionts within this context to exclude disease causation; this leads to further difficulties, as commensals can be opportunistic pathogens (Pérez-Brocal et al., 2013). For this reason, here, symbiotic lifestyles are confined to those with commensalistic, mutualistic or parasitic relationships and exclude pathogens.

Fewer studies have looked at the potential for host microbiomes to mediate disease. However, an interesting example is that of Acute Oak Decline (AOD) in the United Kingdom (Denman et al., 2016; Sapp et al., 2016; Broberg et al., 2018; Denman et al., 2018), a complex decline disease where a combination of several biotic and abiotic factors work in parallel with cumulative effects on host predisposition and health status. Using a combination of traditional culture-based and molecular microbiology techniques, these studies deciphered a bacterial origin of stem tissue necrosis, the primary symptom of AOD, but also identified several taxa that were consistently abundant within the healthy oak cauloplane microbiota, with distinct communities from those recovered within necrotic oak lesions. This switch in taxonomic abundance of specific microbiota indicates dysbiosis, with a consistent microbiota before a transition to pathogenicity in trees with the characteristic symptoms of AOD (Denman et al., 2014, 2018). This shift is marked with high metagenome read counts of epiphytes such as *Perigladula* (Stein et al., 2016) and *Burkholderia* (non-pathogenic here as it is depleted in necrotic lesions; Estrada-De Los Santos et al., 2001), to dominance by the phytopathogenic genus *Brenneria* (Denman et al., 2018). Furthermore, microbiome analysis of horse chestnut (*Aesculus hippocastanum*) stem tissue demonstrated greater diversity of stem microbiota in healthy trees, with a loss of microbial diversity and associated microbiome shift associated with disease (Koskella et al., 2017). These data suggest a protective effect of the healthy host microbiome, with a loss of diversity in symptomatic trees analogous to those observed in human dysbiosis (Feau & Hamelin, 2017).

There is considerable interest in the role of plant microbiomes in protecting hosts from disease due to the potential to exploit these interactions for crop protection (see Section 7.3.1). Examples include the disease-suppressive properties of plant growth–promoting rhizobacteria (e.g. members of the Pseudomonadaceae group) in soils (Mendes et al., 2012; Gopal et al., 2013) through competitive exclusion and the production of antimicrobial compounds. In addition, protective soil microbiomes can also alter the metabolic signatures of above-ground parts of the plant to reduce larval feeding of insect herbivores (Badri et al., 2013). Recently, a remarkable symbiotic interaction has been revealed between a cereal crop, finger millet (*Eleusine coracana*), and a bacterial endophyte (an *Enterobacter* sp. designated 'M6') that confers resistance to the toxin-producing fungal pathogen *Fusarium graminearum* (Mousa et al., 2016). In this novel plant-defence mechanism, the bacterial endophyte (M6) that is associated with the root hairs swarms towards the fungus and causes root hairs to bend in a parallel fashion to the root axis. The resulting multi-layer root hair endophyte stack (RHESt) represents a physical barrier that prevents entry of the fungus, but also provides a habitat where biofilm-like bacterial microcolonies produce fungicidal compounds and demonstrate resistance to antibiotics produced by *Fusarium*. Finger millet is a widely grown cereal crop in Africa and India, and while other cereal crops such as wheat and maize are highly susceptible to disease by *F. graminearum*, finger millet is widely resistant to pathogen infection. The anti-*Fusarium* activity observed in this endophyte–finger millet interaction may therefore be translatable to other cereal species of economic importance (Mousa et al., 2016).

7.2.2 Wildlife

Microbes are part of the defensive repertoire of all wild animals, and research in this area is a rapidly developing field. For example, our knowledge about defensive microbes in invertebrate systems is growing. In pea aphids (*Acyrthosiphon pisum*), defensive microbes and their associated phages can confer protection to their eggs against parasitoid wasps, while other species of bacteria can protect pea aphids against pathogenic fungi (Oliver et al., 2003). There are also examples of insects being protected by bacteria from nematodes and spiders (Oliver et al., 2014), and bacterial species in the cuticle of leafcutter ants produce an antibiotic that targets pathogenic fungi that might otherwise contaminate the beneficial fungi that the ants culture for food (Currie et al., 1999, 2006; Harris et al., 2006). Members of the genus *Hydra* have bacterial species in their epithelium that play a role in defence against pathogenic fungi (Bosch et al., 2009). Similar patterns have also been identified in vertebrates. Bacteria that inhibit the highly lethal *Pseudogymnoascus destructans* (Pd) fungus of North American bats have been identified (Hoyt et al., 2015), such as an inhibitory species of *Rhodococcus* that emits volatile organic compounds that can kill the pathogen, although efficacy in nature has not yet been demonstrated (Cornelison et al., 2014). Other bacterial species inhibit the pathogen in vitro, and concentrations of the bacteria and the pathogen are important in determining the degree of inhibition (Hoyt et al., 2015). Here, we use the case study of amphibians to demonstrate the positive effects of the microbiota on wildlife health.

Most work on defensive microbes and probiotics of vertebrates has been on the amphibian cutaneous microbiota. This work was spurred by the devastating effects of two species of pathogenic chytrid fungi in the genus *Batrachochytrium* (*B. dendrobatidis* and, later, *B. salamandrivorans* – Bd and Bsal, respectively), which have caused global population declines and extinctions across the whole class of amphibians (Scheele et al., 2019). There is considerable variation in how host species are affected by Bd and Bsal, with some species seemingly immune while others readily succumb to the infection, leading to decimated populations and extinction. Therefore, an open question is the degree to which microbial defences are responsible for variation in susceptibility. Most studies to date relate to interactions between the bacterial component of the microbiome and Bd; however, ongoing work is looking at the fungal component of the microbiome, as well as interactions with Bsal (Bates et al., 2019) and ranavirus (Campbell et al., 2019).

One framing hypothesis is that many commensal bacteria on the skin are in fact mutualistic, i.e. the bacteria gain a suitable habitat in terms of space and resources, and the bacteria provide a protective function. A model by Scheuring and Yu (2012) shows that given adequate resources from the host, commensal bacteria grow in population size to the point where they compete via the production of antimicrobial metabolites. Thus, protection of the host from pathogenic invasion may result as a by-product of interference competition of resident bacterial species. This is an appealing model, but it has not been fully tested in the amphibian system, or any other system, to our knowledge. However, aspects of the model have been tested. For example, it has been shown that when two bacterial species from amphibian skin are cultured together in vitro, they produce antibiotic metabolites that are not produced by either species when in monoculture (Loudon et al., 2014a), suggesting that combinations of specific symbiotic bacteria may increase the diversity of antibiotic metabolites that can provide protective function for the host, although this may depend on the pathogen genotype or phenotype (Antwis & Harrison, 2018).

One of the earliest studies of defensive bacteria on amphibians was conducted by Austin (2000) with *Plethodon ventralis* salamanders. Skin bacteria were found to be largely distinct from soil bacteria based on morphological identification, and some were able to inhibit soil bacteria and a fungus (*Cunninghamella echinulate*) isolated from the host gut. Pathogenic fungi that infect embryos are likely to be a major selection factor for amphibians, and it was speculated that antifungal bacteria were vertically transferred to embryos in the nest to reduce mortality. Banning et al. (2008) found that communal nests of *Hemidactylium scutatum* salamanders were more likely than solitary nests to have at least one female with antifungal bacteria, and that females transmitted antifungal bacteria to embryos in their nests. In addition, once a nest was visibly infected with fungi, the presence of antifungal bacteria was significantly positively correlated with embryonic survival. Furthermore, in boreal toads (*Anaxyrus boreas*), bacterial communities on the skin of aquatic larval tadpoles have significantly higher proportion of antifungal taxa relative to later developmental stages, which harboured more diverse fungal taxa (Kueneman et al., 2016). Larval tadpoles do not have fully developed immune functions and recruiting protective skin bacteria, such as the Burkholderiales, during the vulnerable early developmental stages may signal an adaptive strategy for the host. The finding that larval amphibians have different bacterial symbiont communities relative to post-metamorphic life stages has now been observed in a range of host species (Kohl et al., 2013; Kueneman et al., 2014; Vences et al., 2016). Whether larval host stages tend to have bacterial communities selected towards protection from pathogens as a broad pattern across amphibian taxa remains unknown.

Defensive skin microbes of amphibians have been found to inhibit the lethal pathogens Bd and Bsal, starting with a study by Harris et al. (2006). Since then, research into amphibian microbiomes and their interactions with Bd has been a very active field (reviewed in Bletz et al., 2013; Rebollar et al., 2016). Findings have indicated that amphibian cutaneous microbiota could be part of their defensive repertoire and offered the possibility of probiotic manipulation to treat or prevent Bd infections. The protective nature of the skin microbiota was indicated through surveys of bacterially produced metabolites on salamander species in the wild (Brucker et al., 2008). The skins of redback salamanders (*Plethodon cinereus*) had concentrations of violacein and indole-3-carboxaldehyde high enough to inhibit Bd according to minimum inhibitory concentration (MIC) estimates from the laboratory. These metabolites are not known to be produced by vertebrates, but a bacterial species that does produce these (*Janthinobacterium lividum*) was found on the salamanders. In addition, the production of these metabolites suggested that the bacterial producers were at a relatively high population density. Bacterially-produced metabolites may also inhibit pathogen colonisation because Bd displays negative chemotaxis towards some of these (Lam et al., 2011). That said, experimental removal of the microbiome and subsequent infection by Bd in two amphibian hosts (*P. cinereus* and *Lithobathes catesbeiana*) did not lead to decreased survivorship or increased infection intensities compared with hosts with their microbiome intact, although growth rates were negatively affected in both (Harris et al., 2009b; Becker & Harris, 2010). However, there is convincing evidence of microbial signatures of resistance to Bd from laboratory and field trials. Jani and Briggs (2014) used a matched laboratory and field study to show that particular bacterial taxa were systematically more (*Rubrivivax*, *Undibacterium*) or less (*Rhodococcus*, *Sanguibacter*, *Stentrophomonas*, *Pseudomonas*, *Microbacterium*, *Methylotenera*) abundant in experimentally and naturally infected populations of *Rana sierrae*. Becker et al. (2015) found that the microbiota on Panamanian golden frogs (*Atelopus zeteki*) before exposure to Bd strongly predicted survival, with members of the families Flavobacteriaceae, Sphingobacteriaceae, Commonadaceae and Rhodocyclaceae enriched in the communities of surviving frogs. Similarly, Walke et al. (2015) found that bacterial community structure before infection was found to be correlated with Bd infection intensity, which was related to growth rate of bullfrogs (*L. catesbeianus*). Together these studies indicate that particular microbes are involved in pathogenic infection success, but that infection by the pathogen is also likely to be a strong selective factor on microbiome composition (Jani & Briggs, 2014; Jani et al., 2017). However, skin-associated microbes show wide variation in ability to inhibit different genetic isolates of Bd (Antwis et al., 2015; Antwis & Weldon, 2017; Antwis & Harrison, 2018), suggesting responses of amphibian microbiomes to different variants of the pathogen are variable. Experimental studies are required to determine if there are signatures of microbial resistance across pathogen variation.

Selection on the microbiome caused by Bd and other pathogens could work in at least two ways: first, through selection on microbial community structure based on its effect on host survival and reproduction, which is related to the holobiont concept. Second, infection could select for OTUs on the skin that are, for example, competitively dominant to Bd, without an effect on host fitness. The lethal skin fungus Bd is known to have moved in a wave as an invasion front (Lips et al., 2006). The cutaneous microbiotas on *Craugastor fitzingeri* in a Bd-present area and in a Bd-naïve area ahead of the invasion front were compared using 16S rRNA gene sequencing on the Illumina platform (Rebollar et al., 2016). The microbiota in the Bd-naïve area was more diverse, whereas the microbiota in the Bd-present area was enriched for several taxa that are known producers of antimicrobial compounds including antifungal metabolites. This suggests that selection had occurred for a protective microbial community and for increased abundance of a few key species, and that diversity per se was not selected for. Interestingly, in the Bd-naïve area, some individuals had a microbial community structure similar to those in the Bd-present area. Thus, there was variation in bacterial communities among individuals that selection could act on. However, a response to selection requires a heritable basis to bacterial community structure, and although explicit evidence for this is lacking in amphibians, host genotype has been shown to influence microbiome composition in one species (Griffiths et al., 2018). However, host-produced antimicrobial peptides and microbiome-derived compounds were found to be synergistic in inhibiting Bd in vitro, i.e. the effect was greater than additive. This suggests that hosts can achieve a higher fitness by selecting microbial partners with which they can interact synergistically, especially when selection pressure from pathogens is high. In mammals, skin bacteria can affect the adaptive immune system, e.g. by keeping T cells recruited in the epidermis (Hooper et al., 2012; Naik, 2012). Skin bacteria can also influence innate immunity by signalling keratinocytes to increase secretion of antimicrobial peptides at the site of a wound or perhaps to maintain a baseline level of section. Given that animals evolve in an environment that includes microbes, it is not surprising that reciprocal interactions have evolved.

7.2.3 Humans

Human–microbiome interactions include both infectious and non-infectious associations. For instance, humans have been bombarded with new microbial threats over millennia (e.g. Middle East respiratory syndrome (MERS) coronavirus, H7N9 avian influenza virus) as well as the re-emergence of others (e.g. rabies, cryptococcal disease, hepatitis B and HIV) (Morens & Fauci, 2013). Consequently, defining features of infectious diseases include changes in microbial function, the environment and/or hosts, which can give way to new diseases, persistent diseases or render pathogens ineffective in their ability to be symptomatic (Casadevall et al., 2011). Fortunately, with constant surveillance, research and counter-measurements (i.e. vaccines, diagnosis and treatments), selected infectious diseases are becoming better controlled (Morens & Fauci, 2013).

Additionally, human–microbiome interactions can be attributed to microbial dysbiosis; shifts in microbial community structure that may be specific to a given disease (Nath & Raveendran, 2013; Carding et al., 2015). The immune system has evolved to manage these intense microbial interactions to retain microbes that have favourable traits. For example, intestinal regulatory T cells promote bacterial diversity by managing IgA production, which bind microbes and manage their location within the gut (Kawamoto et al., 2014). With the developing commensal microbiome, ongoing interactions between intestinal epithelial and lymphoid cells are required for normal gut and immune function. Apoptotic stimuli, reactive oxygen synthesis and toll-like receptor signalling are all induced by commensal bacteria to produce a state of controlled inflammation that helps develop innate immune defences and promote pathogen recognition by both innate and adaptive immunity (Jakaitis & Denning, 2014). Perhaps one of the most interesting and intriguing findings to date is the interactions between the NLRP6 inflammasome and the microbiota (Elinav et al., 2011; Henao-Mejia et al., 2012; Levy et al., 2015, 2017). The NLRP6 inflammasome comprises pattern-recognising multiprotein complexes residing in the cytoplasmic matrix. These recognise cellular damage and initiate responses to microbial molecules via damage- and pathogen-associated molecular patterns. The NLRP6 inflammasome has long been considered a key component of overall gut homeostasis (Levy et al., 2015). Given the daily interaction between microbes and the host within the gastrointestinal tract, it would seem natural to assume that one important process through which we interact with the microbial community within us is through the NLRP6 inflammasome (Levy et al., 2017). Studies with mice suggest that metabolites from commensal bacteria induce production of the NLRP6 inflammasome to activate antimicrobial peptides (AMPs) by upregulating the secretion of a proinflammatory cytokine known as interleukin-18 (Levy et al., 2015). Disruption of the NLRP6–IL18–AMP interaction can have profound impacts on host health. Similarly, many recent studies have correlated changes in the microbiota with chronic diseases, including diabetes (Wang & Jia, 2016), Alzheimer's disease (Cockburn et al., 2012), autism (Strati et al., 2017), chronic obstructive pulmonary disease (Hilty et al., 2010; Sze et al., 2012), asthma (Arrieta et al., 2015), multiple sclerosis (Miyake et al., 2015), among others. This has the potential to provide valuable information about how diseases establish, and key ways by which treatments could be made to help alleviate or inhibit inflammation or disease (McCoy et al., 2016).

Even neurological disease can result from microbial disruption (see Chapter 6 for more details). Autism spectrum disorder (ASD) has been associated with differences in the faecal microbiota, yet specific biomarkers have proven difficult to identify due to the huge variability in symptomology and comorbidities associated with this disorder. There is evidence of genetic predisposition in ASD with an individual's behavioural traits showing marked correlation with the genome (Sahin & Sur, 2015). Yet the environmental interaction, and likely the microbiome, plays a substantial role in shaping the aetiology of the disease (Kang et al., 2013; McDonald et al., 2015) and animal models have been used to demonstrate the mechanistic activity of bacterial metabolites in mediating autism-like behaviours (Hsiao et al., 2013). The complexity of this disorder, as well as the increased incidence (1 in 60 children are diagnosed with ASD in the USA each year) suggests a stronger influence of environmental factors in shaping this disease. Importantly, new data also point to a pregnancy interaction, whereby the microbial–immune interaction during mouse pregnancy can influence infection-derived placental damage, which in turn can influence neurodevelopment in the foetus (Kim et al., 2017).

While human genetics can explain the aetiology of a number of important disease states, the rise in obesity has proven to be difficult to assign to genetic factors. Genetic studies have not been able to explain the population-scale variance in body mass index (BMI), for example. Although a study with >300,000 individuals identified 97 BMI-associated human genotype loci associated with the disease, these only explained 2.7% of BMI variation (Locke et al., 2015). However, variance in the composition and structure of the microbiome can be used to predict individuals as lean or obese with over 90% accuracy (Knights et al., 2011), although strikingly, these patterns are almost invisible in the raw data (Turnbaugh et al., 2009). Some members of the human microbiota do show substantial heritability and are also associated with BMI and weight loss. For example, *Christensenella* was found to be significantly enriched in lean twins (when compared to their obese twin), and could protect from obesogenic challenge when fed to mice (Goodrich et al., 2014). Consequently, some of the human genetic influence might even be exerted via its effects on the microbiome. However, it is likely that this influence is through genetic influence on immune function (Schirmer et al., 2016).

The incidence of allergic and autoimmune disease has risen dramatically in western populations during the last few decades. Diseases such as childhood-onset asthma along with food and skin allergies are now pervasive within our communities. Similarly, inflammatory bowel disease and type 1 diabetes has been increasing globally, which cannot be explained by surveillance differences. There is now substantial evidence that microbiome disruption may play a role in the onset of these diseases, their exacerbation, or even their treatment. Inflammatory bowel disease patients (Knights et al., 2014) and children at risk for type 1 diabetes (Uusitalo et al., 2015) show a substantial association between the loss of microbial diversity and disease. That these diseases appear to be related to disruption of the microbial ecosystem, rather than infection from a specific pathogen, is important in our understanding of ecological disturbance and its influence on host health. Disturbance, especially early in life, could be a critical issue in the development of many diseases. A Canadian study involving >300 infant faecal microbiome profiles found substantial differences in the microbiota of infants who went on to develop allergic sensitisation and wheezing at age two when compared to subjects who did not (Arrieta et al., 2015). Similarly, disruption in microbial exposure, such as that associated with a farmyard environment, can have profound influence on asthma rates in a population, and microbial exposure associated with these environments has been shown to protect against allergen challenge in sensitised mice (Stefka et al., 2014). All of these studies suggest that there is a window in early life that profoundly influences immune development and the likely onset of allergic disease.

Some of the first reports on colorectal cancer (CRC) and the microbiota focused almost exclusively on specific bacteria (Wu et al., 2009; Goodwin et al., 2011; Arthur et al., 2012; Kostic et al., 2013; Abed et al., 2016). However, it is clear that CRC is associated with a select set of bacterial organisms (Flynn et al., 2016). Perhaps more intriguing, though, is another group of studies that show the importance of the overall community in increasing polyp burden in animal models of CRC (Zackular et al., 2013, 2015; Baxter et al., 2014). Although many studies have shown that specific bacteria associated with *Fusobacterium*, *Parvimonas*, *Peptostreptococcus* and *Porphyromonas* are also associated with CRC (Flynn et al., 2016), many of these same bacteria are not found during earlier stages of the disease (Hale et al., 2017; Sze et al., 2017). However, these specific microbes may not be acting synergistically, because models built to classify individuals based on their microbiota do not include all of these (Baxter et al., 2016; Sze et al., 2017). Interestingly, not all individuals who have CRC have these specific bacteria (Kostic et al., 2012), suggesting that they may represent a proxy for a dysbiotic community and the presence of specific bacteria may not be important. This idea of a small-scale local disturbance that then gives way to large-scale ecological turnover is not a new concept (Flynn et al., 2016). However, many of the studies that investigated this used faecal samples, which may not be able to detect localised bacterial community changes at the site of the polyp growth itself, although studies that have examined the microbiota on polyps have been inconclusive (Lu et al., 2016). Thus, the question remains, how do these CRC-associated bacteria gain an initial foothold within the community? Specifically, what needs to change within the community to allow this foothold to take place? There may be changes that occur initially in the host that may switch the gastrointestinal environment to one that is more favourable to these specific bacteria (Theodoratou et al., 2017; Wright et al., 2017). These changes could initially be driven by diet (Schwingshackl & Hoffmann, 2015; Shivappa et al., 2017). For example, protein-heavy diets, specifically red meat, are a known risk factor for CRC (Tuan & Chen, 2016). These diets tend to produce lower levels of short-chain fatty acids (SCFAs), particularly butyrate, while diets high in resistant starch are known to generate higher levels of these SCFAs that contain antitumorigenic properties (O'Keefe, 2016; Tuan & Chen, 2016). However, within normal individuals there is wide variation in SCFA production that may transcend this diet-based effect (Venkataraman et al., 2016).

Within the fast-growing field of human microbiome research, some of the most exciting findings involve bacteria, their metabolism and the impact on drug treatment. There are many examples by which bacteria can interfere with drug delivery (Maurice et al., 2013; Spanogiannopoulos et al., 2016). One of the most recent examples demonstrates how bacteria within the microbial community can metabolise and deactivate specific chemotherapy drugs (García-González et al., 2017; Scott et al., 2017; Yu et al., 2017). However, members of the microbial community are constantly metabolising compounds, and understanding how these metabolites interact with the human host is only just beginning. One of the most interesting examples of this is the case of trimethylamine-N-oxide (TMAO). High levels of this compound have been correlated with an elevated risk of atherosclerosis (Tang et al., 2013). Diets rich in phosphatidylcholine (a precursor to TMAO), typically found in high meat diets, has also been correlated with atherosclerosis risk (Tuohy et al., 2014). A study using stable-isotope–tracer feeding of phosphatidylcholine provided evidence that the microbiota was a key component of the conversion of this compound to TMAO (Tang et al., 2013). Further, TMAO levels significantly lowered when using broad-spectrum antibiotics to reduce the gut microbiota (Tang et al., 2013). This is fascinating, because it suggests that there may be many current diseases in which the microbiota may metabolise compounds to metabolites that are harmful or cause disease. Conversely, there may also be an equal number of metabolites that may be beneficial, butyrate being a prime example of one. Another exciting avenue is the generation of gamma-aminobutyric acid (GABA) by the microbial community (Dinan & Cryan, 2012; Mazzoli & Pessione, 2016). This may offer an important way in which our mind is influenced by microbes (Dinan & Cryan, 2012; Mazzoli & Pessione, 2016). This area of research is in its infancy, but it offers an exciting way forward in which to link the microbial community to its human host, and to manipulate the microbiome to improve the efficacy of drugs (see Section 7.3.3).

7.3 Manipulating the microbiome to prevent disease

As touched on above, the potential to artificially select engineered or evolved microbiomes to influence host health and fitness is a promising approach for the prevention and treatment of disease in plants and animals. Host-mediated microbiome selection may allow researchers and practitioners to leverage host traits that influence the microbiome. Consequently, using host phenotypes to gauge how microbiome functions influence host fitness is a powerful tool for the maintenance of health and fitness (Mueller & Sachs, 2015). This new research horizon is transforming the fields of medicine, conservation and agriculture, providing unprecedented opportunities to improve health and productivity. Several strategies for manipulating the microbiomes of plants and animals to improve disease outcomes are discussed in the following sections, with specific examples of contemporary approaches for microbiome manipulation. These approaches are also discussed in other contexts in Chapter 9.

7.3.1 Engineering plant microbiomes

One approach for plant disease management is the transfer of microbiomes from disease-suppressive soils to disease-conducive soils in order to promote disease resistance, in a manner analogous to human faecal transplants (see below). The rhizosphere microbiome plays a key role in plant health through the presence of plant growth–promoting rhizobacteria (PGPR) that confer disease suppressive properties to soils, particularly members of the Pseudomonadaceae (Mendes et al., 2012; Gopal et al., 2013). However, there is growing recognition through application of contemporary microbiome analyses that understanding the composition and function of the entire microbial assemblage in the rhizosphere microbiome is critical (Gopal et al., 2013).

The ability to transfer soil microbiomes in order to confer disease resistance in plants was demonstrated by Mendes et al. (2012), who mixed disease-suppressive soil with a disease-conducive soil in order to suppress infection of sugar beet plants with the pathogenic soil fungus *Rhizoctonia solani*. Although members of the Actinobacteria, Firmicutes (Lactobacillaceae) and Proteobacteria (particularly Pseudomonadaceae, Burkholderiaceae and Xanthamonadales) were strongly associated with disease-suppressive soils, more than 33,000 bacterial and archaeal species were identified in the soils through metagenomic and PhyloChip-based analysis, demonstrating the importance of integrating 'omics' technologies for microbiome-wide analysis. In particular, Pseudomonadaceae played an important role in disease suppression, and transposon mutagenesis of *Pseudomonas* spp. isolated from disease-suppressive soil revealed that a non-ribosomal peptide synthetase encoding a putative chlorinated lipopeptide was important to protect sugar beet seedlings from *R. solani* infection (Mendes et al., 2012). Other studies have also demonstrated the role of PGPRs in disease suppression by producing antimicrobial compounds, such as the antibiotics 2,4-DAPG produced by fluorescent pseudomonads, and iturin and surfactin produced by *Bacillus subtilis*, all of which protect against soil-borne pathogens in disease-suppressive soil through competitive exclusion (Chaparro et al., 2012).

Other examples of PGPRs acting antagonistically towards phytopathogens include the biocontrol activity of *Pseudomonas fluorescens* against the oomycete pathogen *Pythium ultimum*. *Pseudomonas fluorescens* protects cucumber from disease by this oomycete and possesses a type III secretion system (T3SS) also found in the phytopathogen *P. synrigae*, for which expression is stimulated in vitro by the oomycete and not the plant (Rezzonico et al., 2005). Inactivation of the *hrcV* gene of the T3SS reduced the biocontrol activity of *P. fluorescens* against *P. ultimum*, demonstrating that the T3SS in *P. fluorescens* has a role in plant protection against oomycete pathogens, rather than phytopathogenic activity (Rezzonico et al., 2005).

Hu et al. (2016) amended the natural microbial communities of the tomato rhizosphere microbiome with defined consortia of *Pseudomonas* containing one to eight species, and assessed their survival rate and activity in suppressing the plant pathogen *Ralstonia solanacearum*. They demonstrated that high *Pseudomonas* diversity reduced pathogen density in the rhizosphere and resulted in a lower incidence of disease within the host. This was due to intensified resource competition and direct interference with the pathogen. Interestingly, although an eight-species *Pseudomonas* consortium demonstrated the most effective disease suppression through reducing pathogen density and increased pseudomonad density in the microbiome, no single species was found to have a major influence on disease suppression, suggesting that community richness and synergistic effects are a major determinant of disease suppression (Hu et al., 2016). These data fit with the general pattern that suggests diverse plant rhizosphere communities promote enhanced disease suppression, and that low-diversity communities may be augmented with diverse probiotic consortia to ultimately improve host function (Chaparro et al., 2012; Hu et al., 2016). Interestingly, application of soil microbiota to plant roots can also confer alterations to metabolic signatures of above-ground parts of the plant. Badri et al. (2013) demonstrated that amendment of the soil microbiome of *Arabidopsis thaliana* enhanced plant growth and altered the metabolic properties of the leaves, which in turn reduced larval feeding of insect herbivores on the leaves.

Despite the promise of microbiome transfers and microbial inoculants demonstrated through pot experiments, there has been limited success under field conditions (see Chapter 9 for more). However, the transfer of artificially cultivated core microbiomes comprising a specifically selected consortium of microorganisms designed based on insights from microbiome studies may represent one approach to reduce the noise associated with transfer of entire and complex microbiomes, and should be a future research priority (Gopal et al., 2013).

7.3.2 Engineering wildlife microbiomes

7.3.2.1 *Bacterial manipulations in invertebrates*

Manipulations of microbes have been successful in controlling vector-transmitted diseases that affect humans (Hoffmann et al., 2011). A strain of *Wolbachia* can shorten mosquito lifespan and susceptibility to infection by pathogens such as the virus that causes dengue fever. A field trial in Australia demonstrated that when a strain of *Wolbachia* (wMel) was inoculated into mosquitos, it replaced all or nearly all other strains of *Wolbachia* in the population through maternal transmission. Females without this inoculated strain then died when mated with males with the strain (Hoffmann et al., 2011). This manipulation is predicted to reduce the probability of pathogen transmission to humans. A similar approach that involved genetic manipulation of bacterial species in the genus *Serratia* shows promise in reducing the transmission of malaria to humans by reducing successful infection of the mosquito vector (Wang et al., 2017).

7.3.2.2 *Bacterial manipulations in amphibians*

There have been a number of laboratory studies looking at the potential to augment the amphibian microbiota with disease-inhibiting microbes. In the amphibian–chytridiomycosis system, however, results of probiotic experiments have been mixed. The first two published studies showed positive results in the laboratory (Harris et al., 2009a, 2009b). A single addition of *Pseudomonas reactans* and *Janthinobacterium lividum* to the salamander *P. cinereus* and the frog *R. muscosa*, respectively, prior to Bd infection led to enhanced growth rate and/or survival compared to individuals exposed to Bd only (Harris et al., 2009a, 2009b). In the case of probiotic addition to *R. muscosa*, survival rate with the probiotic and Bd was 100%, while all individuals with Bd-only died or were very morbid at the end of the experiment. In a laboratory trial with the boreal toad (*Anaxyrus boreas*), multiple probiotic (*J. lividum*) additions significantly increased survival by 40% over toads without the probiotic when Bd was present (Augustin et al., 2017). A two-year field trial in California also indicated an increased survival rate of 39% in the probiotic-treated group compared to the untreated control group (unpublished data).

One mechanism of protection was identified via a laboratory study involving the frog *R. muscosa* and the probiotic *J. lividum*, which produces the antifungal compound violacein (Becker et al., 2009). The concentration of violacein on the host's skin was assessed at the end of the experiment and found to be elevated in two treatments where *J. lividum* was added (probiotic-alone and probiotic followed by Bd) compared to untreated controls (Becker et al., 2009). As noted above, the addition of the probiotic led to a dramatic increase in survival compared to frogs exposed to the pathogen alone. This result suggests that the mechanism of protection was the production of violacein. Adding an experimental treatment of a non–violacein-producing *J. lividum* would be necessary to test this mechanistic hypothesis experimentally. In another study with the salamander *P. cinereus*, it was found that violacein concentration on the skin, either from the naturally occurring skin microbiota or from probiotic additions of *J. lividum*, was strongly associated with survival when exposed to Bd (Becker & Harris, 2010). In experimental work with toads, the same individuals were exposed during two sequential Bd challenges (Kueneman et al., 2016; Augustin et al., 2017). During the first Bd exposure, the toads in all treatment groups and controls already had a high proportion of protective bacteria (*Chryseobacterium*), likely as a result of this strain replicating to high abundance in captive conditions. Thus, *J. lividum*–treated toads did not differ from control frogs during the first Bd challenge (all groups had high survival and low Bd loads). By the second Bd exposure, *Chryseobacterium* abundances had decreased precipitously and *J. lividum*–treated toads had significantly higher survival relative to the controls. Together, these experiments support the hypothesis that the cutaneous microbiota is protective and that probiotic addition can lead to protection from Bd.

Despite these successes, other probiotic addition experiments did not lead to increased survival against Bd (e.g. Woodhams et al., 2012). In most cases it is unclear why protection was not achieved, but one reasonable explanation is that the probiotic species did not persist on the skin. For example, it was found that Bd abundance on Panamanian golden frogs was low while *J. lividum* abundance was high, but Bd abundance rapidly increased as *J. lividum* abundance decreased (Becker et al., 2011). Similarly, *J. lividum* was no longer established on the skin of *Atelopus zeteki* two weeks after inoculation and did not improve the survival of frogs in comparison to controls when infected with Bd (Becker et al., 2011), indicating inoculation is not necessarily permanent. In a study with the critically endangered Panamanian golden frog (*Atelopus zeteki*), the population size of the probiotic *J. lividum* began to decrease after inoculation, although it stabilised at a population density that was apparently too low to achieve protection (Harris et al., 2006). Furthermore, Muletz et al. (2012) showed that inoculating soil with *J. lividum* leads to increases in the concentrations of bacteria on the skin of *P. cinereus*, with Bd prevalence reduced by half in individuals maintained with inoculated soil compared to controls; however, the introduced *J. lividum* had cleared from salamanders 42 days post-treatment. Furthermore, there is evidence that host species actively upregulate peptide production in order to clear probiotic treatments (Küng et al., 2014). In addition, treating already-infected individuals with probiotics may not be effective; *Rana muscosa* already infected with

Bd and inoculated with *Pedobacter cryoconitis* did not have higher survival in comparison to control or intraconizole-treated frogs (Woodhams et al., 2012). Together, these problems indicate that probiotic treatments will be complex to develop, and a species-specific approach may be required. In the laboratory or in a captive setting, reapplication of the probiotic is easy to do, but in a natural setting it would be difficult or impossible. Exceptions could be highly managed populations of frogs that are easily recaptured, such as those that live in a pond year-round, or if the probiotic can be added to the amphibians' environment. An ideal solution would be a self-disseminating system of probiotic bacteria that exists in the environment and on the at-risk host species. It is suggested from several studies that amphibians rely on environmental bacteria to maintain their cutaneous microbiota (Brucker et al., 2008; Fitzpatrick & Allison, 2014). For example, salamanders brought into the laboratory and placed into a container with moist paper towels experienced a dramatic drop in bacterial species diversity and the eventual dominance of just several OTUs, whereas salamanders housed in natural soil retained much of the cutaneous bacterial diversity (Loudon et al., 2014b). Augmenting a probiotic into the soil in a laboratory study was an effective method to inoculate redback salamanders (*P. cinereus*) (Lips et al., 2006). Furthermore, individuals inoculated with *J. lividum* via the soil were significantly less likely to be infected with Bd, and environmental inoculation of water was also effective for probiotic transmission in the tadpole stage of a frog species (Rebollar et al., 2016). This suggests that environmental inoculation with a probiotic may be a feasible method to reapply the probiotic to at risk amphibian species (but see Chapter 9 for potential issues surrounding this approach). Augmenting locally occurring strains of protective bacteria may avoid or minimise effects on non-target organisms.

7.3.2.3 *Probiotics in bats*

A number of bacteria that inhibit Pd have been identified (e.g. Hoyt et al., 2015), although probiotic manipulation in bats is in its infancy. In an experiment with little brown bats (*Myotis lucifugus*), inoculation with the anti-Pd bacterial species *P. fluorescens* led to a 40% increase in survival over untreated controls when both were exposed to Pd (Cheng et al., 2017). Application of the probiotic before experimental infection with Pd did not improve survival. Therefore, timing of probiotic application was important for efficacy, as also indicated in studies with amphibians. The difference in results could be explained by the possibility that the probiotic did not persist on the bats for a long period of time, thereby requiring simultaneous exposure. This comparison suggests that the probiotic delivered potent anti-Pd metabolites that inhibited the fungus before the probiotic numbers decreased. Future work would involve a test of efficacy of the probiotic when it is applied while active infections are occurring.

7.3.3 Engineering the human microbiome

7.3.3.1 *Probiotics and the human microbiome*

The use of probiotics to alter the human microbiome idea has been around since at least 1907 when Élie Metchnikoff hypothesised lactic acid–producing bacteria could implant in the gastrointestinal tract to enhance longevity (Gordon, 2008). Today, the probiotic landscape is still dominated by lactic acid–producing bacteria, specifically the genus *Lactobacillus*, although it is now appreciated that their beneficial properties are not limited to the production of a single metabolite, and that other potential probiotic bacteria could affect various outcomes through multiple means (Bron et al., 2012). Because the application of microorganisms is highly specific with regard to both agent and effect, the use of precision probiotics will likely be necessary. Devices now exist for isolating microorganisms based on metabolic output (Gavrish et al., 2016), and work is being done to identify probiotic bacteria that produce particular compounds of therapeutic potential (Strandwitz et al., 2019). This may include compounds whose efficacies are contingent on the route of administration, for example those that are inactive orally. Furthermore, probiotics are being bioengineered to expand their range and mode of action, as well as their robustness and incorporation capabilities (Amalaradjou & Bhunia, 2013). However, it is important to keep in mind that interactions with diet, established microbiota and genetics are all known to modulate overall health outcomes, if not specific effects and mechanisms of probiotics (Bron et al., 2012). Therefore, effective patient classification and stratification is required for best results. The success of this approach will require detailed insights into metagenomic potential and ecological interactions of presumptive probiotic bacteria, making precision probiotic development a task of considerable difficulty, but one that has already seen demonstrable results (Buffie et al., 2015). Concurrently, the effectiveness of probiotics is contingent on their ability to successfully colonise the gut and overcome the relatively low residence time (5–8 days) in their targeted area, such as the gut or oral cavity (Flichy-Fernández et al., 2010; Ramos et al., 2016). Precision probiotics must therefore overcome the transient behaviour of selected microorganisms in a given individual for successful colonisation (see Chapter 9 for more on this).

7.3.3.2 *Faecal microbiome transplants*

Recurrent *Clostridium difficile* infection (CDI) is a pervasive disease that leads to comprehensive disruption of the gut microbiome. A healthy microbiome engages in active metabolism of host bile acids, and the secondary metabolic products of this activity can inhibit the germination of *C. difficile* spores and hence prevent CDI (Pamer, 2016). As a result, antibiotic treatment may lead to dysbiosis and the onset of CDI. Thus, subsequent antibiotic treatment of the disease could exacerbate the infection by preventing the microbiota from mediating bile acid metabolism that would inhibit the development and recurrence of the disease. However, using a faecal microbiota transplant, whereby the restoration of microbial ecosystem function is managed by direct faecal microbial infusion into the damaged gut environment, can produce an extremely rapid return to a 'healthy' faecal microbial community (Weingarden et al., 2015). This effect size is much greater than any human genetic variation in the stool microbiome that has yet been observed, and perhaps explains the high efficacy of stool transplants relative to standard antibiotic treatments (Kassam et al., 2013). In fact, a recent clinical trial in persons with recurrent CDI had to be stopped early given the >90% efficacy of faecal transplant versus the <30% efficacy of antibiotics, making it unethical to continue withholding faecal transplants (van Nood et al., 2013). That said, there has been mixed success when using faecal microbiome transplants for other diseases (Qazi et al., 2017). A potential reason may be in the actual preparation of the transplants themselves, in that the anaerobic bacteria that comprise the majority of the community are not protected from aerobic conditions (The Human Microbiome Consortium, 2012; Cammarota et al., 2017; Lloyd-Price et al., 2017). For CDI, missing these members may not be important, but for diseases such as inflammatory bowel disease, they may be crucial. Another potential reason is that there really is no consensus of what a 'normal' microbiota constitutes. For example, some healthy individuals have little to no Bacteroidetes or Firmicutes (The Human Microbiome Consortium, 2012; Lloyd-Price et al., 2017). For CDI, the filling of niches to exclude a particular species may be sufficient for treatment; however, when diseases are a complex mix between a dysfunctional host and a dysfunctional microbial community, knowing how the 'normal' host and its microbiota communicate with each other may be the key in treatment of the disease.

7.3.3.3 Prebiotics

Instead of targeting the microbiome to reduce or eliminate deleterious bacteria, one could aim to indirectly increase the levels of beneficial bacteria or otherwise positively alter the structure or function of the microbiome via substrates that promote the growth of desirable members. Substances applied in this way are often referred to as prebiotics. However, the types of prebiotics currently studied are limited in scope – usually non-digestible fibre compounds that stimulate growth of *Bifidobacterium* and other taxa to produce SCFAs including butyrate and propionate (Petschow et al., 2013). Although this is promising as a broad treatment for several conditions (Candela et al., 2010), efforts for precision medicine in this sphere will require the expansion of the scope of prebiotics. Given that metagenomic and metabolomic advances continue to better characterise the metabolic potential of the microbiome, dietary compounds that stimulate alternative beneficial bacteria towards useful metabolic endpoints will undoubtedly be discovered (Preidis & Versalovic, 2009).

More audaciously, one might aim to fine-tune the interactions between members of the gut microbiome. The microbiome is a complex, co-evolved ecosystem that produces many bioactive compounds, often for intercellular communication (Donaldson et al., 2015). These compounds could be mined to find those that modulate the microbiome in a beneficial way, thus unearthing novel prebiotics (Garber, 2015). While microbial community disruption is often the consequence of both xenobiotic and microbiome-targeted drug metabolism, these types of prebiotics might provide a gentler perturbation than possible with the former by harnessing already existing biological pathways. This goal certainly seems distant, but as dynamic systems approaches to studying the microbiome continue to develop, we may find that treating certain dysbiotic states requires perturbations of varying magnitudes or delicate maintenance of the stability of the microbiome, especially in at-risk populations (Gerber, 2014).

7.3.3.4 *Personalised microbiome medicine*

The unique nature of the human microbiome is a central element of precision medicine. The discoveries that led to the development of high-throughput sequencing technologies that enabled the personal genomics revolution is now influencing the personal microbiome revolution. Similarly, the analytical and statistical approaches developed to handle genomic data have been augmented and diversified to deal with the differential complexities of microbiome data. The fact that the microbiome has such interpersonal diversity, even between identical twins (Franzosa et al., 2015), and because, unlike the host genome, the microbiome undergoes such dramatic shifts even within an individual (David et al., 2014), the microbial community in each person is primed for manipulation to prevent disease. While there is great promise, the complexity of the microbial ecology in the human body is extraordinary and currently limits our ability to formulate approaches to precision medicine (Gilbert et al., 2016). That said, substantial research effort is now underway to determine whether these inter-personal differences, which are greater than differences within an individual over time (Lax et al., 2014; Ollberding et al., 2016), may be used to accurately predict susceptibility to disease, determine and improve the response to treatment, and augment microbial ecological stability through prebiotics and probiotics (Kuntz & Gilbert, 2017).

Many drug modifications and a huge majority of adverse drug events have no known aetiology. It is possible, therefore, that microbial drug modification, through metabolism or signalling changes, could play a substantial role in biotransformation, a chemical modification of the drug within the body. This is especially true for low-solubility and low-permeability compounds (Sousa et al., 2008). There are >60 different drugs that have known interactions with microbial metabolism (ElRakaiby et al., 2014), and this is likely a massive underestimation (Carmody & Turnbaugh, 2014). While conjugation and oxidation are the primary mechanisms of drug modification by human metabolism, microbial metabolism is also dominated by reduction and hydrolysis reactions (Sousa et al., 2008). In many cases, this microbial metabolism is actually part of the treatment, hence the use of prodrugs: biologically inactive drug compounds that become pharmacologically active following metabolic activity by the gut microbiota (Rautio et al., 2008). In many cases, prodrug activation results in improved bioavailability to the host, and therefore it is essential that we consider microbial activity when calculating dose responses for these drugs. However, microbial metabolism can also influence the efficacy and potential unintended consequences for particular drugs. A well-understood example is acetaminophen toxicity, a drug response side effect that is hugely variable within the human population (Watkins et al., 2006). Microbial metabolism appears to play a role in this side effect whereby bacteria from the genus *Clostridium* (among others) can metabolise acetaminophen to produce *p*-cresol, which outcompetes acetominophen as a substrate for the human live enzyme (SULT1A1) that breaks down the painkiller (Clayton et al., 2009). As a result of a reduction in the breakdown of acetaminophen, there is an increase in the concentration of NAPQI in the liver, which causes necrosis through hepatotoxicity. Another great example is in the metabolism of digoxin, which can be toxic with the wrong dosage. *Eggerthella lenta* has strain-level variants that may have the potential to degrade digoxin, thereby decreasing its effect and essentially changing the dose (Haiser & Turnbaugh, 2013). Interestingly, other drugs may have substantial effects on the microbiome itself, such as antipsychotic medication, which is known to have side effects by specifically affecting the microbial composition of the gut (Davey et al., 2013). Cataloguing these microbiota–xenobiotic interactions is essential if we are to understand how to use drugs appropriately, but it also requires active monitoring and characterisation of a patient's microbiota to determine the appropriate strategy.

We are already influencing human health by using drugs targeted to affect the microbiome, and indeed we have been doing this for many years; antibiotics are used to prevent the spread of disease-causing organisms, but in turn have a substantial influence on the rest of the microbiome, with the possibility of these changes influencing human health outcomes. It is already well established that one of the progenitors of secondary infections such as *C. difficile* is the use of antibiotics (Worsley, 1998). Interestingly, the way in which antibiotic use can both reduce and increase inflammation under different scenarios may be in part due to their influence on the immune–microbiome relationship (Rubin & Tamaoki, 2005). For example, animal models have shown that antibiotics can substantially reduce the levels of stress-related cytokines in circulation (Bailey et al., 2011). Other drugs and chemicals can have negative outcomes (Maurice et al., 2013), and the influence of many drugs on human health may derive all or part of their efficacy from interactions with the microbiome. Antibiotics, however, remain our most common method of altering the microbiome, and are becoming the preferred method of reducing the biomass of indigenous flora so as to determine the influence of a microbiome transplant on host phenotype. However, a precision micro- biome medicine therapy that involves modulation of the microbiome would have broad clinical relevance. For example, the development of antibiotics that targeted only a single species of bacteria, or even a single strain (subspe- cies), would have a huge influence on healthcare. Leveraging compounds that influence enzyme activity in single species would be a vast improvement on existing technology. One example includes the fusion of an antimicrobial peptide domain with broad species selectivity with a species-specific peptide domain that allows for targeted killing, as has already been developed for *Streptococcus mutans* (Eckert et al., 2006).

A final approach for targeted antimicrobials has been successfully employed for approximately 100 years (Nobrega et al., 2015). Phage therapy was devel- oped predominantly in Russia and was effectively used to control outbreaks of gastrointestinal diseases in Russian armies in World Wars I and II (Summers, 2012). The basic premise is that many bacterial species, and maybe even each strain (subspecies), are predated upon by a unique phage (Koskella & Meaden, 2013). The phage targets bacteria cell-membrane protein and sugar complexes that are unique to each bacterial taxon. Therefore, by identifying the correct phage it should be possible to surgically remove a specific bacterial species from an assemblage. This could enable accurate restructuring of a microbiome so as to precisely augment the functional properties of that consortium. In fact, recent evidence from the commercial sector suggests that the same mechanisms employed by the phage to target and penetrate bacterial cells can be programmed into nanoparticles that mimic these phage properties to infect and kill specific cells (Jeffrey Miller, UCLA, personal communication). In this new future, we may have ultimate control over the microbiome.

7.4 Conclusions

The microbiome plays a crucial role in host health and disease, the progression of which is influenced by host factors (including genetics, physiology and immunity), environmental factors (including biotic and abiotic agents) and microbiota–microbiota interactions. Advances in technical and analytical approaches for microbiome research have transformed our understanding of the role of the microbiome in disease resistance and susceptibility, driving a revolution of microbiome research focused on the diagnosis, prevention, and treatment of disease. Such progress is catalysing the era of microbiome engineering, where the opportunity to directly manipulate the host microbiota is a genuine prospect, with significant potential for disease suppression and treatment. These advances make the mechanistic and ecological analysis of host microbiomes a central component of future applications in plant and animal husbandry and medical practice.

References

Abed J, Emgård JEM, Zamir G, et al. (2016) Fap2 mediates *Fusobacterium nucleatum* colorectal adenocarcinoma enrichment by binding to tumor-expressed Gal-GalNAc. *Cell Host and Microbe*, 20, 215–225.

Amalaradjou MAR, Bhunia AK. (2013) Bioengineered probiotics, a strategic approach to control enteric infections. *Bioengineered*, 4, 379–387.

Antwis RE, Weldon C. (2017) Amphibian skin defences show variation in ability to inhibit growth of *Batrachochytrium dendrobatidis* isolates from the global panzootic lineage. *Microbiology*, 163, 1835–1838.

Antwis RE, Harrison XA. (2018) Probiotic consortia are not uniformly effective against different amphibian chytrid pathogen isolates. *Molecular Ecology*, 27, 577–589.

Antwis RE, Preziosi RF, Harrison XA, et al. (2015) Amphibian symbiotic bacteria do not show a universal ability to inhibit growth of the global panzootic lineage of *Batrachochytrium dendrobatidis*. *Applied and Environmental Microbiology*, 81, 3706–3711.

Arrieta MC, Stiemsma LT, Dimitriu PA, et al. (2015) Early infancy microbial and metabolic alterations affect risk of childhood asthma. *Science Translational Medicine*, 7, 307ra152.

Arthur JC, Perez-Chanona E, Mühlbauer M, et al. (2012) Intestinal inflammation targets cancer-inducing activity of the microbiota. *Science*, 338, 120–123.

Augustin R, Schröder K, Rincón AP, et al. (2017) A secreted antibacterial neuropeptide shapes the microbiome of *Hydra*. *Nature Communications*, 8, 698.

Austin RM. (2000) Cutaneous microbial flora and antibiosis in *Plethodon ventralis*. In: Bruce RC, Jaeger RG. (Eds.) *The Biology of Plethodontid Salamanders*. Dordrecht: Kluwer Academic/Plenum.

Autenrieth IB. (2017) The microbiome in health and disease: A new role of microbes in molecular medicine. *Journal of Molecular Medicine*, 95, 1–3.

Badri DV, Zolla G, Bakker MG, et al. (2013) Potential impact of soil microbiomes on the leaf metabolome and on herbivore feeding behavior. *New Phytologist*, 198, 264–273.

Bailey MT, Dowd SE, Galley JD, et al. (2011) Exposure to a social stressor alters the structure of the intestinal microbiota: Implications for stressor-induced immunomodulation. *Brain, Behavior, and Immunity*, 25, 397–407.

Banning JL, Weddle AL, Wahl GW, et al. (2008) Antifungal skin bacteria, embryonic survival, and communal nesting in four-toed salamanders, *Hemidactylium scutatum*. *Oecologia*, 156, 423–429.

Bates KA, Shelton JMG, Mercier VL, et al. (2019) Captivity and infection by the fungal pathogen *Batrachochytrium salamandrivorans* perturb the amphibian skin microbiome. *Frontiers in Microbiology*, 10, 1834.

Baxter NT, Ruffin MT, Rogers MAM, et al. (2016) Microbiota-based model improves the sensitivity of fecal immunochemical test for detecting colonic lesions. *Genome Medicine*, 8, 37.

Baxter NT, Zackular JP, Chen GY, et al. (2014) Structure of the gut microbiome following colonization with human feces determines colonic tumor burden. *Microbiome*, 2, 20.

Becker MH, Brucker RM, Schwantes CR, et al. (2009) The bacterially produced metabolite violacein is associated with survival of amphibians infected with a lethal fungus. *Applied and Environmental Microbiology*, 75, 6635–6638.

Becker MH, Harris RN. (2010) Cutaneous bacteria of the redback salamander prevent morbidity associated with a lethal disease. *PLoS ONE*, 5, e10957.

Becker MH, Harris RN, Minbiole KPC, et al. (2011) Towards a better understanding of the use of probiotics for preventing chytridiomycosis in Panamanian golden frogs. *EcoHealth*, 8, 501–506.

Becker MH, Walke JB, Cikanek S, et al. (2015) Composition of symbiotic bacteria predicts survival in Panamanian golden frogs infected with a lethal fungus. *Proceedings of the Royal Society B: Biological Sciences*, 282, 20142881.

Berg G. (2009) Plant–microbe interactions promoting plant growth and health: Perspectives for controlled use of microorganisms in agriculture. *Applied Microbiology and Biotechnology*, 84, 11–18.

Berg G, Grube M, Schloter M, et al. (2014) The plant microbiome and its importance for plant and human health. *Frontiers in Microbiology*, 5, e491.

Berg G, Rybakova D, Grube M, et al. (2016) The plant microbiome explored: Implications for experimental botany. *Journal of Experimental Botany*, 67, 995–1002.

Bletz MC, Loudon AH, Becker MH, et al. (2013) Mitigating amphibian chytridiomycosis with bioaugmentation: Characteristics of effective probiotics and strategies for their selection and use. *Ecology Letters*, 16, 807–820.

Bosch TCG, Augustin R, Anton-Erxleben F, et al. (2009) Uncovering the evolutionary history of innate immunity: The simple metazoan *Hydra* uses epithelial cells for host defence. *Developmental and Comparative Immunology*, 4, 559–569.

Broberg M, Doonan J, Mundt F, et al. (2018) Integrated multi-omic analysis of host-microbiota interactions in acute oak decline. *Microbiome*, 6, 21.

Bron PA, Van Baarlen P, Kleerebezem M. (2012) Emerging molecular insights into the interaction between probiotics and the host intestinal mucosa. *Nature Reviews Microbiology*, 10, 66–78.

Brucker RM, Baylor CM, Walters RL, et al. (2008) The identification of 2,4-diacetylphloroglucinol as an antifungal metabolite produced by cutaneous bacteria of the salamander *Plethodon cinereus*. *Journal of Chemical Ecology*, 34, 39–43.

Buffie CG. Bucci V, Stein RR, et al. (2015) Precision microbiome reconstitution restores bile acid mediated resistance to *Clostridium difficile*. *Nature*, 517, 205–208.

Byrd BAL, Segre JA. (2016). Adapting Koch's postulates. *Science*, 351, 224–226.

Cammarota G, Ianiro G, Tilg H, et al. (2017) European consensus conference on faecal microbiota transplantation in clinical practice. *Gut*, 66, 569–580.

Campbell LJ, Garner TWJ, Hopkins K, et al. (2019) Outbreaks of an emerging viral disease covary with differences in the composition of the skin microbiome of a wild United Kingdom amphibian. *Frontiers in Microbiology*, 10, 1245.

Candela M, Maccaferri S, Turroni S, et al. (2010) Functional intestinal microbiome, new frontiers in prebiotic design. *International Journal of Food Microbiology*, 140, 93–101.

Carding S, Verbeke K, Vipond DT, et al. (2015) Dysbiosis of the gut microbiota in disease. *Microbial Ecology in Health and Disease*, 26, 26191.

Carmody RN, Turnbaugh PJ. (2014) Host–microbial interactions in the metabolism of therapeutic and diet-derived xenobiotics. *Journal of Clinical Investigation*, 124, 4173–4181.

Casadevall A, Fang FC, Pirofski L. (2011) Microbial virulence as an emergent property: Consequences and opportunities. *PLoS Pathogens*, 7, e100213.

Chaparro JM, Sheflin AM, Manter DK, et al. (2012) Manipulating the soil microbiome to increase soil health and plant fertility. *Biology and Fertility of Soils*, 48, 489–499.

Cheng TL, Mayberry H, McGuire LP, et al. (2017) Efficacy of a probiotic bacterium to treat bats affected by the disease white-nose syndrome. *Journal of Applied Ecology*, 54, 701–708.

Clayton TA, Baker D, Lindon JC, et al. (2009) Pharmacometabonomic identification of a significant host–microbiome metabolic interaction affecting human drug metabolism. *Proceedings of the National Academy of Sciences*, 106, 14728–14733.

Cockburn AF, Dehlin JM, Ngan T, et al. (2012) High throughput DNA sequencing to detect differences in the subgingival plaque microbiome in elderly subjects with and without dementia. *Investigative Genetics*, 3, 19.

Cornelison CT, Keel MK, Gabriel KT, et al. (2014) A preliminary report on the contact-independent antagonism of *Pseudogymnoascus destructans* by *Rhodococcus rhodochrous* strain DAP96253. *BMC Microbiology*, 14, 1–7.

Currie CR, Scott JA, Summerbell RC, et al. (1999) Fungus-growing ants use antibiotic producing bacteria to control garden parasites. *Nature*, 398, 701–704.

Currie CR, Poulsen M, Mendenhall J, et al. (2006) Coevolved crypts and exocrine glands support mutualistic bacteria in fungus-growing ants. *Science*, 311, 81–83.

Davey KJ, Cotter PD, O'Sullivan O, et al. (2013) Antipsychotics and the gut microbiome: Olanzapine-induced metabolic dysfunction is attenuated by antibiotic administration in the rat. *Translational Psychiatry*, 3, e309.

David LA, Maurice CF, Carmody RN, et al. (2014) Diet rapidly and reproducibly alters the human gut microbiome. *Nature*, 505, 559–563.

Denman S, Brown N, Kirk S, et al. (2014) A description of the symptoms of Acute Oak Decline in Britain and a comparative review on causes of similar disorders on oak in Europe. *Forestry*, 87, 535–551.

Denman S, Plummer S, Peace A, et al. (2016) Isolation studies reveal a shift in the cultivable microbiome of oak affected with Acute Oak Decline. *Systematic and Applied Microbiology*, 39, 484–490.

Denman S, Doonan J, Ransom-Jones E, et al. (2018) Microbiome and infectivity studies reveal complex polyspecies tree disease in Acute Oak Decline. *The ISME Journal*, 12, 386–399.

Dinan TG, Cryan JF. (2012) Regulation of the stress response by the gut microbiota: Implications for psychoneuroendocrinology. *Psychoneuroendocrinology*, 37, 1369–1378.

Donaldson GP, Lee SM, Mazmanian SK. (2015) Gut biogeography of the bacterial microbiota. *Nature Reviews Microbiology*, 14, 20–32.

Eckert R, He J, Yarbrough DK, et al. (2006) Targeted killing of *Streptococcus mutans* by a pheromone-guided 'smart' antimicrobial peptide. *Antimicrobial Agents and Chemotherapy*, 50, 3651–3657.

Elinav E, Strowig T, Kau AL, et al. (2011) NLRP6 inflammasome regulates colonic microbial ecology and risk for colitis. *Cell*, 145, 745–757.

ElRakaiby M, Dutilh BE, Rizkallah MR, et al. (2014) Pharmacomicrobiomics: The impact of human microbiome variations on systems pharmacology and personalized therapeutics. *OMICS: A Journal of Integrative Biology*, 18, 402–414.

Estrada-De Los Santos P, Bustillos-Cristales R, Caballero-Mellado J. (2001) *Burkholderia*, a genus rich in plant-associated nitrogen fixers with wide environmental and geographic distribution. *Applied and Environmental Microbiology*, 67, 2790–2798.

Evans AS. (1976) Causation and disease: The Henle–Koch postulates revisited. *Yale Journal of Biology and Medicine*, 49, 175–195.

Falkow S. (1988) Molecular Koch's postulates applied to microbial pathogenicity. *Reviews of Infectious Diseases*, 10, S274–S276.

Feau N, Hamelin RC. (2017) Say hello to my little friends: How microbiota can modulate tree health. *New Phytologist*, 215, 508–510.

Finkel OM, Castrillo G, Herrera Paredes S, et al. (2017) Understanding and exploiting plant beneficial microbes. *Current Opinion in Plant Biology*, 38, 155–163.

Fitzpatrick BM, Allison AL. (2014) Similarity and differentiation between bacteria associated with skin of salamanders (Plethodon jordani) and free-living assemblages. *FEMS Microbiology Ecology*, 88, 482–494.

Flichy-Fernández AJ, Alegre-Domingo T, Peñarrocha-Oltra D, et al. (2010) Probiotic treatment in the oral cavity: An update. *Medicina Oral, Patologia Oral y Cirugia Bucal*, 15, e677–680.

Flynn KJ, Baxter NT, Schloss PD. (2016) Metabolic and community synergy of oral bacteria in colorectal cancer. *mSphere*, 1, e00102–116.

Franzosa EA, Huang K, Meadow JF, et al. (2015) Identifying personal microbiomes using metagenomic codes. *Proceedings of the National Academy of Sciences*, 112, E2930–E2938.

Fredericks DN, Relman DA. (1996) Sequence-based identification of microbial pathogens: A reconsideration of Koch's postulates. *Clinical Microbiology Reviews*, 9, 18–33.

Garber K. (2015) Drugging the gut microbiome. *Nature Biotechnology*, 33, 228–231.

García-González AP, Ritter AD, Shrestha S, et al. (2017) Bacterial metabolism affects the *C. elegans* response to cancer chemotherapeutics. *Cell*, 169, 431–441.

Gavrish EK, Lewis K, Epstein SS. (2016) Devices and Methods for the Selective Isolation of Microorganisms. Google Patents US20070275451A1.

Gerber GK. (2014). The dynamic microbiome. *FEBS Letters*, 588, 4131–4139.

Gilbert JA, Quinn RA, Debelius J, et al. (2016) Microbiome-wide association studies link dynamic microbial consortia to disease. *Nature*, 535, 94–103.

Goodrich JK, Waters JL, Poole AC, et al. (2014). Human genetics shape the gut microbiome. *Cell*, 159, 789–799.

Goodwin AC, Shields CED, Wu S, et al. (2011) Polyamine catabolism contributes to enterotoxigenic *Bacteroides fragilis*-induced colon tumorigenesis. *Proceedings of the National Academy of Sciences*, 108, 15354–15359.

Gopal M, Gupta A, Thomas GV. (2013) Bespoke microbiome therapy to manage plant diseases. *Frontiers in Microbiology*, 4, 10–13.

Gopalakrishnan V, Spencer CN, Nezi L, et al. (2018) Gut microbiome modulates response to anti-PD-1 immunotherapy in melanoma patients. *Science*, 359, 97–103.

Gordon S. (2008) Elie Metchnikoff: Father of natural immunity. *European Journal of Immunology*, 38, 3257–3264.

Griffiths SM, Harrison XA, Weldon C, et al. (2018) Genetic variability and ontogeny predict microbiome structure in a disease-challenged montane amphibian. *The ISME Journal*, 12, 2506–2517.

Haiser HJ, Turnbaugh PJ (2013). Developing a metagenomic view of xenobiotic metabolism. *Pharmacological Research*, 69, 21–31.

Hale VL, Chen J, Johnson S, et al. (2017) Shifts in the fecal microbiota associated with adenomatous polyps. *Cancer Epidemiology Biomarkers and Prevention*, 26, 1–10.

Harris RN, Brucker RM, Walke JB, et al. (2009a) Skin microbes on frogs prevent morbidity and mortality caused by a lethal skin fungus. *The ISME Journal*, 3, 818–824.

Harris RN, James TY, Lauer A, et al. (2006) Amphibian pathogen *Batrachochytrium dendrobatidis* is inhibited by the cutaneous bacteria of amphibian species. *EcoHealth*, 3, 53–56.

Harris RN, Lauer A, Simon MA, et al. (2009b) Addition of antifungal skin bacteria to salamanders ameliorates the effects of chytridiomycosis. *Diseases of Aquatic Organisms*, 83, 11–16.

Henao-Mejia J, Elinav E, Jin C, et al. (2012) Inflammasome-mediated dysbiosis regulates progression of NAFLD and obesity. *Nature*, 482, 179–185.

Hentschel U, Steinert M, Hacker J. (2000) Common molecular mechanisms of symbiosis and pathogenesis. *Trends in Microbiology*, 8, 226–231.

Hilty M, Burke C, Pedro H, et al. (2010) Disordered microbial communities in asthmatic airways. *PLoS ONE*, 5, e8578.

Hoffmann AA, Montgomery BL, Popovici J, et al. (2011) Successful establishment of *Wolbachia* in *Aedes* populations to suppress dengue transmission. *Nature*, 476, 454–459.

Hooper LV, Littman DR, Macpherson AJ. (2012) Interactions between the microbiota and the immune system the gut microbiota interactions between the microbiota and the immune system. *Science*, 336, 1268–1273.

Hoyt JR, Cheng TL, Langwig KE, et al. (2015) Bacteria isolated from bats inhibit the growth of *Pseudogymnoascus destructans*, the causative agent of white-nose syndrome. *PLoS ONE*, 10, 1–12.

Hsiao EY, McBride SW, Hsien S, et al. (2013) Microbiota modulate behavioral and physiological abnormalities associated with neurodevelopmental disorders. *Cell*, 155, 1451–1463.

Hu J, Wei Z, Friman VP, et al. (2016) Probiotic diversity enhances rhizosphere microbiome function and plant disease suppression. *mBio*, 7, e01790–16.

Jakaitis BM, Denning PW. (2014) Commensal and probiotic bacteria may prevent NEC by maturing intestinal host defenses. *Pathophysiology*, 21, 47–54.

Jani AJ, Briggs CJ. (2014) The pathogen *Batrachochytrium dendrobatidis* disturbs the frog skin microbiome during a natural epidemic and experimental infection. *Proceedings of the National Academy of Sciences*, 111, E5049–E5058.

Jani AJ, Knapp RA, Briggs CJ. (2017) Epidemic and endemic pathogen dynamics correspond to distinct host population microbiomes at a landscape scale. *Proceedings of the Royal Society B: Biological Sciences*, 284, 20170944.

Kang DW, Park JG, Ilhan ZE, et al. (2013) Reduced incidence of *Prevotella* and other fermenters in intestinal microflora of autistic children. *PLoS ONE*, 8, e68322.

Kassam Z, Lee CH, Yuan Y, et al. (2013) Fecal microbiota transplantation for *Clostridium difficile* infection: Systematic review and meta-analysis. *The American Journal of Gastroenterology*, 108, 500–508.

Kawamoto S, Maruya M, Kato LM, et al. (2014) Foxp3+T cells regulate immunoglobulin a selection and facilitate diversification of bacterial species responsible for immune homeostasis. *Immunity*, 41, 152–165.

Kim S, Kim H, Yim YS, et al. (2017) Maternal gut bacteria promote neurodevelopmental abnormalities in mouse offspring. *Nature*, 549, 528–532.

Knights D, Parfrey LW, Zaneveld J, et al. (2011) Human-associated microbial signatures: Examining their predictive value. *Cell Host and Microbe*, 10, 292–296.

Knights D, Silverberg MS, Weersma RK, et al. (2014) Complex host genetics influence the microbiome in inflammatory bowel disease. *Genome Medicine*, 6, 107.

Kohl KD, Cary TL, Karasov WH, et al. (2013) Restructuring of the amphibian gut microbiota through metamorphosis. *Environmental Microbiology Reports*, 5, 899–903.

Koskella B, Meaden S. (2013) Understanding bacteriophage specificity in natural microbial communities. *Viruses*, 5, 806–823.

Koskella B, Hall LJ, Metcalf CJE. (2017) The microbiome beyond the horizon of ecological and evolutionary theory. *Nature Ecology and Evolution*, 1, 1606–1615.

Kostic AD, Gevers D, Pedamallu CS, et al. (2012) Genomic analysis identifies association of *Fusobacterium* with colorectal carcinoma. *Genome Research*, 22, 292–298.

Kostic AD, Chun E, Robertson L, et al. (2013) *Fusobacterium nucleatum* potentiates intestinal tumorigenesis and modulates the tumor-immune microenvironment. *Cell Host and Microbe*, 14, 207–215.

Kueneman JG, Parfrey LW, Woodhams DC, et al. (2014) The amphibian skin-associated microbiome across species, space and life history stages. *Molecular Ecology*, 23, 1238–1250.

Kueneman JG, Woodhams DC, Van Treuren W, et al. (2016) Inhibitory bacteria reduce fungi on early life stages of endangered Colorado boreal toads (*Anaxyrus boreas*). *The ISME Journal*, 10, 934–944.

Küng D, Bigler L, Davis LR, et al. (2014) Stability of microbiota facilitated by host immune regulation: Informing probiotic strategies to manage amphibian disease. *PLoS ONE*, 9, e87101.

Kuntz TM, Gilbert JA. (2017) Introducing the microbiome into precision medicine. *Trends in Pharmacological Sciences*, 38, 81–91.

Lam BA, Walton DB, Harris RN. (2011). Motile zoospores of *Batrachochytrium dendrobatidis* move away from antifungal metabolites produced by amphibian skin bacteria. *EcoHealth*, 8, 36–45.

Lax S, Smith DP, Hampton-Marcell J, et al. (2014) Longitudinal analysis of microbial interaction between humans and the indoor environment. *Science*, 345, 1048–1052.

Levy M, Shapiro H, Thaiss CA, et al. (2017) NLRP6: A multifaceted innate immune sensor. *Trends in Immunology*, 38, 248–260.

Levy M, Thaiss CA, Zeevi D, et al. (2015) Microbiota-modulated metabolites shape the intestinal microenvironment by regulating NLRP6 inflammasome signaling. *Cell*, 163, 1428–1443.

Lips KR, Brem F, Brenes R, et al. (2006) From the cover: Emerging infectious disease and the loss of biodiversity in a Neotropical amphibian community. *Proceedings of the National Academy of Sciences*, 103, 3165–3170.

Lloyd-Price J, Mahurkar A, Rahnavard G, et al. (2017) Strains, functions and dynamics in the expanded Human Microbiome Project. *Nature*, 550, 61–66.

Locke A, Kahali B, Berndt S, et al. (2015) Genetic studies of body mass index yield new insights for obesity biology. *Nature*, 518, 197–206.

Loudon AH, Holland JA, Umile TP, et al. (2014a) Interactions between amphibians' symbiotic bacteria cause the production of emergent anti-fungal metabolites. *Frontiers in Microbiology*, 5, 1–8.

Loudon AH, Woodhams DC, Parfrey LW, et al. (2014b) Microbial community dynamics and effect of environmental microbial reservoirs on red-backed salamanders (*Plethodon cinereus*). *The ISME Journal*, 8, 830–840.

Lu Y, Chen J, Zheng J, et al. (2016) Mucosal adherent bacterial dysbiosis in patients with colorectal adenomas. *Scientific Reports*, 6, 26337.

Maurice CF, Haiser HJ, Turnbaugh PJ. (2013) Xenobiotics shape the physiology and gene expression of the active human gut microbiome. *Cell*, 152, 39–50.

Mazzoli R, Pessione E. (2016) The neuro-endocrinological role of microbial glutamate and GABA signaling. *Frontiers in Microbiology*, 7, 1934.

McCoy SS, Stannard J, Kahlenberg JM. (2016) Targeting the inflammasome in rheumatic diseases. *Translational Research*, 167, 125–137.

McDonald D, Hornig M, Lozupone C, et al. (2015). Towards large-cohort comparative studies to define the factors influencing the gut microbial community structure of ASD patients. *Microbial Ecology in Health & Disease*, 26, 28168.

Mendes R, Kruijt M, de Bruijn I, et al. (2012) Deciphering the rhizosphere microbiome. *Science*, 1097, 1097–1100.

Miyake S, Kim S, Suda W, et al. (2015) Dysbiosis in the gut microbiota of patients with multiple sclerosis, with a striking depletion of species belonging to clostridia XIVa and IV clusters. *PLoS ONE*, 10, e137429.

Morens DM, Fauci AS. (2013) Emerging infectious diseases: Threats to human health and global stability. *PLoS Pathogens*, 9, e1003467.

Mousa WK, Shearer C, Limay-Rios V, et al. (2016) Root-hair endophyte stacking in finger millet creates a physicochemical barrier to trap the fungal pathogen *Fusarium graminearum*. *Nature Microbiology*, 1, 1–12.

Mueller UG, Sachs JL. (2015) Engineering microbiomes to improve plant and animal health. *Trends in Microbiology*, 23, 606–617.

Muletz CR, Myers JM, Domangue RJ, et al. (2012) Soil bioaugmentation with amphibian cutaneous bacteria protects amphibian hosts from infection by Batrachochytrium dendrobatidis. *Biological Conservation*, 152, 119–126.

Muletz Wolz CR, Yarwood SA, Campbell Grant EH, et al. (2017) Effects of host species and environment on the skin microbiome of Plethodontid salamanders. *Journal of Animal Ecology*, 87, 341–353.

Naik S. (2012) Compartmentalized control of skin. *Science*, 1115, 1115–1120.

Nath S, Raveendran R. (2013) Microbial dysbiosis in periodontitis. *Journal of Indian Society of Periodontology*, 17, 543–545.

Nobrega FL, Costa AR, Kluskens LD, et al. (2015) Revisiting phage therapy: New applications for old resources. *Trends in Microbiology*, 23, 185–191.

O'Keefe SJD. (2016) Diet, microorganisms and their metabolites, and colon cancer. *Nature Reviews Gastroenterology and Hepatology*, 13, 691–706.

Olesen SW, Alm EJ. (2016) Dysbiosis is not an answer. *Nature Microbiology*, 25, 16228.

Oliver KM, Russell JA, Moran NA, et al. (2003) Facultative bacterial symbionts in aphids confer resistance to parasitic wasps. *Proceedings of the National Academy of Sciences*, 100, 1803–1807.

Oliver KM, Smith AH, Russell JA. (2014) Defensive symbiosis in the real world – Advancing ecological studies of heritable, protective bacteria in aphids and beyond. *Functional Ecology*, 28, 341–355.

Ollberding NJ, Völgyi E, Macaluso M, et al. (2016) Urinary microbiota associated with preterm birth: Results from the conditions affecting neurocognitive development and learning in early childhood (CANDLE) study. *PLoS ONE*, 11, e162302.

Pamer EG. (2016) Resurrecting the intestinal microbiota to combat antibiotic-resistant pathogens. *Science*, 352, 535–538.

Pérez-Brocal V, Latorre A, Moya A. (2013) Symbionts and pathogens: What is the difference? *Current Topics in Microbiology and Immunology*, 358, 215–243.

Petschow B, Doré J, Hibberd P, et al. (2013) Probiotics, prebiotics, and the host microbiome: The science of translation. *Annals of the New York Academy of Sciences*, 1306, 1–17.

Poiani A. (2010) Do cloacal pathogenic microbes behave as sexually transmitted parasites in birds? *The Open Ornithology Journal*, 3, 72–85.

Preidis GA, Versalovic J. (2009) Targeting the human microbiome with antibiotics, probiotics, and prebiotics: Gastroenterology enters the metagenomics era. *Gastroenterology*, 136, 2015–2031.

Qazi T, Amaratunga T, Barnes EL, et al. (2017) The risk of inflammatory bowel disease flares after fecal microbiota transplantation: Systematic review and meta-analysis. *Gut Microbes*, 8, 574–588.

Ramos PE, Abrunhosa L, Pinheiro A, et al. (2016) Probiotic-loaded microcapsule system for human *in situ* folate production: Encapsulation and system validation. *Food Research International*, 90, 25–32.

Rautio J, Kumpulainen H, Heimbach T, et al. (2008). Prodrugs: Design and clinical applications. *Nature Reviews Drug Discovery*, 7, 255–270.

Raveh-Sadka T, Thomas BC, Singh A, et al. (2015) Gut bacteria are rarely shared by co-hospitalized premature infants, regardless of necrotizing enterocolitis development. *eLife*, 4, e05477.

Rebollar EA, Hughey MC, Medina D, et al. (2016) Skin bacterial diversity of Panamanian frogs is associated with host susceptibility and presence of *Batrachochytrium dendrobatidis*. *The ISME Journal*, 10, 1682–1695.

Rezzonico F, Binder C, Défago G, et al. (2005) The type III secretion system of biocontrol

Pseudomonas fluorescens KD targets the phytopathogenic *Chromista pythium ultimum* and promotes cucumber protection. *Molecular Plant–Microbe Interactions*, 18, 991–1001.

Rivers TM. (1937) Viruses and Koch's postulates. *Journal of Bacteriology*, 33, 1–12.

Rubin BK, Tamaoki J. (2005) Antibiotics as anti-inflammatory and immunomodulatory agents. In: *Progress in Inflammation Research*. Basel: Birkhäuser Basel.

Sahin M, Sur M. (2015) Genes, circuits, and precision therapies for autism and related neurodevelopmental disorders. *Science*, 350, 926.

Sapp M, Lewis E, Moss S, et al. (2016) Metabarcoding of bacteria associated with the Acute Oak Decline syndrome in England. *Forests*, 7, 95.

Scheele BC, Pasmans F, Skerratt LF, et al. (2019) Amphibian fungal panzootic causes catastrophic and ongoing loss of biodiversity. *Science*, 363, 1459–1463.

Scheuring I, Yu DW. (2012) How to assemble a beneficial microbiome in three easy steps. *Ecology Letters*, 15, 1300–1307.

Schirmer M, Smeekens SP, Vlamakis H, et al. (2016) Linking the human gut microbiome to inflammatory cytokine production capacity. *Cell*, 167, 1125–1136.

Schwingshackl L, Hoffmann G. (2015) Adherence to Mediterranean diet and risk of cancer: An updated systematic review and meta-analysis of observational studies. *Cancer Medicine*, 4, 1933–1947.

Scott TA, Quintaneiro LM, Norvaisas P, et al. (2017) Host–microbe co-metabolism dictates cancer drug efficacy in *C. elegans*. *Cell*, 169, 442–456.

Shivappa N, Godos J, Hébert JR, et al. (2017) Dietary inflammatory index and colorectal cancer risk – A meta-analysis. *Nutrients*, 9, 1043.

Sousa T, Paterson R, Moore V, et al. (2008) The gastrointestinal microbiota as a site for the biotransformation of drugs. *International Journal of Pharmaceutics*, 363, 1–25.

Spanogiannopoulos P, Bess EN, Carmody RN, et al. (2016) The microbial pharmacists within us: A metagenomic view of xenobiotic metabolism. *Nature Reviews Microbiology*, 14, 273–287.

Stefka AT, Feehley T, Tripathi P, et al. (2014) Commensal bacteria protect against food allergen sensitization. *Proceedings of the National Academy of Sciences*, 111, 13145–13150.

Stein MM, Hrusch CL, Gozdz J, et al. (2016) Innate immunity and asthma risk in Amish and Hutterite farm children. *The New England Journal of Medicine*, 375, 411–421.

Strandwitz P, Kim KH, Terekhova D, et al. (2019). GABA-modulating bacteria of the human gut microbiota. *Nature Microbiology*, 4, 396–403.

Strati F, Cavalieri D, Albanese D, et al. (2017) New evidences on the altered gut microbiota in autism spectrum disorders. *Microbiome*, 5, 24.

Summers WC. (2012) The strange history of phage therapy. *Bacteriophage*, 2, 130–133.

Sze MA, Baxter NT, Ruffin MT, et al. (2017). Normalization of the microbiota in patients after treatment for colonic lesions. *Microbiome*, 5, 150.

Sze MA, Dimitriu PA, Hayashi S, et al. (2012) The lung tissue microbiome in chronic obstructive pulmonary disease. *American Journal of Respiratory and Critical Care Medicine*, 185, 1073–1080.

Tang WHW, Wang Z, Levison BS, et al. (2013) Intestinal microbial metabolism of phosphatidylcholine and cardiovascular risk. *New England Journal of Medicine*, 368, 1575–1584.

The Human Microbiome Consortium. (2012) Structure, function and diversity of the healthy human microbiome. *Nature*, 486, 207–214.

Theodoratou E, Timofeeva M, Li X, et al. (2017) Nature, nurture, and cancer risks: Genetic and nutritional contributions to cancer. *Annual Review of Nutrition*, 37, 293–320.

Tuan J, Chen YX. (2016) Dietary and lifestyle factors associated with colorectal cancer risk and interactions with microbiota: Fiber, red or processed meat and alcoholic drinks. *Gastrointestinal Tumors*, 3, 17–24.

Tuohy KM, Fava F, Viola R. (2014) 'The way to a man's heart is through his gut microbiota' – Dietary pro- and prebiotics for the management of cardiovascular risk. *Proceedings of the Nutrition Society*, 73, 172–185.

Turnbaugh PJ, Hamady M, Yatsunenko T, et al. (2009) A core gut microbiome in obese and lean twins. *Nature*, 457, 480–484.

Turner TR, James EK, Poole PS. (2013) The plant microbiome. *Genome Biology*, 14, 209.

Uusitalo U, Liu X, Yang J, et al. (2015) Association of early exposure of probiotics and islet autoimmunity in the TEDDY study. *JAMA Pediatrics*, 33612, 1–9.

van Nood E, Vrieze A, Nieuwdorp M, et al. (2013) Duodenal infusion of donor feces for recurrent *Clostridium difficile*. *New England Journal of Medicine*, 368, 407–415.

Vences M, Lyra ML, Kueneman JG, et al. (2016) Gut bacterial communities across tadpole ecomorphs in two diverse tropical anuran faunas. *Die Naturwissenschaften*, 103, 25.

Venkataraman A, Sieber JR, Schmidt AW, et al. (2016) Variable responses of human microbiomes to dietary supplementation with resistant starch. *Microbiome*, 4, 33.

Walke JB, Becker MH, Loftus SC, et al. (2015) Community structure and function of amphibian skin microbes: An experiment with bullfrogs exposed to a chytrid fungus. *PLoS ONE*, 10, e139848.

Wang J, Jia H. (2016) Metagenome-wide association studies: Fine-mining the microbiome. *Nature Reviews Microbiology*, 14, 508–522.

Wang S, Dos-Santos ALA, Huang W, et al. (2017) Driving mosquito refractoriness to *Plasmodium falciparum* with engineered symbiotic bacteria. *Science*, 357, 1399–1402.

Watkins PB, Kaplowitz N, Slattery JT, et al. (2006) Aminotransferase elevations in healthy adults receiving 4 grams of acetaminophen daily: A randomized controlled trial. *Journal of the American Medical Association*, 296, 87–93.

Weingarden A, González A, Vázquez-Baeza Y, et al. (2015) Dynamic changes in short- and long-term bacterial composition following fecal microbiota transplantation for recurrent *Clostridium difficile* infection. *Microbiome*, 3, 10.

Woodhams DC, Geiger CC, Reinert LK, et al. (2012) Treatment of amphibians infected with chytrid fungus: learning from failed trials with itraconazole, antimicrobial peptides, bacteria, and heat therapy. *Diseases of Aquatic Organisms*, 98, 11–25.

Worsley MA. (1998). Infection control and prevention of *Clostridium difficile* infection. *Journal of Antimicrobial Chemotherapy*, 41, 59–66.

Wright M, Beaty JS, Ternent CA. (2017) Molecular markers for colorectal cancer. *Surgical Clinics of North America*, 97, 683–701.

Wu S, Rhee KJ, Albesiano E, et al. (2009) A human colonic commensal promotes colon tumorigenesis via activation of T helper type 17 T cell responses. *Nature Medicine*, 15, 1016–1022.

Young VB. (2017) The role of the microbiome in human health and disease: An introduction for clinicians. *British Medical Journal*, 356, j831.

Yu TC, Guo F, Yu Y, et al. (2017) *Fusobacterium nucleatum* promotes chemoresistance to colorectal cancer by modulating autophagy. *Cell*, 170, 548–563.

Zackular JP, Baxter NT, Iverson KD, et al. (2013) The gut microbiome modulates colon tumorigenesis. *mBio*, 4, e00692–13.

Zackular JP, Baxter NT, Chen GY, et al. (2015) Manipulation of the gut microbiota reveals role in colon tumorigenesis. *mSphere*, 1, e00001–15.

Zhu A, Sunagawa S, Mende DR, et al. (2015) Inter-individual differences in the gene content of human gut bacterial species. *Genome Biology*, 18, 82.

CHAPTER EIGHT

Adapting to environmental change

ELLEN L. FRY
University of Manchester
FENG ZHU
Chinese Academy of Sciences and Netherlands Institute of Ecology
and
BETHAN GREENWOOD
University of Essex

8.1 Introduction

In the twenty-first century, unprecedented climate change, pollutants and habitat alterations are causing abiotic stress across all plants and animals. This stress has and will continue to shift the host–microbiome relationship in unpredictable ways, and is likely to have far-reaching consequences for host metabolism, immunity to disease, community assembly and, beyond the host, for delivery of ecosystem functions and services. The importance of host–microbe partnerships to the integrated responses and adaptations of organisms to environmental change is being increasingly recognised (Singh & Trivedi, 2017; David et al., 2018; Pita et al., 2018). For example, there is some evidence that plants only make close associations with microbes when they are already stressed, which could mean increasingly close links with microbes as environmental change intensifies (Mendes et al., 2011; Pineda et al., 2013). This may be, in part, due to the autotrophic nature of plants, which means they may be less reliant upon a co-evolved microbiome for nutrients in comparison to animals. By contrast, aquatic and terrestrial animals are innately reliant on their associated microbiome, partly because of the benefits they offer in terms of nutrient release from external food sources. This could lead to unexpected effects as abiotic pressures increase on animal and human populations. While the direct impacts of atmospheric and ocean warming, elevated carbon dioxide (eCO_2), precipitation changes and pollution have been studied fairly extensively for plants, animals and ecosystems, focus is now turning to the influence of environmental change on host microbiomes, and what this means for host function.

In this chapter, we first consider the direct effects of environmental change on the microbiome and the cascading effects on a variety of plant and animal hosts. We will draw on examples from the plant kingdom, corals (as an indicator taxon for the response of marine life) and terrestrial fauna from insects to humans. Where appropriate, we consider whether there are unifying principles between the groups. We also consider the overall effects of environmental changes at larger scales, using outcomes of environmental changes from a plant health perspective as a primary example. There is a large body of research on plant health because of their importance as the basis for food security, and environmental changes are likely to affect them strongly and rapidly. The second part of the chapter will discuss the potential for the microbiome to mitigate against environmental change for the host organism, again considering plants, corals and terrestrial animals in turn.

8.2 Effects of environmental changes on the microbiome and subsequent impacts on the host

8.2.1 Plants

The plant microbiome offers the same broad functions as that of animals: improving intake and use of nutrients and water (Philippot et al., 2013), protection from predators and pathogens (Berendsen et al., 2012) and altering tolerance to changing conditions (Berg et al., 2016). The plant microbiome consists of: (1) the external, i.e. those inhabiting the root surface and zone, known as the rhizosphere, and those inhabiting the leaf and shoot surface and zone, known as the phyllosphere, which is composed of microbial epiphytes; and (2) the internal, i.e. those that inhabit leaf and root tissues (endophytes) and those that primarily inhabit the root tissues, including mycorrhizal fungi and rhizobial bacteria (Figure 8.1). The plant microbiome is largely neutral or beneficial (Sánchez-Cañizares et al., 2017), but changing conditions can result in decoupling of the plant–microbe relationship (Johnson et al., 2008; Vacher et al., 2016). The effect of environmental change on the plant microbiome is likely to occur directly through abiotic changes that alter microbial performance or community composition, or indirectly through changes to the plant, which will result in altered inputs through plant morphology, root exudates, root sloughing and litter.

The effects of environmental change on the epiphytic microbes of the phyllosphere are likely to be considerable, but this habitat is largely understudied. Part of the reason for the oversight of the phyllosphere is because the leaf surface is a much more ephemeral environment than the root surface, usually lasting only through the growing season (Vacher et al., 2016). It is also a slightly controversial classification because the leaf surface is so easily penetrated through stomata and wounds; therefore, many microbial epiphytes live both on and in the leaf. At the microscale, the phyllosphere environment is very heterogeneous, and so microbial epiphytes have evolved a number of adaptations to cope with environmental stress that is encountered on a diurnal basis. The main stresses are ultraviolet (UV) radiation,

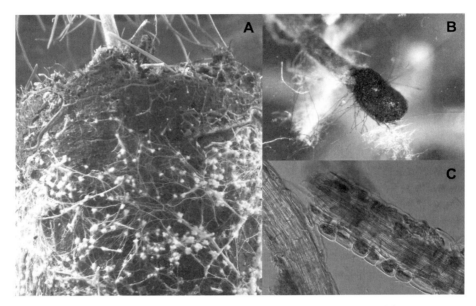

Figure 8.1 Mycorrhizal colonisation of plant roots at different scales. (A) Ectomycorrhizal fungal colonisation of *Pinus sylvestris* (photo credit: Joshua Harrop); (B) ectomycorrhizal fungal colonisation of *Cenococcum geophilum* (black) on *Pinus sylvestris* roots, with a second ectomycorrhizal coloniser visible (white) (photo credit: David Johnson); (C) ericoid mycorrhizal colonisation of *Vaccinium vitis-idaea* root, with mycorrhiza stained blue (photo credit: Ully Kritzler). (A black and white version of this figure will appear in some formats. For the colour version, please refer to the plate section.)

desiccation and oxygen release from photosynthesis, which results in the formation of reactive oxygen species (ROS) that can impair biochemical machinery in the epiphytes (Jacobs & Sundin, 2001; Vorholt, 2012). Future changes in cloud cover, light intensity and rainfall could all increase these stresses past physiological limits, impacting the beneficial epiphytes that prevent colonisation of harmful groups such as *Pseudomonas* spp., which could lead to increased plant disease (Babic et al., 1996; Vacher et al., 2016). For example, at high concentrations, ROS can switch from useful signalling molecules that can help regulate plant–microbial interactions to agents of disruption or inhibition of cellular processes in plant organs including chloroplasts (similar to zooxanthellae in corals, see below), which can negatively affect plant growth and homeostatic regulation (Nath et al., 2017). Increases in UV radiation are also linked with mutations of epiphytic microbes, which could have consequences for microbial community interactions on the leaf, as well as potential changes to interactions between plants and microbial epiphytes (Vorholt, 2012). Further, some sugars and inorganic nutrients from photosynthetic activity can pass through the cuticle and provide an energy source for microbial epiphytes. If photosynthetic activity decreases due to environmental change, this is likely to shape the community composition of the phyllosphere. In terms of climatic changes, it seems that the most important change for microbial epiphytes will be that of drought and warming, with less effect of CO_2 and ozone (O_3) enrichment (Rico et al., 2014; Bálint et al. 2015; Ueda et al. 2016). Additionally, there is evidence that microbial epiphytes are highly reactive to pollutants and chemical changes (Khanna, 1986). However, evidence that this will impact the plant is lacking, and until their true role in plant function is described, it will be difficult to ascertain the effect of climate or pollution-driven changes (Vacher et al., 2016).

The role of endophytic microbes in above-ground plant tissues is understudied, and therefore their response to environmental change can mainly only be inferred through understanding changes in plant physiology and chemistry in a context-dependent manner (Pineda et al., 2013). Moreover, colonisation tends to occur through seeds or roots, and so environmental changes that might impact infection rates could have far-reaching impacts on the host. Currently, most literature is focused on the benefits that an endophyte can confer upon the plant, with very little empirical evidence of the impact of environmental change on the microbe itself (Rodriguez & Redman, 2008; Hardoim et al., 2015). The current paradigm is that plants and endophytes exist in a kind of 'balanced antagonism', which would mean that if the health of the host was compromised, endophytes are likely to become pathogenic (Saona et al., 2010). The main direct effect of environmental change, therefore, is probably on the mode and efficacy of transmission of the endophyte, and its ability to colonise the plant. Drought, increases in UV light and changes in soil stoichiometry are all inhibitory to endophytic penetration of tissues, and future changes in abiotic drivers through climate change or pollution may cause reductions in colonisation (Hardoim et al., 2015). Endophytes are known to use photosynthate from the plant and compete with mycorrhizae for C. If stressful conditions mean that photosynthesis is reduced, particularly in species that use a C_3 pathway, the presence of the endophyte could be detrimental to the plant–mycorrhizal association, which could in turn mean that the mycorrhiza becomes parasitic or withholds N and P from the plant (Liu et al., 2017). The resources that plants offer may become a battleground for different microbial groups under abiotic stress, and more research is needed to incorporate these interactions into future-proofing plans. Other forms of global change may have subtler, or possibly undetectable, effects. A recent study has shown that eCO_2 has minimal effect on an endophytic fungal species and its relationship with the host plant (in this case aspen), indicating that while the endophyte does not incur any cost to the plant, eCO_2 will also not trigger an antagonistic response in this case (Randriamanana et al., 2018). More experimental work is needed to ascertain whether this is a general rule and whether multiple stresses could alter host–endophyte relationships.

Research into the effect of environmental change on plant microbiomes has largely looked at relationships between the rhizosphere community and the plant, with a focus on mycorrhizal fungi and plant-growth promoting (PGPR) bacteria. This is chiefly because of the well-characterised links between colonisation of these groups and plant growth, particularly from a food security perspective (Berg et al., 2014). Ultimately, soil microbes are likely to be directly affected through changes in water availability, temperature, and concentrations of atmospheric, liquid, and solid gases and pollutants. Changes in water availability will impact PGPR more rapidly than mycorrhizae because single-celled organisms are more vulnerable to osmotic stress, changes in nutrient supply and loss of connectivity through pore water (Kaisermann et al., 2017). To some extent they may be shielded from the worst of the effects of drought through their association with the plant; some plants may exhibit hydraulic lift, redistributing water to upper soil layers, while most will leave liquid exudates in the soil, which will alleviate drought in the short term, although these may become more unpredictable as drought continues (Preece & Peñuelas, 2016). Flooding, however, may cause problems by leaching bacteria into deeper soil layers or increasing accessibility of soil pathogens to roots (Callahan et al., 2017). With regard to warming, evidence suggests that the soil microbial community may adapt rapidly through shifts in the community or physiological adaptation, which will increase as warming continues (Romero-Olivares et al., 2017).

Mycorrhizal fungi engage in close symbiotic relationships with plant roots, where nitrogen (N) and phosphorus (P) in the soil is traded with the plant for photosynthetically derived carbon (C). This relationship is highly context-dependent as it is modulated by a range of abiotic and biotic factors. Thus, environmental changes will impact mycorrhizae both directly and indirectly through its relationship with the host (Johnson et al., 2013). For mycorrhizae, most research focuses on the amelioration of stress on the plant, rather than considering the effect on the fungus itself (although see Millar & Bennet, 2016 for a review). Similar to endophytes, the parts of the fungus inside the plant are likely to be indirectly affected by environmental changes, mediated through the plant response. However, one study has shown that under abiotic stress mycorrhizal communities become simplified and the remaining taxa are more resilient to stress (Gehring et al., 2014). Depending on the type of environmental change that occurs, the mycorrhizal relationship could become more or less important to the plant. This will be particularly true if the change in question alters nutrient availability; studies have shown that if N or P become more available in the soil, the plant may not need the symbiosis at all. Because most mycorrhizae are obligately dependent on the host, this could change the nature of the relationship from symbiotic to parasitic (Johnson et al., 2008). Interestingly, eCO_2 could favour the mycorrhizal symbiosis through inducing the plant host to create excess photosynthate, which would in turn favour the plant by increasing N nutrition (Gamper et al., 2005), although this is the subject of some debate (Johnson et al., 2013).

8.2.2 Marine invertebrates

Marine invertebrates, and their associated microbiomes, are threatened by a range of anthropogenically caused environmental changes. In this section we consider the impacts of ocean warming and acidification due to eCO_2, as well as the impacts of pollution on the microbiomes of a group of keystone marine invertebrates: the stony corals. Average sea-surface temperatures (SSTs) of the Pacific, Atlantic and Indian Oceans have increased by 0.31, 0.41 and 0.65°C, respectively, from 1950 to 2009 (Hoegh-Guldberg et al., 2014). A continued trajectory of current greenhouse gas emissions [Representative Concentration Pathway (RCP) 8.5] is predicted to result in an increase in tropical SSTs of 3–4°C by 2100 (Hoegh-Guldberg et al. 2014, 2017; ISRS, 2015). The eCO_2 that has dissolved into the oceans over the past 150 years has decreased pH by 0.1 (representing a 26% increase in hydrogen ions), and decreased carbonate ion concentration by ~30 µmol kg^{-1} seawater (IPCC, 2007; Hoegh-Guldberg et al., 2017). These changes in carbonate chemistry are known to especially impact calcifying organisms (including certain molluscs, echinoderms, corals and plankton) through the process of ocean acidification (Hofmann et al., 2010). Here, we focus on the scleractinian corals as keystone organisms. These build vast calcium carbonate structures and form the foundations of one of the most biodiverse ecosystems on the planet. Coral reefs harbour between a quarter and a third of all known marine species (Connell, 1978), representing diversity which is dwarfed when considering the enormous array of microbiota not counted (Rohwer et al., 2002).

Like plants, corals associate with a diverse microbiome comprised of algae, bacteria, archaea, fungi and viruses, rendering them a meta-organism termed the 'coral holobiont' (Rohwer et al., 2002). In a functioning symbiosis between coral host and microscopic, photosynthetic dinoflagellates called zooxanthellae, the coral host benefits from provision of up to 90% of its energy requirements in the form of autotrophically fixed organic carbon (Muscatine, 1990; Yellowlees et al., 2008). In exchange, the zooxanthellae receive CO_2, essential nutrients and trace elements that are otherwise scarce in the open ocean, and a refuge beneath transparent coral tissues with access to sunlight (Figure 8.2). The bacterial portion of the microbiome within coral tissues has been purported to play roles in N and sulphur (S) cycling, metabolising otherwise unavailable nutrients (Rohwer et al., 2002; Bourne et al., 2016); not unlike the role of cellulose-degrading microbes in ruminant guts (Russell et al., 2009)

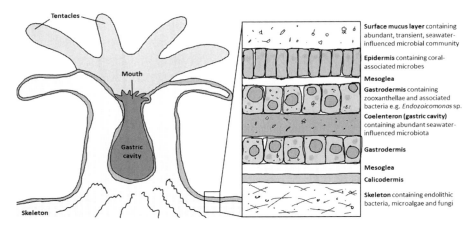

Figure 8.2 Schematic illustration of the coral holobiont depicting a cross-section of a coral polyp and microbial symbionts associated with various compartments: surface mucus layer, epidermis, mesoglea, gastrodermis, gastric cavity, calicodermis and skeleton (illustration by Bethan Greenwood, adapted from Bourne et al., 2016). (A black and white version of this figure will appear in some formats. For the colour version, please refer to the plate section.)

or N-fixing bacteria in legume root nodules (Oldroyd et al., 2011). Without microbial symbiotic associations, corals could not survive in such clear, nutrient-deficient waters as those found around reefs (see Darwin's Paradox, 1842). Due to the functional importance of these symbioses, there is likely a coral host–mediated immune response for selecting beneficial microbes while rejecting pathogens (Krediet et al., 2013).

Perhaps the most obvious effect of environmental change on the coral microbiome, at least visually, is on the coral–zooxanthellae symbiosis, which is vulnerable to increased temperatures (Smith et al., 2004). Like all oxygenic photosynthetic organisms, zooxanthellae risk photo-oxidative damage. Accumulation of ROS in zooxanthellae occurs due to cascading effects of impaired photosynthetic apparatus and continued oxygen production. These lead to oxidative stress, resulting in cellular damage to membranes, proteins and nucleic acids (Lesser, 2006). It is thought that the compromised and damage-causing zooxanthellae are either ejected (exocytosis), eliminated (apoptosis) or eaten (phagocytosis) by the coral host as an innate immune response, resulting in coral bleaching (Weis, 2008). It should be noted that temperature and light are not the only causes of bleaching, and that bleaching is not necessarily always precluded by a build-up of photosynthetically generated ROS (Tolleter et al., 2013; Krueger et al., 2015). There is growing evidence for both host and bacterial involvement in bleaching (Diaz et al., 2016; Pogoreutz et al., 2017). Nevertheless, without the photosynthetically derived nutrition from the algal symbionts, the coral host starves. Moreover, once a coral has bleached, it often exhibits a microbiome different to that of healthy corals (Bourne et al., 2008; Koren & Rosenberg, 2008), although there are exceptions (Hadaidi et al., 2017).

As well as indirectly altering the microbiome by decoupling the coral–zooxanthellae symbiosis, elevated temperatures have been shown to initiate pathogenesis in coral microbiomes (Rosenberg & Ben-Haim, 2002; Vega Thurber et al., 2009), and have been correlated with widespread disease outbreaks (Bruno et al., 2007). There are several examples of pathogenic bacteria whose virulence and spread is temperature-dependent (Cervino et al., 2004; Rosenberg & Falkovitz, 2004; Remily & Richardson, 2006), including *Vibrio coralliilyticus* attacking its coral host *Pocillopora damicornis* (Ben-Haim et al., 2003). Under normal conditions, the coral mucus layer and associated coral microbiota offer a line of defence to the host by inhibiting pathogenic infection (Ritchie, 2006; Shnit-Orland & Kushmaro, 2009; Kvennefors et al., 2012). However, this antibiotic ability is diminished at higher temperatures (as evidenced after unusually high summer temperatures: Ritchie, 2006; and under experimental warming conditions: Rypien et al., 2010), thereby indirectly altering the microbiome. Metagenomics approaches have revealed that elevated temperatures can shift coral microbiomes to disease-associated states with higher pathogenic bacteria and fungi, as well as increases in virulence genes (Vega Thurber et al., 2009; Littman et al., 2011). Increased SSTs cause a compositional shift in the coral microbiome from a normally commensal community with the ability to exclude pathogens towards dominance by opportunistic potential pathogens (Figure 8.3). Consequently, more-frequent high SST anomalies predicted with climate change could select for pathogenic taxa and increase the susceptibility of corals to disease (Bruno et al., 2007).

The effects of increased SSTs on the coral microbiome can be mediated by other environmental conditions. For at least some coral pathogens, there exists a synergistic effect of pH and temperature; with increasing temperature, the causative pathogen of white plague disease expanded its minimum pH tolerance from pH 6 down to pH 5 (Remily & Richardson, 2006). Some local stressors such as nutrient pollution and overfishing interact with temperature to further disrupt coral microbiomes, thereby increasing coral disease and mortality (Zaneveld et al., 2016; Wang et al., 2018). However, other environmental conditions, such as water flow, can buffer temperature-induced microbiome changes (Lee et al., 2017).

Comparatively little research has focused on the impacts of ocean acidification on coral microbiota. Recent findings indicate that increasing acidity of seawater can have a similar effect to temperature increases, whereby the coral microbiome is shifted to a disease-associated state with associated increases in microbial diversity (Vega Thurber et al., 2009). However, a field study of the

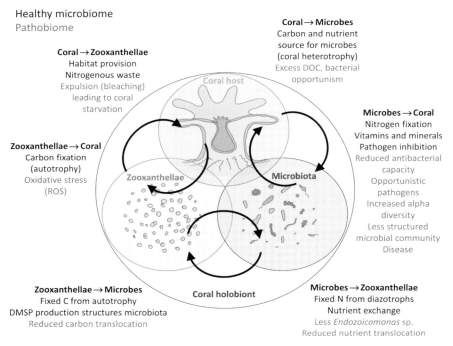

Figure 8.3 Conceptual figure showing purported roles of the coral host and associated microbiome, including both zooxanthellae and other microbiota within the coral holobiont. Functions of a healthy microbiome are shown in black text, and impaired functions due to a disease-associated microbiome or 'pathobiome' (Sweet & Bulling, 2017) during times of environmental stress in pale grey (illustration by Bethan Greenwood, adapted from Vega Thurber et al., 2009). (A black and white version of this figure will appear in some formats. For the colour version, please refer to the plate section.)

corals *Balanophyllia europaea* and *Cladocora caespitosa* translocated across a natural pH gradient caused by CO_2 vents in the Mediterranean found that low pH had no impact on microbial community structure, and no pathogenic bacteria were detected (Meron et al., 2012). A lack of restructuring in the coral microbiome in response to reduced pH could be explained by natural exposure to pH fluctuations, both through natural processes on the reef (Guadayol et al., 2014), as well as internal changes within coral tissues (ranging from pH 7.3 at night to pH 8.5 in the day) (Kuhl et al., 1995; Venn et al., 2011). For many known pathogens, their growth optima already lie within the natural pH range of the coral microhabitat (e.g. Remily & Richardson, 2006). Thus, the effects of ocean acidification on coral microbiota are not conclusive; while some coral hosts appear to maintain a stable microbiome (Meron et al., 2012; Webster et al., 2016), others exhibit shifts when exposed to lowered pH (Vega Thurber et al., 2009; Meron et al., 2011). However, it should be noted that these and many other acidification experiments overshoot the next-century predictions of a 0.4 pH unit decrease (IPCC, 2013).

Pollution is another human-driven change to the reef environment, but usually at a more local scale. Coastal development can increase sedimentation and turbidity through dredging and building activities, while sewage discharge and agricultural run-off both exacerbate nutrient loading on these nutrient-poor ecosystems. There is evidence that even while corals appear healthy, those living in polluted sites can exhibit specific bacterial signatures, manifested as changes in bacterial symbiont diversity and increases in opportunists (Ziegler et al., 2016). For example, the mucus of Caribbean corals *Montastraea faveolata* and *Porites astreoides* host more diverse bacterial communities with a higher relative abundance of disease-associated taxa at sites closer to the mainland, i.e. more anthropogenically influenced reefs (Morrow et al., 2012). Research into the potential for microbial contamination of Florida's coral microbiota by land-based sources of pollution revealed that oceanic outfalls of municipal wastewater treatment plants influenced microbial community structure of water overlying nearby reefs, as well as the mucus and tissue microbiomes of coral hosts *P. astreoides* and *Siderastrea siderea* (Staley et al., 2017). Nutrient enrichment can also disrupt the coral–algal symbiosis (Pogoreutz et al., 2017). In some cases, despite causing bleaching and tissue loss to the coral host, nutrient enrichment does not alter the composition of other microbiota (Pogoreutz et al., 2018). The bacterial community of this host, *Pocillopora verrucosa*, was previously found to be relatively invariant when compared to another, *Acropora hemprichii*, across reef sites experiencing different exposure to nutrients from sedimentation and sewage (Ziegler et al., 2016). Coral hosts may therefore lie on a continuum of microbiome flexibility, with some hosts able to change their microbiome to suit the environment, and others exhibiting stable microbial associations unable to adapt or acclimatise to environmental change (Pogoreutz et al., 2018).

In general, stressors to coral reefs, including increased SSTs, ocean acidification and pollution, have been found to increase taxa richness of coral-associated bacteria (McDevitt-Irwin et al., 2017). A likely explanation for this is that bacteria not normally present within coral microbiomes invade opportunistically under a change in conditions, leading to a more taxa-rich microbiome (Figure 8.3). Global and local stressors have also been associated with changes in evenness within the coral microbiome, indicating shifts in the dominant bacterial taxa (McDevitt-Irwin et al., 2017). Decreased bacterial evenness has similarly been found in plant rhizospheres subjected to heat disturbance (van der Voort et al., 2016). As coral-associated microbes have been implicated in nutrient cycling (Raina et al., 2009; Rädecker et al., 2015) and antimicrobial activity (Ritchie, 2006), compositional changes in microbiota likely have consequences for coral host functioning, health and ultimately, survival. Environmentally induced changes in the coral microbiome are likely to have consequences not only for the host, but for associated food webs and interactions. For example, simulated nutrient pollution in a manipulated field study altered the outcome of parrotfish predation on corals by increasing bacterial opportunism (Zaneveld et al., 2016). Corals that had been bitten and were nutrient-enriched exhibited microbiome shifts towards Proteobacteria dominance and subsequently died, whereas bitten corals that were not experimentally nutrient-polluted showed no microbial shifts and survived predation (Zaneveld et al., 2016). By impacting reefs through knock-on effects, the consequences of pollution can be complex.

8.2.3 Terrestrial animals

One key difference between the microbiomes of different animal taxa arises through the mode of acquisition; mammals receive their internal microbiome during their live birth, while insects, birds, amphibians and reptiles may be more dependent on their environment and food sources to instil the microbiome. In addition, host diet is one of the key factors that shape the composition and structure of animal gut microbiome (see Chapter 5). Consequently, animal microbiomes may change over generations as the environment and food availability alters. For example, the cascading effects on nutritional value of plant and animal-derived food sources are likely to have complex impacts on gut microbiota of all animals as the environment changes. Understanding these effects may become crucial for maintaining healthy ecosystems and animal populations in the future. According to current models, expected consequences of climate change include extreme rainfall events, severe heatwaves, and habitat destruction and fragmentation. These rapid environmental changes may alter host fitness if the microbiome and physiological limits of the host cannot adapt sufficiently. In this section, we mainly focus on temperature-induced changes in the microbiome, because literature is sparse on other forms of global change, and changes in water availability are likely to be mediated by the homeostatic mechanisms of the host.

Given that studies have suggested seasonal variations alter host–microbe associations in a wide range of animals and humans (Wei et al., 2014), it is reasonable to assume that environmental changes may directly affect the animal microbiome and thereby indirectly affect host fitness. For example, in some extreme cases, mammalian symbionts may act as opportunistic pathogens under unfavourable environmental conditions, thus reducing host fitness directly (Cerf-Bensussan & Gaboriau-Routhiau, 2010). While empirical evidence for direct effects of environmental changes on the microbiome is sparse, a recent mass mortality event in saiga antelope (*Saiga tatarica*) in which 200,000 individuals died over a three-week period in central

Kazakhstan has been attributed to unusually high temperatures and humidity that turned the usually commensal bacterium *Pasteurella multocida* pathogenic, causing population-wide hemorrhagic septicemia in the host (Kock et al., 2018). Aside from this, most examples of environmental influences on microbiomes are confined to insect hosts. Insects are generally sensitive to extreme temperatures, and thermal tolerance can vary significantly within insect groups. In aphids, temperature-mediated mutations in *Buchnera* spp. can alter the thermal tolerance of the host (Dunbar et al., 2007; Wernegreen, 2012). Further, there is evidence that a second bacterial symbiont, *Serratia symbiotica*, can shield both the host and *Buchnera* from the effects of warming (Burke et al., 2010). However, in other insect groups, it has long been recognised that high temperatures reduce the survival of endosymbionts across a range of insect hosts (Buchner, 1965). For example, the mutualistic relationship between the mountain pine beetle and its fungal partners is restricted to cool conditions; increasing temperatures leads to marginalisation or loss of the beetle–fungal mutualism (Addison et al., 2013). Moreover, some bacterial symbionts also seem to be constrained by thermal adaptation. It has been demonstrated that the bacterial symbiont can be eliminated from stinkbug (*Acrosternum ilare* and *Murgantia histrionica*) hosts by experimentally increasing air temperatures (Prado et al., 2010). The decoupling of the host–microbe association causes a reduction in the fitness of the insect host, expressed as a reduction in growth rates and size (Kikuchi et al., 2016). In these examples, the impact of environmental change on host fitness is caused by symbiont mortality, not a direct effect of heat on host itself. In larger animals, there is very little literature on the effect of warming on the microbiome. This could be because the worst effects of warming are mitigated by the host itself through homeostatic or behavioural adjustments, or otherwise attenuated by more important variables such as diet choice. The same may be true for changes in water availability.

A second role of the animal microbiome is to protect the host against disease or pathogens, and to overcome plant defence chemicals. Plant defence chemicals are likely to be highly susceptible to changes in climate or other environmental changes, and thus should be the focus of substantial research efforts. Some insect gut symbionts may facilitate detoxification of defensive allelochemicals in their host plant, benefiting both host and microbial fitness (Hammer & Bowers, 2015; Berasategui et al., 2017). Colorado potato beetle (*Leptinotarsa decemlineata*) relies on microbial symbionts residing in the beetle's oral secretions to suppress defence responses in tomato (Chung et al., 2013). However, under certain conditions such as eCO_2, plant-induced defence is increased (Noctor & Mhamdi, 2017). Therefore, under future climate-change scenarios there is potential for an 'arms race' between herbivorous insects, their gut microbiota and plants. Interestingly, insect-associated microbes may also indirectly affect insect–plant interactions by altering insect physiology, rendering future interactions unpredictable (Shikano et al., 2017). In mammals, particularly humans, the rise of allergies and intolerances is linked with increases of atmospheric pollution in the form of ROS and reactive nitrogen species, such as O_3 and nitrous oxides. These increase oxidative stress to cellular lipids, proteins and nucleic acids. As these pollutants continue to be released, the role of the microbiome may become increasingly important to mitigate their effects (Reinmuth-Selzle et al., 2017). Other forms of pollution may also impact animal microbiomes depending on the route of contact, including heavy metals, pesticides, organic pollutants such as sewage, and many more.

8.3 How could the microbiome aid host survival in response to environmental change?

8.3.1 Plants

The holobiont theory suggests that during periods of environmental change, the best combination of host and associated microbiome are selected for (Zilber-Rosenberg & Rosenberg, 2008). However, observed shifts in the relationship between plants and microbes towards the antagonistic end of the continuum under stressful conditions indicate that this theory may not hold true for an entire community, or potentially during periods of rapid change (Douglas & Werren, 2016). Nevertheless, there is mounting evidence that host–microbe interactions will often lead to induced host tolerance of abiotic stress such as temperature increases, drought and salinity (Dimkpa et al., 2009; Aroca et al., 2013). This is likely to occur through microbially induced chemical signalling and increased plant growth (Pineda et al., 2013).

Endophytic fungi have differing roles in the host, and there are varying reports on their ability to protect the host from environmental changes. It is thought that many strains that are pathogenic or otherwise deleterious under normal conditions can become beneficial under stressful conditions (Bacon et al., 2008). Furthermore, there is some evidence that residing in a host can increase stress tolerance for both parties (Rodriguez & Redman, 2008). That said, clavicipitaceous fungal endophytes (class 1) found in grasses offer no net improvement in drought tolerance to their grass hosts, although this may be highly context-dependent (Cheplick, 2004). Conversely, non-clavicipitaceous endophytes appear to offer stress tolerance properties to their hosts (Rodriguez & Redman, 2008). This is attributed to observational findings that colonised plants use less water than non-colonised plants, so may be more drought-tolerant, and they are slower to lose chlorophyll function when exposed to ROS. Moverover, maintenance of cell turgor under drought occurs through endophyte-mediated production of osmolytes including proline (Hare & Cress, 1997; Gagné-Bourque et al., 2016).

Most work to determine the protective nature of the plant microbiome has concerned arbuscular mycorrhizal (AM) fungi. There is substantial evidence showing that AM fungi are instrumental in reducing the harm to the plant arising through abiotic stress, despite fungal diversity being lower than in unstressed soils (Lenoir et al., 2016). AM fungi have been shown to scavenge ROS and reinforce antioxidant defences, thus alleviating the symptoms of stress, but there is much work still needed to characterise this interaction (Kapoor & Singh, 2017; Nath et al., 2017). Nevertheless, AM fungi have been identified as key mitigators of abiotic stress including drought (Fouad et al., 2014), pollutants such as cadmium (Garg & Bandari, 2012) and excess salinity (Kumar et al., 2014; Saxena et al., 2017). Mycorrhizal fungi have also been widely reported to offer increased drought tolerance to their plant host, and one mechanism is through induced expression of the phytohormone abscisic acid, which improves stomatal control (Aroca et al., 2008). There is also some indication that association with AM fungi in lettuce and tomato plants improves efficiency of Photosystem II (part of the photosynthetic apparatus) under drought stress (Ruiz-Lozano et al., 2016). More work is needed to incorporate these effects into larger-scale models.

Under eCO_2, carbon is usually no longer limiting for photosynthetic activity, known as the CO_2 fertilisation effect. In many systems, N then becomes the limiting factor for plant growth. Mycorrhizal associations can alleviate this stress by increasing N supply to the plant, and in turn, their growth is increased by eCO_2 (Compant et al., 2010; Terrer et al., 2017). This is particularly noted in ectomycorrhizal plants, which are often trees, because ectomycorrhizae seem to lower the costs of N uptake to the plant (Figure 8.1). AM fungi, which often colonise grassland species and rainforest trees, do not seem to offer the same benefits. A large-scale synthesis has shown that ectomycorrhizae improves plant growth under eCO_2 regardless of N availability, while AM fungi seem not to aid uptake of N when N is limiting, thus also reducing the fertilisation effect of eCO_2 (Terrer et al., 2017). However, a caveat to this is that under eCO_2, there may be less need for the mycorrhiza to colonise the plant because they are obtaining C substrate from the air, which could lead to a detrimental effect on the plant (Tang et al., 2009). This has been particularly observed in C_3 plants compared with C_4, which could change competitive interactions between plants in mixed swards. Additionally, there are conflicting reports of the direct importance of mycorrhizae in plant growth under eCO_2, which could indicate a more complex relationship if the increase in CO_2 does not technically result in plant stress (Jakobsen et al., 2016).

8.3.2 Marine invertebrates

Amid the 2015–2016 'Godzilla El Niño', anomalously high SSTs caused the third and most severe global coral bleaching event since bleaching records began (Hughes et al., 2017). While many mobile taxa, famously birds and butterflies, have responded to rapid climate change by shifting their range (Parmesan & Yohe, 2003), corals cannot quickly escape unfavourable conditions as they are sessile. Due to their longevity, there are also concerns that traditional Darwinian adaptation over generational time might not allow corals to keep up with climate change, so must use alternatives to survive a changing climate, or risk extinction (Carpenter et al., 2008). In this respect, the vast numbers, high turnover and short generation times of the diverse coral microbiota may afford opportunities for faster acclimatisation and adaptation to new climatic conditions (Torda et al., 2017).

Single-celled symbiotic zooxanthellae may aid the coral host in surviving fast-paced environmental change through their own rapid evolution, as demonstrated after only two and a half years of laboratory thermal selection (Chakravarti et al., 2017). Alternatively, corals, as meta-organisms, can respond to their environment by changing the composition of their symbiotic community (Berkelmans & van Oppen, 2006). This plastic change in genotype frequencies can be considered a sort of rapid intermediate response between phenotypic acclimatisation and genetic adaptation. Many corals are capable of hosting more than one type of zooxanthellae, and different zooxanthellae–host combinations exhibit different thermal tolerances (e.g. Howells et al., 2016). Thus, it has been theorised that coral bleaching might provide an opportunity for a coral to substitute a disadvantageous algal clade for more tolerant *Symbiodinium* algae from the local environment (the 'adaptive bleaching hypothesis' by Buddemeier & Fautin, 1993). Support for this theory was obtained after the 1998 El Niño event, where a global molecular screen of *Symbiodinium* indicated that corals associated with *Symbiodinium* clade D were more abundant on reefs that had suffered severe mass-bleaching events (Baker et al., 2004). Meanwhile, coral–*Symbiodinium* associations on previously severely affected reefs closely resembled those found in naturally elevated temperature environments such as the Persian–Arabian Gulf, thus pointing to an SST-induced adaptive shift in symbionts towards thermal tolerance (Baker et al., 2004). The Persian–Arabian Gulf harbours corals are able to withstand remarkably high salinities and temperatures exceeding 35°C, which is partly explained by their association with a recently discovered symbiont, *S. thermophilum* (subclade C3) (D'Angelo et al., 2015; Hume et al., 2016). The authors suggest the symbiont was naturally selected by extreme temperatures in the Holocene.

Although there has been a lot of attention around the promise of the adaptive bleaching hypothesis for rapid adaptation to fast-paced climate change, a consensus has not yet been reached. The main argument centres on how the *Symbiodinium* community within a coral holobiont shifts. Some adult corals have been shown to take up *Symbiodinium* from the environment (Lewis & Coffroth, 2004), known as 'symbiont switching', but whether the new associations remain stable or the new symbionts are able to become dominant in the holobiont is unknown. Coral hosts also seem to exhibit high fidelity to certain clades (Rodriguez-Lanetty et al., 2004; Goulet, 2006; Sampayo et al., 2016) and therefore changes in the relative abundance of existing symbionts, known as 'symbiont shuffling', may be the more prevalent mechanism of symbiont change.

In additional to algal symbionts, certain bacterial attributes, including their wide metabolic scope, rapid community turnover, short generation times and potential for horizontal gene transfer (McFall-Ngai et al., 2013), could contribute to the adaptive capacity of coral hosts facing imminent environmental change. There is some contention over the role of bacteria in the coral holobiont, because historically research has tended to show that bacteria are associated with harmful bleaching and disease. The controversial concept known as the 'bacterial bleaching hypothesis' was presented after evidence was published showing that annual bleaching of the Mediterranean/Red Sea coral *Oculina patagonica* was caused by the pathogenic bacterium *Vibrio shiloi* (Kushmaro et al., 1996), and bleaching of *Pocillopora damicornis* was caused by *V. coralliilyticus* (Ben-Haim et al., 2003). Controversy arising from this work, based on findings that *V. shiloi* no longer caused bleaching in *O. patagonica*, led to the 'coral probiotic hypothesis' (Reshef et al., 2006): due to changes in the relative abundances of microbes in the coral holobiont, the coral had adapted to new conditions. The hypothesis states that symbiotic microorganisms exist in a dynamic state that enables rapid community turnover under changing environmental conditions, resulting in a more advantageous coral microbial community. Change in bacterial community composition over seasons was previously recorded in *O. patagonica* (Koren & Rosenberg, 2006), and from this, Reshef et al. (2006) surmised that environmental conditions could select for advantageous changes in bacterial community far faster than classical Darwinian gene mutation and selection in the coral host alone. There is some empirical evidence from a 17-month transplantation experiment that coral holobionts can adjust their microbiome based on thermal environment, irrespective of host genotype (Ziegler et al., 2017). It remains to be seen whether indicator associations between certain bacterial taxa and heat-tolerant corals are due to the same heat-based selection pressures acting in parallel on both coral host and bacteria, or whether differences in coral thermotolerance are caused by the microbial community hosted. Evidence for the latter possibility was provided by Gilbert et al. (2012), who showed that removal of α and γ-Proteobacteria by antibiotics caused severe tissue loss during heat stress, whereas corals with intact microbiomes only suffered typical heat-induced declines in photosynthetic efficiency.

Should a successful community of microbes provide stress tolerance to the coral, it would be advantageous for this microbiome to be inherited by future generations. Zooxanthellae have been shown to be transmitted from the parents (vertical transmission) via the eggs of broadcast spawning corals (Padilla-Gamiño et al., 2012) as well as the planula larvae of brooding corals (Serrano et al., 2016). However, a paradox remains in that many corals do not pass on their algal symbionts, but instead rely on acquisition from the environment (horizontal transmission) (Hartmann et al., 2017), including even brooders (Quigley et al., 2018). In broadcast-spawning corals whose larvae travel further (Quigley et al., 2016), horizontal transmission potentially allows uptake of locally adapted symbionts from the new settlement habitat. While vertical transmission has been revealed as a mode of bacterial transfer in the brooding coral *Porites astreoides* (Sharp et al., 2012), it has been rejected in the spawner *Pocillopora meandrina* (Apprill et al., 2009). This was corroborated by a separate study where bacteria were not detected in the eggs, sperm or larvae of seven mass-spawning coral species, but were present in the early settled stages of polyps (Sharp et al., 2010), suggesting that uptake from the environment may be important throughout a coral's lifespan. As bacterial colonisation appears to occur after settlement in several corals, there is huge potential to experimentally manipulate the bacterial assemblages of corals. However, understanding the acquisition and transmission of coral-associated microbes are key areas yet to be fully understood. While these examples indicate how microbes could, in theory, enable the coral host to keep up with rapid environmental change, more direct experimental research is needed. The dinoflagellate *Symbiodinium* spp. and bacterial portion of the coral microbiome are being relatively well-researched as the default using ITS2 and 16S rDNA sequencing studies. However, the potential for fungal, archaeal and even viral portions of the coral microbiome to aid the host to survive environmental change remain underexplored.

8.3.3 Terrestrial animals

The host microbiome contains massive genetic potential that may be beneficial to the host in order to cope with specific environmental challenges. As stated before, the mobility of most terrestrial animals means that they can potentially evade the worst consequences of environmental change (habitat allowing), but changes to food quality or contamination and pathogen or parasite outbreaks could be important considerations in the future. Many host–microbe mutualisms have gone through long-term co-evolution, experiencing periods when extreme environmental changes occurred. It is unclear how those historical events of environmental change affected host–microbe associations, or whether mutations in microbial symbionts or secondary symbionts might have played important roles during those periods. Protection of the host from the direct effects of climate change has been shown in insect guilds, where strong obligate mutualisms between the host and a particular microbial taxon have been identified. For instance, heat sensitivity and the fitness of aphids are related to a mutation of a regulatory gene *ibpA* in the bacterial symbiont *Buchnera*. This mutation interferes with the expression of a homopolymer heat shock protein, thereby affecting host fitness in a temperature-dependent manner, resulting in a reduced heat-shock response of *Buchnera* (Dunbar et al., 2007). Aphids hosting *Buchnera* with this mutation show reduced fitness under heat stress (Harmon et al., 2009). Further exploration of natural variation of this recurrent mutation in *Buchnera* revealed that it occurs infrequently in natural populations of aphids, indicating that natural selection favours the expression of *ibpA* (Burke et al., 2010). Moreover, experimental replacement of *Buchnera* in the pea aphid, *Acyrthosiphon pisum*, with a selectively bred strain of the bacterium dramatically increased heat tolerance in the host aphid (Moran & Yun, 2015). Together, these results suggest that genetic variation in microbial symbionts offer their hosts opportunities to adapt to current environmental changes.

The increasing pressures of habitat loss, pathogens and species invasions are likely to be exacerbated through the interactive effects of environmental change. For example, amphibian populations are currently under particular stress due to widespread fungal chytridiomycosis infections, and research is urgently needed to determine whether changes in climatic factors or anthropogenic pollution could alter microbiome structure or function in a manner that could affect the virulence of the fungus (Jiménez & Sommer, 2017). Ecological theory mandates that if the microbiome of the host is species-rich, functional and healthy, it is less likely to be invaded by deleterious microbes such as pathogens (Lawley & Walker, 2013). This idea, known as 'colonisation resistance', has resulted in some attempts to reduce the virulence of chytridiomycosis by adding cultures of healthy bacteria to the skin of amphibians, although success in preventing infection has been limited (Holden et al., 2015). However, rather than simply being a numbers game, the host microbiome also combats pathogenic invasion through a combination of induced host immune responses, competition for nutrients and metabolic changes (Young, 2017; see Chapter 7). Therefore, any climate or pollution-induced alteration in the host microbiome could offer a potentially deadly opportunity to these pathogens. Infections and diseases across other animal host groups may also become more virulent under climate change, and there is recent concerning evidence that environmental pollution and climate change can cause epigenetic changes that appear over successive generations

(Guerrero-Bosagna & Jensen, 2015). There is some evidence that the micro-biome, particularly in the gut, can alleviate these problems, but research is patchy and consensus has not been reached (Dinan & Cryan, 2012).

Finally, diet changes as a result of changing abiotic conditions are becoming increasingly likely, and the animal host will likely increase reliance on its gut microbiota to optimise nutrient uptake (Raiten & Aimone, 2017). As a result, there is increasing evidence that changes in diet selects for different assemblages. This has been demonstrated in animals as diverse as honeybees (Zhao et al., 2018), amphibians (Antwis et al., 2014), land and marine iguanas (Kohl et al., 2017), and humans (Blaser et al., 2016). Furthermore, temperature increases lead directly to shifts in the community composition of gut microbiota in northern leopard frog tadpoles (*Lithobates pipiens*), and in particular the pathogenic *Mycobacterium*, although the overall effects on fitness are unclear (Kohl & Yahn, 2016). Ultimately, much of this research is in the early stages, and a better understanding of the mode of action of the gut microbiome is needed in order to disentangle the complex interactions between abiotic stress, changes in diet and/or host range, and the gut microbiota, before we have a comprehensive understanding of the impacts on host communities, and how these may mitigate environmental change.

8.4 Conclusions

As human impacts on the natural world become increasingly widespread and intense, the search for tools that might potentially mitigate these effects is gaining importance in scientific research (Antwis et al., 2017). It is clear that one of the most powerful and non-invasive tools is the host's own microbiome. Therefore, as methods of characterising and manipulating microbial communities increase in accessibility, researchers and biotechnological practitioners are beginning to consider the possibility of altering host microbiomes in order to achieve various objectives. Considering biological control strategies against plant pathogens and manipulation of root-associated microbes to promote plant growth are already used in farming (Dobbelaere et al., 2003), and probiotic formulations are widely used in veterinary and human medicine (Fathi et al., 2017; Ochoa-Hueso, 2017), the use of beneficial native bacteria for promoting coral health might not be so far-fetched in the search for solutions to the coral bleaching crisis (Peixoto et al., 2017). Environmental change is a multifaceted, complex problem, which will affect host–microbiome interactions in a number of unpredictable ways. There are still large knowledge gaps in almost every area, and these need to be urgently addressed so we can apply conservation efforts in a judicious manner. However, it is becoming increasingly clear that preservation of the microbiome is likely to be the key to maintaining healthy ecosystems in an uncertain future.

References

Addison AL, Powell JA, Six DL, et al. (2013) The role of temperature variability in stabilizing the mountain pine beetle–fungus mutualism. *Journal of Theoretical Biology*, 335, 40–50.

Antwis RE, Haworth RL, Engelmoer DJP, et al. (2014) *Ex situ* diet influences the bacterial community associated with the skin of red-eyed tree frogs (*Agalychnis callidryas*). *PLoS ONE*, 9, e85563.

Antwis RE, Griffiths SM, Harrison XA, et al. (2017) Fifty important research questions in microbial ecology. *FEMS Microbiology and Ecology*, 93, fix044.

Apprill A, Marlow HQ, Martindale MQ, et al. (2009) The onset of microbial associations in the coral *Pocillopora meandrina*. *The ISME Journal*, 3, 685–699.

Aroca R, Vernieri P, Ruiz-Lozano JM. (2008) Mycorrhizal and non-mycorrhizal *Lactuca sativa* plants exhibit contrasting responses to exogenous ABA during drought stress and recovery. *Journal of Experimental Biology*, 59, 2029–2041.

Aroca R, Ruiz-Lozano JM, Zamarreño ÁM, et al. (2013) Arbuscular mycorrhizal symbiosis influences strigolactone production under salinity and alleviates salt stress in lettuce plants. *Journal of Plant Physiology*, 170, 47–55.

Babic I, Roy S, Watada AE, et al. (1996) Changes in microbial populations on fresh cut spinach. *Food Microbiology*, 31, 107–119.

Bacon CW, Glenn AE, Yates IE. (2008) *Fusarium verticillioides*: Managing the endophytic association with maize for reduced fumonisins accumulation. *Toxin Reviews*, 27, 411–446.

Baker AC, Starger CJ, McClanahan TR, et al. (2004) Coral reefs: Corals' adaptive response to climate change. *Nature*, 430, 741.

Bálint M, Bartha L, O'Hara RB, et al. (2015) Relocation, high-latitude warming and host genetic identity shape the foliar fungal microbiome of poplars. *Molecular Ecology*, 24, 235–248.

Ben-Haim Y, Zicherman-Keren M, Rosenberg E. (2003) Temperature-regulated bleaching and lysis of the coral *Pocillopora damicornis* by the novel pathogen *Vibrio coralliilyticus*. *Applied and Environmental Microbiology*, 69, 4236–4242.

Berasategui A, Salem H, Paetz C, et al. (2017) Gut microbiota of the pine weevil degrades conifer diterpenes and increases insect fitness. *Molecular Ecology*, 26, 4099–4110.

Berendsen RL, Pieterse CMJ, Bakker PAHM. (2012) The rhizosphere microbiome and plant health. *Trends in Plant Science*, 17, 478–486.

Berg G, Erlacher A, Grube M. (2014) Plant-associated microbial diversity: Human food and health issues. In: Lugtenberg B. (Ed.) *Principles of Plant–Microbe Interactions*. Cham: Springer.

Berg G, Rybakova D, Grube M, et al. (2016) The plant microbiome explored: Implications for experimental botany. *Journal of Experimental Botany*, 67, 995–1002.

Berkelmans R, van Oppen MJH. (2006) The role of zooxanthellae in the thermal tolerance of corals: A 'nugget of hope' for coral reefs in an era of climate change. *Proceedings of the Royal Society B: Biological Sciences*, 273, 2305–2312.

Blaser MJ, Cardon ZG, Cho MK, et al. (2016) Toward a predictive understanding of earth's microbiomes to address 21st century challenges. *mBio*, 7, e00714–16.

Bourne D, Iida Y, Uthicke S, et al. (2008) Changes in coral-associated microbial communities during a bleaching event. *The ISME Journal*, 2, 350–363.

Bourne DG, Morrow KM, Webster NS. (2016) Insights into the coral microbiome: Underpinning the health and resilience of reef ecosystems. *Annual Review of Microbiology*, 70, 317–340.

Bruno JF, Selig ER, Casey KS, et al. (2007) Thermal stress and coral cover as drivers of coral disease outbreaks. *PLoS Biology*, 5, e124.

Buchner P. (1965) *Endosymbiosis of Animals with Plant Microorganisms*. Geneva: Interscience Publishers Inc.

Buddemeier RW, Fautin DG. (1993) Coral bleaching as an adaptive mechanism – A testable hypothesis. *BioScience*, 43, 320–326.

Burke GR, McLaughlin HJ, Simon JC, et al. (2010) Dynamics of a recurrent *Buchnera* mutation that affects thermal tolerance of pea aphid hosts. *Genetics*, 186, 367–577.

Callahan MT, Micallef SA, Buchanan RL. (2017) Soil type, soil moisture, and field slope influence the horizontal movement of *Salmonella enterica* and *Citrobacter freundii* from floodwater through soil. *Journal of Food Protection*, 80, 189–197.

Carpenter KE, Abrar M, Aeby G, et al. (2008) One-third of reef-building corals face elevated extinction risk from climate change and local impacts. *Science*, 321, 560–563.

Cerf-Bensussan N, Gaboriau-Routhiau V. (2010) The immune system and the gut microbiota: Friends or foes? *Nature Reviews Immunology*, 10, 735–744.

Cervino JM, Hayes RL, Polson SW, et al. (2004) Relationship of *Vibrio* species infection and elevated temperatures to yellow blotch/band disease in Caribbean corals. *Applied and Environmental Microbiology*, 70, 6855–6864.

Chakravarti LJ, Beltran VH, van Oppen MJH. (2017) Rapid thermal adaptation in photosymbionts of reef-building corals. *Global Change Biology*, 23, 4675–4688.

Cheplick GP. (2004) Recovery from drought stress in *Lolium perenne* (Poaceae): Are fungal endophytes detrimental? *American Journal of Botany*, 91, 1960–1968.

Chung SH, Rosa C, Scully ED, et al. (2013) Herbivore exploits orally secreted bacteria to suppress plant defenses. *Proceedings of the National Academy of Sciences*, 110, 15728–15733.

Compant S, Van Der Heijden MGA, Sessitsch A. (2010) Climate change effects on beneficial plant–microorganism interactions. *FEMS Microbiology Ecology*, 73, 197–214.

Connell JH. (1978) Diversity in tropical rain forests and coral reefs. *Science*, 199, 1302–1310.

D'Angelo C, Hume BCC, Burt J, et al. (2015) Local adaptation constrains the distribution potential of heat-tolerant *Symbiodinium* from the Persian/Arabian Gulf. The *ISME Journal*, 9, 1–10.

Darwin's Paradox (1842) *The Structure and Distribution of Coral Reefs. Being the First Part of the Geology of the Voyage of the Beagle, Under the Command of Capt. Fitzroy, R.N. During the Years 1832 To 1836*. Smith Elder and Co.

David AS, Thapa-Magar KB, Afkami ME. (2018) Microbial mitigation–exacerbation continuum: A novel framework for microbiome effects on hosts in the face of stress. *Ecology*, 99, 517–523.

Diaz JM, Hansel CM, Apprill A, et al. (2016) Species-specific control of external superoxide levels by the coral holobiont during a natural bleaching event. *Nature Communications*, 7, 13801.

Dimkpa C, Weinand T, Asch F. (2009) Plant–rhizobacteria interactions alleviate abiotic stress conditions. *Plant, Cell and Environment*, 32, 1682–1694.

Dinan TG, Cryan, JF. (2012) Regulation of the stress response by the gut microbiota: Implications for psychoneuroendocrinology. *Psychoneuroendocrinology*, 37, 1369–1378.

Dobbelaere S, Vanderleyden J, Okon Y. (2003) Plant growth-promoting effects of Diazotrophs in the rhizosphere. *Critical Reviews in Plant Sciences*, 22, 107–149.

Douglas AE, Werren JH. (2016) Holes in the hologeome: Why host–microbe symbioses are not holobionts. *mBio*, 7, e02099–15.

Dunbar HE, Wilson ACC, Ferguson NR, et al. (2007) Aphid thermal tolerance is governed by a point mutation in bacterial symbionts. *PLoS Biology*, 5, 1006–1015.

Fathi MM, Ebeid TA, Al-Homidan I, et al. (2017) Influence of probiotic supplementation on immune response in broilers raised under hot climate. *Immunology, Health and Disease*, 58, 512–516.

Fouad OM, Essahibi A, Benhiba L, et al. (2014) Effectiveness of arbuscular mycorrhizal fungi in the protection of olive plants against oxidative stress induced by drought. *Spanish Journal of Agricultural Research*, 12, 763–771.

Gagné-Bourque F, Bertrand A, Claessens A, et al. (2016) Alleviation of drought stress and metabolic changes in timothy (*Phleum pratense* L.) colonized with *Bacillus subtilis* B26. *Frontiers in Plant Science*, 7, 584.

Garg N, Bhandari P. (2012) Influence of cadmium stress and arbuscular mycorrhizal fungi on nodule senescence in *Cajanus cajan* (L) Millsp. *International Journal of Phytoremediation*, 14, 62–74.

Gamper H, Hartwig UA, Leuchtmann A. (2005) Mycorrhizas improve nitrogen nutrition of *Trifolium repens* after 8 yr of selection under elevated atmospheric CO_2 partial pressure. *New Phytologist*, 167, 531–542.

Gehring CA, Mueller RC, Haskins KE, et al. (2014) Convergence in mycorrhizal fungal communities due to drought, plant competition, parasitism, and susceptibility to herbivory: Consequences for fungi and host plants. *Frontiers in Microbiology*, 5, 306.

Gilbert JA, Hill R, Doblin MA, et al. (2012) Microbial consortia increase thermal tolerance of corals. *Marine Biology*, 159, 1763–1771.

Goulet TL. (2006) Most corals may not change their symbionts. *Marine Ecology Progress Series*, 321, 1–7.

Guadayol Ò, Silbiger NJ, Donahue MJ, et al. (2014) Patterns in temporal variability of temperature, oxygen and pH along an environmental gradient in a coral reef. *PLoS ONE*, 9, e85213.

Guerrero-Bosagna C, Jensen P. (2015) Globalisation, climate change and transgenerational epigenetic inheritance: Will our descendants be at risk? *Clinical Epigenetics*, 7, 8.

Hadaidi G, Röthig T, Yum LK, et al. (2017) Stable mucus-associated bacterial communities in bleached and healthy corals of *Porites lobate* from the Arabian Seas. *Scientific Reports*, 7, 45362.

Hammer TJ, Bowers MD. (2015) Gut microbes may facilitate insect herbivory of chemically defended plants. *Oecologia*, 179, 1–14.

Hardoim PR, van Overbeek LS, Berg G, et al. (2015) The hidden world within plants: Ecological and evolutionary considerations for defining functioning of microbial endophytes. *Microbiology and Molecular Biology Reviews*, 79, 293–320.

Hare PD, Cress WA. (1997) Metabolic implications of stress-induced proline accumulation in plants. *Plant Growth Regulation*, 21, 79–102.

Harmon JP, Moran NA, Ives AR. (2009) Species response to environmental change: impacts of food web interactions and evolution. *Science*, 323, 1347–1350.

Hartmann AC, Baird AH, Knowlton N, et al. (2017) The paradox of environmental symbiont acquisition in obligate mutualisms. *Current Biology*, 27, 3711–3716.

Hoegh-Guldberg O, Cai R, Poloczanska ES, et al. (2014) *The Ocean Climate Change 2014: Impacts, Adaptation, and Vulnerability Part B: Regional Aspects Contribution of Working Group II to the Fifth Assessment Report of the Intergovernmental Panel on Climate Change*. New York, NY: Cambridge University Press.

Hoegh-Guldberg O, Poloczanska ES, Skirving W, et al. (2017) Coral reef ecosystems under climate change and ocean acidification. *Frontiers in Marine Science*, 4, 158.

Hofmann GE, Barry JP, Edmunds PJ, et al. (2010) The effect of ocean acidification on calcifying organisms in marine ecosystems: An organism-to-ecosystem perspective. *Annual Review of Ecology, Evolution, and Systematics*, 41, 127–147.

Holden WM, Reinert LM, Hanlon SM, et al. (2015) Development of antimicrobial peptide defenses of southern leopard frogs, *Rana sphenocephala*, against the pathogenic chytrid fungus, *Batrachochytrium dendrobatidis*. *Developmental and Comparative Immunology*, 48, 65–75.

Howells EJ, Abrego D, Meyer E, et al. (2016) Host adaptation and unexpected symbiont partners enable reef-building corals to tolerate extreme temperatures. *Global Change Biology*, 22, 2702–2714.

Hughes TP, Kerry JT, Álvarez-Noriega M, et al. (2017) Global warming and recurrent mass bleaching of corals. *Nature*, 543, 373–377.

Hume BCC, Voolstra CR, Arif C, et al. (2016) Ancestral genetic diversity associated with the rapid spread of stress-tolerant coral symbionts in response to Holocene climate change. *Proceedings of the National Academy of Sciences*, 113, 4416–21.

ISRS, International Society for Reef Studies. (2015) Consensus statement on climate change and coral bleaching. Available at www.openchannels.org/news/news/isrs-consensus-statement-climate-change-and-coral-bleaching-paris-climate-change-targets.

IPCC. (2007) *Climate Change 2007: The Physical Science Basis*. Cambridge: Cambridge University Press.

IPCC. (2013) *IPCC, 2013: Climate Change 2013: The Physical Science Basis. Contribution of Working Group I to the Fifth Assessment Report of the Intergovernmental Panel on Climate Change*, edited by Stocker T, Qin D, Plattner G, et al. New York, NY: Cambridge University Press.

Jacobs JL, Sundin GW. (2001) Effect of solar UV-B radiation on a phyllosphere bacterial community. *Applied and Environmental Microbiology*, 67, 5488–5496.

Jakobsen I, Smith SE, Smith FA, et al. (2016) Plant growth responses to elevated atmospheric CO_2 are increased by phosphorus sufficiency but not by arbuscular mycorrhizas. *Journal of Experimental Botany*, 67, 6173–6186.

Jiménez RR, Sommer S. (2017) The amphibian microbiome: Natural range of variation,

pathogenic dysbiosis, and role in conservation. *Biodiversity and Conservation*, 26, 763–786.

Johnson N, Rowland D, Corkidi L, et al. (2008) Plant winners and losers during grassland N-eutrophication differ in biomass allocation and mycorrhizas. *Ecology*, 89, 2868–2878.

Johnson NC, Angelard C, Sanders IC, et al. (2013) Predicting community and ecosystem outcomes of mycorrhizal responses to global change. *Ecology Letters*, 16, 140–153.

Kaisermann A, de Vries FT, Griffiths RI, et al. (2017) Legacy effects of drought on plant–soil feedbacks and plant–plant interactions. *New Phytologist*, 215, 1413–1424.

Kapoor R, Singh N. (2017) Arbuscular mycorrhiza and reactive oxygen species. In: Wu QS. (Ed.) *Arbuscular Mycorrhizas and Stress Tolerance of Plants*. Singapore: Springer.

Khanna KK. (1986) Phyllosphere microflora of certain plants in relation to air pollution. *Environmental Pollution Series A*, 42, 191–200.

Kikuchi Y, Tada A, Musolin DL, et al. (2016) Collapse of insect gut symbiosis under simulated climate change. *mBio*, 7, e01578–16.

Kock RA, Orynbayev M, Robinson S, et al. (2018) Saigas on the brink: Multidisciplinary analysis of the factors influencing mass mortality events. *Scientific Advances*, 4, eaao2314.

Kohl KD, Yahn J. (2016) Effects of environmental temperature on the gut microbial communities of tadpoles. *Environmental Microbiology*, 18, 1561–1565.

Kohl KD, Brun A, Magallanes M, et al. (2017) Gut microbial ecology of lizards: Insights into diversity in the wild, effects of captivity, variation across gut regions and transmission. *Molecular Ecology*, 26, 1175–1189.

Koren O, Rosenberg E. (2006) Bacteria associated with mucus and tissues of the coral *Oculina patagonica* in summer and winter. *Applied and Environmental Microbiology*, 72, 5254–5259.

Koren O, Rosenberg E. (2008) Bacteria associated with the bleached and cave coral *Oculina patagonica*. *Microbial Ecology*, 55, 523–529.

Krediet CJ, Ritchie KB, Paul VJ, et al. (2013) Coral-associated micro-organisms and their roles in promoting coral health and thwarting diseases. *Proceedings of the Royal Society B: Biological Sciences*, 280, 20122328.

Krueger T, Hawkins TD, Becker S, et al. (2015) Differential coral bleaching – Contrasting the activity and response of enzymatic antioxidants in symbiotic partners under thermal stress. *Comparative Biochemistry and Physiology Part A: Molecular & Integrative Physiology*, 190, 15–25.

Kuhl M, Cohen Y, Dalsgaard T, et al. (1995) Microenvironment and photosynthesis of zooxanthellae in scleractinian corals studied with microsensors for O_2, pH and light. *Marine Ecology Progress Series*, 117, 159–172.

Kumar A, Dames JF, Gupta A, et al. (2014) Current developments in arbuscular mycorrhizal fungi research and its role in salinity stress alleviation: A biotechnological perspective. *Critical Reviews in Biotechnology*, 35, 461–474.

Kushmaro A, Loya Y, Fine M, et al. (1996) Bacterial infection and coral bleaching. *Nature*, 380, 396–396.

Kvennefors ECE, Sampayo E, Kerr C, et al. (2012) Regulation of bacterial communities through antimicrobial activity by the coral holobiont. *Microbial Ecology*, 63, 605–618.

Lawley TD, Walker AW. (2013) Intestinal colonization resistance. *Immunology*, 356, 1–11.

Lee STM, Davy SK, Tang S-L, et al. (2017) Water flow buffers shifts in bacterial community structure in heat-stressed *Acropora muricata*. *Scientific Reports*, 7, 43600.

Lenoir I, Fontaine J, Sahraoui AL-H. (2016) Arbuscular mycorrhizal fungal responses to abiotic stresses: A review. *Phytochemistry*, 123, 4–15.

Lesser MP. (2006) Oxidative stress in marine environments: Biochemistry and physiological ecology. *Annual Review of Physiology*, 68, 253–278.

Lewis CL, Coffroth MA. (2004) The acquisition of exogenous algal symbionts by an octocoral after bleaching. *Science*, 304, 1490–1492.

Littman R, Willis BL, Bourne DG. (2011) Metagenomic analysis of the coral holobiont during a natural bleaching event on the Great Barrier Reef. *Environmental Microbiology Reports*, 3, 651–660.

Liu H, Chen W, Wu M, et al. (2017) Arbuscular mycorrhizal fungus inoculation reduces the drought-resistance advantage of endophyte-infected versus endophyte-free *Leymus chinensis*. *Mycorrhiza*, 27, 791–799.

McDevitt-Irwin JM, Baum JK, Garren M, et al. (2017) Responses of coral-associated bacterial communities to local and global stressors. *Frontiers in Marine Science*, 4, 262.

McFall-Ngai M, Hadfield MG, Bosch TCG, et al. (2013) Animals in a bacterial world, a new imperative for the life sciences. *Proceedings of the National Academy of Sciences*, 110, 3229–3236.

Mendes R, Kruijt M, de Bruijn I, et al. (2011). Deciphering the rhizosphere microbiome for disease-suppressive bacteria. *Science*, 332, 1097–1100.

Meron D, Atias E, Iasur Kruh L, et al. (2011) The impact of reduced pH on the microbial community of the coral, *Acropora eurystoma*. *The ISME journal*, 5, 51–60.

Meron D, Rodolfo-Metalpa R, Cunning R, et al. (2012) Changes in coral microbial communities in response to a natural pH gradient. *The ISME Journal*, 6, 1775–1785.

Millar NS, Bennett AE. (2016) Stressed out symbiotes: Hypotheses for the influence of abiotic stress on arbuscular mycorrhizal fungi. *Oecologia*, 182, 625–641.

Moran NA, Yun Y. (2015) Experimental replacement of an obligate insect symbiont. *Proceedings of the National Academy of Sciences*, 112, 2093–2096.

Morrow KM, Moss AG, Chadwick NE, et al. (2012) Bacterial associates of two Caribbean coral species reveal species-specific distribution and geographic variability. *Applied and Environmental Microbiology*, 78, 6438–6449.

Muscatine L. (1990) The role of symbiotic algae in carbon and energy flux in reef corals. In: Dubinsky Z. (Ed.) *Ecosystems of the World 25 Coral Reefs*. Amsterdam: Elsevier Science BV.

Nath M, Bhatt D, Prasad R, et al. (2017) Reactive oxygen species (ROS) metabolism and signaling in plant–mycorrhizal association under biotic and abiotic stress conditions. In: Varma A, Prasad R, Tuteja N (Eds.) *Mycorrhiza – Eco-Physiology, Secondary Metabolites, Nanomaterials*. Cham: Springer International Publishing.

Noctor G, Mhamdi A. (2017) Climate change, CO_2, and defense: The metabolic, redox and signalling perspectives. *Trends in Plant Science*, 22, 857–870.

Ochoa-Hueso R. (2017) Global change and the soil microbiome: A human-health perspective. *Frontiers in Ecology and Evolution*, 5, 71.

Oldroyd GED, Murray JD, Poole PS, et al. (2011) The rules of engagement in the legume–rhizobial symbiosis. *Annual Review of Genetics*, 45, 119–144.

Padilla-Gamiño JL, Pochon X, Bird C, et al. (2012) From parent to gamete: Vertical transmission of *Symbiodinium* (Dinophyceae) ITS2 sequence assemblages in the reef building coral *Montipora capitata*. *PLoS ONE*, 7, e38440.

Parmesan C, Yohe G. (2003) A globally coherent fingerprint of climate change impacts across natural systems. *Nature*, 421, 37–42.

Peixoto RS, Rosado PM, Leite DC, et al. (2017) Beneficial microorganisms for corals (BMC): Proposed mechanisms for coral health and resilience. *Frontiers in Microbiology*, 8, 341.

Philippot L, Raaijmakers JM, Lemanceau P, et al. (2013) Going back to the roots: The microbial ecology of the rhizosphere. *Nature Reviews Microbiology*, 11, 789–799.

Pineda A, Dicke M, Pieterse CMJ, et al. (2013) Beneficial microbes in a changing environment: Are they always helping plants to deal with insects? *Functional Ecology*, 27, 574–586.

Pita L, Rix L, Slaby BM, et al. (2018) The sponge holobiont in a changing ocean: From microbes to ecosystems. *Microbiome*, 6, 46.

Pogoreutz C, Rädecker N, Cárdenas A, et al. (2017) Sugar enrichment provides evidence for a role of nitrogen fixation in coral bleaching. *Global Change Biology*, 23, 3838–3848.

Pogoreutz C, Rädecker N, Cárdenas A, et al. (2018) Dominance of *Endozoicomonas* bacteria throughout coral bleaching and mortality suggests structural inflexibility of the *Pocillopora verrucosa* microbiome. *Ecology and Evolution*, 8, 2240–2252.

Prado SS, Hung KY, Daugherty MP, et al. (2010) Indirect effects of temperature on stink bug fitness, via maintenance of gut-associated symbionts. *Applied and Environmental Microbiology*, 76, 1261–1266.

Preece C, Peñuelas J. (2016) Rhizodeposition under drought and consequences for soil communities and ecosystem resilience. *Plant and Soil*, 409, 1–17.

Quigley KM, Willis BL, Bay LK. (2016) Maternal effects and *Symbiodinium* community composition drive differential patterns in juvenile survival in the coral *Acropora tenuis*. *Royal Society Open Science*, 3, 160471.

Quigley KM, Warner PA, Bay LK, et al. (2018) Unexpected mixed-mode transmission and moderate genetic regulation of *Symbiodinium* communities in a brooding coral. *Heredity*, 121, 524–536.

Rädecker N, Pogoreutz C, Voolstra CR, et al. (2015) Nitrogen cycling in corals: The key to understanding holobiont functioning? *Trends in Microbiology*, 23, 490–497.

Raina J-B, Tapiolas D, Willis BL, et al. (2009) Coral-associated bacteria and their role in the biogeochemical cycling of sulfur.

Applied and Environmental Microbiology, 75, 3492–3501.

Raiten DJ, Aimone AM. (2017) The intersection of climate/environment, food, nutrition and health: Crisis and opportunity. *Current Opinion in Biotechnology*, 44, 52–62.

Randriamanana TR, Nissinen K, Ovaskainen A, et al. (2018) Does fungal endophyte inoculation affect the responses of aspen seedlings to carbon dioxide enrichments? *Fungal Ecology*, 33, 24–31.

Reinmuth-Selzle K, Kampf CJ, Lucas K, et al. (2017) Air pollution and climate change effects on allergies in the anthropocene: Abundance, interaction, and modification of allergens and adjuvants. *Environmental Science and Technology*, 51, 4119–4141.

Remily ER, Richardson LL. (2006) Ecological physiology of a coral pathogen and the coral reef environment. *Microbial Ecology*, 51, 345–352.

Reshef L, Koren O, Loya Y, et al. (2006) The coral probiotic hypothesis. *Environmental Microbiology*, 8, 2068–2073.

Rico L, Ogaya R, Terradas J, et al. (2014) Community structures of N_2-fixing bacteria associated with the phyllosphere of a Holm oak forest and their response to drought. *Plant Biology*, 16, 586–593.

Ritchie KB. (2006) Regulation of microbial populations by coral surface mucus and mucus-associated bacteria. *Marine Ecology Progress Series*, 322, 1–14.

Rodriguez R, Redman R. (2008) More than 400 million years of evolution and some plants still can't make it on their own: Plant stress tolerance via fungal symbiosis. *Journal of Experimental Botany*, 59, 1109–1114.

Rodriguez-Lanetty M, Krupp D, Weis V. (2004) Distinct ITS types of *Symbiodinium* in Clade C correlate with cnidarian/dinoflagellate specificity during onset of symbiosis. *Marine Ecology Progress Series*, 275, 97–102.

Rohwer F, Seguritan V, Azam F, et al. (2002) Diversity and distribution of coral-associated bacteria. *Marine Ecology Progress Series*, 243, 1–10.

Romero-Olivares AL, Allison SD, Treseder KK. (2017) Soil microbes and their response to experimental warming over time: A meta-analysis of field studies. *Soil Biology and Biochemistry*, 107, 32–40.

Rosenberg E, Ben-Haim Y. (2002) Microbial diseases of corals and global warming. *Environmental Microbiology*, 4, 318–326.

Rosenberg E, Falkovitz L. (2004) The *Vibrio shiloi/Oculina patagonica* model system of coral bleaching. *Annual Review of Microbiology*, 58, 143–159.

Ruiz-Lozano JM, Aroca R, Zamarreño ÁM, et al. (2016) Arbuscular mycorrhizal symbiosis induces strigolactone biosynthesis under drought and improves drought tolerance in lettuce and tomato. *Plant, Cell & Environment*, 39, 441–452.

Russell JB, Muck RE, Weimer PJ. (2009) Quantitative analysis of cellulose degradation and growth of cellulolytic bacteria in the rumen. *FEMS Microbiology Ecology*, 67, 183–197.

Rypien KL, Ward JR, Azam F. (2010) Antagonistic interactions among coral-associated bacteria. *Environmental Microbiology*, 12, 28–39.

Sampayo EM, Ridgway T, Franceschinis L, et al. (2016) Coral symbioses under prolonged environmental change: Living near tolerance range limits. *Scientific Reports*, 6, 36271.

Sánchez-Cañizares C, Jorrin B, Poole PS, et al. (2017) Understanding the holobiont: The interdependence of plants and their microbiome. *Current Opinion in Microbiology*, 38, 188–196.

Saona NM, Albrechtsen BR, Ericson L, et al. (2010) Environmental stresses mediate endophyte–grass interactions in a boreal archipelago. *Journal of Ecology*, 98. 470–479.

Saxena B, Shukla K, Giri B. (2017) Arbuscular mycorrhizal fungi and tolerance of salt stress in plants. In: Wu QS (Ed.) *Arbuscular Mycorrhizas and Stress Tolerance of Plants*.

Singapore: Springer International Publishing, pp.67–97.

Serrano XM, Baums IB, Smith TB, et al. (2016) Long distance dispersal and vertical gene flow in the Caribbean brooding coral *Porites astreoides*. *Scientific Reports*, 6, 21619.

Sharp KH, Ritchie KB, Schupp PJ, et al. (2010) Bacterial acquisition in juveniles of several broadcast spawning coral species. *PLoS ONE*, 5, e10898.

Sharp KH, Distel D, Paul VJ. (2012) Diversity and dynamics of bacterial communities in early life stages of the Caribbean coral *Porites astreoides*. *The ISME Journal*, 6, 790–801.

Shikano I, Rosa C, Tan CW, et al. (2017) Tritrophic interactions: Microbe-mediated plant effects on insect herbivores. *Annual Review of Phytopathology*, 55, 313–331.

Shnit-Orland M, Kushmaro A. (2009) Coral mucus-associated bacteria: A possible first line of defense. *FEMS Microbiology Ecology*, 67, 371–380.

Singh BK, Trivedi P. (2017) Microbiome and the future for food and nutrient security. *Microbial Biotechnology*, 10, 50–53.

Smith DJ, Sugget DJ, Baker NR. (2004) Is photoinhibition of zooxanthellae photosynthesis the primary cause of thermal bleaching in corals? *Global Change Biology*, 11, 1–11.

Staley C, Kaiser T, Gidley ML, et al. (2017) Differential impacts of land-based sources of pollution on the microbiota of Southeast Florida coral reefs. *Applied and Environmental Microbiology*, 83, e03378–16.

Sweet MJ, Bulling MT. (2017) On the importance of the microbiome and pathobiome in coral health and disease. *Frontiers in Marine Science*, 4, 9.

Tang J, Xu L, Chen X, et al. (2009) Interaction between C_4 barnyard grass and C_3 upland rice under elevated CO_2: Impact of mycorrhizae. *Acta Oecologia*, 35, 227–235.

Terrer C, Vicca S, Hungate BA, et al. (2017) Mycorrhizal association as a primary control of the CO_2 fertilisation effect. *Science*, 353, 72–74.

Tolleter D, Seneca FOO, Denofrio JC, et al. (2013) Coral bleaching independent of photosynthetic activity. *Current Biology*, 23, 1782–1786.

Torda G, Donelson JM, Aranda M, et al. (2017) Rapid adaptive responses to climate change in corals. *Nature Climate Change*, 7, 627–636.

Ueda Y, Frindte K, Knief C, et al. (2016) Effects of elevated tropospheric ozone concentration on the bacterial community in the phyllosphere and rhizoplane of rice. *PLoS ONE*, 11, e0163178.

Vacher C, Hampe A, Porté AJ, et al. (2016) The phyllosphere: Microbial jungle at the plant–climate interface. *Annual Review of Ecology, Evolution, and Systematics*, 47, 1–24.

van der Voort M, Kempenaar M, van Driel M, et al. (2016) Impact of soil heat on reassembly of bacterial communities in the rhizosphere microbiome and plant disease suppression. *Ecology Letters*, 19, 375–382.

Vega Thurber R, Willner-Hall D, Rodriguez-Mueller B, et al. (2009) Metagenomic analysis of stressed coral holobionts. *Environmental Microbiology*, 11, 2148–2163.

Venn A, Tambutté E, Holcomb M, et al. (2011) Live tissue imaging shows reef corals elevate pH under their calcifying tissue relative to seawater. *PLoS ONE*, 6, e20013.

Vorholt JA. (2012) Microbial life in the phyllosphere. *Nature Reviews Microbiology*, 10, 828–840.

Wang L, Shantz AA, Payet JP, et al. (2018) Corals and their microbiomes are differentially affected by exposure to elevated nutrients and a natural thermal anomaly. *Frontiers in Marine Science*, 5, 101.

Webster NS, Negri AP, Botté ES, et al. (2016) Host-associated coral reef microbes respond to the cumulative pressures of ocean warming and ocean acidification. *Scientific Reports*, 6, 19324.

Wei T, Ishida R, Miyanaga K, et al. (2014) Seasonal variations in bacterial communities and antibiotic-resistant strains associated with green bottle flies

(Diptera: Calliphoridae). *Applied Microbiology and Biotechnology*, 98, 4197–4208.

Weis VM. (2008) Cellular mechanisms of Cnidarian bleaching: Stress causes the collapse of symbiosis. *The Journal of Experimental Biology*, 211, 3059–3066.

Wernegreen JJ. (2012) Mutualism meltdown in insects: Bacteria constrain thermal adaptation. *Current Opinion in Microbiology*, 15, 255–262.

Yellowlees D, Rees TA, Leggat W. (2008) Metabolic interactions between algal symbionts and invertebrate hosts. *Plant, Cell and Environment*, 31, 679–694.

Young VB. (2017) The role of the microbiome in human health and disease: An introduction for clinicians. *BMJ*, 356, j831.

Zaneveld JR, Burkepile DE, Shantz AA, et al. (2016) Overfishing and nutrient pollution interact with temperature to disrupt coral reefs down to microbial scales. *Nature Communications*, 7, 11833.

Zhao Y, Chen Y, Li Z, et al. (2018) Environmental factors have a strong impact on the composition and diversity of the gut bacterial community of Chinese black honeybees. *Journal of Asia–Pacific Entomology*, 21, 261–267.

Ziegler M, Roik A, Porter A, et al. (2016) Coral microbial community dynamics in response to anthropogenic impacts near a major city in the central Red Sea. *Marine Pollution Bulletin*, 105, 629–640.

Ziegler M, Seneca FO, Yum LK, et al. (2017) Bacterial community dynamics are linked to patterns of coral heat tolerance. *Nature Communications*, 8, 1–8.

Zilber-Rosenberg I, Rosenberg E. (2008) Role of microorganisms in the evolution of animals and plants: The hologenome theory of evolution. *FEMS Microbiology Reviews*, 32, 723–735.

CHAPTER NINE

Microbial biotechnology

RACHAEL E. ANTWIS
University of Salford
ELLEN L. FRY
University of Manchester
CHLOË E. JAMES AND NATALIE FERRY
University of Salford

9.1 Introduction

The rapid pace of societal development in the twentieth and twenty-first centuries has led to a dramatic decline in the functioning of global ecosystems (Ripple et al., 2017). An expanding human population has resulted in widespread conversion of habitats for food production, leading to environmental degradation and a significant loss of global biodiversity (Crist et al., 2017). The ever-increasing demands for higher productivity from these systems, which are reliant on unsustainable inputs, has greatly exacerbated these crises, and livestock production and chemical fertilisers are major contributors to greenhouse gas emissions. Reliance on antibiotics, pesticides and herbicides damage environmental ecosystems and drive the evolution of resistance, exacerbating challenges in tackling infectious disease. This intensification of agriculture has further reduced biodiversity and environmental quality (Crist et al., 2017). Sustainable production of food for a growing human population is high on political and environmental agendas, and within this, an ability to maximise yields while minimising land-use change and soil degradation is required (Dwivedi et al., 2017; Huws et al., 2018). One significant constraint on food production is crop disease, which severely limits productivity. Although a range of preventative measures and treatments aimed at eradication are often available, these are usually at odds with long-term sustainable production of crops due to their impact on the broader environment (Crist et al., 2017). Similarly, the use of antibiotics to minimise infection outbreaks and increase overall productivity has been widespread in intensive animal farming, which is unsustainable and undesirable, in part due to the development of antibiotic resistance (Tang et al., 2017).

Alongside habitat degradation and land-use change, wildlife disease is also a major contributor to the loss of global biodiversity. The last 50 years have seen the emergence of a number of hypervirulent wildlife pathogens (Tompkins et al., 2015). Such pathogens have decimated wildlife populations globally, with amphibian, fish and tree species particularly at risk (Tompkins et al., 2015; Stephens et al., 2016). Such diseases are very difficult to control in the wild, and broad-scale treatments are usually either unavailable or hard to implement (Sleeman, 2013). Given the extraordinary functional diversity contained within host and environmental microbial communities (as discussed in previous chapters), these provide enormous potential to solve a wide range of environmental and medical problems (Antwis et al., 2017). For example, microbial bioaugmentation strategies (also termed 'probiotics' or 'synthetic microbial communities'; forthwith 'microbial inputs') have been proposed to address the range of issues highlighted above, and have been used to some success to reduce agricultural, livestock, human and wildlife disease (reviewed by McKenzie et al., 2018); replace antibiotics (Nunes et al., 2012; Allen et al., 2013); increase agricultural productivity and food quality (reviewed in Menendez & Garcia-Fraile, 2017 and Jiménez-Gómez & Sommer, 2017); and reduce environmental contamination (Varjani, 2017). In addition, the removal of highly methanogenic microbes from ruminant guts may reduce the unsustainable carbon footprint of the meat industry (Seshadri et al., 2018). 'Microbiome engineering', whereby microbial communities can be altered through environmental or biological manipulations, also offers a promising approach to address various issues, particularly in the context of food production (Mueller & Sachs, 2015; Bender et al., 2016; Sheth et al., 2016). Furthermore, products derived from microorganisms have long been used for the benefit of humanity, most notably since the discovery of penicillin in 1928, synthesised by *Penicillium notatum* (Ligon, 2004). Since then, over 100 microbially derived antibiotics have been commercialised. However, the increase of antimicrobial resistance is well-documented, responsible for killing an estimated 700,000 people per annum and threatening several Sustainable Development Goals (HM Government, 2019). As such, there is an urgent need to identify new products and approaches to ensure humans continue to benefit from the enormous improvements in health care achieved in the twentieth and twenty-first centuries. Microbially derived products are also being used to improve biofuel production, crop health and human gut health (Lian et al., 2018), and 'microbiome prospecting' can be used to identify a range of ways to improve environmental health and human existence.

In this chapter, we will look at a range of examples of microbial inputs, microbiome engineering, microbiome prospecting, and the benefits and limitations associated with these various approaches. Policy issues relating to broad-scale use of these will also be explored. Given the infancy of this field, this chapter will present many more questions than it will answer.

9.2 Microbial inputs

9.2.1 Examples of current uses

On the surface, microbial inputs present a relatively low-cost and low-tech possibility for making use of existing biological traits to provide a particular function in a specific system. As such, microbial inputs are being used in a range of contexts to effectively improve productivity and reduce disease incidence (McKenzie et al., 2018; see Table 9.1 for further examples). In particular, their use is increasing in the context of food production, including agriculture, aquaculture and livestock farming. Altering plant and soil micro-biomes to enhance plant productivity is an ancient practice dating back to around 300 BC, and since the first commercial bioinoculant was developed in 1896, hundreds of commercial microbial inoculants and products registered for use in crop production (Finkel et al., 2017). Application of plant growth–promoting rhizobacteria (PGPRs) in an agricultural setting has potential to increase microbiome diversity, fill vacant niches in the soil and increase the niche breadth of the host. PGPR, endo- and ectomycorrhizal fungi (AMF and ECM, respectively) and cyanobacteria have all been used to mobilise nutrients from the soil, fix atmospheric nitrogen, limit pathogenic infection, promote phytohormone biosynthesis, confer salt and drought tolerance, and promote plant growth (reviewed in Bhardwaj et al., 2014; Di Benedetto et al., 2017; Menendez & Garcia-Fraile, 2017; Kaminsky et al., 2018). Greenhouse studies using tomato plants have demonstrated that inoculation of plants with PGPR and mycorrhizal fungi reduced the fertiliser requirement of the system; inoculated plants that received 75% less fertiliser than uninoculated controls (which received a full fertiliser treatment) generated the same yields (Adesemoye et al., 2009). In field experiments using tomato plants treated with PGPR, mycorrhizal fungi and 50% fertiliser addition, yields were greater than the control treatments, where only 100% fertiliser was applied (Hernández & Chailloux, 2004). Microbial inputs have also been tested on other crops including rice, wheat, sugarcane, peppers, soybean and others, with a number of commercial products currently available on the market (reviewed in Menendez & Garcia-Fraile, 2017 and Jiménez-Gómez & Sommer, 2017). In honeybees (*Apis mellifera*), there is evidence that microbial treatments can mitigate *Paenibacillus larvae* (Mudroňová et al., 2011) and *Nosema ceranae* (El Khoury et al., 2018, but also see Ptaszyńska et al., 2016). Microbial inputs can also increase egg-laying in hens (Denev et al., 2013), promote weight gain and health in cattle (Uyeno et al. 2015), and optimise feed conversion, facilitate reproduction and reduce pathogen incidence in aquaculture of numerous commercial fish species (Martínez Cruz et al., 2012).

The use of microbial inputs is also being investigated to address a number of emerging wildlife pathogens, with some evidence of successful prophylaxis and/or treatment of fungal pathogens. These include *Pseudogymnoascus*

(*Geomyces*) *destructans*, the causative agent of white-nose syndrome in bats in North America (Hoyt et al., 2015); *Batrachochytrium* spp., which cause chytridiomycosis disease in a phenomenal range of amphibian genera and species (Bletz et al., 2013, 2017; Rebollar et al., 2016); and *Ophiostoma novo-ulmi*, the Dutch elm pathogen (Blumenstein et al., 2015), to name a few examples. However, extensive field trials are lacking in most cases (see Chapter 7 for a more complete overview of this subject).

In humans, the use of probiotic therapies has increased dramatically over the last 10 years (Draper et al., 2017). Live bacteria consumption has had reported benefits for general health, weight management, allergy control and a range of gastrointestinal, cardiovascular and psychological conditions (Cuello-Garcia et al. 2015; Sun & Buys, 2016; Thushara et al., 2016; Zhang et al., 2016; McKean et al., 2017; Lin et al., 2018). Probiotic therapies are also prescribed to reduce the impacts of antibiotics (Hempel et al., 2012), and microbial inputs can be used to stimulate host immune responses (Naik et al., 2012; Colombo et al., 2015), and prevent or treat disease. For example, *Streptococcus salivarius* strains have been developed for the treatment or prevention of a range of oral and upper respiratory tract disorders such as halitosis, tooth decay, periodontitis, pharyngitis and otitis media (Wescombe et al., 2012). These strains originate from the oral cavity of healthy individuals and are commonly viewed as beneficial oral bacteria that secrete a range of bacteriocins as competitive agents to inhibit pathogens such as *S. mutans* (major causative agent of tooth decay) and *S. pyogenes* (pharyngitis). The effects of these inhibitory species are strain-specific and include the promotion of innate immune responses, reduced inflammatory responses, enhanced antiviral responses and competitive inhibition (Wescombe et al., 2012). Despite commercial production of these species in formulations such as lozenges and chewing gum, most evidence to support the claims of health benefits rely heavily on in vitro studies and a few small-scale clinical trials.

Alternative microbial inputs for humans include bacteriophages and bacterial predators. Bacteriophages are viruses that can infect and kill bacteria, and their therapeutic value was realised soon after their discovery over 100 years ago (1915–1917). Phages are highly specific and ubiquitous, and outnumber their bacterial hosts in every niche by at least 10:1. In addition, once they encounter their target bacterial hosts, they amplify at the site of infection, constituting a highly effective and specific treatment that is non-toxic to the host. Phage therapy was largely superseded by antibiotics in the 1940s, but remained a mainstay of bacterial infection treatment in the former Soviet Union. Until recently, reliable evidence of efficacy through controlled clinical trials was severely lacking. However, their therapeutic application is attracting increased attention as the rate of antimicrobial resistance becomes unsustainable. This type of approach is also being used outside of humans.

Commercially available bacteriophage suspensions are available for a range of applications including clinical treatment, livestock decolonisation and reduction of bacterial load on processed meat (Cisek et al., 2017). For example, the bacterial predator *Bdellovibrio bacteriovorus* can be found naturally in most environments, including the human gut, and feeds on Gram-negative bacteria, such as *Escherichia coli* and *Salmonella*. When orally administered live to young chicks, *B. bacteriovorus* significantly reduces *S. enterica* sv *enteritidis* numbers and caecal inflammation (Atterbury et al., 2011). There is, however, concern that the evolution of resistance to increased predation in the host environment might select for increased virulence (Gagliardi et al., 2018). Furthermore, the current European regulatory framework for medical product development requires a fixed chemical composition. This is a problem for live bacteriophage formulations, because actively replicating bacteriophages are subject to mutation. Efficient bacteriophage therapy also requires a tailored approach for each individual patient, in which different bacteriophages should be optimised, depending on the specific bacterial strain causing the infection. There have thus been calls for changes in policies for the development of antimicrobials (Verbeken et al., 2014).

9.2.2 How can we select microbial inputs?

In order to develop effective microbial inputs, there are two main aspects for consideration: identifying microorganisms that are capable of producing the desired trait (e.g. resisting pathogenic invasion or reducing pathogen growth, degrading an environmental contaminant, restoring healthy microbial consortia, increasing crop yields, etc.), and whether they can establish long-term in or on the host or environment. Candidate microbial inputs can be identified through traditional culturing directly from a given host or environment, coupled with high-throughput in vitro screening (e.g. inhibition assays or tolerance tests; Wescombe et al., 2012; Bletz et al., 2013; De Roy et al., 2014). Sanger sequencing can then be used to identify microorganisms that confer the required trait, and frozen stocks maintained using glycerol for further in vivo or in situ testing. For those candidates that cannot be isolated using classical culture media (up to 99% of all microbial species in the natural environment), new devices, such as the iChip, have been developed to grow microorganisms in situ. This approach identified the previously uncharacterised soil bacterium *Eleftheria terrae* that produces a teixobactin, representing a novel class of antibiotics (Ling et al., 2015).

Next-generation sequencing is another key tool in identifying microorganisms of interest for use as microbial inputs (see Chapter 2). Amplicon sequencing is a particularly quick and cost-effective method of taxonomically identifying microorganisms associated with a particular trait of interest. For

Table 9.1 *Examples of microbial input uses and applications.*

Problem	Purpose of intervention	Target taxon/ ecosystem	Probiotic taxa applied	Mode of application	Success rate	Reference
Low yield	Plant growth promotion	Bean plants	*Rhizobium*–PGPR consortium vs. individual taxa	Soil inoculated with liquid culture mixed with humus as inoculum carrier	*Rhizobium–Pseudomonas* 41% more growth than *Rhizobium* alone. Depends on soil type	Remans et al., 2008; Colás Sánchez et al., 2014
Fusarium wilt affects graminaceous crops, and can also cause disease in horses and pigs, and oesophageal cancer in humans	Reduce disease, increase crop yield	Graminaceous plants	*Arthrobacter, Azotobacter, Pseudomonas, Bacillus subtilis*	Seed treatment	*Azotobacter armeniacus* results in total inhibition at 10^6–10^7 cell ml^{-1}. Other taxa less successful	Cavaglieri et al., 2004
Rhizoctonia solani; tomato fungal pathogen	Reduce disease, increase crop yield	Tomato plants	*Aureobasidium pullulans, Paraconiothyrium sporulosum*	Syringe used to apply inoculum to soil	Almost total inhibition of *R. solani* growth on tomato comparable to uninfected control	Miles et al., 2012
Honeybees are increasingly vulnerable to pests and pathogens, e.g. Gram-positive bacterium *Paenbacillus larvae*	Induce an immune response (abaecin expression)	Honeybees	Bacterial consortium: *Bifidobacterium; Lactobacillus rhamnosus; L. casei; L. plantarum; L. acidophilus; B. lungum; B. breve*	2×10^6 cells per ml food, fed to larvae	Some success, but very variable	Evans & Lopez, 2004
Enteric bacteria causing colony collapse through infected food or nurse worker bees	Reduce enteric bacteria	Honeybees	Bee prebiotics: lactic or acetic acid; probiotics: Enterolactis Plus containing *Lactobacillus casei*, or enterobiotics containing *Lactobacillus acidophilus* and *Bifidobacterium lactis*	Colony fed 1:1 sugar water solution containing probiotics in different concentrations in early spring	Pre- and probiotics work together complementarily. The prebiotics reduce pathogen load early in the season. Probiotic concentration is critical to success. Largest increase in beneficial gut microbes is when Enterlactis Plus is added at a concentration of 2.4 g per 1.4 l sugar solution	Pătruică & Mot, 2012

Table 9.1 (*cont.*)

Problem	Purpose of intervention	Target taxon/ecosystem	Probiotic taxa applied	Mode of application	Success rate	Reference
Pollen substitutes, added when pollen is scarce, can shorten bee lifespans through introducing unnatural proteins and excessive sterilisation which reduces beneficial gut microbes	Need for nutritious pollen substitutes that improve bee lifespan	Honeybees	Biogen-N containing bacterial species: *Pediococcus acidilactici*, *Lactobacillus acidophilus*, *Enterococcus faecium*, *Bifidobacterium bifidum*, and Trilac contains *L. acidophilus*, *L. delbrueckii* spp. *bulgaricus*, *B. bifidum*	Two days with 1 mg probiotic to 100 g pollen substitute then 12 days without, or 14 days with probiotic	30–50% increase in bee survival across probiotic treatments	Kaznowski et al., 2004
Chytridiomycosis: *Batrachochytrium dendrobatidis* (Bd) fungal skin pathogen	Reduce pathogenicity, ideally with broad-spectrum inhibition of Bd (>80%). Alleviate extinction risk of various frog, toad and salamander species	Amphibians	Individual bacterium: *Stenotrophomonas*, *Aeromonas*, *Pseudomonas*	Only tested in vitro. Application would consist of painting culture onto skin	Proportion of inhibitory isolates: 100%, 77% and 73%, respectively	Becker et al., 2015
Chytridiomycosis: *Batrachochytrium dendrobatidis* (Bd) fungal skin pathogen	Reduce pathogenicity, ideally with broad-spectrum inhibition of Bd (>80%). Alleviate extinction risk of various frog, toad and salamander species	Amphibians	Individual bacterium: *Enterobacteriaceae*, *Pseudomonadaceae*, *Xanthamonadaceae*	Only tested in vitro. Application would consist of painting culture onto skin	Proportion of inhibitory isolates: 84%, 80% and 75%, respectively	Bletz et al., 2017

Disease/pathogen	Aim	Host	Treatment	Method	Outcome	Reference
Chytridiomycosis: *Batrachochytrium dendrobatidis* (Bd) fungal skin pathogen	Reduce pathogenicity, ideally with broad-spectrum inhibition of Bd (>80%). Alleviate extinction risk of various frog, toad and salamander species	Amphibians	Bacterial consortium: *Pseudoclavibacter helvolus*, *Chryseobacterium indoltheticum*, *Chryseobacterium aquaticum*, *Exiguobacterium*, *Serratia fonticola*, *Stenotrophomonas rhizophila*	Only tested in vitro. Application would consist of applying culture directly to skin	Much greater inhibition when all six present, compared with 1, 2 or 3 species	Piovia-Scott et al., 2017
White-nose syndrome: *Pseudogymnoascus destructans* fungal skin pathogen	Reduce extinction risk to bat populations, especially *Myotis septentrionalis*	Bats	Six *Pseudomonas* spp., cultured from bats	Tested in vitro	Up to 100% in some strains at high bacterial concentrations	Hoyt et al., 2015
Inflammatory bowel disease, e.g. Crohn's, ulcerative colitis	Alleviation of symptoms: suppress inflammation, activate immunity	Humans	Bifidobacteria and lactic acid bacteria (LAB)	Oral administration	Very variable success rate, possibly because of differences between strains	Saez-Lara et al., 2015
Eczema	Alleviation of symptoms in infants	Humans	*Lactobacillus rhamnosus*, *L. reuteri*, *L. fermentum*	Topical	No significant evidence of improvement. Some reports of sepsis and bowel problems from probiotics	Boyle et al., 2009
Clostridium difficile infection	Treatment for recurrent infection	Humans	Faecal infusion	Surgical intervention	Overall 97% success rate, but only 69% of sample cured by one infusion. Depends on severity of infection	Ianiro et al., 2017
Diet-induced insulin resistance	Characteristic of type 2 diabetes and obesity	Humans	*Lactobacillus casei*	Consumption of probiotic yoghurts twice a day	It appears to maintain insulin action during a high-fat diet, but limited study	Hulston et al., 2015

example, using 16S rRNA metabarcoding of bacterial communities, Jani and Briggs (2014) identified six genera (*Rhodococcus*, *Sanguibacter*, *Stentrophomonas*, *Pseudomonas*, *Microbacterium* and *Methylotenera*) significantly associated with low or absent *Batrachochytrium dendrobatidis* infection intensities on Sierra Nevada yellow-legged frogs (*Rana sierrae*). This suggests these genera may be effective microbial inputs for protecting frogs from *B. dendrobatidis* in the wild. Thus, this type of approach may be useful for identifying groups from which probiotics could be developed, and then genera of interest can be selectively cultured, combined, and tested in vitro, in vivo or in situ. Similarly, agricultural microbial inputs often belong to the genera *Rhizobium*, *Frankia*, *Pseudomonas*, *Trichoderma*, *Lysobacter* and *Bacillus* (Carro & Nouioui, 2017), and in gastrointestinal applications, *Lactobacillus* spp. and *Bacillus* spp. are common components of probiotic formulations (Hong et al., 2005). However, caution must be taken in the interpretation of different microbial community profiles. For example, it can be difficult to determine whether the differences in microbial community composition observed are a driver of a particularly host/environment condition, or whether the associated host/environmental condition caused the shift in community composition (i.e. it is hard to dissociate cause and effect using these types of data). A further limitation of both culturing-based and amplicon-sequencing approaches is that taxonomy does not necessarily accurately map on to function. Broad-scale taxonomic identity is unlikely to be a useful indicator of function (e.g. Antwis & Harrison, 2018), and even strains of the same bacterial 'species' do not exhibit the same antipathogen abilities and/or gene expression in vitro (De Le Fuente et al., 2006; Antwis et al., 2015; Carro & Nouioui, 2017; Antwis & Harrison, 2018). In addition, amplicon sequencing does not distinguish between active and dormant members of the microbial community. In soils, dormancy can be extremely high; up to 90% in very nutrient-poor systems (Jones & Lennon, 2010; Lennon & Jones, 2011; Salazar et al., 2018). Thus, identifying microbial inputs based on taxonomy alone may result in wasted development efforts and inadvertent exclusion of valuable possibilities.

A better approach may be to target functional genes or enzyme expression of interest, for example through the use of metagenomic or metatranscriptomic approaches, from which candidate microbes can subsequently be identified (Rebollar et al., 2016; Trivedi et al., 2016; Carro & Nouioui, 2017; Knight et al., 2018). These approaches use full sequences from microbial DNA or RNA extracted from a given environment to either reconstruct metabolic pathways or perform targeted searches for genes of particular function (see Chapter 2 for more details). For example, metatranscriptomic analysis of a polluted field site might be used to identify microbial genes associated with degradation of that pollutant. Using the more expansive data sets provided by these 'omics' methods, in comparison to amplicon sequencing, entire metabolic pathways can also be reconstructed to identify previously poorly defined nutritional requirements to better inform optimal culturing conditions (Gutleben et al., 2018). That said, the development of new bioinformatics tools may mean that entire metabolic pathways aren't necessarily needed, and draft metabolic reconstructions can be used to identify novel microbe–habitat interactions with their habitat, in turn bridging our gap in knowledge about how specific microbial contributions affect ecosystem-scale processes (Hamilton et al., 2017).

9.2.3 Microbial consortia

An increasing body of research is showing that the use of 'consortia' microbial inputs improves the desired outcome (Sarma et al., 2015; Lindemann et al., 2016). This involves the use of multiple microorganisms applied simultaneously, rather than single species. For example, consortia can increase inhibition of *B. dendrobatidis* growth through increased competition and the production of emergent metabolites (Loudon et al., 2014; Piovia-Scott et al., 2017), and these may also provide greater inhibitory capabilities across a wider range of pathogen genotypes (Antwis & Harrison, 2018). Similar results have been seen for a range of plants, whereby increased complexity of the microbial consortia leads to increased inhibition of pathogens and enhanced growth (e.g. de Boer et al., 2007; Hu et al., 2016, 2017). Cross-kingdom consortia may also provide a particularly novel and effective method to achieve the desired trait. For example, co-inoculation of Scots pine (*Pinus sylvestris* L.) with ectomycorrhizal fungi and endophytic *Methylobacterium* can improve growth and nutrient uptake (Pohjanen et al., 2014). Ideal probiotic treatments could therefore include complex microbial mixtures that coordinate multiple cooperative properties, including immune stimulation, gut barrier restoration, improved metabolic activity and competition with pathogenic microorganisms (Gagliardi et al., 2018). Co-occurrence network analysis of amplicon or metagenomic data could be used to inform consortium development by identifying groups of microbes that occur together and are associated with a trait of interest (Williams et al., 2014).

9.2.4 Improving the establishment of microbial inputs

The inability of microbial inputs to persist in the target organism or environment has been a common theme across systems and host species (Ouwehand & Salminen, 2009; Weimer et al., 2010; Muletz et al., 2012; Y. Liu et al., 2018a). For example, even when the amphibian skin microbiome is removed prior to inoculation, persistence of microbial inputs rarely exceeds ~40 days, and cross-inoculation of bacteria isolated from different host species has shown relatively little success in improving pathogen resistance (Muletz et al., 2012; Woodhams et al., 2012; Rebollar et al., 2016). A similar problem has been observed for soil additions, where the invasion success of existing soil micro-biomes by beneficial organisms is low, and as such, microbial inputs are not currently considered an economically viable solution to plant health and soil fertility in field conditions (Emam, 2016; Hu et al., 2017; Kaminsky et al., 2018). The need to understand how microbial inputs integrate and establish within the resident microbiome has been repeatedly highlighted (Bender et al., 2016; Rebollar et al., 2016; Busby et al., 2017; Kaminsky et al., 2018). There could be several interacting reasons for the poor success rate, including a lack of avail-able niche space or inhospitable abiotic conditions, or host-specific traits that inhibit establishment. For example, host genotype can influence the effective-ness of microbial inputs. Martín and Macaya-Sanz (2015) identified a significant effect of host genotype on the efficacy of microbial inputs to protect elm trees (*Ulmus minor*) from Dutch elm disease, meaning that such treatments will only work for some individuals. The specific mechanisms underlying these genetic × microbiome interactions require further research to improve the efficacy of microbial inputs. Many different host taxa, from plants to amphibians to humans, produce exudates, peptides or proteins that can either promote or inhibit microbes from establishing (Zasloff, 2002; Oldroyd et al., 2013; Walder & van der Heijden, 2015; Hancock et al., 2016). The composition and production of these are often, in part, genetically deter-mined, but in any case, the production of host-associated inhibitory com-pounds may even by upregulated if microbial inputs are perceived as 'invaders'. Targeting microbes that comprise the core microbiome (the set of microbes that are ubiquitous across all individuals of that host population) for development of microbial inputs may also mean the host (and existing micro-biome; see below) is more likely to recognise the microbial input as commen-sal or symbiotic (Busby et al., 2017).

It is becoming clear that one key factor regulating the establishment of microbial inputs is the existing community, whereby antagonism by existing microbes hinders the microbial newcomers. Existing microbiomes often represent diverse and complex communities that are resistant to invasion, in a similar way to macro-ecological systems where multicellular organisms can resist invasive species. Antimicrobial capabilities are widespread across bacteria, fungi and other microorganisms (e.g. Kennedy et al., 2009; Zhao et al., 2011; Becker at al., 2015), suggesting that these organisms exhibit generalist inhibitory capabilities. This reduces the potential for other microorganisms, both pathogenic and beneficial, to invade. Generally speaking, low commu-nity relatedness, high species richness and high bacterial abundance all increase the resistance of the community to invaders (Jousset et al., 2011; Eisenhauer et al., 2012, 2013). For example, van Elsas et al. (2012) demon-strated an inverse relationship between the invasion capacity of *Escherichia coli* and the diversity of the existing soil microbial community. However, Wei et al.

(2015) found that resource competition networks are more accurate predictors of invasion success than extant community diversity in bacterial rhizosphere communities.

Consortia microbial inputs may be more effective at establishing than single-strain inputs as they may be more stable and resilient to the existing microbiome (Hu et al., 2016). In addition, consortia often have higher niche differentiation and secondary metabolite production than single species, and so may be more effective at infiltrating the existing community (Jousset et al., 2014; Lindemann et al., 2016). Introducing a more diverse range of choice microorganisms through the use of consortia may also allow the host to select their own recruits and, thus, increase the potential for establishment. Furthermore, members of the consortia could be carefully selected for their complementarity. For example, within the well-characterised polymicrobial biofilms of the human oral cavity, communities are built by stepwise establishment of primary pioneer species, followed by cooperative bridging species, then late colonisers (James, 2013). While production of inhibitory molecules, such as bacteriocins, can provide a competitive edge for successful residents or invaders, expression of compatible surface adhesion molecules and metabolic cross-feeding are crucial for successful establishment in the community (James, 2013). For example, a close relationship has been observed between the pioneer species *S. gordonii* and the later colonising anaerobic pathogen *Porphyromonas gingivalis* (James, 2013). Both species possess the LuxS quorum sensing system that enables cross-species communication via auto-inducer2 (AI-2). Recognition of this signal molecule enables stronger physical interactions by the upregulation of surface adhesion molecules such as fimbriae (James, 2013). Thus, specific cooperative interactions between microbes may facilitate establishment. Similarly, bacterial adhesions and protein secretion systems of microbial inputs may facilitate establishment, and much of the knowledge from pathogenic and commensal microbes may be transferable to improve the success of synthetic communities (Dale & Moran, 2006; Kline et al., 2009; Chagnot et al., 2013).

Indeed, to improve establishment, we also need to understand how an existing microbial community recognises an invader. Social dynamics and antimicrobial properties of microbial communities are determined through the recognition of metabolites produced by other microbes in that community. Existing communities are likely to respond differently according to the genotype or metabolite profile of an invader, regardless of whether it is pathogenic or 'probiotic'. For example, antimicrobial metabolite production may be upregulated by the existing community on recognition of invader-specific metabolites (Mitri & Foster, 2013). This relies on two things: (1) cell–cell communication between closely related and/or cooperative species (governed by the production of metabolites in a density-dependent process known as quorum sensing); and

(2) the recognition of invader metabolite profiles, or rather, recognition that the metabolite profile is not similar to their own, and so an invader must be present (Scheuring & Yu, 2012; Mitri & Foster, 2013). More broadly speaking, cooperation theory predicts that a given microbe may allow the persistence of closely related microbes (Mitri & Foster, 2013). Indeed, the colonisation of pathogens in the gut is correlated with the abundance of related species (Stecher et al., 2010). Thus, communities may allow related species to become established and attempt to reject dissimilar species, which has been demonstrated for both pathogenic and commensal bacteria in mice (Stecher et al., 2010). Similarly, kin recognition can improve cooperation in rhizobia populations (Zee & Bever, 2014). This may also mean that the higher the abundance of introduced microbes, the greater the chance of inhibitory compounds being produced by the existing community. Therefore, counter-intuitively, the persistence of microbial inputs may be greater when introduced at lower abundances, although it is important to ensure these can then replicate to sufficient densities to achieve the desired outcome, or that they have the potential to confer the desired trait at low densities (i.e. act as keystone species). That said, some resident microbiomes are harsher than others. For example, in ruminants, strong host-specificity causes microbial community composition and fermentation profiles to quickly return to pre-inoculation composition in the rumen (Weimer et al., 2010). In these types of highly competitive environments, microbial inputs may never establish, whereas microbial inputs may be more successful in systems (host or environmental) that exert less selection pressure on the resident microbiome. Limitations to establishment may be further overcome by identifying traits associated with the microorganisms themselves that confer increased ability to invade and persist. For example, analysis of high- and low-persistence strains of *Lactobacillus johnsonii* NCC533 using comparative genomics identified three gene loci specific to the high-persistence strain, which when knocked-out and trialled in mice, were associated with reduced persistence (Denou et al., 2008).

Another strategy to avoid rejection is to overwhelm the existing microbial community with a vast quantity of microbial input in the hope that it will contain enough beneficial representatives of the microbial community to have the desired outcome. Examples include the application of manure or sewage sludge on soils (e.g. Quaye et al., 2011), or faecal transplants in humans for recurrent *Clostridium difficile* infection (Bakken et al., 2011, but see also Spector & Knight, 2015). Indeed, particular success has been reported in the clinical use of faecal transplants to restore the gut microbiota of patients suffering from *C. difficile* infections after broad-spectrum antibiotic treatment. In such cases, the faecal matter of a healthy donor is delivered directly into the patient gut with relatively little prior processing. This approach presents challenges in: (1) identifying suitable healthy donors; (2) testing each sample for safety; and (3) developing the procedure for broader, more palatable use (Kelly & Tebas, 2018). This strategy of overwhelming an existing community is an extremely blunt approach that may introduce problematic microbes to the system. Furthermore, prior removal of the existing microbial community is often still required to reduce competition (e.g. Bakken et al., 2011; Quaye et al., 2011; Muletz et al., 2012; Holden et al., 2015), but is not necessarily feasible on a wide scale, such as in agriculture or wildlife settings. Identifying the groups of microbes that confer the desired outcome may fine-tune this approach. For example, an artificial bacterial consortium of 100 species that mimic the healthy gut microbiota has been used to successfully modulate intestinal microbiota of elderly individuals (Gagliardi et al., 2018). Others have developed a combination of 33 species, with the aim of restoring a healthy gut microbiota after recurrent *C. difficile* infection (Petrof et al., 2013). Evidence from these investigations confirms that a delicate balance of complex microbial consortia is required. Thus, the use of microbial consortia, as discussed above, may provide a more refined approach to overwhelming the existing microbial community, in addition to maximising functional capabilities of a microbial input.

A nice example of a novel approach to the application of microbial inputs for soils, similar to the microbiome transplant approach, is through the use of earthworm excreta. Earthworms are highly efficient ecosystem engineers, and may offer a unique solution to many of the cost and extraction efficiency issues associated with soil probiotics (Forey et al., 2018). Compost turned over by earthworms, known as vermicompost, has long been used by horticulturalists to improve soil quality. While they are known bioturbators, improving the quality of the soil through tunnelling and aeration, there is less recognition for the value of their excreta, or 'casts'. However, there is likely to be a commercial benefit to using the casts alone to improve soil on a larger scale after degradation or intensive agriculture. Compost can be problematic because it may have high levels of N, P or K, which is not always desirable, especially in a restoration framework. It can also cause mechanical problems – a heavy layer of compost may reduce seedling establishment. Earthworm casts are rich in beneficial microbes such as nitrogen-fixing or phosphate-solubilising bacteria (Hussain et al., 2016), and phytohormones that aid plant growth and establishment (Wong et al., 2016). In particular, beneficial microorganisms (including *Enterobacter*, *Aeromonas* and *Bacillus*) have a key role in suppressing pathogenic or parasitic microbes and nematodes, thus improving soil health (Mishra et al., 2017; Mu et al., 2017). Therefore, a solution made from worm casts could be a simple and cheap way of adding microbial inoculum where needed (Arraktham et al., 2016).

Identifying efficient strategies for the physical application of microbial inputs will also likely improve their success, such as applying microbial inputs at a particular time of year, or under particular pH, water or nutrient conditions (De Roy et al., 2014). Identifying a particular time point in host development may also improve establishment. Amphibians undergo significant skin microbiome restructuring on metamorphosis, which may provide an opportunity to inoculate for disease protection (Walke & Belden, 2016). Manipulating the microbiome before it has sufficiently colonised, such as during early life, is also being explored for ruminants (e.g. Yáñez-Ruiz et al., 2015). Several differences in human gut microbiota have been linked to events in early life, such as vaginal versus caesarean birth, or breast-fed versus formula-fed infants (Neu et al., 2011; Timmerman et al., 2017), emphasising the point that early-stage interventions can have long-lasting effects. Furthermore, agricultural or grassland inocula may work best if inserted into the soil rather than placed on top (Middleton & Bever, 2012). The use of arbuscular mycorrhizal fungi (AMF) is particularly challenging as large-scale cultivation of these organisms is complex (Vosátka et al., 2012; Berruti et al., 2016). However, novel application methods are being developed, such as seed coating, co-inoculation with rhizobia and biostimulants (e.g. phytohormones) that encourage growth of AMF (Vosátka et al., 2012). Seed coating may be particularly effective because the resident community is not as established compared with later stages of development. Concurrently, inoculation of flowers to encourage probiotics to establish inside seeds may also prove successful (Mitter et al., 2017). Inoculation of soil communities may be improved by using seedlings as a 'carrier', and the establishment of inoculants may be maintained through the use of cover-crops (Lehman et al., 2012; Middleton & Bever, 2012). However, there is unlikely to be a 'silver bullet' approach to the application of microbial inputs and as with the inputs themselves, this will most likely need to be determined on a case-by-case basis.

9.3 Microbiome engineering

The use of microbial inputs requires cultured strains and/or consortia for direct application and integration to the organism or environment of interest. This can be hard to achieve due to the complexities of integrating microbial inputs with the existing community, as described above, and because only a small proportion of the resident microbes are culturable and so obtaining microbes of interest may not be possible (Gutleben et al., 2018). 'Microbiome engineering' is gaining traction as an alternative approach to microbial inputs because it potentially allows circumnavigation of both of these problems. Microbiome engineering is the manipulation of host or environmental microbial communities in situ, often making use of host traits that influence microbiome composition and function to obtain the desired microbial community and associated traits (Mueller & Sachs, 2015; Sheth et al., 2016). Indeed, the use of microbial inputs, antibiotics, antifungals and bacteriophages all represent forms of microbiome engineering (Quiza et al., 2015; Foo et al., 2017). However, alternative approaches with greater potential for successful outcomes without negative consequences are increasingly being investigated.

One novel and potentially sophisticated approach to microbiome engineering includes the use of prebiotics or biostimulants, such as phytochemicals, root exudates or short-chain fatty acids, which encourage the growth of desirable microbes or discourage the growth of undesirable strains (Quiza et al., 2015; Bender et al., 2016; Thijs et al., 2016; Foo et al., 2017). The use of prebiotics in humans is growing, particularly oligosaccharides including fructooligosaccharides, (*trans*)galacto-oligosaccharides and xylo-oligosaccharides, and polysaccharides such as inulin, either commercially manufactured or derived from natural sources such as chicory (Kellow et al., 2014; Pandey et al., 2018). The aim of these is to stimulate growth of health-promoting bacteria within the colon; typical targets include *Bifidobacterium* or *Lactobacillus* (Kellow et al., 2014). However, their efficacy remains mixed. A meta-analysis of 26 randomised controlled trials involving 831 human participants indicated that prebiotics were effective at reducing self-perceived levels of hunger and regulating post-consumption glucose and insulin, although effects on other metabolic functions and immune function were contradictory (Kellow et al., 2014). As with all microbiome biotechnologies, the success of different approaches will vary between individuals, particularly for a host species as complex and diverse as humans. Prebiotics or 'dietary interventions' have also been used to improve microbiome function in livestock ruminants (Huws et al., 2018). Feeding animals with red clover and other high-quality forage, or supplementing diets with tannins, saponins, bicarbonate, essential oils and unsaturated fats (among other things), have improved productivity and milk quality, prevented rumen acidosis, and reduced methane production (Huws et al., 2018). Thus, prebiotics have the potential to increase food conversion efficiency and reduce greenhouse gas emissions in the ever-growing meat industry (Huws et al., 2018). In plants, prebiotics in the form of extrinsically applied root exudates or other carbon-based substrates can reduce microbial dormancy and improve the recruitment of root symbionts, such as AMF or rhizobia, thus stimulating a range of otherwise inaccessible metabolic functions (De Nobili et al., 2001; Oldroyd, 2013). Biochemical stimulants ranging from red grape extract to hydrolosates and nitrophenolate have been shown to improve yields for a number of crop species, and the industry is thought to be worth around $2 billion (Calvo et al., 2014; Brown & Saa, 2015). Humic and fulvic acids have been identified and synthesised as plant additives, and have been shown to improve the performance of 16 crop species (Calvo et al., 2014). These are slow to decompose and thus offer a steady input of available nutrients to soil organisms and plants. As such, stimulating existing microbial communities through the addition of microbially or plant-derived natural products may provide a realistic alternative to environmentally damaging fertilisers, herbicides and pesticides.

Another approach to microbiome engineering involves the use of management practices that encourage the growth of desired microbes or encourages the establishment of microbial inputs (Adam et al., 2016). Due to the nature of the approach, this is currently more widely used in agriculture rather than the context of wildlife or humans. Modern conventional farming practices involving the widespread use of chemical-based fertilisers, herbicides and pesticides has, generally speaking, negatively affected soil microbial biodiversity and associated function (Flohre et al., 2011; Chaudhry et al., 2012; Hartmann et al., 2015; Pershina et al., 2015; Ishaq et al., 2017). Examples of management strategies that can be used to restore the soil microbiome include the use of organic practices such as no-till, crop rotations and inter- or cover-cropping (Quiza et al., 2015; Bender et al., 2016; Foo et al., 2017). For example, Lehman et al. (2012) showed a number of different cover crops increased AMF propagules in agricultural soil, with forage oats (*Avena sativa* L.) proving the most effective. A meta-analysis conducted by Bowles et al. (2017) across multiple crop species and continents indicated the use of cover-crops can increase AMF by around 30%. Brennan and Acosta-Martinez (2017) also showed an increase in soil microbial biomass, carbon and nitrogen as a result of cover-cropping, although cover-crop type and frequency had implications for this. Intercropping increases yields of many crop species (Schmidt et al., 2016) and there is some indication this is related to microbial community composition (Zhang et al., 2010). However, the microbial mechanisms of this are poorly understood. The potential for such management techniques to improve microbial diversity and subsequent yield returns is an underexplored and promising area of research.

Selective breeding of hosts for desirable microbial community functions is a third method of microbiome engineering (Quiza et al., 2015; Bender et al., 2016; Thijs et al., 2016; Foo et al., 2017). A topical example is the incompatible insect technique (IIT), which is being trialled to control vector-borne diseases of humans including malaria, dengue and Zika (Lees et al., 2015; Flores & O'Neill, 2018). This approach involves the selective breeding and release of *Wolbachia*-infected male mosquitos that results in the death of offspring when mated to females carrying a different *Wolbachia* strain, or none at all, due to cytoplasmic incompatibility (Lees et al., 2015; Flores & O'Neill, 2018). In the majority of cases, selective breeding for microbiome composition requires some degree of genetic control over host microbiome composition that can be identified and selected for, and, ideally, heritability of host microbiomes (e.g. Schweitzer et al., 2008; Walters et al., 2018) to ensure the desired microbiome composition or function is passed on to subsequent generations. Kittelmann et al. (2014) identified two bacterial community types in sheep that are linked to low methane production, and Roehe et al. (2016) have developed methods for selecting cattle based on host genotype effects on bacterial communities and subsequent methane production. Thus, it may be possible to breed ruminants with a lower carbon footprint (although it should be noted that a considerable reduction in consumption of red meat will ultimately be required to reduce anthropogenic carbon emissions to the levels needed to avoid substantial climate change; Tuomisto, 2019). Furthermore, root exudates of plants are genetically controlled and have a major influence on rhizosphere communities, affecting their capacity to absorb nutrients and resist disease, among other traits (Chaparro et al., 2013; Quiza et al., 2015). Therefore, selective breeding of plants based on phytochemical production may allow us to improve crop yields or protect valuable agroforestry or endangered species.

More contrived approaches to microbiome engineering include engineering of the microbes themselves, such as genetically engineering microorganisms that seek out and inhibit pathogens, or the use of plasmids or phages that deliver genes and other mobile genetic elements to resident bacteria to stimulate biofilm growth and subsequent exclusion of pathogens (Sheth et al., 2016; Foo et al., 2017). In some cases, microbes can also be used to deliver drugs, reducing side effects experienced with systemic routes of drug administration (LeBlanc et al., 2013). These bacteria are also genetically tractable and are therefore becoming increasingly considered as mucosal delivery vehicles for DNA vaccines and therapeutic peptides. Daniel et al. (2009) demonstrated protection of mice by intranasal immunisation with *Lactococcus lactis* engineered to secrete the low-calcium response V (LcrV) antigen of *Yersinia pseudotuberculosis*. The recombinant strain stimulated both humoral and cellular immune responses against *Y. pseudotuberculosis*. The potential to induce both systemic and mucosal immune responses is a very desirable trait for effective vaccination. Both IgM- and IgA-specific antibody responses were triggered in mice immunised with recombinant *L. lactis* expressing *Brucella abortus* Cu–Zn superoxide dismutase (SOD), which protected hosts against a virulent *B. abortus* (Sáez et al., 2012). Others have engineered *L. lactis* to secrete the anti-inflammatory cytokine interleukin 10 (IL10) to alleviate irritable bowel syndrome and chronic colitis, or mouse insulin-like growth factor-I (IGF-I) with potential to treat diabetes or neurodegenerative diseases (LeBlanc et al., 2013). *Lactobacillus* species have also been engineered to secrete anti-HIV-I chemokines or HIV-1 antigens to stimulate antiviral responses and reduce transmission of the virus in the vaginal mucosa. There has also been some success of recombinant *L. rhamnosus* enhancing tumour regression in a model of bladder cancer (LeBlanc et al., 2013).

As with microbial inputs, microbiome engineering is currently limited by our understanding of the mechanisms that control microbiome composition and function, and the ability to reproduce these over variable environmental conditions and timescales (Sheth et al., 2016). However, it may be that we can actually bypass the microorganisms themselves, and instead identify the bioactive products of interest to produce the desired outcome, much like the use of microbially derived antibiotics. Such 'bioprospecting' is another area of research that has been unlocked through technological advances, although care must be taken to avoid the same problems associated with antibiotics. We will now explore these aspects in more detail.

9.4 Bioprospecting microbiomes

There is an increasing need to discover novel or modified bioactive compounds, such as peptides, enzymes and secondary metabolites, for use in medicine, agriculture, industry, sustainable development and environmental protection. Bioprospecting has been reinvigorated by advances in genomics, high-throughput screening tools, microfluidic bioreactor cultivation and mass spectroscopy (Wohlleben et al., 2016). Using DNA recovered directly from environmental samples, microbial metabolic diversity can be assessed without the need for cells. These techniques have enabled the discovery of novel compounds produced by many previously uncultivable microorganisms from the enormous biodiversity hidden in terrestrial, marine and host microbiomes, from rhizospheres to sea sponges to humans. Furthermore, the ease of generating sequence data and the development of bioinformatics tools, such as ClustScan (https://omictools.com/clustscan-professional-tool), which identifies biosynthetic gene clusters in assembled genomes and predicts their molecular products based upon conserved biosynthetic domains, has dramatically expanded our knowledge of microbial biosynthetic diversity. Armed with these new tools, bioprospectors are set to infinitely extend this with microbial candidates that have previously been overlooked. Here, we focus on antimicrobial products, describing examples of antimicrobial peptides, enzybiotics and secondary metabolites that have potential uses in human and plant disease management. In addition, we finish this section by looking at how bioprospecting is revolutionising the biofuel industry.

9.4.1 Antimicrobial peptides and secondary metabolites

Most antibiotics and statins are secondary metabolites produced by microorganisms from a relatively small pool of genera. For example, nisins are bacteriocidal peptides (class I bacteriocins) naturally produced by several strains of *Lactococcus* and *Streptococcus*, first identified in fermented milk cultures in 1928. Nisins are 'generally regarded as safe' (GRAS) by the Food and Drug Administration (FDA) and have been used for over 30 years as food preservatives. These broad-spectrum antimicrobial peptides effectively inhibit the growth of multi–drug-resistant strains of *S. aureus*, *S. pneumoniae*, *Enterococcus*, and *C. difficile*. Bioengineered variants of nisin with modified spectrums of activity have been developed for several biomedical applications such as anti-biofilm, immunomodulatory and antitumour treatments (Shin et al., 2016). Furthmore, genome mining has been used to discover new types of nisin, such as nisinP that was identified in the genome of *Streptococcus gallolyticus* subsp. *pasteurianus* from the ruminant alimentary tract (Zhang et al., 2012). Nisins belong to a broader family of lantibiotics including lacticin 3147 and 481, whose genes have been incorporated together into commercial strains of *L. lactis* to develop multi-bacteriocin cheese starter systems (Mills et al., 2017). Matrix-assisted laser desorption/ionisation time-of-flight mass spectrometry (MALDI-TOF MS) has been applied to rapidly screen *Lactococcus* isolates for the production of lantibiotics (García-Cayuela et al., 2017). These approaches may represent useful tools for identifying novel bacteriocin producers that could be developed further. However, the broad spectrum of activity means that lantibiotics would not be suitable as orally administered therapeutics, as they could negatively impact the healthy microbiota. Other antimicrobial peptides have been isolated from soil bacteria, such as ADEP-1, an acyldepsipeptide produced by *Streptomyces hawaiiensis* that is active against Gram-positive bacteria and shows promising antisporulation activity against *C. difficile* (Petrosillio et al., 2018). Such peptides belong to a wide range of microbially derived compounds that have been termed 'post-biotics', produced by the metabolic activity of probiotic bacteria and important in regulating the healthy microbiota. Many such compounds have been developed for use in purified forms, or bioengineered to be produced by commercial strains of probiotic bacteria.

The current antibiotic crisis may also require us to search novel environments for potential compounds of interest. Marine invertebrate microbiomes represent a huge and largely untapped source of pharmaceutically and biotechnologically useful metabolites including antimicrobial, anticancer, anti-inflammatory, antioxidant, and antifouling compounds and nutraceuticals. For example, marine Actinomycetes and cyanobacteria boast a huge repertoire of secondary metabolites, including non-ribosomal peptides (NRPs) and polyketides (PKs) that act as antibiotics, immunosuppressants, antitumour agents, toxins and siderophores. Genome mining, coupled with mass spectrometry and NMR, have been used to discover novel NRPs, PKs and other bioactive compounds from marine microbiomes of soft corals, tunicates and sponges (Amoutzias et al., 2016). This approach enabled the discovery of salinilactam A, an antifungal macrolactam, from the actinomycete *Salinispora tropica* (Udwary et al., 2007).

Plant-associated microbiomes also represent an underexploited source of secondary metabolites that could be used to better manage the spread of infectious disease in crops (Müller et al., 2016). A range of endophytic bacteria (e.g. members of the genera *Paenibacillus*, *Citrobacter*, *Bacillus*, *Clostridium*, *Enterobacter*, *Pantoea*, *Methylobacteria*, *Pseudomonas*, *Burkholderia*, *Erwinia* and *Microbacterium*) have been reported to produce fungal antagonists. For example, Mousa et al. (2015) screened 215 bacterial endophytes of wild and domesticated maize and identified four that produced fungicidal antagonists of *F. graminearum*, which causes *Gibberella* ear rot in maize. Interestingly, the endophytes isolated from wild maize exhibited a broader spectrum of activity than those isolated from modern maize, suggesting co-evolutionary selection (Mousa et al., 2015). Three of the four effective endophytes were thought to be strains of *Paenibacillus polymyxa*, which is known to produce an impressive arsenal of antagonists including polymyxins, fusaricidins, colistins, volatiles and lytic enzymes (Mousa et al., 2015). The fusaricidins not only exhibited fungicidal properties, but also enhanced the plant host immune system by boosting flavonoid expression, making these excellent candidates for broader use (Mousa et al., 2015). Many other such antagonists have been described from endophytic, root-associated and free-living soil microorganisms. For example, *Pseudomonas fluorescens* strains produce 2,4-diacetylphloroglucinol (DAPG), phenazines (PHZ), pyrrolnitrin (PRN) and hydrogen cyanide (HCN), which have been detected in the field and may aid disease suppression (for more examples see Mousa & Raizada, 2015). In addition, the elicitor acetoin (3-hydroxy-2-butanone) produced by *Bacillus subtilis* can be applied to trigger induced systemic resistance in plants, conferring plant protection against *Pseudomonas syringae* pv. (Rudrappa et al., 2008). However, these studies often omit the complex biotic and abiotic interactions that affect antimicrobial production in the rhizosphere (Imperiali et al., 2017). The application of purified antagonists might circumvent these issues, but few have been tested in the field and there is little information on how to sustainably and safely use these compounds or enzymes, and at what rate resistance might develop.

9.4.2 Enzybiotics

Bacteriophages are abundant members of microbiomes and most rely on an ability to lyse bacterial cells. Bacteriophage-encoded lysins hydrolyse bacterial peptidoglycan cell walls, releasing fresh phage progeny after replication. These enzymes have been commercially purified and developed as new therapeutic endolysin molecules. Such purified enzymes are bactericidal and can completely lyse a dense bacterial broth culture in seconds (Fischetti, 2008). Because lysins target peptidoglycan, they are mostly of use against Gram-positive bacteria. However, a few variants have been isolated with key properties that enable their diffusion across the Gram-negative outer membrane. Furthermore, lysin variants have been engineered to include a highly positively charged C-terminal domain (artilysins), enabling transport across the outer membrane, thus broadening the spectrum of activity and making these effective treatments for both Gram-positive and -negative bacteria (Briers et al., 2014). Thus, these therapeutic enzymes, termed 'enzybiotics' (of which lysins are just one group), have potential activity against broad communities rather than just single species, as is the case with bacteriophage. Databases such as phiBIOTICS (Hojckova et al., 2013) have been compiled to share information on these enzymes. The exploration of interactions between bacteriophages and their bacterial hosts also enabled the discovery of CRISPR-CAS systems, which bacteria and archaea use as phage-defence mechanisms and are at the cutting edge of genome editing for wide-ranging applications in biotechnology and medicine (Sander & Joung, 2014; Donohoue et al., 2018).

9.4.3 Biofuel production

The screening of understudied environments for pharmacologically active molecules using metagenomic approaches is increasing; however, these approaches can also yield novel enzymes of biotechnological significance beyond the medical field. Microorganisms are natural sources of plant cell wall degrading enzymes (Batista-García et al., 2016), and aerobic and anaerobic lignocellulosic degrading microorganisms can be found in a variety of ecosystems such as mammal and insect guts, compost, soil, manure, biogas reactors and rumen (Silva et al., 2018 and Table 9.2). Bioprospecting of these has identified enzymes with great commercial and industrial relevance, particularly for the biofuel industry and the conversion of plant biomass into mixed sugars (see Table 9.2 for examples).

Bioprospecting studies using metagenomic approaches to search for cellulolytic enzymes have been conducted on soils, composts, watercourses and animal rumens (Table 9.2). The key features for novel enzymes are resistance to shear and fluctuations in temperature and pH, high specific activity on complex biomass substrate, and adsorption on cellulose, synergism with other enzymes, and low susceptibility to inhibition by lignocellulose degrading end products (Knauf & Moniruzzaman, 2004; Viikari et al., 2012). Microorganisms able to degrade lignocellulose include fungi from the Ascomycete and Basidiomycete divisions, such as brown-rot fungi, white-rot fungi and some anaerobic fungi found in rumens (Rana & Rana, 2017). Anaerobic bacteria associated with ruminants produce enzymes that degrade plant material pre-processed by mechanical disruption by the host rumen (Douglas, 2013), and therefore ruminants are not necessarily the best source of lignocellulose-degrading bacteria. Insect and mollusc guts are often much more efficient at plant material degradation, which occurs without a 'preparation' stage (Genta et al., 2006; Warnecke et al., 2007; Hansen & Moran, 2014). Insects and molluscs also present much more variability in their bacterial assemblages, which help them feed on a wider range of plant material, including grass and wood (Shi et al., 2011, 2013). The study of the insect–microorganism

Table 9.2 *Examples of enzymes discovered through bioprospecting strategies.*

Enzyme	Application	Source(s)	Reference(s)
Amylase	Starch degradation	Soil, groundwater, compost	Richardson et al., 2002; Voget et al., 2003; Yun et al., 2004; Lämmle et al., 2007
Cellulase	Plant biomass degradation	Lake water, soda lake sediment, rabbit cecum, insect and mollusc gut, mammalian gut	Rees et al., 2003; Voget et al., 2003, 2006; Grant et al., 2004; Feng et al., 2007; Allgaier et al., 2010; Joynson et al., 2017; Cardoso et al., 2012a
Chitinase	Fungal cell wall degradation	Seawater	Cottrell et al., 1999
Cyclodextrinase	Modified starch	Bovine rumen	Ferrer et al., 2005
Endo β 1,4-glucanase	Plant biomass degradation	Bovine rumen	Ferrer et al., 2005
Esterase	Plant biomass degradation	Bovine rumen, oil-contaminated soil, drinking water biofilm	Rees et al., 2003; Ferrer et al., 2005; Elend et al., 2006; Kim et al., 2006; Hess et al., 2011
Pectate lyase	Plant biomass degradation	Soil	Voget et al., 2003
Xylanase	Plant biomass degradation	Insect and mollusc gut, manure waste (dairy farm), soil, mammalian gut	Brennan et al., 2004; Lee et al., 2006; Allgaier et al., 2010; Joynson et al., 2017
De-branching enzymes	Plant biomass degradation	Insect and mollusc gut, mammalian gut	Voget et al., 2003; Allgaier et al., 2010; Cardoso et al., 2012b; Joynson et al., 2017

mutualism as a natural biodegrading system not only allows the discovery of new enzymes, but by also understanding its mechanism of action, strategies can be planned to emulate it and enhance biofuel production (Shi et al., 2011). For example, xylophagous coleopterans have an array of adaptations to feed on woody material such as gut structures, digestive enzymes and a numerous group of microorganisms associated with their guts (Watanabe & Tokuda, 2010; Poelchau et al., 2016). Many species have the capacity to colonise a wide range of tree hosts due to their highly diverse and plastic gut communities (Scully et al., 2013). Some of the beetle species studied, such as *Anoplophora glabripennis*, efficiently decompose lignin-enriched wood, which is one of the most complicated polymers to degrade from lignocellulose (Scully et al., 2013; Xu et al., 2014; Poelchau et al., 2016). Other adaptations of coleopterans include the storage of symbiotic yeasts and bacteria in specialised cells (mycetocytes) located in the midgut caeca, and the presence of a fermentation chamber inhabited by microorganisms. Several species have developed fungus-farming symbioses, and others produce endogenous xylanases and have unique gut physiologies such as high alkalinity, all of which contribute to lignocellulose degradation (Calderón-Cortés et al., 2012). Another group exceptionally efficient at degrading lignocellulose includes the terrestrial slugs and snails (Davidson, 1976; Reich et al., 2018). Studies on the gut and faecal microbiomes of gastropods have found lignocellulose-degrading taxa that allow the host to feed on plant material (Cardoso et al., 2012a, 2012b; Joynson et al., 2017). Their plastic microbiota allows them to populate a wide range of ecosystems that can range from tropical forests to savannahs as well as aquatic environments (Dar et al., 2017). Termites, perhaps one of the most well-studied groups, have enormous capacity for ligno-cellulosic digestion (C. Liu et al., 2018b). A complex array of microorganisms is present in their guts; mainly bacteria and archaea in higher termites, and cellulolytic flagellates in lower termites (Ohkuma, 2003). The rich number of enzymes produced by the host and associated microorganisms makes termites an appealing model for biofuel production. However, even with the profusion of enzymatic information obtained from the termite model alone, the biological processing of plant material remains a techno-economic hurdle for the production of biofuel, partly driven by cost but also due to the inability of single recombinant enzymes to replicate the conditions in the insect gut (Rana & Rana, 2017). Thus, extensive research is required from a greater variety of other natural biodegrading systems, not only to discover new enzymes, but also to compare their function and to design better biomass-processing mechanisms (Shi et al., 2011).

Recent reports suggest that the establishment of industrially relevant enzyme collections from environmental genomes has become a routine procedure (Ferrer et al., 2016). A detailed overview of genes with high biotechnological potential discovered through metagenomic approaches was recently published by Alves et al. (2018), providing a comprehensive overview of genes screened from metagenomic studies with roles in plant cell-wall degradation for the biofuel industry, as well as laccases used for decolourising industrial dyes, oxygenases used to treat contaminated soils, cutinases for PET degradation, phenol hydroxylases for aromatic compound degradation, lipase/protease/hemolysins/biosurfactants with antimicrobial activity, genes that confer resistance to extreme conditions (e.g. acid, salt), promotor sequences that can be used as 'biobricks', pathways/systems/operons for drug or pollutant degradation, and of course, bioactive molecules with antibiotic or other pharmacological potential. However, despite early success with the omics approaches, function-based metagenome screening and sequence-based metagenome data mining have limitations (Li et al., 2009), including reliance on known conserved sequences for homology-based identification of genes. Thus, studies may fail to uncover non-homologous enzymes or to detect fundamentally different novel genes.

9.5 Ethics and policy

As we have explored in this chapter, microbial biotechnologies have the potential to address wide-ranging global challenges and improve the success of a number of the Aichi Biodiversity Targets and Sustainable Development Goals (Redford et al., 2013). However, as new and exciting possibilities for microbially derived solutions to global challenges become available (e.g. see Bender et al., 2017), there are important considerations regarding the ethics and legislation surrounding the use of these (see Machado et al., 2016). A major concern surrounds undesirable responses of hosts and unintended targets. For example, adverse effects were recorded in 28.5% of human faecal microbiome transplant cases, ranging from abdominal discomfort to death (Wang et al., 2016). In addition, strains of *Bacillus* used as agricultural biopesticides are thought to have caused illness in farm workers (Hong et al., 2005). Another example is that of insecticidal *Bacillus thuringiensis* (Bt) biopesticide formulations, which have been used widely in agriculture for pest control (notably against Lepidopteran and Coleopteran larvae; Lambert & Peferoen, 1992). While the toxins produced by subspecies of the bacterium are highly specific to an insect order, this specificity exerts high selection pressure for the evolution of resistance in pest populations. Indeed, resistance to Bt biopesticides was noted as early as the 1980s in the diamondback moth, *Plutella xylostella*, in Hawaii (Tabashnik, 1994), thus demonstrating that sustained use of biopesticides follows the chemical pesticide resistance paradigm.

Similarly, the environmental implications of using live microbes or derived synthetic products require careful assessment. Microbes that are beneficial to one organism may not be so to another and may, in fact, be pathogenic (Redman et al., 2001; Daskin & Alford, 2012). Long-term environmental monitoring may be more tangible or realistic in highly managed systems, such as agricultural fields or livestock production, but in wildlife or natural populations, the response of the environment and other associated organisms to microbial inputs may be harder to predict or monitor. In addition, declines or extirpations of non-target species in the wild may go unnoticed in some taxa, although evidence of this is limited due to a lack of studies. *Bacillus thuringiensis* var. *israelensis* and *Bacillus sphaericus* spores can be used to control mosquitoes and blackfly (Lacey, 2007). These products are applied to water and have been highly successful in selectively killing mosquito larvae (Lacey,

2007). However, poor stability requires repeat applications, prompting the more recent development of long-lasting formulations with sustained release over a six-month period. Derua et al. (2017) investigated the indirect effects of these products on broad ecosystem diversity around three Kenyan villages over a five-month period. The study concluded that one round of the long-lasting treatment did not significantly alter the abundance or diversity of aquatic vertebrates or other invertebrates. They noted that the treatments could accumulate and thus reduce the abundance of mosquitoes in the ecosystem.

It is also possible that introduced microbes may switch from being beneficial to pathogenic or detrimental in response to different environmental conditions, particularly in the context of anthropogenic climate change. The metabolic activity of microbes in vitro can differ wildly to their activity in vivo or in situ (e.g. Gram et al., 2001; De Roy et al., 2014; Becker et al., 2015; Blajman et al., 2015; Martín et al., 2015). Thus, candidate microbial inputs and their derivatives require broad-scale in vivo and in situ screening that reflects the diverse spatial, temporal and physiological conditions experienced by the host or system (Bletz et al., 2013; Rebollar et al., 2016). Adame-Álvarez et al. (2014) found that the growth of pathogenic *Pseudomonas syringae* pv. *syringae* was inhibited when fungal endophytes were applied to wild lima bean (*Phaseolus lunatus*) first, but facilitated when the bacterial pathogen was allowed to colonise prior to application. Moreover, probiotics for protecting amphibians against the chytrid fungus have been shown to lose antifungal capabilities at different temperatures (Daskin et al., 2014), and it may be that these could actually switch to promoting the growth of the pathogen. Thus, the use of microbially derived biotechnologies will require strict testing prior to widespread use, accompanied by long-term and wide-ranging surveying before, during and after use. Even then, the unpredictability of the systems may render these approaches unfeasible (Machado et al., 2016; Kaminsky et al., 2018).

An additional consideration for microbial technologies that specifically target pathogens (i.e. wildlife or agricultural) is their propensity to inhibit genetically or phenotypically diverse targets. For example, amphibian probiotics are not able to universally inhibit the growth of all chytrid isolates (Antwis et al., 2015; Antwis & Harrison, 2017), and thus, large-scale roll out of microbial inputs will need to be tested for efficacy. These applications may also alter the evolutionary trajectory of pathogens, potentially making them more virulent, akin to the use of antibiotics in humans. For example, suppression of invading pathogens by probiotic gut bacteria has the potential to drive evolutionary changes in disease severity (Ford et al., 2016; Stacy et al., 2016). Ensuring that a microbially derived product is effective against the target, or appropriate for the intended income, will require thorough risk assessment and associated legislation. Regulatory bodies such as the European Food Safety

Authority (EFSA), the Food and Agriculture Organisation of the United States (FAO), the Food and Drug Administration (FDA) or the World Health Organization (WHO) are involved in setting standards and requirements for probiotics for human use (Hong et al., 2005; Glanville et al., 2015). A similar approach should be taken for microbial inoculants designed for agriculture and wildlife. However, it is also important to ensure assessment methods are fit for purpose and based on evidence. In the USA, probiotic strains for human oral consumption must be classified as GRAS by the FDA. This is demonstrated by showing the presence of the strain in the normal healthy microbiota and the absence of association with disease, virulence factors, antibiotic resistance or production of deleterious by-products (Venugopalan et al., 2010). Such criteria would need to be reviewed and updated as new evidence comes to light, and additional policies will also need to be developed for the registration of novel microbial biotechnologies across the diverse range of contexts highlighted throughout this chapter.

A particularly important ethical consideration, albeit relatively novel in terms of policy, is that of intellectual property and knowledge ownership. The Nagoya Protocol on Access to Genetic Resources and the Fair and Equitable Sharing of Benefits Arising from their Utilisation to the Convention on Biological Diversity (also known as the Nagoya Protocol on Access and Benefit Sharing, or ABS) was set up in 2010 and ratified in 2014 to ensure that the benefits arising from genetic resources are shared with the originating country. This means that, for example, microbial inoculants developed through genetic material obtained internationally cannot then be used commercially in another country without first obtaining permission from the originating country, and potentially sharing any outcomes, be it academic outputs, commercial products or profits. This is an important step in recognising the intellectual property of historically marginalised or overlooked groups of people, and it is important that benefit-sharing continues to be implemented in scientific research and commercial development, microbial and otherwise.

9.6 Conclusions

Microbes provide a diverse source of functional traits that can be used to address a whole range of human and environmental problems, from agriculture and farming, to human and wildlife health, to energy production and climate change mitigation. Although microbes and their derivatives have been used for decades in some contexts, recent advances in sequencing and other technologies have allowed us to identify and understand novel sources and applications. Despite the wide range of examples of successful microbial augmentation strategies, however, their use is still fraught with complications and controversies. In particular, microbial inputs often fail to establish across a range of hosts and environments. This may be due to the complex factors that regulate microbial colonisation, such as host biochemical production, environmental factors and, critically, host genotype × environmental interactions. Furthermore, the existing community is also likely to be key in determining the propensity for a microbial input to establish and work effectively. Microbes related to the resident microbiota, or those from the core microbiome, may have greater chance of establishing. Microbial inputs made up of many members (consortia) may be more successful than those comprised of individual microbes. In addition, selection of microbes with the necessary adhesions and protein secretion systems may facilitate establishment. There is unlikely to be a one-size-fits-all approach to microbial input development, and indeed, to improve the success of microbial inputs, a targeted and strategic approach will likely be required, similar to the use of personalised medicine in humans. Other forms of microbial biotechnology include the use of microbiome engineering such as prebiotics, biostimulants, management practices, or selective breeding of hosts for a desired microbiome composition and function. Furthermore, there is considerable scope for the use of microbial derivatives to improve human health and biofuel production. Although microbial biotechnology has significant potential to do good, the potential for harm must also be considered throughout development and implementation.

References

Adam E, Groenenboom AE, Kurm V, et al. (2016) Controlling the microbiome: Microhabitat adjustments for successful biocontrol strategies in soil and human gut. *Frontiers in Microbiology*, 7, 1079.

Adame-Álvarez RM, Mendiola-Soto J, Heil M. (2014) Order of arrival shifts endophyte–pathogen interactions in bean from resistance induction to disease facilitation. *FEMS Microbiology Letters*, 355, 100–107.

Adesemoye AO, Torbert HA, Kloepper JW. (2009) Plant growth-promoting rhizobacteria allow reduced application rates of chemical fertilizers. *Microbial Ecology*, 58, 921–929.

Allen HK, Levine UY, Looft T, et al. (2013) Treatment, promotion, commotion: Antibiotic alternatives in food-producing animals. *Trends in Microbiology*, 21, 114–119.

Allgaier M, Reddy A, Park J, et al. (2010) Targeted discovery of glycoside hydrolases from a switchgrass-adapted compost community. *PLoS ONE*, 5, e8812.

Alves LdF, Westmann CA, Lovate GL, et al. (2018) Metagenomic approaches for understanding new concepts in microbial science. *International Journal of Genomics*, 2018, 2312987.

Amoutzias GD, Chaliotis A, Mossialos D. (2016) Discovery strategies of bioactive compounds synthesized by nonribosomal peptide synthetases and type-I polyketide synthases derived from marine microbiomes. *Marine Drugs*, 14, 80.

Antwis RE, Preziosi RF, Harrison XA, et al. (2015) Amphibian symbiotic bacteria do not show a universal ability to inhibit growth of the global panzootic lineage of *Batrachochytrium dendrobatidis*. *Applied and Environmental Microbiology*, 81, 3706–3711.

Antwis RE, Harrison XA. (2018) Probiotic consortia are not uniformly effective against different amphibian chytrid pathogen isolates. *Molecular Ecology*, 27, 577–589.

Antwis RE, Griffiths SM, Harrison XA, et al. (2017) Fifty important research questions in microbial ecology. *FEMS Microbiology Ecology*, 93, fix044.

Arraktham S, Tancho A, Niamsup P, et al. (2016) The potential of bacteria isolated from earthworm intestines, vermicompost and liquid vermicompost to produce indole-3-acetic acid (IAA). *Journal of Agricultural Technology*, 12, 229–239.

Atterbury RJ, Hobley L, Till R, et al. (2011) Effects of orally administered *Bdellovibrio bacteriovorus* on the well-being and *Salmonella* colonization of young chicks. *Applied and Environmental Microbiology*, 77, 5794–5803.

Bakken JS, Borody T, Brandt LJ, et al. (2011) Treating *Clostridium difficile* infection with fecal microbiota transplantation. *Clinical Gastroenterology and Hepatology*, 9, 1044–1049.

Batista-García RA, del Rayo Sánchez-Carbente M, Talia P, et al. (2016) From lignocellulosic metagenomes to lignocellulolytic genes: Trends, challenges and future prospects. *Biofuels, Bioproducts and Biorefining*, 10, 864–882.

Becker MH, Walke JB, Murrill L, et al. (2015) Phylogenetic distribution of symbiotic bacteria from Panamanian amphibians that inhibit growth of the lethal fungal pathogen *Batrachochytrium dendrobatidis*. *Molecular Ecology*, 24, 1628–1641.

Bender SF, Wagg C, van der Heijden MGA. (2016) An underground revolution: Biodiversity and soil ecological engineering for agricultural sustainability. *Trends in Ecology & Evolution*, 31, 440–452.

Bender SF, Wagg C, van der Heijden MGA. (2017) Strategies for environmentally sound soil ecological engineering: A reply to Machado et al. *Trends in Ecology & Evolution*, 32, 10–12.

Berruti A, Lumini E, Balestrini R, et al. (2016) Arbuscular mycorrhizal fungi as natural biofertilizers: Let's benefit from past successes. *Frontiers in Microbiology*, 6, 1–13.

Bhardwaj D, Ansari MW, Sahoo RK, et al. (2014) Biofertilizers function as key player in sustainable agriculture by improving soil fertility, plant tolerance and crop productivity. *Microbial Cell Factories*, 13, 1–10.

Blajman J, Gaziano C, Zbrun MV, et al. (2015) *In vitro* and *in vivo* screening of native lactic acid bacteria toward their selection as a probiotic in broiler chickens. *Research in Veterinary Science*, 101, 50–56.

Bletz MC, Loudon AH, Becker MH, et al. (2013) Mitigating amphibian chytridiomycosis with bioaugmentation: Characteristics of effective probiotics and strategies for their selection and use. *Ecology Letters*, 16, 807–20.

Bletz MC, Myers J, Woodhams DC, et al. (2017) Estimating herd immunity to amphibian chytridiomycosis in Madagascar based on the defensive function of amphibian skin bacteria. *Frontiers in Microbiology*, 8, 1751.

Blumenstein K, Albrectsen BR, Martín JA, et al. (2015) Nutritional niche overlap potentiates the use of endophytes in biocontrol of a tree disease. *BioControl*, 60, 655–667.

Bowles TM, Jackson LE, Loeher M, et al. (2017) Ecological intensification and arbuscular mycorrhizas: A meta-analysis of tillage and cover crop effects. *Journal of Applied Ecology*, 54, 1785–1793.

Boyle RJ, Bath-Hextall FJ, Leonardi-Bee J, et al. (2009) Probiotics for the treatment of eczema: Asystematic review. *Clinical and Experimental Allergy*, 39, 1117–1127.

Brennan EB, Acosta-Martinez V. (2017) Cover cropping frequency is the main driver of soil microbial changes during six years of organic vegetable production. *Soil Biology and Biochemistry*, 109, 188–204.

Brennan Y, Callen WN, Christoffersen L, et al. (2004) Unusual microbial xylanases from insect guts. *Applied and Environmental Microbiology*, 70, 3609–3617.

Briers Y, Walmagh M, Van Puyenbroeck V, et al. (2015) Engineered endolysin-based 'artilysins' to combat multidrug-resistant Gram-negative pathogens. *mBio*, 5, e01379–14.

Brown P, Saa S. (2015) Biostimulants in agriculture. *Frontiers in Plant Science*, 6, 671.

Busby PE, Soman C, Wagner MR, et al. (2017) Research priorities for harnessing plant microbiomes in sustainable agriculture. *PLoS Biology*, 15, 1–14.

Calderón-Cortés N, Quesada M, Watanabe H, et al. (2012) Endogenous plant cell wall digestion: A key mechanism in insect evolution. *Annual Review of Ecology, Evolution, and Systematics*, 43, 45–71.

Calvo P, Nelson L, Kloepper JW. (2014) Agricultural uses of plant biostimulants. *Plants and Soil*, 383, 3–41.

Cardoso AM, Cavalcante JJ, Cantão ME, et al. (2012a) Metagenomic analysis of the microbiota from the crop of an invasive snail reveals a rich reservoir of novel genes. *PLoS ONE*, 7, e48505.

Cardoso AM, Cavalcante JJV, Vieira RP, et al. (2012b) Gut bacterial communities in the giant landsnail *Achatina fulica* and their modification by a sugarcane-based diet. *PLoS ONE*, 7, e33440.

Carro L, Nouioui I. (2017) Taxonomy and systematics of plant probiotic bacteria in the genomic era. *AIMS Microbiology*, 3, 383–412.

Cavaglieri LR, Passone A, Etcheverry MG. (2004) Correlation between screening procedures to select root endophytes for biological control of *Fusarium verticillioides* in *Zea mays* L. *Biological Control*, 31, 259–267.

Chagnot C, Zorgani MA, Astruc T, et al. (2013) Proteinaceous determinants of surface colonization in bacteria: Bacterial adhesion and biofilm formation from a protein secretion perspective. *Frontiers in Microbiology*, 4, 1–26.

Chaparro JM, Badri DV, Bakker MG, et al. (2013) Root exudation of phytochemicals in *Arabidopsis* follows specific patterns that are developmentally programmed and correlate with soil microbial functions. *PLoS ONE*, 8, e55731.

Chaudhry V, Rehman A, Mishra A, et al. (2012) Changes in bacterial community structure of agricultural land due to long-term organic and chemical amendments. *Microbial Ecology*, 64, 450–460.

Cisek AA, Dąbrowska I, Gregorczyk KP, et al. (2017) Phage therapy in bacterial infections treatment: One hundred years after the discovery of bacteriophages. *Current Microbiology*, 74, 277–283.

Colás Sánchez A, Torres Gutiérrez R, Cupull Santana R, et al. (2014) Effects of co-inoculation of native *Rhizobium* and *Pseudomonas* strains on growth parameters and yield of two contrasting *Phaseolus vulgaris* L. genotypes under Cuban soil conditions. *European Journal of Soil Biology*, 62, 105–112.

Colombo BM, Scalvenzi T, Benlamara S, et al. (2015) Microbiota and mucosal immunity in amphibians. *Frontiers in Immunology*, 6, 111.

Cottrell MT, Moore JA, Kirchman DL. (1999) Chitinases from uncultured marine microorganisms. *Applied and Environmental Microbiology*, 65, 2553–2557.

Crist E, Mora C, Engelman R. (2017) The interaction of human population, food production, and biodiversity protection. *Science*, 264, 260–264.

Cuello-Garcia C.A, Brozek JL, Fiocchi A, et al. (2015) Probiotics for the prevention of allergy: A systematic review and meta-analysis of randomized controlled trials. *Journal of Allergy and Clinical Immunology*, 136, 952–961.

Dale C, Moran NA. (2006) Molecular interactions between bacterial symbionts and their hosts. *Cell*, 126, 453–465.

Daniel C, Sebbane F, Poiret S, et al. (2009) Protection against *Yersinia pseudotuberculosis* infection conferred by a *Lactococcus lactis* mucosal delivery vector secreting LcrV. *Vaccine*, 27, 1141–1144.

Dar MA, Pawar KD, Pandit RS. (2017) Gut microbiome analysis of snails: A biotechnological approach. In: Ray S (Ed.) *Organismal and Molecular Malacology*. London: InTech Open.

Daskin JH, Alford RA. (2012) Context-dependent symbioses and their potential roles in wildlife diseases. *Proceedings of the Royal Society B: Biological Sciences*, 279, 1457–1465.

Daskin JH, Bell SC, Schwarzkopf L, et al. (2014) Cool temperatures reduce antifungal activity of symbiotic bacteria of threatened amphibians – Implications for disease management and patterns of decline. *PLoS ONE*, 9, e100378.

Davidson DH. (1976) Assimilation efficiencies of slugs on different food materials. *Oecologia*, 26, 267–273.

De Boer W, Wagenaar AM, Klein Gunnewiek, PJA, et al. (2007) *In vitro* suppression of fungi caused by combinations of apparently non-antagonistic soil bacteria. *FEMS Microbiology Ecology*, 59, 177–185.

De La Fuente L, Mavrodi DV, Landa BB, et al. (2006) phlD-based genetic diversity and detection of genotypes of 2,4-diacetylphloroglucinol-producing *Pseudomonas fluorescens*. *FEMS Microbiology Ecology*, 56, 64–78.

De Nobili M, Contin M, Mondini C, et al. (2001) Soil microbial biomass is triggered into activity by trace amounts of substrate. *Biology and Fertility of Soils*, 33, 1163–1170.

De Roy K, Marzorati M, Van den Abbeele P, et al. (2014) Synthetic microbial ecosystems: An exciting tool to understand and apply microbial communities. *Environmental Microbiology*, 16, 1472–1481.

Denev S, Chevaux E, Demey ECV. (2013) Efficacite du probiotique Pediococcus acidilactici sur les performances zootechniques de poules pondeuses. *Dixièmes Journées de la Recherche Avicole et Palmipèdes à Foie Gras*, 2013, 943–946.

Denou E, Pridmore RD, Berger B, et al. (2008) Identification of genes associated with the long-gut-persistence phenotype of the probiotic *Lactobacillus johnsonii* strain NCC533 using a combination of genomics and transcriptome analysis. *Journal of Bacteriology*, 190, 3161–3168.

Derua YA, Kahindi SC, Mosha FW, et al. (2018) Microbial larvicides for mosquito control: Impact of long lasting formulations of *Bacillus thuringiensis* var. *israelensis* and *Bacillus sphaericus* on non-target organisms in western Kenya highlands. *Ecology and Evolution*, 8, 7563–7573.

Di Benedetto AN, Rosaria Corbo M, Campaniello D, et al. (2017) The role of plant growth promoting bacteria in improving nitrogen use efficiency for sustainable crop production: A focus on wheat. *AIMS Microbiology*, 3, 413–434.

Donohoue PD, Barrangou R, May AP. (2018) Advances in industrial biotechnology using CRISPR-Cas systems. *Trends in Biotechnology*, 36, 134–146.

Douglas AE. (2013) Microbial brokers of insect-plant interactions revisited. *Journal of Chemical Ecology*, 39, 952–961.

Draper K, Ley C, Parsonnet J. (2017) Probiotic guidelines and physician practice: A cross-sectional survey and overview of the literature. *Beneficial Microbes*, 8, 507–519.

Dwivedi SL, Van Bueren ETL, Ceccarelli S, et al. (2017) Diversifying food systems in the pursuit of sustainable food production and healthy diets. *Trends in Plant Science*, 22, 842–856.

Eisenhauer N, Scheu S, Jousset A. (2012) Bacterial diversity stabilizes community productivity. *PLoS ONE*, 7, e34517.

Eisenhauer N, Schulz W, Scheu S, et al. (2013) Niche dimensionality links biodiversity and invasibility of microbial communities. *Functional Ecology*, 27, 282–8.

El Khoury S, Rousseau A, Lecoeur A, et al. (2018) Deleterious interaction between honeybees (*Apis mellifera*) and its microsporidian intracellular parasite *Nosema ceranae* was mitigated by administrating either endogenous or allochthonous gut microbiota strains. *Frontiers in Ecology and Evolution*, 6, 58.

Elend C, Schmeisser C, Leggewie C, et al. (2006) Isolation and biochemical characterization of two novel metagenome-derived esterases. *Applied and Environmental Microbiology*, 72, 3637–3645.

Emam T. (2016) Local soil, but not commercial AMF inoculum, increases native and non-native grass growth at a mine restoration site. *Restoration Ecology*, 24, 35–44.

Evans JD, Lopez DL. (2004) Bacterial probiotics induce an immune response in the honey bee (Hymenoptera: Apidae). *Journal of Economic Entomology*, 97, 752–756.

Feng YD, Duan CJ, Pang H, et al. (2007) Cloning and identification of novel cellulase genes from uncultured microorganisms in rabbit cecum and characterization of the expressed cellulases. *Applied Microbiology and Biotechnology*, 75, 319–328.

Ferrer M, Golyshina OV, Chernikova TN, et al. (2005) Novel hydrolase diversity retrieved from a metagenome library of bovine rumen microflora. *Environmental Microbiology*, 7, 1966–2010.

Ferrer M, Martínez-Martínez M, Bargiela R, et al. (2016) Estimating the success of enzyme bioprospecting through metagenomics: Current status and future trends. *Microbial Biotechnology*, 9, 22–34.

Finkel OM, Castrillo G, Herrera Paredes S, et al. (2017) Understanding and exploiting plant beneficial microbes. *Current Opinion in Plant Biology*, 38, 155–163.

Fischetti VA. (2010) Bacteriophage endolysins: A novel anti-infective to control Gram-positive pathogens. *International Journal of Medical Microbiology*, 300, 357–362.

Flohre A, Rudnick M, Traser G, et al. (2011) Does soil biota benefit from organic farming in complex vs. simple landscapes? *Agriculture, Ecosystems and Environment*, 141, 210–214.

Flores HA, O'Neill SL. (2018) Controlling vector-borne diseases by releasing modified mosquitoes. *Nature Reviews Microbiology*, 16, 508–518.

Foo JL, Ling H, Lee YS, et al. (2017) Microbiome engineering: Current applications and its future. *Biotechnology Journal*, 12, 1–11.

Ford SA, Kao D, Williams D, et al. (2016) Microbe-mediated host defence drives the evolution of reduced pathogen virulence. *Nature Communications*, 7, 13430.

Forey E, Chauvat M, Coulibaly SFM, et al. (2018) Inoculation of an ecosystem engineer (Earthworm: *Lumbricus terrestris*) during experimental grassland restoration: Consequences for above and belowground soil compartments. *Applied Soil Ecology*, 125, 148–155.

Gagliardi A, Totino V, Cacciotti F, et al. (2018) Rebuilding the gut microbiota ecosystem. *International Journal of Environmental Research and Public Health*, 15, 1679.

García-Cayuela T, Requena T, Martínez-Cuesta MC, et al. (2017) Rapid detection of *Lactococcus lactis* isolates producing the lantibiotics nisin, lacticin 481 and lacticin 3147 using MALDI-TOF MS. *Journal of Microbiology Methods*, 139, 138–142.

Genta FA, Dillon RJ, Terra WR, et al. (2006) Potential role for gut microbiota in cell wall digestion and glucoside detoxification in *Tenebrio molitor* larvae. *Journal of Insect Physiology*, 52, 593–601.

Glanville J, King S, Guarner F, et al. (2015) A review of the systematic review process and its applicability for use in evaluating evidence for health claims on probiotic foods in the European Union. *Nutrition Journal*, 14, 16.

Gram L, Løvold T, Nielsen J, et al. (2001) *In vitro* antagonism of the probiont *Pseudomonas fluorescens* strain AH2 against *Aeromonas salmonicida* does not confer protection of salmon against furunculosis. *Aquaculture*, 199, 1–11.

Grant S, Sorokin DY, Grant WD, et al. (2004) A phylogenetic analysis of Wadi el Natrun soda lake cellulase enrichment cultures and identification of cellulase genes from these cultures. *Extremophiles*, 8, 421–429.

Gutleben J, Chaib De Mares M, van Elsas JD, et al. (2018) The multi-omics promise in context: From sequence to microbial isolate. *Critical Reviews in Microbiology*, 44, 212–229.

Hamilton JJ, Garcia SL, Brown BS, et al. (2017) Metabolic network analysis and metatranscriptomics reveal auxotrophies and nutrient sources of the cosmopolitan freshwater microbial lineage acI. *mSystems*, 2, 1–13.

Hancock REW, Haney EF, Gill EE. (2016) The immunology of host defence peptides: Beyond antimicrobial activity. *Nature Reviews Immunology*, 16, 321–334.

Hansen AK, Moran NA. (2014) The impact of microbial symbionts on host plant utilization by herbivorous insects. *Molecular Ecology*, 23, 1473–1496.

Hartmann M, Frey B, Mayer J, et al. (2015) Distinct soil microbial diversity under long-term organic and conventional farming. *The ISME Journal*, 9, 1177–1194.

Hempel S, Newberry SJ, Maher AR, et al. (2012) Probiotics for the prevention and treatment of antibiotic-associated diarrhea. *JAMA*, 307, 1959–1969.

Hernández M, Chailloux M. (2004) Las micorrizas arbusculares y las bacterias rizosféricas como alternativa a la nutrición mineral del tomate. *Cultivos Tropicales*, 25, 5–12.

Hess M, Sczyrba A, Egan R, et al. (2011) Metagenomic sequencing of biomass-degrading microbes from cow rumen reveals new carbohydrate-active enzymes. *Science*, 28, 463–467.

HM Government. (2019) Contained and controlled: The UK's 20-year vision for antimicrobial resistance. Available at: https://assets.publishing.service.gov.uk /government/uploads/system/uploads/ attachment_data/file/773065/uk-20-year-vision-for-antimicrobial-resistance.pdf

Hojckova K, Stano M, Klucar L. (2013) PhiBIOTICS: Catalogue of therapeutic enzybiotics, relevant research studies and practical applications. *BMC Microbiology*, 13, 53.

Holden WM, Hanlon SM, Woodhams DC, et al. (2015) Skin bacteria provide early protection for newly metamorphosed southern leopard frogs (*Rana sphenocephala*) against the frog-killing fungus, *Batrachochytrium dendrobatidis*. *Biological Conservation*, 187, 91–102.

Hong HA, Le HD, Cutting SM. (2005) The use of bacterial spore formers as probiotics. *FEMS Microbiology Reviews*, 29, 813–835.

Hoyt JR, Cheng TL, Langwig KE, et al. (2015) Bacteria isolated from bats inhibit the growth of *Pseudogymnoascus destructans*, the causative agent of white-nose syndrome. *PLoS ONE*, 10, e0121329.

Hu J, Wei Z, Friman VP, et al. (2016) Probiotic diversity enhances rhizosphere microbiome function and plant disease suppression. *mBio*, 7, 1–8.

Hu J, Wei Z, Weidner S, et al. (2017) Probiotic *Pseudomonas* communities enhance plant growth and nutrient assimilation via diversity-mediated ecosystem functioning. *Soil Biology and Biochemistry*, 113, 122–129.

Hulston CJ, Chrunside AA, Venables MC. (2015) Probiotic supplementation prevents high-fat, overfeeding-induced insulin resistance in human subjects. *British Journal of Nutrition*, 113, 595–602.

Hussain N, Singh A, Saha S, et al. (2016) Excellent N-fixing and P-solubilizing traits in earthworm gut-isolated bacteria: A vermicompost based assessment with vegetable market waste and rice straw feed mixtures. *Bioresource Technology*, 222, 165–174.

Huws SA, Creevey CJ, Oyama LB, et al. (2018) Addressing global ruminant agricultural challenges through understanding the rumen microbiome: Past, present and future. *Frontiers in Microbiology*, 9, 2161.

Ianiro G, Valerio L, Mascucci L, et al. (2017) Predictors of failure after single faecal microbiota transplantation in patients with recurrent *Clostridium difficile* infection: Results from a 3-year, single-centre cohort study. *Clinical Microbiology and Infection*, 23, 337.

Imperiali N, Dennert F, Schneider J, et al. (2017) Relationships between root pathogen resistance, abundance and expression of *Pseudomonas* antimicrobial genes, and soil properties in representative Swiss agricultural soils. *Frontiers in Plant Science*, 8, 1–22.

Ishaq SL, Johnson SP, Miller ZJ, et al. (2017) Impact of cropping systems, soil inoculum, and plant species identity on soil bacterial community structure. *Microbial Ecology*, 73, 417–434.

James CE. (2013) Recent advances in studies of polymicrobial interactions in oral biofilms. *Current Oral Health Reports*, 1, 59–69.

Jani AJ, Briggs CJ. (2014) The pathogen Batrachochytrium dendrobatidis disturbs the frog skin microbiome during a natural epidemic and experimental infection. *Proceedings of the National Academy of Sciences*, 111, E5049–5058.

Jiménez RR, Sommer S. (2017) The amphibian microbiome: Natural range of variation, pathogenic dysbiosis, and role in conservation. *Biodiversity and Conservation*, 26, 763–786.

Jones SE, Lennon JT. (2010) Dormancy contributes to the maintenance of microbial diversity. *Proceedings of the National Academy of Sciences*, 107, 5881–5886.

Jousset A, Schulz W, Scheu S, et al. (2011) Intraspecific genotypic richness and relatedness predict the invasibility of microbial communities. *The ISME Journal*, 5, 1108–1114.

Jousset A, Becker J, Chatterjee S, et al. (2014) Biodiversity and species identity shape the antifungal activity of bacterial communities. *Ecology*, 95, 1184–1190.

Joynson R, Pritchard L, Osemwekha E, et al. (2017) Metagenomic analysis of the gut microbiome of the common black slug *Arion ater* in search of novel lignocellulose degrading enzymes. *Frontiers in Microbiology*, 8, 2181.

Kaminsky LM, Trexler RV, Malik RJ, et al. (2018). The inherent conflicts in developing soil microbial inoculants. *Trends in Biotechnology*, 37, 140–151.

Kaznowski A, Szymas B, Jazdzinska E, et al. (2004) The effects of probiotic supplementation on the content of intestinal microflora and chemical composition of worker honey bees (*Apis mellifera*). *Journal of Apicultural Research*, 44, 10–14.

Kellow NJ, Coughlan MT, Reid CM. (2014) Metabolic benefits of dietary prebiotics in human subjects: A systematic review of randomised controlled trials. *British Journal of Nutrition*, 111, 1147–1161.

Kelly BJ, Tebas P. (2018) Clinical practice and infrastructure review of faecal microbiota transplantation for *Clostridium difficile* infection. *Chest*, 153, 266–277.

Kennedy J, Baker P, Piper C, et al. (2009) Isolation and analysis of bacteria with antimicrobial activities from the marine sponge *Haliclona simulans* collected from Irish waters. *Marine Biotechnology*, 11, 384–396.

Kim J, Choi GS, Kim SB, et al. (2006) Screening and characterization of a novel esterase from a metagenomic library. *Protein Expression and Purification*, 45, 315–323.

Kittelmann S, Pinares-Patiño CS, Seedorf H, et al. (2014) Two different bacterial community types are linked with the low-methane emission trait in sheep. *PLoS ONE*, 9, 1–9.

Kline KA, Fälker S, Dahlberg S, et al. (2009) Bacterial adhesins in host–microbe interactions. *Cell Host and Microbe*, 5, 580–592.

Knauf M, Moniruzzaman M. (2004) Lignocellulosic biomass processing: A perspective. *International Sugar Journal*, 106, 147–150.

Knight R, Navas J, Quinn RA, et al. (2018) Best practices for analysing microbiomes. *Nature Reviews Microbiology*, 16, 410–422.

Lacey LA. (2007) *Bacillus thuringiensis* serovariety *israelensis* and *Bacillus sphaericus* for mosquito control. *Journal of the American Mosquito Control Association*, 23, 133–163.

Lambert B, Peferoen M. (1992) Insecticidal promise of *Bacillus thuringiensis*: Facts and mysteries about a successful biopesticide. *Bioscience*, 42, 112–122.

Lämmle K, Zipper H, Breuer M, et al. (2007) Identification of novel enzymes with different hydrolytic activities by metagenome expression cloning. *Journal of Biotechnology*, 127, 575–592.

LeBlanc JG, Aubry C, Cortes-Perez NG, et al. (2013) Mucosal targeting of therapeutic molecules using genetically modified lactic acid bacteria: An update. *FEMS Microbiology Letters*, 344, 1–9.

Lee CC, Kibblewhite-Accinelli RE, Wagschal K, et al. (2006) Cloning and characterization of a cold-active xylanase enzyme from an environmental DNA library. *Extremophiles*, 10, 295–300.

Lees RS, Gilles JR, Hendrichs J, et al. (2015) Back to the future: The sterile insect technique against mosquito disease vectors. *Current Opinion in Insect Science*, 10, 156–162.

Lehman RM, Taheri WI, Osborne SL, et al. (2012) Fall cover cropping can increase arbuscular mycorrhizae in soils supporting intensive agricultural production. *Applied Soil Ecology*, 61, 300–304.

Lennon JT, Jones SE. (2011) Microbial seed banks: The ecological and evolutionary implications of dormancy. *Nature Reviews Microbiology*, 9, 119–130.

Li LL, McCorkle SR, Monchy S, et al. (2009) Bioprospecting metagenomes: Glycosyl hydrolases for converting biomass. *Biotechnology for Biofuels*, 2, 10.

Lian J, Wijffels RH, Smidt H, et al. (2018) The effect of the algal microbiome on industrial production of microalgae. *Microbial Biotechnology*, 11, 806–818.

Ligon BL. (2004) Penicillin: Its discovery and early development. *Seminars in Pediatric Infectious Diseases*, 15, 52–57.

Lin J, Zhang Y, He C, et al. (2018) Probiotics supplementation in children with asthma: A systematic review and meta-analysis. *Journal of Paediatrics and Child Health*, 54, 953–961.

Lindemann SR, Bernstein HC, Song HS, et al. (2016) Engineering microbial consortia for controllable outputs. *The ISME Journal*, 10, 2077–2084.

Ling LL, Schneider T, Peoples AJ, et al. (2015) A new antibiotic kills pathogens without detectable resistance. *Nature*, 517, 455–459.

Liu C, Zou G, Yan X, et al. (2018b) Screening of multimeric β-xylosidases from the gut microbiome of a higher termite, *Globitermes brachycerastes*. *International Journal of Biological Sciences*, 14, 608.

Liu Y, Li X, Zhang L, et al. (2018a) Response of the wheat rhizosphere soil nematode community in wheat/walnut intercropping system in Xinjiang, Northwest China. *Applied Entomology and Zoology*, 53, 297–306.

Loudon AH, Woodhams DC, Parfrey LW, et al. (2014) Microbial community dynamics and effect of environmental microbial reservoirs on red-backed salamanders (*Plethodon cinereus*). *The ISME Journal*, 8, 830–840.

Machado AAS, Valyi K, Rillig MC. (2016) Potential environmental impacts of an 'Underground Revolution'. *Trends in Ecology & Evolution*, 31, 2016–2018.

Martín JA, Macaya-Sanz D. (2015) Strong *in vitro* antagonism by elm xylem endophytes is not accompanied by temporally stable in planta protection against a vascular pathogen under field conditions. *European Journal of Plant Pathology*, 142, 185–196.

Martínez Cruz P, Ibáñez AL, Monroy Hermosillo OA, et al. (2012) Use of probiotics in aquaculture. *ISRN Microbiology*, 2012, 1–13.

McKean J, Naug H, Nikbakht E, et al. (2017) Probiotics and subclinical psychological symptoms in healthy participants: A systematic review and meta-analysis. *The Journal of Alternative and Complementary Medicine*, 23, 249–258.

McKenzie VJ, Kueneman JG, Harris RN. (2018) Probiotics as a tool for disease mitigation in wildlife: Insights from food production and medicine. *Annals of the New York Academy of Sciences*, 1429, 18–30.

Menendez E, Garcia-Fraile P. (2017) Plant probiotic bacteria: Solutions to feed the world. *AIMS Microbiology*, 3, 747–748.

Middleton EL, Bever JD. (2012) Inoculation with a native soil community advances succession in a grassland restoration. *Restoration Ecology*, 20, 218–226.

Miles LA, Lopera CA, González S, et al. (2012) Exploring the biocontrol potential of fungal endophytes from an Andean Colombian Paramo ecosystem. *BioControl*, 57, 697–710.

Mills S, Griffin C, O'Connor PM, et al. (2017) A multibacteriocin cheese starter system, comprising nisin and lacticin 3147 in *Lactococcus lactis*, in combination with plantaricin from *Lactobacillus plantarum*. *Applied and Environmental Microbiology*, 83, 1–17.

Mishra S, Wang KH, Sipes BS, et al. (2017) Suppression of root-knot nematode by vermicompost tea prepared from different curing ages of vermicompost. *Plant Disease*, 101, 734–737.

Mitri S, Foster KR. (2013) The genotypic view of social interactions in microbial communities. *Annual Review of Genetics*, 47, 247–273.

Mitter B, Pfaffenbichler N, Flavell R, et al. (2017) A new approach to modify plant microbiomes and traits by introducing beneficial bacteria at flowering into progeny seeds. *Frontiers in Microbiology*, 8, 1–10.

Mousa WK, Raizada MN. (2015) Biodiversity of genes encoding anti-microbial traits within plant associated microbes. *Frontiers in Plant Science*, 6, 231.

Mousa WK, Shearer CR, Limay-Rios V, et al. (2015) Bacterial endophytes from wild maize suppress *Fusarium graminearum* in modern maize and inhibit mycotoxin accumulation. *Frontiers in Plant Science*, 6, 1–19.

Mu J, Li X, Jiao J, et al. (2017) Biocontrol potential of vermicompost through antifungal volatiles produced by indigenous bacteria. *Biological Control*, 112, 49–54.

Mudroňová D, Toporčák J, Nemcová R, et al. (2011) *Lactobacillus* sp. as a potential probiotic for the prevention of *Paenibacillus* larvae infection in honey bees. *Journal of Apicultural Research*, 50, 323–324.

Mueller UG, Sachs JL. (2015) Engineering microbiomes to improve plant and animal health. *Trends in Microbiology*, 23, 1–12.

Muletz CR, Myers JM, Domangue RJ, et al. (2012) Soil bioaugmentation with amphibian cutaneous bacteria protects amphibian hosts from infection by *Batrachochytrium dendrobatidis*. *Biological Conservation*, 152, 119–126.

Müller CA, Obermeier MM, Berg G. (2016) Bioprospecting plant-associated microbiomes. *Journal of Biotechnology*, 235, 171–180.

Naik S, Bouladoux N, Wilhelm C, et al. (2012) Compartmentalized control of skin immunity by resident commensals. *Science*, 337, 1115–1119.

Neu J, Rushing J. (2011) Cesarean versus vaginal delivery: Long-term infant outcomes and the hygiene hypothesis. *Clinics in Perinatology*, 38, 321–331.

Nunes RV, Scherer C, Pozza PC, et al. (2012) Use of probiotics to replace antibiotics for broilers. *Revista Brasileira de Zootecnia*, 41, 2219–2224.

Ohkuma M. (2003) Termite symbiotic systems: Efficient bio-recycling of lignocellulose. *Applied Microbiology and Biotechnology*, 61, 1–9.

Oldroyd GED. (2013) Speak, friend, and enter: Signalling systems that promote beneficial symbiotic associations in plants. *Nature Reviews Microbiology*, 11, 252–263.

Ouwehand AC, Salminen S, Ouwehand AC, et al. (2009) *In vitro* adhesion assays for probiotics and their *in vivo* relevance: A review. *Microbial Ecology in Health and Disease*, 15, 175–184.

Pandey G, Pandey AK, Pandey SS, et al. (2018) Microbiota in immune pathogenesis and the prospects for pre and probiotic dietetics in psoriasis. *Biomedical Research Journal*, 2, 220.

Pătruică S, Mot D. (2012) The effect of using prebiotic and probiotic products on intestinal micro-flora of the honeybee (*Apis mellifera carpatica*). *Bulletin of Entomological Research*, 102, 619–623.

Pershina E, Valkonen J, Kurki P, et al. (2015) Comparative analysis of prokaryotic communities associated with organic and conventional farming systems. *PLoS ONE*, 10, 1–16.

Petrof EO, Gloor GB, Vanner SJ, et al. (2013) Stool substitute transplant therapy for the eradication of *Clostridium difficile* infection: 'RePOOPulating' the gut. *Microbiome*, 1, 3.

Petrosillo N, Granata G, Cataldo MA. (2018) Novel antimicrobials for the treatment of *Clostridium difficile* infection. *Frontiers in Medicine*, 5, 1–16.

Piovia-Scott J, Rejmanek D, Woodhams DC, et al. (2017) Greater species richness of bacterial skin symbionts better suppresses the amphibian fungal pathogen *Batrachochytrium dendrobatidis*. *Microbial Ecology*, 74, 217–226.

Poelchau MF, Coates BS, Childers CP, et al. (2016) Agricultural applications of insect ecological genomics. *Current Opinion in Insect Science*, 13, 61–69.

Pohjanen J, Koskimäki JJ, Sutela S, et al. (2014) Interaction with ectomycorrhizal fungi and endophytic *Methylobacterium* affects nutrient uptake and growth of pine seedlings *in vitro*. *Tree Physiology*, 34, 993–1005.

Ptaszyńska AA, Borsuk G, Zdybicka-Barabas A, et al. (2016) Are commercial probiotics and prebiotics effective in the treatment and prevention of honeybee nosemosis C? *Parasitology Research*, 115, 397–406.

Quaye AK, Volk TA, Hafner S, et al. (2011) Impacts of paper sludge and manure on soil and biomass production of willow. *Biomass and Bioenergy*, 35, 2796–2806.

Quiza L, St-Arnaud M, Yergeau E, et al. (2015) Harnessing phytomicrobiome signaling for rhizosphere microbiome engineering. *Frontiers in Plant Science*, 6, 1–11.

Rana V, Rana D. (2017) Role of microorganisms in lignocellulosic biodegradation. In: *Renewable Biofuels: Bioconversion of*

Lignocellulosic Biomass by Microbial Community. Cham: Springer.

Rebollar EA, Antwis RE, Becker MH, et al. (2016) Using 'omics' and integrated multi-omics approaches to guide probiotic selection to mitigate chytridiomycosis and other emerging infectious diseases. *Frontiers in Microbiology*, 7, 68.

Redford KH, Adams W, Mace GM. (2013) Synthetic biology and conservation of nature: Wicked problems and wicked solutions. *PLoS Biology*, 11, 2–5.

Redman RS, Dunigan D, Rodriguez RJ, et al. (2001) Fungal symbiosis from mutualism to parasitism: Who controls the outcome, host or invader? *New Phytologist*, 151, 705–716.

Rees HC, Grant S, Jones B, et al. (2003) Detecting cellulase and esterase enzyme activities encoded by novel genes present in environmental DNA libraries. *Extremophiles*, 7, 415–421.

Reich I, Ijaz UZ, Gormally M, et al. (2018) 16S rRNA sequencing reveals likely beneficial core microbes within faecal samples of the EU protected slug *Geomalacus maculosus*. *Scientific Reports*, 8, 10402.

Remans R, Ramaekers L, Schelkens S, et al. (2008) Effect of *Rhizobium–Azospirillum* coinoculation on nitrogen fixation and yield of two contrasting *Phaseolus vulgaris* L. genotypes cultivated across different environments in Cuba. *Plant and Soil*, 312, 25–37.

Richardson TH, Tan X, Frey G, et al. (2002) A novel, high performance enzyme for starch liquefaction. Discovery and optimization of a low pH, thermostable alpha-amylase. *Journal of Biological Chemistry*, 277, 26,501–26,507.

Ripple WJ, Wolf C, Newsome TM, et al. (2017) World scientists warning to humanity: A second notice. *BioScience*, 67, 1026–1028.

Roehe R, Dewhurs, RJ, Duthie CA, et al. (2016) Bovine host genetic variation influences rumen microbial methane production with best selection criterion for low methane emitting and efficiently feed converting hosts based on metagenomic gene abundance. *PLoS Genetics*, 12, e1005846.

Rudrappa T, Czymmek KJ, Pare PW, et al. (2008) Root-secreted malic acid recruits beneficial soil bacteria. *Plant Physiology*, 148, 1547–1556.

Sáez D, Fernández P, Rivera A, et al. (2012) Oral immunization of mice with recombinant *Lactococcus lactis* expressing Cu, Zn superoxide dismutase of *Brucella abortus* triggers protective immunity. *Vaccine*, 30, 1283–1290.

Saez-Lara MJ, Gomez-Llorente C, Plaza-Diaz P, et al. (2015) The role of probiotic lactic acid bacteria and bifidobacteria in the prevention and treatment of inflammatory bowel disease and other related diseases: A systematic review of randomized human clinical trials. *BioMed Research International*, 2015, 505878.

Salazar A, Sulman BN, Dukes JS. (2018) Microbial dormancy promotes microbial biomass and respiration across pulses of drying-wetting stress. *Soil Biology and Biochemistry*, 116, 237–244.

Sander JD, Joung JK. (2014) CRISPR-Cas systems for editing, regulating and targeting genomes. *Nature Biotechnology*, 32, 347–350.

Sarma BK, Yadav SK, Singh S, et al. (2015) Microbial consortium-mediated plant defense against phytopathogens: Readdressing for enhancing efficacy. *Soil Biology and Biochemistry*, 87, 25–33.

Scheuring I, Yu DW. (2012) How to assemble a beneficial microbiome in three easy steps. *Ecology Letters*, 15, 1300–1307.

Schmidt JE, Bowles TM, Gaudin ACM. (2016) Using ancient traits to convert soil health into crop yield: Impact of selection on maize root and rhizosphere function. *Frontiers in Plant Science*, 7, 1–11.

Schweitzer JA, Bailey JK, Fischer DG, et al. (2008) Plant–soil–microorganism interactions: Heritable relationship between plant genotype and associated soil microorganisms. *Ecology*, 89, 773–781.

Scully ED, Geib SM, Hoover K, et al. (2013) Metagenomic profiling reveals lignocellulose degrading system in a microbial community associated with a wood-feeding beetle. *PLoS ONE*, 8,e73827.

Seshadri R, Leahy SC, Attwood GT, et al. (2018) Cultivation and sequencing of rumen microbiome members from the Hungate1000 collection. *Nature Biotechnology*, 36, 359–367.

Sheth RU, Cabral V, Chen SP, et al. (2016) Manipulating bacterial communities by *in situ* microbiome engineering. *Trends in Genetics*, 32, 189–200.

Shi W, Ding SY, Yuan JS. (2011) Comparison of insect gut cellulase and xylanase activity across different insect species with distinct food sources. *Bioenergy Research*, 4, 1–10.

Shi W, Xie S, Chen X, et al. (2013) Comparative genomic analysis of the endosymbionts of herbivorous insects reveals eco-environmental adaptations: Biotechnology applications. *PLoS Genetics*, 9, e1003131.

Shin JM, Gwak JW, Kamarajan P, et al. (2016) Biomedical applications of nisin. *Journal of Applied Microbiology*, 120, 1449–1465.

Silva CO, Vaz RP, Filho EX. (2018) Bringing plant cell wall-degrading enzymes into the lignocellulosic biorefinery concept. *Biofuels, Bioproducts and Biorefining*, 12, 277–289.

Sleeman JM. (2013) Has the time come for big science in wildlife health? *EcoHealth*, 10, 335–338.

Spector T, Knight R. (2015). Faecal transplants. *BMJ*, 351, 1–2.

Stacy A, McNally L, Darch SE, et al. (2016) The biogeography of polymicrobial infection. *Nature Reviews Microbiology*, 14, 93–105.

Stecher B, Chaffron S, Käppeli R, et al. (2010) Like will to like: Abundances of closely related species can predict susceptibility to intestinal colonization by pathogenic and commensal bacteria. *PLoS Pathogens*, 6, e1000711.

Stephens PR, Altizer S, Smith KF, et al. (2016) The macroecology of infectious diseases: A new perspective on global-scale drivers of pathogen distributions and impacts. *Ecology Letters*, 19, 1159–1171.

Sun J, Buys NJ. (2016) Glucose- and glycaemic factor-lowering effects of probiotics on diabetes: A meta-analysis of randomised placebo-controlled trials. *British Journal of Nutrition*, 115, 1167–1177.

Tabashnik BE. (1994) Evolution of resistance to *Bacillus thuringiensis*. *Annual Review of Entomology*, 39, 47–79.

Tang KL, Caffrey NP, Nóbrega DB, et al. (2017) Articles restricting the use of antibiotics in food-producing animals and its associations with antibiotic resistance in food-producing animals and human beings: A systematic review and meta-analysis. *The Lancet*, 5196, 9–11.

Thijs S, Sillen W, Rineau F, et al. (2016) Towards an enhanced understanding of plant–microbiome interactions to improve phytoremediation: Engineering the metaorganism. *Frontiers in Microbiology*, 7, 1–15.

Thushara RM, Gangadaran S, Solati Z, et al. (2016) Cardiovascular benefits of probiotics: a review of experimental and clinical studies. *Food and Function*, 7, 632–642.

Timmerman HM, Rutten NBMM, Boekhorst J, et al. (2017) Intestinal colonisation patterns in breastfed and formula-fed infants during the first 12 weeks of life reveal sequential microbiota signatures. *Scientific Reports*, 7, 1–10.

Tompkins DM, Carver S, Jones ME, et al. (2015) Emerging infectious diseases of wildlife: A critical perspective. *Trends in Parasitology*, 31, 149–159.

Tuomisto HL. (2019) The complexity of sustainable diets. *Nature Ecology and Evolution*, 3, 720–721.

Trivedi P, Delgado-Baquerizo M, Trivedi C, et al. (2016) Microbial regulation of the soil carbon cycle: Evidence from gene–enzyme relationships. *The ISME Journal*, 10, 2593–2604.

Udwary DW, Zeigler L, Asolkar RN, et al. (2007) Genome sequencing reveals complex secondary metabolome in the marine actinomycete *Salinispora tropica*. *Proceedings of the National Academy of Sciences*, 104, 10376–10381.

Uyeno Y, Shigemori S, Shimosato T. (2015) Effect of probiotics/prebiotics on cattle health and productivity. *Microbes and Environments*, 30, 126–132.

van Elsas JD, Chiurazzi M, Mallon CA, et al. (2012) Microbial diversity determines the invasion of soil by a bacterial pathogen. *Proceedings of the National Academy of Sciences*, 109, 1159–1164.

Varjani SJ. (2017) Microbial degradation of petroleum hydrocarbons. *Bioresource Technology*, 223, 277–286.

Venugopalan V, Shriner KA, Wong-Beringer A. (2010) Regulatory oversight and safety of probiotic use. *Emerging Infectious Diseases*, 16, 1661–1665.

Verbeken G, Huys I, Pirnay JP, et al. (2014) Taking bacteriophage therapy seriously: A moral argument. *BioMed Research International*, 2014, 1–8.

Viikari L, Vehmaanperä J, Koivula A. (2012) Lignocellulosic ethanol: From science to industry. *Biomass and Bioenergy*, 46, 13–24.

Voget S, Leggewie C, Uesbeck A, et al. (2003) Prospecting for novel biocatalysts in a soil metagenome. *Applied and Environmental Microbiology*, 69, 6235–6242.

Voget S, Steele HL, Streit WR. (2006) Characterization of a metagenome-derived halotolerant cellulase. *Journal of Biotechnology*, 126, 26–36.

Vosátka M, Látr A, Gianinazzi S, et al. (2012) Development of arbuscular mycorrhizal biotechnology and industry: Current achievements and bottlenecks. *Symbiosis*, 58, 29–37.

Walder F, Van Der Heijden MGA. (2015) Regulation of resource exchange in the arbuscular mycorrhizal symbiosis. *Nature Plants*, 1, 1–7.

Walke JB, Belden LK. (2016) Harnessing the microbiome to prevent fungal infections: Lessons from amphibians. *PLoS Pathogens*, 12, e1005796.

Walters WA, Jin Z, Youngblut N, et al. (2018) Large-scale replicated field study of maize rhizosphere identifies heritable microbes. *Proceedings of the National Academy of Sciences*, 115, 7368–7373.

Wang S, Xu M, Wang W, et al. (2016) Systematic review: Adverse events of fecal microbiota transplantation. *PLoS ONE*, 11, e0161174.

Warnecke F, Luginbühl P, Ivanova N, et al. (2007) Metagenomic and functional analysis of hindgut microbiota of a wood-feeding higher termite. *Nature*, 450, 560.

Watanabe H, Tokuda G. (2010) Cellulolytic systems in insects. *Annual Review of Entomology*, 55, 609–632.

Wei Z, Yang T, Friman VP, et al. (2015) Trophic network architecture of root-associated bacterial communities determines pathogen invasion and plant health. *Nature Communications*, 6, 8413.

Weimer PJ, Stevenson DM, Mantovani HC, et al. (2010) Host specificity of the ruminal bacterial community in the dairy cow following near-total exchange of ruminal contents. *Journal of Dairy Science*, 93, 5902–5912.

Wescombe PA, Hale JD, Heng NC, et al. (2012) Developing oral probiotics from *Streptococcus salivarius*. *Future Microbiology*, 7, 1355–1371.

Williams RJ, Howe A, Hofmockel KS. (2014) Demonstrating microbial co-occurrence pattern analyses within and between ecosystems. *Frontiers in Microbiology*, 5, 1–10.

Wohlleben W, Mast Y, Stegmann E, et al. (2016) Antibiotic drug discovery. *Microbial Biotechnology*, 9, 541–548.

Wong WS, Tan SN, Ge L, et al. (2016) The importance of phytohormones and microbes in biostimulants: Mass spectrometric evidence and their positive effects on plant growth. *Acta Horticulturae*, 1148, 49–60.

Woodhams DC, Geiger CC, Reinert LK, et al. (2012) Treatment of amphibians infected with chytrid fungus: Learning from failed trials with itraconazole, antimicrobial peptides, bacteria, and heat therapy. *Diseases of Aquatic Organisms*, 98, 11–25.

Xu C, Arancon RAD, Labidi J, et al. (2014) Lignin depolymerisation strategies: Towards valuable chemicals and fuels. *Chemical Society Reviews*, 43, 7485–7500.

Yáñez-Ruiz DR, Abecia L, Newbold CJ. (2015) Manipulating rumen microbiome and fermentation through interventions during early life: A review. *Frontiers in Microbiology*, 6, 1–12.

Yun J, Kang S, Park S, et al. (2004) Characterization of a novel amylolytic enzyme encoded by a gene from a soil-derived metagenomic library. *Applied and Environmental Microbiology*, 70, 7229–7235.

Zasloff M. (2002) Antimicrobial peptides of multicellular organisms. *Nature*, 415, 389–395.

Zee PC, Bever JD. (2014) Joint evolution of kin recognition and cooperation in spatially structured rhizobium populations. *PLoS ONE*, 9, e95141.

Zhang NN, Sun YM, Li L, et al. (2010) Effects of intercropping and *Rhizobium* inoculation on yield and rhizosphere bacterial community of faba bean (*Vicia faba* L.). *Biology and Fertility of Soils*, 46, 625–639.

Zhang GQ, Hu HJ, Liu CY, et al. (2016) Probiotics for prevention of atopy and food hypersensitivity in early childhood: A PRISMA-compliant systematic review and meta-analysis of randomized controlled trials. *Medicine (Baltimore)*, 95, 1–10.

Zhang Q, Yu Y, Velasquez JE, et al. (2012) Evolution of lanthipeptide synthetases. *Proceedings of the National Academy of Sciences*, 109, 18361–18366.

Zhao K, Penttinen P, Guan T, et al. (2011) The diversity and anti-microbial activity of endophytic actinomycetes isolated from medicinal plants in Panxi Plateau, China. *Current Microbiology*, 62, 182–190.

CHAPTER TEN

Synthesis and future directions

RACHAEL E. ANTWIS
University of Salford
XAVIER A. HARRISON
University of Exeter
MICHAEL J. COX
University of Birmingham

Our knowledge of the structure and function of complex host-associated communities has grown exponentially in the last decade, particularly due to reductions in the sequencing costs of both amplicon-based and shotgun metagenomic approaches, and advances in computational methods for tackling large metagenomic data sets (Quince et al., 2017; Thomas & Segata, 2019). However, despite the large volume of research directed at profiling microbial communities living in association with animals, plants and soils, we still lack a complete understanding of the extensive patterns of diversity they contain (Thomas & Segata, 2019). The uncertainty in our diversity estimates occurs at two levels. First, at broad taxonomic scales, the non-bacterial components of microbiomes have been poorly characterised across the majority of hosts and environmental contexts. The fungal, archaeal and even viral portions of the animal microbiome remain underexplored, and so our knowledge of the strength and direction of cross-kingdom microbial interactions remains limited (de Menezes et al., 2017). Understanding these interactions may be key to developing biotechnological approaches to human medicine, food and fuel production, and wildlife conservation, to name a few (Layeghifard et al., 2017). Second, even within distinct microbial groups such as bacteria, we often fail to characterise extensive strain-level diversity comprising the pangenomes of individual bacterial species (Thomas & Segata, 2019). Measuring this cryptic taxonomic diversity is vital, because among-individual variation in the presence of bacterial strains may have marked functional consequences for hosts (e.g. Vatanen et al., 2019). Recent work has estimated that even within a paradigm as well-studied as the human microbiome, 20% of sequences match no known microbial genomes, and 40% of genes lack a match in functional databases (Thomas & Segata, 2019). Likewise, only 1.5% of bacteria and 7% of fungi have been described for soil communities (Orgiazzi et al., 2016). There is clearly a lot of work to do to address these gaps in our knowledge across multiple hosts and environmental contexts. Understanding within-kingdom taxonomic and functional diversity and characterising pan-kingdom interactions among microbial communities can only be possible through improvement of existing reference databases. Recently developed sequencing and bioinformatic approaches now allow us to target under-represented groups such as viruses directly (Warwick-Dugdale et al., 2019), which will be invaluable for ecosystems where taxonomic groups of interest may occur at relatively low abundance and be hard to capture with traditional shotgun sequencing. Likewise, large-scale metagenomic assembly projects can uncover thousands of novel microbial species genomes, as has recently been undertaken for the human microbiome (Pasolli et al., 2019). However, we note that the microbiome literature is still largely dominated by key model organisms such as humans, laboratory mice, the fruit fly *Drosophila melanogaster*, and crop and nitrogen-fixing plants. Although studies of wild animals including birds and insects are increasing (Pascoe et al., 2017), further studies across a broad taxonomic range of wild species are needed. In addition, greater understanding of how laboratory-based findings relate to field or real-world systems are needed (e.g. Jani & Briggs, 2014; Knowles et al., 2019).

Correlations between microbiome structure and traits of individual health abound in the literature, but the mechanisms underlying such correlations remain to be determined. Many studies have identified patterns in microbiome variation (often derived from amplicon sequencing) that correlate with a disease, a behaviour or some aspect of physiology. However, from these data, directionality is still very difficult to determine; do differences in microbiome composition drive the physiological, epidemiological or behavioural differences we see, or vice versa? For example, studies of host–pathogen systems often detect an apparent link between microbiome diversity and pathogen susceptibility, where individuals with lower diversity exhibit higher pathogen burdens or rates of infection (e.g. Bates et al., 2018). But does such a pattern emerge because low microbiome diversity is 'bad' and weakens host immune defences, or does the act of pathogenic infection itself depress microbiome diversity? Quantifying the directionality of these relationships is often difficult in correlative studies performed on natural systems. Experimental evidence of diversity–disease relationships from model organisms is perhaps more convincing. Laboratory mice treated with antibiotics exhibit lower gut microbiome diversity and an altered gut metabolome that favours the invasion of *Clostridium difficile*, leading to higher infection rates (Theriot et al., 2014). Elucidating the mechanism(s) by which host–microbe interactions operate is crucial to our efforts of quantifying the importance of microbes for the optimal health and physiology for their hosts. Distinguishing correlation from causation in host–microbe studies will become easier as the cost of sequencing reduces, and as new methods are developed that allow us to understand the role of individual and groups of microbes within the microbiome (Douglas, 2018). One particularly promising approach to tackle these questions is the use of multi-omic tools to microbiome research (e.g. Mallick et al., 2017). For example, combining metagenomic and metatranscriptomic techniques allows us to distinguish between which genes are simply present in a community and which are actively transcribed. More importantly, we may predict that the map between gene presence and transcription may be altered by ecological factors of interest, such as exposure to a pathogen. Applying such techniques to systems where previously we have simply been busy describing taxonomic composition should be a major priority for future research, especially in wild species where knowledge of functional relationships remains limited. Finally, the importance of controlled experimental systems as tractable models for probing directionality and causality in host–microbe interactions cannot be overstated (e.g. see King et al., 2016).

The impact of community diversity on emergent community function remains an unsolved puzzle in microbial ecology. Insights into diversity–function relationships in microbial species assemblages may be gleaned from comparisons to eukaryotic communities. However, two unique traits of microbial communities set these communities apart from traditional ecological systems (Koskella et al., 2017), including the production of 'public goods' that facilitate microbe–microbe mutualisms, and marked levels of functional redundancy due to horizontal gene transfer that can blur the distinction between species presence and emergent functional properties (e.g. Moya & Ferrer, 2016; Koskella et al., 2017; Louca et al., 2018). Thus, one key question arises: does it even matter who is there? A more prudent approach may be to skip the 'who' question all together and focus instead on the functional capabilities of microbial communities and the consequences of this for the host. Indeed, direct functional characterisation of microbial communities using tools such as metatranscriptomics can often yield potential mechanistic insights not available from approaches that simply measure taxonomy (e.g. Schirmer et al., 2018). Critically, within this framework, we need to understand how individual members of the microbiome interact to confer function, and how this relates to host biology and genotype, and the multitude of environmental factors that can influence microbiome activity.

Despite these gaps, general patterns are emerging across a diverse taxonomic range of hosts showing the host microbiome is highly plastic, and shaped by a range of intrinsic and extrinsic factors. The consequences of this temporal variation in microbiome structure and function for the host remain poorly understood, and several key questions remain to be answered (Antwis et al., 2017). How does microbiome plasticity affect host physiological processes, and the strength of host–microbe interactions over time? Does microbiome plasticity improve the ability of hosts to respond to environmental change? Variation among individuals in the temporal trajectories of their microbiomes, and the factors driving such variation, are relatively understudied. This is especially the case in wild systems, perhaps with the exception of longitudinal studies of early-life developmental changes in microbiome (e.g. Videvall et al., 2019). Studies detecting single time-point correlations between traits of host health (e.g. parasite burden) and microbiome structure provide a solid basis for hypothesis generation concerning the adaptive value of host–microbe interactions, but it is equally important to ask how temporally stable and resilient to change these associations are. Fully understanding the magnitude of microbiome plasticity and its consequences for host physiology and health requires that we employ repeated sampling under a range of conditions to quantify the shape of within and among-individual variation in microbiome trajectory over time.

We are currently in a period of unprecedented environmental change, and the ability of hosts to adapt and mitigate these changes may depend on their microbiomes. Given the vast numbers, wide metabolic scope, high turnover and short generation times of microbes, microbiomes may allow faster acclimatisation and adaptation of their hosts to new climatic conditions (McFall-Ngai et al., 2013; Torda et al., 2017). Current and future environmental changes are also likely to drive a number of social and economic changes (Crist et al., 2017; Ripple et al., 2017), and microbes may play an important role in managing this. Can microbes be used to extend the existing resource limits of our planet, such as food and fuel production? Will microbial biotechnology allow previously inaccessible land to become available for agriculture, or allow us to reduce our reliance on agrochemicals (Sutherland et al., 2018)? Could microbiome engineering be used to limit insect-vectored diseases, improve personalised medicine in humans or protect wildlife from diseases? A number of biological and ethical issues still surround biotechnology initiatives that use microbes; however, these organisms possess enormous functional power that could be used to improve the health and well-being of humans and, critically, our planet.

References

Antwis RE, Griffiths SM, Harrison XA, et al. (2017) 50 important research questions in microbial ecology. *FEMS Microbiology Ecology*, 93, fix044.

Bates KA, Clare FC, O'Hanlon S, et al. (2018) Amphibian chytridiomycosis outbreak dynamics are linked with host skin bacterial community structure. *Nature Communications*, 9, 693.

Crist E, Mora C, Engelman R. (2017) The interaction of human population, food production, and biodiversity protection. *Science*, 264, 260–264.

De Menezes AB, Richardson AE, Thrall PH. (2017) Linking fungal–bacterial co-occurrences to soil ecosystem function. *Current Opinion in Microbiology*, 37, 135–141.

Douglas AE. (2018) What will it take to understand the ecology of symbiotic microorganisms? *Environmental Microbiology*, 20, 1920–1924.

Jani AJ, Briggs CJ. (2014) The pathogen *Batrachochytrium dendrobatidis* disturbs the frog skin microbiome during a natural epidemic and experimental infection. *Proceedings of the National Academy of Sciences*, 111, E5049–5058.

King KC, Brockhurst MA, Vasieva O, et al. (2016) Rapid evolution of microbe-mediated protection against pathogens in a worm host. *The ISME Journal*, 10, 1915.

Knowles SC, Eccles RM, Baltrūnaitė L. (2019) Species identity dominates over environment in shaping the microbiota of small mammals. *Ecology Letters*, 22, 826–837.

Koskella B, Hall LJ, Metcalf CJE. (2017) The microbiome beyond the horizon of ecological and evolutionary theory. *Nature Ecology and Evolution*, 1, 1606–1615.

Layeghifard M, Hwang DM, Guttman DS. (2017) Disentangling interactions in the microbiome: A network perspective. *Trends in Microbiology*, 25, 217–228.

Louca S, Polz MF, Mazel F, et al. (2018) Function and functional redundancy in microbial systems. *Nature Ecology and Evolution*, 2, 936–943.

Mallick H, Ma S, Franzosa EA, et al. (2017) Experimental design and quantitative analysis of microbial community multiomics. *Genome Biology*, 18, 228.

McFall-Ngai M, Hadfield MG, Bosch TCG, et al. (2013) Animals in a bacterial world, a new imperative for the life sciences. *Proceedings of the National Academy of Sciences*, 110, 3229–3236.

Moya A, Ferrer M. (2016). Functional redundancy-induced stability of gut microbiota subjected to disturbance. *Trends in Microbiology*, 24, 402–413.

Orgiazzi A, Bardgett RD, Barrios E. (Eds.) (2016) *Global Soil Biodiversity Atlas*. Luxembourg: Publications Office of the European Union.

Pascoe EL, Hauffe HC, Marchesi JR, et al. (2017) Network analysis of gut microbiota literature: An overview of the research landscape in non-human animal studies. *The ISME Journal*, 11, 2644–2651.

Pasolli E, Asnicar F, Manara S, et al. (2019) Extensive unexplored human microbiome diversity revealed by over 150,000 genomes from metagenomes spanning age, geography, and lifestyle. *Cell*, 176, 649–662.

Quince C, Walker AW, Simpson JT, et al. (2017) Shotgun metagenomics, from sampling to analysis. *Nature Biotechnology*, 35, 833.

Ripple WJ, Wolf C, Newsome TM, et al. (2017) World scientists' warning to humanity: A second notice. *BioScience*, 67, 1026–1028.

Schirmer M, Franzosa EA, Lloyd-Price J, et al. (2018) Dynamics of metatranscription in the inflammatory bowel disease gut microbiome. *Nature Microbiology*, 3, 337.

Sutherland WJ, Broad S, Butchart SHM, et al. (2018) A horizon scan of emerging issues for global conservation in 2019. *Trends in Ecology and Evolution*, 34, 83–94.

Theriot CM, Koenigsknecht MJ, Carlson Jr PE, et al. (2014) Antibiotic-induced shifts in the mouse gut microbiome and metabolome increase susceptibility to *Clostridium difficile* infection. *Nature Communications*, 5, 3114.

Thomas AM, Segata N. (2019) Multiple levels of the unknown in microbiome research. *BMC Biology*, 17, 48.

Torda G, Donelson JM, Aranda M, et al. (2017) Rapid adaptive responses to climate change in corals. *Nature Climate Change*, 7, 627–636.

Vatanen T, Plichta DR, Somani J, et al. (2019) Genomic variation and strain-specific functional adaptation in the human gut microbiome during early life. *Nature Microbiology*, 4, 470.

Videvall E, Song SJ, Bensch HM, et al. (2019) Major shifts in gut microbiota during development and its relationship to growth in ostriches. *Molecular Ecology*, 28, 2653–2667.

Warwick-Dugdale J, Solonenko N, Moore K, et al. (2019) Long-read viral metagenomics captures abundant and microdiverse viral populations and their niche-defining genomic islands. *PeerJ*, 7, e6800.

Index